T0401356

Global Perspectives on Fostering Problem-Based Learning in Chinese Universities

Zhiliang Zhu
Northeastern University, China

Chunfang Zhou
Aalborg University, Denmark

A volume in the Advances in
Higher Education and Professional
Development (AHEPD) Book Series

Published in the United States of America by
    IGI Global
    Information Science Reference (an imprint of IGI Global)
    701 E. Chocolate Avenue
    Hershey PA, USA 17033
    Tel: 717-533-8845
    Fax: 717-533-8661
    E-mail: cust@igi-global.com
    Web site: http://www.igi-global.com

Library of Congress Cataloging-in-Publication Data

Names: Zhu, Zhiliang, 1962- editor. | Zhou, Chunfang, 1980- editor.
Title: Global perspectives on fostering problem-based learning in Chinese
  universities / Zhiliang Zhu and Chunfang Zhou, Editors.
Description: Hershey, PA : Information Science Reference, [2019] | Includes
  bibliographical references and index.
Identifiers: LCCN 2019013147| ISBN 9781522599616 (hardcover) | ISBN
  9781522599623 (softcover) | ISBN 9781522599630 (ebook)
Subjects: LCSH: Problem-based learning--China--Cross-cultural studies. |
  Universities and colleges--China--Cross-cultural studies.
Classification: LCC LB1027.42 .G56 2019 | DDC 378.1/70951--dc23 LC record available at
https://lccn.loc.gov/2019013147

This book is published in the IGI Global book series Advances in Higher Education and Professional Development (AHEPD) (ISSN: 2327-6983; eISSN: 2327-6991)

British Cataloguing in Publication Data
A Cataloguing in Publication record for this book is available from the British Library.

All work contributed to this book is new, previously-unpublished material.
The views expressed in this book are those of the authors, but not necessarily of the publisher.

For electronic access to this publication, please contact: eresources@igi-global.com.

Advances in Higher Education and Professional Development (AHEPD) Book Series

ISSN:2327-6983
EISSN:2327-6991

Editor-in-Chief: Jared Keengwe, University of North Dakota, USA

MISSION

As world economies continue to shift and change in response to global financial situations, job markets have begun to demand a more highly-skilled workforce. In many industries a college degree is the minimum requirement and further educational development is expected to advance. With these current trends in mind, the **Advances in Higher Education & Professional Development (AHEPD) Book Series** provides an outlet for researchers and academics to publish their research in these areas and to distribute these works to practitioners and other researchers.

AHEPD encompasses all research dealing with higher education pedagogy, development, and curriculum design, as well as all areas of professional development, regardless of focus.

COVERAGE

- Adult Education
- Assessment in Higher Education
- Career Training
- Coaching and Mentoring
- Continuing Professional Development
- Governance in Higher Education
- Higher Education Policy
- Pedagogy of Teaching Higher Education
- Vocational Education

IGI Global is currently accepting manuscripts for publication within this series. To submit a proposal for a volume in this series, please contact our Acquisition Editors at Acquisitions@igi-global.com or visit: http://www.igi-global.com/publish/.

Titles in this Series

For a list of additional titles in this series, please visit:
https://www.igi-global.com/book-series/advances-higher-education-professional-development/73681

Handbook of Research on Cross-Cultural Online Learning in Higher Education
Jared Keengwe (University of North Dakota, USA) and Kenneth Kungu (Clayton State University, USA)
Information Science Reference • ©2019 • 400pp • H/C (ISBN: 9781522582861) • US $245.00

Redesigning Higher Education Initiatives for Industry 4.0
Arumugam Raman (Universiti Utara Malaysia, Malaysia) and Mohan Rathakrishnan (Universiti Utara Malaysia, Malaysia)
Information Science Reference • ©2019 • 390pp • H/C (ISBN: 9781522578321) • US $185.00

Handbook of Research on Challenges and Opportunities in Launching a Technology ...
Mehdi Khosrow-Pour, D.B.A. (Information Resources Management Association, USA)
Information Science Reference • ©2019 • 420pp • H/C (ISBN: 9781522562559) • US $275.00

Advanced Web Applications and Progressing E-Learning 2.0 Technologies in Higher Education
Jean-Éric Pelet (ESCE International Business School, France)
Information Science Reference • ©2019 • 271pp • H/C (ISBN: 9781522574354) • US $175.00

Higher Education and the Evolution of Management, Applied Sciences, and Engineering ...
Carolina F. Machado (University of Minho, Portugal) and J. Paulo Davim (University of Aveiro, Portugal)
Engineering Science Reference • ©2019 • 258pp • H/C (ISBN: 9781522572596) • US $185.00

Handbook of Research on Critical Thinking Strategies in Pre-Service Learning Environments
Gina J. Mariano (Troy University, USA) and Fred J. Figliano (Troy University, USA)
Information Science Reference • ©2019 • 657pp • H/C (ISBN: 9781522578239) • US $265.00

Fostering Multiple Levels of Engagement in Higher Education Environments
Kelley Walters (Northcentral University, USA) and Patricia Henry (Northcentral University, USA)
Information Science Reference • ©2019 • 316pp • H/C (ISBN: 9781522574705) • US $185.00

For an entire list of titles in this series, please visit:
https://www.igi-global.com/book-series/advances-higher-education-professional-development/73681

701 East Chocolate Avenue, Hershey, PA 17033, USA
Tel: 717-533-8845 x100 • Fax: 717-533-8661
E-Mail: cust@igi-global.com • www.igi-global.com

Table of Contents

Foreword xii

Preface xiv

Acknowledgment xx

Chapter 1
Fostering Problem-Based Learning (PBL) in Chinese Universities for a
Creative Society 1
    Chunfang Zhou, Aalborg University, Denmark
    Zhiliang Zhu, Northeastern University, China

Chapter 2
Design of Crowd Creative Collaborative Education Model Based on PBL:
Background, Reflection, and Teaching Practice in Northeastern University in
China 32
    Xinbo Sun, Northeastern University, China

Chapter 3
Fostering Practical Developers in Computer Science Classrooms: A PBL
Approach 55
    Yin Zhang, Northeastern University, China

Chapter 4
Rethinking Environmental Education: Reflections on AAU UNESCO Center
Certificate Course of Problem-Based Learning 88
    Fenghua Li, Northeastern University, China

Chapter 5
PBL Implementation in Material Science and Engineering Education at
Chinese Universities 130
    Xiu Song, Northeastern University, China

Chapter 6
The Change Towards PBL: Designing and Applying PBL at a Program
Level...159
    Fei Wang, Northeastern University, China

Chapter 7
An Elective Course-Based Model for the Change of Traditional Engineering
Curriculum Towards PBL in a Chinese University 183
    Xufang Zhang, Northeastern University, China

Chapter 8
Experience and Reflection on PBL and Implementation of Interdisciplinary-
Level PBL Plan 210
    Jingping Song, Northeastern University, China

Chapter 9
Facilitating Cross-Cultural Communication: A Global Dimension to
Fostering International Talents and Innovation in University Foreign Affairs
Management..244
    Mei Li, Northeastern University, China & Aalborg University, Denmark
    Zhiliang Zhu, Northeastern University, China

Chapter 10
Developing Engineering Creativity in STEM Programs in Chinese
Universities 273
    Chunfang Zhou, Aalborg University, Denmark

Glossary 294

Compilation of References 298

Related References...320

About the Contributors 342

Index...348

Detailed Table of Contents

Foreword xii

Preface xiv

Acknowledgment xx

Chapter 1
Fostering Problem-Based Learning (PBL) in Chinese Universities for a
Creative Society 1
Chunfang Zhou, Aalborg University, Denmark
Zhiliang Zhu, Northeastern University, China

Recently, building a creative society has been a new vision of China that brings much discussion on how to foster creative talents and how to improve pedagogic models in Chinese universities. This chapter regards problem-based learning (PBL) as a promising strategy, and accordingly, the following questions will be discussed: 1) How can we understand the context of building a creative society in China? 2) What is a PBL model? 3) How can we understand history of PBL in a global context? 4) What is the theoretical root of PBL? and 5) For Chinese universities, what are boundaries to be broken for facilitating changes towards PBL that benefits to build a creative society? As both challenges and opportunities of fostering PBL in Chinese universities will be revealed, and appropriate strategies of reform will be suggested, this chapter has important significances of pedagogical innovation in Chinese context. In addition, it also implies universities in other cultures for improving innovation strategies in the future.

Chapter 2
Design of Crowd Creative Collaborative Education Model Based on PBL:
Background, Reflection, and Teaching Practice in Northeastern University in
China 32
    Xinbo Sun, Northeastern University, China

The global information technology revolution puts forward the following requirements
for higher education: education mode transforms from experience education to
overall education; education mechanism transforms from traditional management
to comprehensive governance; the educational goal transfers from the traditional
knowledge to the ability training. In such a macro educational background, the
structural contradictions in China's higher education have triggered the supply-side
reform of education. The implementation of this reform to Northeastern University
requires us to vigorously promote the excellent education action plan in view of the
current teaching reality and local difficulties in Northeastern University to change
the logic of unilateral teaching into the logic of co-creating education. Based on
comprehensive learning of PBL education paradigm, the author of this chapter,
based on his own teaching practice and reflection of educational philosophy, puts
forward the collaborative education mode of crowd innovation and gives the basic
framework of this model. On this basis, specific cases and suggestions are given.

Chapter 3
Fostering Practical Developers in Computer Science Classrooms: A PBL
Approach 55
    Yin Zhang, Northeastern University, China

Real-life software development requires practical developers. This chapter discusses
the challenges put by real-life software development on computer science education
of modern universities, and how to face these challenges by changing traditional
teaching and learning to a PBL-based approach. Based on a literature review on
PBL theories, methods and tools, and observations made in classrooms and group
rooms at Aalborg University, this chapter discusses possible aspects to consider when
changing traditional computer science classrooms. A case is then used to demonstrate
the process of changing traditional teaching and learning of a computer science
course named Visual Programming and Applications to a PBL-based approach.

Chapter 4
Rethinking Environmental Education: Reflections on AAU UNESCO Center
Certificate Course of Problem-Based Learning 88
    Fenghua Li, Northeastern University, China

This chapter brings a participatory learning experience on PBL at Aalborg University
in Denmark. Based on the inherent wholeness of the human-nature ecosystem,
interdisciplinary, sustainability-oriented teaching philosophies in environmental

education endeavor for the appeal of more concern the value of life, aiming at promoting greater sensitivity to critical thinking, individual happiness, and social responsibility. Problem-based learning may be an effective way to realize the action competence of students by solving real problems and adjusting their behavior and finally to compass transformative learning and lifelong learning.

Chapter 5

PBL Implementation in Material Science and Engineering Education at Chinese Universities 130
Xiu Song, Northeastern University, China

Traditional university education with ordinary lectures is changing to more practical and actively student-centered learning systems. Materials science and engineering is originally the study of actual engineering materials but now becomes more interdisciplinary and sophisticated in the rapidly advancing industrial society. It is very necessary to cultivate the practical materials engineers and it also becomes a big challenge for Chinese universities to make a change. PBL is one of the potential approaches for Chinese universities. This chapter describes PBL theories, discusses PBL principles, PBL models, and also some PBL experiences at Aalborg University. In addition, this chapter exposes how PBL could be applied to materials science and engineering education in Chinese universities, and a case of PBL implementation has been given to show the process of transformation from traditional education at Chinese universities to PBL in the materials science and engineering field.

Chapter 6

The Change Towards PBL: Designing and Applying PBL at a Program Level.. 159
Fei Wang, Northeastern University, China

This chapter proposes the design of course groups PBL at program level for students from the BSc. programs of Robot Engineering (RE) at Northeastern University (NEU), China. The overall courses are divided into four groups throughout Grades 1 to 4. In this chapter, the authors provide background information about student cultivation and discipline construction in RE, and then they discuss correlation of characteristics between PBL and RE program, which indicates the reasons for applying PBL in RE. Finally, they introduce the detailed design of course groups.

Chapter 7
An Elective Course-Based Model for the Change of Traditional Engineering
Curriculum Towards PBL in a Chinese University 183
    Xufang Zhang, Northeastern University, China

The chapter presents two PBL models for the change of traditional engineering curriculum based on traditional courses across colleges at the Northeastern University in China. A particular focus of the PBL model design is about interdisciplinarity. In this regard, the E2-iPBL model is developed based on general and major elective courses offered across many disciplines, whereas the JD-iPBL model is considered to develop PBL courses by further introducing compulsory major courses for a joint-degree training program. For practical implementations within the traditional engineering curriculum background, the change of the teacher's role for student-centered constructive learning is briefly summarized. Possible realizations and simple cases are illustrated. Finally, a comparative study of the E2-iPBL and JD-iPBL models is outlined.

Chapter 8
Experience and Reflection on PBL and Implementation of Interdisciplinary-
Level PBL Plan 210
    Jingping Song, Northeastern University, China

This chapter introduces the author's own teaching practices, teaching philosophy, and teaching challenges by traditional ways in Northeastern University of China at first. Then it presents the author's experience by participatory learning of PBL in UNESCO center of Aalborg University in Denmark. And the impact and guidance of the course on author's teaching philosophy, challenges, and skills are also given in this chapter. To apply PBL teaching methods, the author proposes future teaching plans with PBL. Moreover, design and implementation of interdisciplinary-level PBL plan is presented. And the implementation plan is expounded by six aspects: students, teaching staff, learning goals, contents, teaching and learning methods, and assessment. Finally, a case is put forward by the implementation plan.

Chapter 9
Facilitating Cross-Cultural Communication: A Global Dimension to
Fostering International Talents and Innovation in University Foreign Affairs
Management...244
    Mei Li, Northeastern University, China & Aalborg University, Denmark
    Zhiliang Zhu, Northeastern University, China

The purpose of this chapter is twofold: 1) to make a brief interpretation of global dimension mainly focusing on the criterion for "international talents" and the requirements for the internationalization of higher education and 2) to address foreign affairs management in universities plays a vital role in promoting the internationalization of teaching, research, and administrative management, which can be regarded as a key diver to develop global dimension of innovation in higher education. Accordingly, this chapter proposes potential strategies for innovation of the foreign affairs management in universities, which has important significances in studies on internationalization of higher education, cross-culture communication, and foreign affairs management.

Chapter 10
Developing Engineering Creativity in STEM Programs in Chinese
Universities 273
        Chunfang Zhou, Aalborg University, Denmark

This chapter aims to formulate a proposal of developing engineering creativity by problem- and project-based pedagogies in STEM programs in university education in China. It will introduce the increasing needs of engineering creativity in China, deepen understanding of the concept of creativity and engineering creativity, and provide a review of diverse models of problem- and project-based pedagogies in STEM programs. This further brings a discussion on how to develop engineering creativity in STEM programs in Chinese universities in order to overcome the barriers caused by traditional education system and culture. A series of strategies will be proposed including supporting student group work, designing interdisciplinary project, facilitating staff development, and developing creative communities, etc. Briefly, this chapter has the significance of developing engineering creativity in China both theoretically and practically, and also implies how to develop problem- and project-based pedagogies in STEM programs in other cultures around the world.

Glossary 294

Compilation of References 298

Related References 320

About the Contributors 342

Index 348

Foreword

During the past decade, China has accelerated the pace of innovation and created an open innovation system. Globalization has been a powerful force for national economic growth; and China has also contributed to put its capital and expertise into global development projects, building on the momentum of the One Belt, One Road initiative. On technology, China has already developed a range of initiatives in establishing strong R&D infrastructure, increasing R&D capacity, and showing its leadership in diverse emerging areas in global innovation. More fundamentally, China has changed itself and changed the world; the past decade appears to have ushered in a new context for China and the world.

Higher education reforms in China are closely align with reforms in the economic sector. To respond to the new context, Chinese educational policies have focused on increasing the technical and cognitive skills of university graduates and building a few world-class research universities with strong links to industry. In June 2018, during the National Work Conference on Undergraduate Education of Higher Education Institutions in the New Era, the Minister of Education of China pointed out that higher education institutions should accelerate the construction of high-level undergraduate education, comprehensively improve the ability to cultivate talents, and regard undergraduate education as the core of talents cultivation, the foundation of teaching and education, and the frontier of educational development in the new era. As 'competency development' is the key issue of fostering qualified talents, Chinese universities are actively exploring appropriate strategies and meanwhile improving current educational systems that meet requirements of creative workforce in managing challenges of technological innovation, industrial upgrading, macroeconomic growth, and globalization.

The interest in Problem-Based Learning (PBL) has been widely grown in higher education around the world, as it advocates learner-centered curriculum design, interdisciplinarity, and locating learning activities in problem-solving contexts. It has been evidenced by a number of studies that successful application of PBL is full of potential to facilitate transformative learning experience. Its core principles motivate active participation of learners by linking theories and practices. Thus it encourages individual reflection and collective endeavor; it emphasizes learning process and quality of learning; and it requires that teaching should be constructive rather than instructive. In a PBL environment, there is keen sense of developing abilities to learn knowledge from ambiguity and uncertainty in problem-solving processes; there is integration of holistic thinking, hybrid subjects, and recognition of life-long learning; and there is aware of emergence by focusing on adaptive, critical and creative learning. This is, on essence, calling for 'learning as change', which engages the whole person and the whole learning institution to foster an ecological paradigm in higher education for sustainable development.

Zhiliang Zhu and Chunfang Zhou have assembled an array of authors who expertly address how to foster PBL in Chinese universities in global context. It involves discussions on a series of issues including curriculum design, organizational change, teaching reflection, student participation, and evaluation system. By taking Northeastern University (NEU) as an example in chapters, this book provides valuable implications of pedagogical innovation for Chinese universities that accelerates the process of internationalization and globalization.

Jianhua Wang
Northeastern University, China

Preface

In a global view, the next generation is facing diverse situations of solving professional problems in a hybrid world in which there is no clear boundary between autonomous, non-human nature and human-generated process. This is due to increasing models of interdisciplinary knowledge production and emerging digital technologies that have shaped an interlinked global innovation environment. So this requires young students to prepare themselves for managing issues of complexity, uncertainty and ambiguity in their professional practice. Accordingly, on of key topics in higher education field is how to foster qualified talents who are able to face growing challenges in their future career that meets development requirements of their national societies as well as global innovation.

Such a topic is undoubtedly reflected and evidenced by Chinese universities that can be seen with a rise number of employing new pedagogical models under supports of recent policies. Chinese students are expected to be main driving forces of building a modern, harmonious, and creative society in a near future and ensuring a deeper integration of Chinese economy into a global context. Increasingly, in a changing process towards introducing advanced elements such as 'learning by doing', 'student-centered learning', 'active learning', 'peer learning', etc. to traditional curriculum system, studies on Problem-Based Learning (PBL) has shown its potential to be applied in Chinese universities. Even though most current efforts focus on medical education, there is a growing attention to design new PBL curriculum in other fields, in particular to STEM (Science, Technology, Engineering, and Mathematics) education in China. Along with curriculum reforms, discussions have also concerned with how to facilitate organizational changes in order to support the new pedagogy, how to equip teaching staff with knowledge and skills of PBL, how to motivate students to adopt the new models, and how to make institutional policies to ensure successful changes. This indicates a call for a systematic research on bringing together with diverse issues and proposals on how to foster PBL in Chinese universities in a global context.

This book responds to the above call and aims to meet current knowledge gaps by a collection of 10 chapters in one column. It is particularly interesting and meaningful that chapters bridge cultures between the East and the West: most of empirical cases of new curriculum designs are drawn from Northeastern University (NEU), which is one of top universities and has a long tradition of STEM education in China; and meanwhile, most of professional reflection is related to contributors' participatory learning experiences of PBL at Aalborg University (AAU), Denmark, which is leading engineering education in Europe and has a popular AAU-PBL model around the world. So all contributors present theories, course designs, and reflections in relation to experience of learning to develop new PBL models by looking at pedagogical innovation in Chinese universities from a global perspective. Thus, this book provides a comprehensive understanding on PBL both theoretically and practically, both locally and internationally. The following lines briefly show the different focuses of the chapters that indicate the important significances and outline the main profile of this book:

Chapter 1, "Fostering Problem-Based Learning (PBL) in Chinese Universities for a Creative Society," explores a discuss under a background of a new vision of building a creative society China. It regards Problem-Based Learning (PBL) as a promising strategy and aims at responds to the following questions: 1) How can we understand the context of building a creative society in China? 2) What is a PBL model? 3) How can we understand history of PBL in a global context? 4) What is the theoretical root of PBL? And 5) For Chinese universities, what are boundaries to be broken for facilitating changes towards PBL that benefits to build a creative society? As both challenges and opportunities of fostering PBL in Chinese universities will be revealed, and appropriate strategies of reform will be suggested, this chapter has important significances of pedagogical innovation in Chinese context. In addition, it also implies universities in other cultures for improving innovation strategies in the future.

Chapter 2, "Design of Crowd Creative Collaborative Education Model Based on PBL: Background, Reflection, and Teaching Practice at Northeast University in China," highlights that the global information technology revolution puts forward the following requirements for higher education: Education mode transforms from experience education to overall education; education mechanism transforms from traditional management to comprehensive governance; the educational goal transfers from the traditional knowledge to the ability training. In such a macro educational background, the structural contradictions in China's higher education have triggered the supply-side reform of education. The implementation of this reform to Northeastern University requires to vigorously promote the excellent education action plan in view of the current teaching reality and local difficulties in China, to change the logic of unilateral teaching into the logic of co-creating education. Based on comprehensive learning of PBL education paradigm, the author of this chapter, based on his own teaching practice and reflection of educational philosophy, puts forward the collaborative education mode of crowd innovation, and gives the basic framework of this model. On this basis, specific cases and suggestions are given.

Chapter 3, "Fostering Practical Developers in Computer Science Classrooms: A PBL Approach," underpins that real-life software development requires practical developers. This chapter discusses the challenges put by real-life software development on Computer Science education of modern universities, and how to face these challenges by changing traditional teaching and learning to a PBL based approach. Based on a literature review on PBL theories, methods and tools, and observations made in classrooms and group rooms at Aalborg University, this chapter discusses possible aspects to consider when changing traditional Computer Science classrooms. A case is then used to demonstrate the process of changing traditional teaching and learning of a Computer Science course named Visual Programming and Applications to a PBL based approach.

Chapter 4, "PBL Implementation in Material Science and Engineering Education at Chinese Universities," addresses that it is a widespread global process of changing traditional university education with ordinary lectures to more practical and actively student-centered learning systems. Materials Science and Engineering is originally the study of actual engineering materials but now becomes more interdisciplinary, and sophisticated in the rapidly advancing industrial society. It is very necessary to cultivate the practical Materials engineers and it also becomes a big challenge for Chinese universities to make a change. PBL is one of the potential approaches for Chinese Universities. This chapter describes PBL theories, discusses PBL principles, PBL models and also some PBL experiences at Aalborg University. In addition, this chapter exposes how PBL could be applied to Materials Science and Engineering education in Chinese Universities, and a case of PBL implementation has been given to show the process of transformation from traditional education at Chinese Universities to PBL in a Materials Science and Engineering field.

Chapter 5, "Rethinking Environmental Education: Reflections on AAU UNESCO Center Certificate Course of Problem-Based Learning," has important significances of integrating PBL into environmental education based on a professional learning reflection at Aalborg University in Denmark. Based on the inherent wholeness of the human-nature ecosystem, interdisciplinary, sustainability-oriented teaching philosophies in environmental education, endeavor has been made for the appeal of more concern the value of life, aiming at promoting greater sensitivity to critical thinking, individual happiness, and social responsibility. Problem-Based Learning may be an effective way to realize the action competence of students by solving real problems and adjusting their behavior and finally to compass transformative learning and lifelong learning. Following this sense, this chapter will provide a theoretical reflection on how to improve environmental education by PBL in the future.

Chapter 6, "The Change Towards PBL: Designing and Applying PBL at a Program Level," proposes the design of course groups on PBL for students from the BSc. programmes of Robot Engineering (RE) at NEU, China. The overall courses are divided into four groups throughout grade 1 to 4. By a discussion step by step, this chapter firstly provides background information about student cultivation and discipline construction in RE, then introduces the correlation of characteristics between PBL and RE programme that lays the reasons for applying PBL in RE. Finally, this chapter introduces the detailed design of course groups by PBL.

Chapter 7, "An Elective Course-Based Model for the Change of Traditional Engineering Curriculum Towards PBL," presents two PBL models for the change of traditional engineering curriculum based on traditional courses across colleges at the Northeastern University in China. A particular focus of the PBL model design is about the interdisciplinarity. In this regard, the E2-iPBL model is developed based on general and major elective courses offered across many disciplines, whereas the JD-iPBL model is considered to develop PBL courses by further introducing compulsory major courses for a joint-degree training program. For practical implementations within the traditional engineering curriculum background, the change of teacher's role for student-centered constructive learning is briefly summarized. Possible realizations and simple cases are illustrated. Finally, a comparative study of the E2-iPBL and JD-iPBL models is outlined.

Chapter 8, "Experience and Reflection on PBL and Implementation of Interdisciplinary-Level PBL Plan," introduces the author's teaching practices, teaching philosophy and teaching challenges by traditional ways in Northeastern University of China at first. Then it presents the author's experience and learning of PBL in UNESCO center of Aalborg University. And the impact and guidance of the course on author's teaching philosophy, challenges and skills are also given in this chapter. To apply PBL teaching methods, the author proposes future teaching plans with PBL. Moreover, design and implementation of interdisciplinary level PBL plan is presented. And the implementation plan is expounded by six aspects, students, teaching staff, learning goals, contents, teaching and learning methods and assessment. Finally, a case is put forward by the implementation plan.

Chapter 9, "Facilitating Cross-Cultural Communication: A Global Dimension to Fostering International Talents and Innovation in University Foreign Affairs

Management," emphasizes that the global integration of universities is profoundly affecting the direction of higher education's development, accepting the idea of international education, promoting the internationalization of higher education, and cultivating high-quality innovative international talents. The purpose of this chapter is twofold: 1) to make a brief interpretation of global dimension mainly focusing on the criterion for "international talents" and the requirements for the internationalization of higher education; and 2) to address foreign affairs management in universities plays a vital role in promoting the internationalization of teaching, research and administrative management, which can be regarded as a key diver to develop global dimension of innovation in higher education. Accordingly, this chapter proposes potential strategies for innovation of the foreign affairs management in universities, which has important significances in studies on internationalization of higher education, cross-cultural communication, and foreign affairs management.

Chapter 10, "Developing Engineering Creativity in STEM Programs in Chinese Universities," aims to formulate a proposal of developing engineering creativity by problem and project-based pedagogies in STEM programmes in university education in China. It will introduce the increasing needs of engineering creativity in China, deepen understanding the concept of creativity and engineering creativity, and provide a review of diverse models of problem and project-based pedagogies in STEM programmes. This further brings a discussion on how to develop engineering creativity in STEM programmes in Chinese universities in order to overcome the barriers caused by traditional education system and culture. A series of strategies will be proposed including supporting student group work, designing interdisciplinary project, facilitating staff development, and developing creative communities, etc. Briefly, this chapter has significances of developing engineering creativity in China and also implies how to develop problem and project-based pedagogies in STEM programmes in other cultures around the world.

As we can see today PBL is widespread across cultures around the world; however, at present in China, it is still in its infancy. Accordingly, contributors involved in this book behave as pioneers of keeping an open mind, exploring innovative strategies, and leading university education changes towards leaner-centered models in China. This book lays a stepping-stone in paving the way of moving on higher education reforms by taking PBL as a reference. It guides audience to unpack a 'black box of PBL' from perspectives interplayed between the Chinese context and the global context. Thus, this book contributes to provide an international forum to encourage more educators, researchers, decision-makers, and practitioners, who are interested in PBL and who are seeking for strategies of contributing university education innovation, to share with knowledge, experience, and insights between each other.

This further benefits to draw significant inspirations and implications of rethinking 'why', 'what', and 'how' to develop PBL for institutions in higher education around the world and improving traditional universities for gaining more core competence and opportunities of sustainable development in the future.

Zhiliang Zhu
Northeastern University, China

Chunfang Zhou
Aalborg University, Denmark

Acknowledgment

This book embodies the significant achievement of a collaboration on *Designing, Participation and Facilitation of Problem and Project-Based Learning (PBL)* between Northeastern University (NEU), China and Aalborg University (AAU), Denmark.

We acknowledge all institutional supports from NEU and AAU for starting up and moving on the collaborative project cross-culturally that brings a strong motivation to foster PBL in Chinese universities in global context.

We acknowledge all the contributors involved in this book project. More specially, we would like to thank all authors for their participation in this book, all reviewers for their valuable insights for improvement of academic quality, and the IGI Global staff for their continuous support during the development of the book. Without their support, this book would not have become a reality.

Zhiliang Zhu
Northeastern University, China

Chunfang Zhou
Aalborg University, Denmark

Chapter 1
Fostering Problem-Based Learning (PBL) in Chinese Universities for a Creative Society

Chunfang Zhou
Aalborg University, Denmark

Zhiliang Zhu
Northeastern University, China

ABSTRACT

Recently, building a creative society has been a new vision of China that brings much discussion on how to foster creative talents and how to improve pedagogic models in Chinese universities. This chapter regards problem-based learning (PBL) as a promising strategy, and accordingly, the following questions will be discussed: 1) How can we understand the context of building a creative society in China? 2) What is a PBL model? 3) How can we understand history of PBL in a global context? 4) What is the theoretical root of PBL? and 5) For Chinese universities, what are boundaries to be broken for facilitating changes towards PBL that benefits to build a creative society? As both challenges and opportunities of fostering PBL in Chinese universities will be revealed, and appropriate strategies of reform will be suggested, this chapter has important significances of pedagogical innovation in Chinese context. In addition, it also implies universities in other cultures for improving innovation strategies in the future.

DOI: 10.4018/978-1-5225-9961-6.ch001

INTRODUCTION

Recently, 'innovation-oriented nation' have been an officially recognized national strategy in China, and it has been a belief that only innovation will afford the nation a leading role in existing and emerging areas of development (Jing & Osborne, 2017). According to the report provided by Mckinsey Global Institute (MGI) in 2017 (https://www.mckinsey.com), China has one of the most active digital-investment and start-up ecosystems in the world, has the potential to set the world's digital frontier in coming decades. We can see that 'creativity', 'design', 'digitalization', 'entrepreneurship', and 'innovation' have become key words in Chinese political discourse. As one of key element of innovation, creativity has been a new strategic choice to combine with technology and market demand to develop high-value-added cultural and creative industries. Cultural creativity and technological innovation have been linked to the 'wheels of a cart and wings of a bird' for economic growth in China (Li, 2011). This underpins that creative industries promote the transformation of economic development model through transformation of resources, value upgrading, structural optimization, and market expansion.

Accordingly, to build a creative society has been one part of a new vision and development strategy in China. As The World Bank (2013) described, by 2030, if managed well, China could become a modern, harmonious, creative, and high-income society. Among a series of key factors of supporting the new strategy, 'creativity' and 'new technology' have been addressed as two key enablers to build a creative society. The new strategy highlights that China sees itself building its future prosperity on innovation in which everyone's creative potential is tapped. Its success will lie in its ability to produce more value, not more products, enabling it to move up the value chain and compete globally in the same product space as advanced countries. In the shift that China is moving towards a creative society, it is a more specific indicator of cultural progress that the slogan 'harmonious society', which is used to refer to all facets of people's lives (Zhou et al., 2017).

Given the role of young talents in technological development, attracting the creative, smart, and highly educated has been a major task for Chinese government in the past decade (The World Bank, 2013). What society really needs is a combination of creative skills and practical capabilities among Chinese students. As Li (2011) addressed, creative industries are an industrialized business operation system covering process of creative planning, production, marketing and consumption. Designers, engineers or technology developers, production crews, agents, marketing professionals, and managers should all be professionally trained. However, creative people cannot be fostered overnight. Creativity among Chinese students are influenced by social values, pedagogical practices and educational testing systems (Zhou, 2018). Although educational reform is underway, most of Chinese universities are still following a teaching way of 'chalk and talk', with large classes and single-discipline, lecture-based delivery of the norm. These are truly traditional pedagogical models and organizational systems.

Thus, to build a creative education mechanism in China, focuses should be on breaking through the boundaries of the traditional education system and establishing a new teaching concept and new curriculum that is required by a creative society. It can be seen that recently, Chinese universities strive to learn advanced pedagogic models from other cultures and introduce them to local contexts, and those new models include, for example, inquiry-based learning, Problem-Based Learning (PBL), service learning, active learning, challenge-based learning, outcome-based education, and CDIO (Conceive, Design, Implement, and Operate), etc (Zhou, 2012; Kolmos, 2013, Zhou, 2018). All of these new models are student-centered in their philosophy and approach to learning; moreover, among them, PBL has been particularly regarded as a promising strategy for fostering creative talents in China (Zhou, 2012; Zhou, 2018).

Under such a background, this chapter explores a discussion focusing on how to foster PBL in Chinese universities that benefits to build a creative society. Based on such a focus, a series of key questions will lead the discussion:

1. How can we understand the context of building a creative society in China?
2. What is a PBL model?
3. What is a history of PBL in a global view?
4. What is the theoretical root of PBL? And
5. For Chinese universities, what are boundaries to be broken for facilitating changes towards PBL that benefits to build a creative society?

As the above questions indicate, the new vision of developing a creative society in China shapes a context for fostering PBL in Chinese universities, and provides opportunities as well as challenges. This chapter has important significances that brings a discussion on potential strategies of applying PBL in a particular context of China based on a comprehensive understanding on PBL in a global view. This also implies universities in other cultures, especially in Asian areas where are also influenced by traditional Confucianism, for rethinking how to improve their pedagogic models and how to step on first stone on the way of changing towards PBL in the future.

A NEW VISION: BUILDING A CREATIVE SOCIETY IN CHINA

From a historical view, in the 1980s, there were much discussions on the transition from the Industrial Society to the Information Society; since 1990s, focus of discussion is on Knowledge Society; however, it does not mean information is not useful when it is transformed into knowledge (Reimeris, 2016). Undoubtedly, knowledge alone is not enough. In today's rapidly changing world, people must continually come up with creative solutions to unexpected problems. Success is based not only on what or how much knowledge we know, but on our abilities to think and act creatively. In short, we are now living in the Creative Society (Purushothaman& Zhou, 2014).

Therefore, we think creative society is an expansion or evolution of information and knowledge society. Ideally such a society reflects an open system model; overcoming one constraints leads to possibilities as well as new challenges (Li, 2011). Although at the moment there is no widespread, solid and universal description of the creative society, there is an agreement that a creative society views creativity as vital to the economy in general and fundamental to a technology-driven global economy in particular (Araya, 2010). So, as mentioned previously, creativity and new technology are two key enablers of a creative society. From a narrow sense, the creative society labels the society as being creative or interchangeably inventive; creativity is just the one of possible features, likely the most important one, which can be attributed to the contemporary society. From a broad sense, the creative society should be understood as a phenomenon; it is a name of the contemporary society, not limited only to one attribute as being creative, but emphasizing the creativity as state of the society, affecting all other attributes (Resnik, 2007).

However, what is creativity? The literature has shown a general definition of creativity is to develop new and useful ideas (Amabile, 1996; Zhou, 2016a). 'Newness' is pointed out as being new with regard to the whole of humanity or to the person's previous ways of thinking; 'usefulness' means to possess relevance and effectiveness and having the ability to satisfy the need for which it is created (Zhou, 2012; Zhou 2018). So creativity is more than just making something, seeing differently, and solving problems successfully, for it also includes innovating and inventing, question posing and meaning-making, and change and transformation (Mullen, 2017). The creative act may be regarded either as a mental or an intellectual phenomenon, known as creative thinking or divergent thinking, or as a process that generates social and cultural products, such as music and works of art, science and technology, a concept known as divergent production (Guilford, 1950; Amabile,

1996). This means firstly, creativity is both a domain-general and a domain-specific ability (Zhou, 2012); and secondly, creative abilities do not stand in isolation and there are a lot of variables influencing the nature and ontogeny of the creative act (Zhou, 2016b). These variables span a wide range of individual and situational attributes, including knowledge, basic cognitive processes, aptitudes and abilities, personality characteristics, environmental perceptions, environmental structure, cultural characteristics, and economic or evaluative considerations (Zhou, 2016a).

In technological context, the most important characteristic of creativity is to perform tasks or solve problems. A problem triggers the context for engagement, curiosity, inquiry, and a quest to address a real-world concern (Tan, 2009). Technology problems can take various forms, such as failure to perform, situations in need of immediate attention or improvement, a need to find better ways to do things, unexplained phenomena or observations, gaps in information and knowledge, decision-making situations, or a need for new designs or innovations (Zhou, 2016a). This means creativity in solving technological problems should not only be measured by outcomes, products, or solutions, it always involves processes that interacts with influencing factors in technology contexts (Zhou, 2017). Furthermore, we can understand new technologies play dual roles in developing a creative society. On one hand, the proliferation of new technologies is quickening the pace of change, accentuating the need for creative thinking in all aspects of people's lives. On the other hand, new technologies have the potential, if properly designed and used, to help people develop as creative thinkers, so that they are better prepared for life in the creative society (Mitchel, 2007).

To build a creative society in China, it means the economic growth is frequently seen as based on the creativity, on the new recipes and new combination of local capital and via innovation centers; attention should be paid to creative workers and creative class that is based on the professionalism delivered by education (Mitchel, 2007; Li, 2011). Meanwhile, technology has emerged as the 'info-structure' for enterprises competing on a global scale, and it has provided the platform on the top of which knowledge-driven organizations create value (Reimeris, 2016). Moving beyond the simple 'one-to-many' liner model of industrial manufacturing, the information and communication networks are facilitating 'many-to-many' production (Ramaswamy & Ozcan, 2014). Building out from specialized communities of practice, there is a noticeable shift from passive consumption to active cultural production (Jing & Osborne, 2017). Fundamental to this shift is an emerging understanding that tools that facilitate design in the context of learning by doing are becoming crucial to the advancement of both culture and economy (Araya, 2010; Pucciarelli & Kaplan, 2016). Briefly, the most important factor in a creative society is education. This point drives this chapter to discuss PBL as a promising strategy to be applied in Chinese universities in the following sections.

PROBLEM-BASED LEARNING (PBL): HOW TO DEFINE IT?

What is PBL? Briefly, it is a student-centered educational model. Theoretically, it reflects social theories of learning. In practice, student learning centers on a complex problem that does not have a single correct answer (Zhou, 2016a). Students work in collaborative groups to identify what they need to learn in order to solve a problem. They engage in self-directed learning and then they apply their new knowledge to the problem and reflect on what they learned and the effectiveness of the strategies employed. The teachers act to facilitate the learning process rather than only to provide knowledge (Zhou, 2017). Meanwhile, curricula are organized to support the development of disciplinary patterns of discourse and representations of a domain, emphasizing the importance of formulating and evaluating, questions, problems, arguments, and explanations (Hmelo-Silver, 2004). Teachers in PBL help to support knowledge construction as students are guided through their problem-solving processes. In order to deepen understanding the process of learning ad facilitating, a learning cycle has been developed (Zhou, et al., 2015) (Figure 1).

In this cycle, the PBL process begins with a discussion on how to solve a real-life problem (Hmelo-Silver, 2004). Students will work in groups towards a shared understanding of the problem presented to them. They then brainstorm ideas about the content area related to the problem using their existing knowledge and prior experiences. Similar types of ideas are grouped into named categories. The most important and actual problem areas among the named categories are determined. The first tutorial session is then held to decide on the learning tasks to undertake and the goals to achieve. Following the tutorial, students engage in information search and self-study, working both individually and in pairs or in small groups depending on the learning tasks and goals as well as the strategy deemed most appropriate for seeking information. The second tutorial is the time for applying the new knowledge acquired, to tackle the learning tasks and to reconstruct the problem in a new way. New and in-depth knowledge is synthesized and integrated to provide a basis for deeper learning. Participants clarify and reflect on the whole problem-solving process in the light of the new knowledge. Assessment is part of every single phase

Figure 1. Problem-based learning cycle

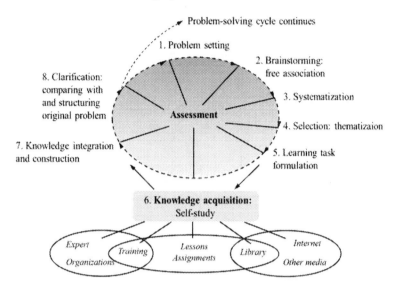

of the process. It is necessary to close the tutorial with feedback about students' own learning, their information-seeking behavior, their problem-solving skills and the group processes so that improvements can be made (Zhou, et al., 2015).

The above process fosters a type of learning environment where produces students who are self-confident in their social roles within a group, willing to take risk in the public social arena of the classroom and willingly collaborate with others to interpret and develop meaning from challenging problems (Zhou, 2012; Zhou, 2017). Meanwhile, PBL advocates experienced-based education (Hmelo-Silver, 2004): it provides students with guided experience in learning through solving complex, real-world problems, and therefore it helps students to: a) construct an extensive and flexible knowledge based, b) develop effective problem-solving skills, c) develop self-directed, lifelong learning skills, d) become effective collaborators, and e) become intrinsically motivated to learn. In order to reach these goals, more specifically, PBL should have the following characteristics (Savery, 2006; Zhou, 2016a):

1. Students must have the responsibility for their own learning.
2. The problem simulations used in PBL must be ill-structured and allow for free inquiry.
3. Learning should be integrated from a wide range of disciplines or subjects.
4. Collaboration is essential.

5. What students learn during their self-directed learning must be applied back to the problem with reanalysis and resolution.

6. A closing analysis of what has been learned from work with the problem and a discussion of what concepts and principles have been learned are essential.

7. Self and peer assessment should be carried out at the completion of each problem and at the end of every curricular unit.

8. The activities carried out in PBL must be those valued in the real world.

9. Student examinations must measure student progress towards the goals of PBL. And,

10. PBL must be the pedagogical base in the curriculum and not part of a didactic curriculum.

Given the above, PBL can be seen as a model in a co-created curriculum. As indicated by Figure1, PBL involves a dynamic and interactive process of teaching and learning, and multiple channels of resource of teaching and learning. It also involves the elements in a co-created curriculum such as students' active and reflective participation, the changes of teachers' role towards facilitation and increased levels of individual and collective students' responsibility for their learning, etc (Zhou, 2014; Zhou, 2017).

A REVIEW IN GLOBAL CONTEXT: HOW IS A HISTORY OF PBL?

History of PBL calls us to look back its development in medical school. This was due to a concern with rigidity and over-emphasis on memorizing of large volumes of information in medical education. In Canada, as early as 1899, Sir William Osler recommended abolishing lectures and allowing medical students more time for self-study. He suggested that a more important role of teachers was to help students develop their skills in observation and reasoning (Khoo, 2003). In 1932, the Commission on Medical Education of the Association of American Colleges stated that medical education should develop sound habits as well as methods of independent study and thought, which will equip the students to continue their self-education through life. This can be brought about only by freeing medical education from some of its present rigidity and uniformity, by reducing classroom overcrowding, and by adapting medical education to more closely meet the educational needs of students (Nandi, et al., 2000).

In 1969, the term Problem-Based Learning (PBL) was originally coined by Don Woods who is based on his work with Chemistry students in McMaster's University in Canada (Zhou, 2016). Since then, many medical schools in USA, Canada and Europe have implemented PBL as part of their curricula. However, acceptance and adoption of PBL in other medical schools was relatively slow process, especially in the early years since its first implementation (Gwee, 2008). Usually, development and change in education can occur at many levels, but there are basically two kinds: one is the individual level which focuses on changing the teachers' attitude towards learning and teaching; and one is the systemic level which focuses on changing the overall foundation of the educational programme by instituting new objectives and methods of teaching and evaluation, along with efforts aimed at cultural change (Kolmos, 2002). But in the changes from a traditional model to PBL, both individual and systematic levels are involved. In fact, PBL is a highly resource-intensive teaching-learning strategy, its adoption and implementation would require a significant change in the mindsets of teachers and students (Gwee, 2008). This is because PBL requires a major shift from a traditional teacher-directed instructional paradigm to a student-centered learning paradigm, and usually, it is not a popular and less readily accepted shift by policy-makers, institutional leaders, teachers and students.

It should be noted that parallel to the birth and development of PBL in the medical schools, in Denmark, a new pedagogical approach to PBL in engineering education emerged in the University of Roskilde in 1972 and Aalborg University in 1974. The Danish PBL approach is a combination of a problem-based and a project-organized approach. The students analyze and define problems within a defined interdisciplinary or subject frame. The students work together in groups on their project and submit a common project report. The project group has a joint examination but the students are given individual marks. Furthermore, in each semester the project and the majority of the courses must relate to the theme of the actual semester, students spend half time in doing project and the other half in courses (Zhou, 2012). The Danish approach to PBL has been evidenced as a well-established concept, since it is also used at Maastricht University in the Netherlands, Linköping University in Sweden. They were all new universities established in 1970s (Kolmos, Fink, & Krogh, 2004).

Until mid-1990s, PBL had spread widely across continents and what started as only a ripple soon became almost a tidal wave, as it gained acceptance by more and more fields. According to an earlier data provide by Samford University in 2000, there were more than 100 undergraduate institutions using PBL around the world. Those institutions involve universities in areas of United States, Australia, Belgium, Canada, Denmark, the Netherlands, Hong Kong, Sweden, Italy, Turkey, India, Singapore, Philippines, Korean, and United Kingdom, etc (Zhou & Shi, 2016). Then we can also find that at about same time, in mid-1990s, many Asian governments were in the search of a new educational paradigm that would ensure the end-product capability acquired from higher education and would be able to match the demands and challenges made on a workforce in a globalized knowledge-based economy in the 21st century (Gwee, 2008; Purushothaman& Zhou, 2014). PBL, with its more holistic approach to education had great appeal to many Asian universities. There were orgnizations begun to host varies PBL conferences, for example, the Asia Pacific Conference on PBL was initiated by the University of Hong Kong; the 6th conference of this organization was hosted by Tokyo Women's Medical University in Tokyo, Japan (Gwee, 2008). Along with development of research network in Asia, studies on PBL accordingly were mainly focused on globalization of PBL, diversity of PBL models, and cross-cultural implications for PBL (Khoo, 2003).

Today, PBL is widespread across the globe. Spreading from America and Europe to Asia, and then from Taiwan and Hong Kong to Mainland China, PBL has been drawn a growing interests among educators who are striving for reforms. However, in Asian areas, most of universities that practise PBL are medical colleges (Lam, Wan & IP, 2006). We can see that from the mid-1980s in Asia, some medical schools began to adopt PBL, with the aim of cultivating students' creativity and practical abilities. In 1986, the first 2 tertiary colleges to introduce PBL to China were Shanghai Second Medical University and Xi'an Medical University. Since 1990s, the number of tertiary colleges adopting PBL gradually increased, with positive results. (Lam, Wan & IP, 2006). Besides medical education, PBL in other fields has also been tried in practice, for example, in Regional Anatomy education at Peking University (Wang et al., 2010), and in Analytical Chemistry education at Ocean University of China (Zhang, 2002). More recently, in October 2018, Tsinghua University organized The 7th International Research Symposium on PBL in Engineering Education (http://www.icee-unesco.org/unesco/news/5). However, even though there are emerging initiatives of fostering PBL in Chinese universities, most cases are still on single course levels and there are little experience of interdisciplinary curriculum design. In one word, PBL in China is still in its infancy.

In addition, the rapid development of Information and Communication Technology (ICT) in the 21st century is demanding swift action to engage students to participate in the mainstream of development. The Web 2.0 era that encouraged the sharing of information, discussion, and video applications virtually, certainly adds to the treasures of germination and dissemination of knowledge all over the world (Daud & Zakaria, 2012). With the emergence of online learning and e-learning initiatives, there has been shaped two major trajectories of the use of technology in PBL: a) distance learning, and b) use of multimedia (Castell, 2011; Purushothaman & Zhou, 2014).

However, studies (Tan, 2009; Verstegen et al., 2016; Zhou & Purushothaman, 2017) have emphasized that to genuinely support PBL, e-learning tools and facilities should support or at least not hinder the PBL principles and processes such as activation of prior knowledge, elaboration, structuring, and restructuring of information, collaborative learning, learning in context, and self-directed learning, etc. This means, digital tools should be as elements being integrated into a PBL environment that also reflect requirements of improvement of digital skills and literacy among students as well as teaching staff (Tan, 2009; Li; 2011; Zhou, 2017).

A THEORITICAL RELFECTION: WHY DOES PBL WORK?

One of the starting points of theoretical reflection on PBL is to define 'what learning is', to rethink 'how we learn', and to then reflect further 'why PBL works but that is supported by its theoretical roots'. In the following lines, we will firstly review definitions of 'learning"; secondly we will take a social perspective to discuss how learning happens; and finally, as a summary of the theoretical reflection on PBL, a 'co-creation' concept will be addressed.

Broadly, learning develops knowledge, abilities, understandings, emotions, attitudes and sociality, which are important elements of the conditions and raw material of society (Zhou, 2017). It involves any process that in living organisms leads to permanent capacity change and which is not solely due to biological maturation or ageing (Illeris, 2007). Such a broad understanding of an definition of learning means many different elements must be taken into consideration if the whole complexity of human learning is to be understood (Zhou, 2012; Zhou, 2016a). Even though the term 'learning' has been used very broadly, but partly, it has different meanings. In general, four different main meaning can be distinguished that most frequently occur when the term learning is used in a non-specific manner in everyday language (Illeris, 2007):

1. The term learning can refer to the outcomes of the learning processes that take place in the individual. Therefore, learning is used to mean what has been learned or the change that has taken place.
2. The term learning can refer to the mental processes that take place in the individual and can lead to such changes or outcomes as covered by meaning a). These may be termed learning processes that learning psychology is concerned with.

3. The term learning can refer to both the interaction processes between individuals and their material and social environment, which, directly or indirectly, are preconditions for the inner learning processes covered by meaning b), and which can lead to the learning covered by meaning a).

4. The term learning is very often employed not only in every language, but also in official and professional contexts, more or less synonymously with the term teaching. This shows that there is a general tendency to confuse the terms for teaching and learning.

Learning is thus understood as a matter that is wide-ranging and complex, and it is impossible to arrive at an adequate understanding of the extensive and complex field of learning without relating to the results achieved in different scholarly approaches (Burr, 1995; Wenger, 1998; Biesta, 2009). Traditionally, learning has been explored first and foremost as a psychological matter, and learning psychology is one of the most classical disciplines of psychology. But other psychological disciplines must be also involved, such as development psychology, cognitive psychology, personality psychology, and social psychology (Illeris, 2007). In recent years, understanding of learning has also been taken up to a considerable extent quite outside of what we traditionally understand as psychology (Mullen, 2017). This has been explored further: on one hand, on a biological basis in connection with understanding the body and brain research; on the other hand, on a social science basis, first and foremost in the 'grey area' between sociology and social psychology. While the literature has shown there are growing interests on such a 'grey area' that links a close discussion on 'how we learn'(Illeris, 2007; Pucciarelli & Kaplan, 2016; Zhou, 2018).

However, how can we understand the meaning of being social? When something is social, it is automatically interconnected and referred to other people (Zhou, 2016b). Weber (1922) defined "social acting" in a way that the sense of the action is related to others' behavior. Social acting is an essential part of our everyday life and also occurs at the workplace and its sequence is always oriented to others (Zhou & Luo, 2012). Accordingly, the social perspective to learning has been discussed much on its relevance with issues such as pedagogical innovation, curriculum design, and assessment. It involves different research branches, for example, social constructionism (Gergen, 1994), community of practice (Wenger, 1998), activity system (Engeström et al., 1999), networks (Fox, 2000), and complexity (Sawyer, 2005; Haggis, 2007). Although there are diverse focuses explored within a common framework, all theorists talk about the 'situation specificity' of behavior; our behavior is viewed as being dependent not upon personality characteristics but upon the nature of the situations in which we find ourselves; behavior is therefore 'specific' to a particular situation (Burr, 1995). Meanwhile, the discussion becomes more and more broadly and right into national economy (Illeris, 2007; Ramaswamy & Ozcan, 2014). This applies, for example, to measures to strengthen adult learning and lifelong learning with a view to economic growth and competitiveness and to improve educational reforms on a national level (Zhou, et al., 2017).

From a social perspective, firstly and most importantly, a keyword of 'interaction' should be addressed. It includes action, communication, and cooperation. This means fundamentally learning is a process mediating between man as biologically and genetically developed species and the societal structures developed by man. Learning is not something that only takes place in the single individual; on the contrary, learning is always embedded in a social and societal context that provides impulses and sets the frames for what can be learned and how (Illeris, 2007). As addressed by Wenger (1998), learning is the interplay between social competence and personal experience, which is a dynamic, two-way relationship between people and the social learning systems in which they participate. A social theory of learning integrates the components necessary to characterize social participation as a process of learning and knowing. These components include a) meaning, b) practice, c) community, and d) identity. Similarly, Illeris (2007) has described that there are three dimensions involved in all learning: namely a) the content and the incentive, which have to do with the individual acquisition process; b) the emotional or psychodynamic dimension is the dimension encompassing mental energy, feelings and motivations; and c) the social and societal dimension, to do with the interaction processes between the individual and the environment. The three dimensions frames a learning circle that indicates learning always takes place within the frames of an outer societal context, which on the general level, is decisive for the learning possibilities. Thus, learning combines personal transformation with the evolution of social structures.

A social perspective to learning suggests learning cannot be apart from 'practice'. According to Wenger (1998), 'practice' can be regarded as the learners' shared historical and social resources, frameworks, and perspectives that can sustain their mutual engagement in action in certain community. It involves the skilled practice that uses experience, knowledge and inquiry processes to increase our capability to intervene, interpret, and act positively on successes, problems, issues, and significant questions. So practice is therefore associated with learners' reflection. The reflective practices help us to understand the links between feeling, thinking and doing and the links between what we do and how we might improve our effectiveness by developing new insights (Tan, 2009). This further facilitates 'transformative learning' that refers to the process by which we transform our take-for-granted frames of reference (meaning perspectives, habits of mind, mind-sets), to make them more inclusive, discriminating, open, emotionally capable of change, and reflective so that they may generate beliefs and opinions that will prove more true or justified to guide action (Mezirow, 2000). Through transformative learning, personality-integrated knowledge is developed on the basis of which associations can be freely made in all subjectively relevant contexts (Illeris, 2007).

Following the key point of 'learning by practice', it underpins 'learning by doing', which also means, learning is learned by 'experience'. According to Dewey (1965), there are two central principles of experience: one is continuity, and one is interaction. The principle of continuity of experience means that every experience both takes up something from those which have gone before and modifies in some way the quality of those which come after. Interaction means a transaction is taking place between an individual and what, at the same time, constitutes his environment (Illeris, 2007). From a broader sense, Olesen (1989) suggests experience is the process whereby we as human beings, individually and collectively master reality, and the ever-living understanding of this reality and our relation to it. Experiences in the plural exist, as in everyday language, but they are to be understood as partial products of this process. Experience is thus a subjective process as it is seen from the point of view of the person experiencing. It is also a collective process because when we experience as individuals we also do so through a socially structured consciousness. It is, finally, an active, critical and creative process where we both see and adapt (Illeris, 2007). The understanding on what experience is leads us to recognize that learning requires learners' active engagement though communication between each other and participation, and meanwhile learning involves situated activities that are always learning-in-context (Biesta, 2009). In this regard, we can say context is not the external situation in which learning occurs, but rather the engagement with the environment through which learning happens (Pucciarelli & Kaplan, 2016).

However, to learn knowledge by practice in a context is always full of complexity. As Sáenz (2009) suggested, contextual knowledge is related to everyday-life problems in the real world and enters the learning situation through the presentation of the problem in a context with its own story. It does not appear when the problems are presented using much more than mathematical symbols with numbers, operators and variables. In the process of problem-solving in any professional practice, it is not an instrumental process but influenced by diverse factors in contextual system; there is neither a routine solution nor a defined script for doing the work. Accordingly, we can say the complexity in a learning context stimulates learners' sensitivity in solving problems and facilitates them to understand the interrelated conditions and circumstances that will support or hinder the potential solutions, and therefore gain knowledge from multiple dimensions (Zhou, 2016a). Then we can also say the complexity underpins 'interdisciplinarity'. It involves interaction among two or more different disciplines, and the interaction may range from simple communication of ideas to the mutual integration of organizing concepts, methodology, procedures, epistemology, terminology, data, and organization of research and education in a fairly large field (Lattuca, 2002). Finally, we can say, one of best way of learning is to learn by 'interdisciplinarity'. This could happen in an interdisciplinary group that consist of persons trained in different fields of knowledge. Through organizing learning tasks into common efforts and goals, members from an interdisciplinary group will continuously intercommunicate and make endeavor together (Zhou, 2018).

Furthermore, learning is always for personal competency development and therefore that is beneficial to society development. While competency refers to a person's being qualified in a broader sense. It is not merely that a person masters a professional area, but also that a person can apply this professional knowledge and more than that, apply it in relation to the requirements inherent in a situation which perhaps in addition is uncertain and unpredictable (Jørgensen, 1999; Sawyer, 2005). Thus competence also includes the person's assessments and attitudes, and ability to draw on a considerable part of his/her more personal qualifications (Zhou, 2016a). This drives to reflect that pedagogical design by a social perspective to learning may facilitate competency development, as it highlights conceptions such as interaction, practice, experience, reflection, learning-in-context, active engagement, and interdisciplinarity, etc. All these conceptions are all align with principles and characteristics of PBL, for example, student-centered learning, problem-oriented learning, group learning, peer learning, and interdisciplinary learning, etc (Tan, 2009). Meanwhile, this also helps to understand PBL as a systematic creative environment (Zhou, 2012), as it provides a learning context where is conducive to creativity by reflecting the qualities of exploration, play, taking risks, reflection, flexibility, focus, commitment and sensitivity for valuing the endeavors of individuals and group work (Hmelo-Silver, 2004; Savery, 2006;Zhou, 2014).

If we briefly describe PBL as the learning which results from the process of working towards the understanding of, or resolution of, a problem in situated context (Savery, 2006; Tan, 2009), then it is more a methodology of learning than an instructional method (Zhou, 2014). As a problem refer to what is problematic about a situation (Zhou, 2016a); it is generally shorthand for a cluster, network or set of interrelated problems and related contextual conditions (Hmelo-Silver, 2004). It encourages open-minded, reflective, critical and active learning, and meanwhile it reflects the nature of knowledge – that is, knowledge is complex and changes as a result of responses by communities of persons to problems they perceive in their worlds (Wenger, 1998; Zhou et al., 2015). This further drivers us to rethink in the changes from a traditional lecture-led educational model to a PBL model, a systematic effort is required; it is naturally to change towards a co-creation paradigm by breaking traditional boundaries in higher education, for example, in Chinese universities.

BREAKING BOUNDARY: HOW TO CHANGE TOWARDS PBL IN CHINESE UNIVERSITIES?

As mentioned, in the wake of China's integration into the global economy, regional development is occurring in many parts of China, where reform is the operative principle of economic, social and cultural development (The World Bank, 2013). This includes a number of ongoing conceptual changes, from example, the transformation from economic growth to economic development. While growth and development are two different concepts. Economic growth focuses on quantity and it relates to the increased output caused by variations in input (Jing & Osborne, 2017). The objective of development is of benefit to the general population, since it relates to a broader and deeper than simple economic growth, and it relates to systemic and a combination of quantitative and qualitative changes, which include not only transformations in production inputs but also elements which are the driving forces of development including structure, quality, efficiency, employment, distribution, consumption, ecology, and environment (Li, 2011).

Higher education is a place where the teachers try to understand the world in all its rich complexity and glorious detail, but it is also a place where teachers prepare students for a lifetime of working with their own complex issues and problems (Jackson, 2006; Illeris, 2007). Under a shift towards a creative society, Chinese universities should reflect their roles in re-modelling education mechanism that should be centered on 'people-oriented development' (Li, 2011). Higher education requires not only work under a shift of creativity research from 'how to make people creative', 'why people becomes creative' and 'when people becomes creative', but also work on a paradigm shift in the mindset of authority (Zhou, 2018). This determines 'what' and 'how' young generation will learn according to their demands. Therefore, the design of education needs a significant change that has to be towards a learner-centered design, whose prime focus is allow one's own self-realization, rather than a teacher-centered design whose prime purpose is to imprint a convenient model on students (Pucciarelli & Kaplan, 2016). This also takes the belief that the curriculum design should be combination of theory and practice that provides opportunities of students to learn more to be a practitioner and a researcher than a knowledge receiver. Undoubtedly, all these points are highlighting necessity of PBL.

As discussed, by taking a social perspective to learning, PBL motives students' active and reflective participation, changes of teachers' role towards facilitation, increases levels of individual and collective students' responsibility for their learning (Zhou, 2016b). However, it indicates in the changes towards PBL in Chinese universities, institutions should involve cooperation between multiple PBL elements into one new framework. These elements include knowledge delivery, student projects, examinations, staff development, collaboration with industries, organizational management, and so on. This is, accordingly, Chinese universities should seek for appropriate strategies of integrating multi-dimensional resources. This demands to develop a new profile of 'entrepreneurial university' engaging in collaboration with other actors such as industrial networks, public institutions, and private sectors, etc. As Zhou (2013) figured out, PBL locates all learners in a community of practice where there is an aggregation of people who, through joint engagement in some enterprise, come to develop and share ways of doing things, ways of talking, beliefs, values – in short, practice. Therefore, it requires a wide range of capabilities – knowing facts, concepts, and principles; understanding social relations and norms of interaction; knowing how to communicate and how to interpret documents and other information sources (Wenger, 1998). Thus, to change towards a PBL model means to build up a joint platform of engagement by (and for) multiple stakeholders of an education mechanism (Zhou, 2018), which also means it is calling for a change towards a co-creation paradigm. This requires shift in our thinking to build ecosystems of capabilities together with other private, public, and social sector enterprises to expand wealth-welfare-wellbeing in the economy and in society as a whole (Ramaswamy & Ozcan, 2014).

Given the above, for Chinese universities, first, boundary of traditional relationship between teachers and students should be broken, which means, Chinese teachers should change their professional identity from knowledge providers to facilitator of problem solvers and group collaborators. Such a boundary is influenced by traditional Confucianism. According to Zhou & Shi (2016), on one hand, Confucianism inhibits creativity as the principle of Hierarchical Relationships decrease creativity through unequal relationships, rigid social structure, gender role expectations, and authoritarian relationship between teachers and students; on the other hand, there are also strengths of fostering creativity by collectivism: Chinese learners are good at meeting a shared standard so as to maintain harmony in one's relationships to the group, which leads the groups are to be high in collaboration and achievement of collective goals (Zhou, et al., 2017). By taking these cultural elements into account, Chinese teachers should pick off their 'masks of knowledge authority' given by traditional Confucianism, sit among groups of students together, and encourage students to manage challenge and support with each other (Zhou, 2018). This will meet what PBL requires that involves all learners' active engagement, during which process teachers behave as learner experts who are able to share learning experience with students.

Second, boundary between traditional disciplines should be broken. As suggested by Gibbons and his colleagues (1994), modern university should change its model of knowledge production from single disciplines to trans-disciplines and inter-disciplines. This change should involve a diverse range of specialists with a focus on learning process of solving practical problems collaboratively. In order to break disciplinary boundaries, management structure of institutions that is built upon traditional disciplines should also be re-built for developing transdisciplinary and interdisciplinary programmes in Chinese universities. University management and scholars, should take on a central role in the design of a new assessment framework, promoting bottom-up initiatives and think tanks to bring concrete proposals to political and institutional decision makers, which take into account the learner-centric and knowledge-centric focus of higher education (Pucciarelli & Kaplan, 2016). Moreover, the quality of university management should increasingly be considered in terms of what staff and students need; the need includes both 'hard resource' (such as physical capital and advanced equipment) and 'soft resource' (such as methods of knowledge management and assessment)(Zhou, et al., 2017). Based on a concept of 'people-oriented development', Chinese universities should pay more attention to a dynamic generated by interplay between 'hard resource' and 'soft resource' that further brings a great power of innovation.

Third, boundary of traditional organizations should be broken, which means, universities should go towards open innovation and increase interactions and value co-creation with multiple stakeholders and partners locally and globally. This is to say, universities will not live in 'ivory towers' any longer; instead, 'being entrepreneurial universities' will be a way of gaining more research resources by corporations with industries for and increased number of applied projects (Zhou, et al., 2017). Such a strategy will further lead to increased partnership between universities, and between universities and industries. In other words, attention should be paid to build 'innovation communities', which is the foundation of a co-creation paradigm, as it provides opportunities of developing cross-disciplinary innovation initiatives and a joint platform of engagement for synthesis of resources. Within an university, this will benefit to more opportunities of research projects as well as student projects. However, the research culture in Chinese universities is highly competitive; researchers must obtain research funding and disseminate the results of their research through peer-reviewed publications. This makes it important for university administrators to build institutions that can support both the processes dissemination and commercialization of research outcomes and student research abilities. Accordingly, for Chinese universities, to ensure building a 'healthy innovation community', policy efforts are needed to ensure quality of research, teaching, and learning, as well as equality between learners, researchers, and collaborative partners.

Fourth, boundary between cultures should be broken that underlines a trend of internationalization of Chinese universities. Considering widespread of PBL around the world, Kolmos (2013) figured out quite a lot of international networks have been already established, for example, the Pan-American Network for Problem-Based Learning, the International PBL Symposium organized by Republic Polytechnic in Singapore, and the Aalborg Center for Problem-Based Learning in Engineering Science and Sustainability under the Auspices of UNESCO. These well-established networks provide Chinese universities opportunities of joining in an 'international PBL society' and exploring new forms of international collaboration for sustainable growth. Meanwhile, besides meeting with international partners physically, new emerging digital technologies will increase connections and interactions. As suggested by The World Bank (2013), China will reply more on innovations in Information and Communication Technology (ICT) and pedagogical techniques involving greater use of multimedia and flexible online training customized to the varying needs of students. In other words, there are needs of new design of PBL by digital infrastructures aiming at co-learning through highly responsible pedagogies and deeper integration of Web 2.0 into multimedia classrooms. This will further facilitate the creation of new international networks, giving rise to an expansion and reconfiguration of collaboration between cultures, overcoming the limitations of traditional forms of cooperation (Castells, 2011; Zhou & Purushothaman, 2017).

Last but not least, and to summarize, any change cannot happen overnight, so the above suggested strategies on breaking traditional boundaries require a systematic effort by a long-term plan. For Chinese universities, the reform and the innovation should be incrementally, and therefore the focuses are on a) a self-evaluation of strength and weakness of own pedagogic model in fostering qualified talents, b) identifying an appropriate strategy for improvement of current situation, and c) taking actions step by step. As suggested by The World Bank (2013), in the long run, the objective of developing a creative society should be to develop a system that stimulates broad-based creativity and innovation in China. Meanwhile, self-reflection, evaluation, and improvement should be always along with the process of reform. What is most important is that in the process of change towards PBL and a co-creation paradigm, it requires strong leadership and commitment, steady implementation with a determined will, coordination across ministries and sectors, and effective management of a consultation process. This will ensure multi-dimensional supports and participation in the design, implementation, and oversight of the reform process in Chinese universities.

CONCLUSION

Universities are used to be considered public good, provided by nonprofit organizations that are unexposed to market pressure and have clear societal missions. However, such a traditional thinking should be changed as higher education is becoming a global service delivered by quasi-companies in an ever-more complex environment and competitive knowledge marketplace. Today, as the new vision of building a creative society is underway in China, innovation and technological development are assigned central roles in making long-term five-year plans. Globalization and new development policies bring Chinese universities both challenges and opportunities of pedagogic innovation. Changes of pedagogic models from 'teacher-led education' to 'student-centered learning' have been driven, which meanwhile has grown the interests of PBL. As any educational model has been shaped by its social-cultural environment, the most successful pedagogic model is the one that meets the needs of fostering qualified talents for society for sustainable development and meanwhile fits its local and global contexts. Therefore, for Chinese educators and institution managers, one of most urgent tasks is to develop an appropriate PBL model for Chinese students. This requires to break boundaries such as traditional relationship between teachers and students, between traditional disciplines, between organizations, and between cultures. Beyond a pedagogic model, PBL also requires a synthesized and systematic effort of developing a co-creation platform where involves stakeholders and multi-dimensional resources into one framework. This indicates the reform in Chinese universities should be interplays between bottom-up and up-bottom, so both active participation among teaching staff and strong leadership are required. As the action should be taken step by step, there should be calls for diverse methods and designs of PBL in (or across) different disciplines or different levels. The calls should also involves strong motivation among teaching staff who take pilot PBL studies into their pedagogical practice. The policy makers should accordingly improve the measure system of pedagogical innovation that should include both 'hard' indicators and 'soft' ability or innovation environment, both quantitatively and qualitatively. All these endeavors are what a creative society is striving for in China, centered on a core concept of 'people-oriented development', reflected by new visions of Chinese universities.

REFERENCES

Amabile, T. M. (1996). *Creativity in Context: Update to the Social Psychology of Creativity*. New York: Crown.

Araya, D. (2010). Educational policy in the creative economy. In D. Araya & M. A. Peters (Eds.), *Education in the Creative Economy: Knowledge and Learning in the Age of Innovation* (pp. 3–28). New York: Peter Lang.

Biesta, G. (2009). Pragmatism's contribution to understanding learning-in-context. In R. Edwards, G. Biesta, & M. Thorpe (Eds.), *Rethinking Contexts for Learning and Teaching* (pp. 61–72). London: Routledge.

Burr, V. (1995). *An Introduction to Social Constructionism*. London: Routledge. doi:10.4324/9780203299968

Castells, M. (2011). *The Rise of Network Society*. London: Wiley-Blackwell.

Daud, M. Y., & Zakaria, E. (2012). Web 2.0 application and cultivate creativity in ICT literacy. *Procedia: Social and Behavioral Sciences*, *59*, 459–466. doi:10.1016/j.sbspro.2012.09.301

Dewey, J. (1965). *Experience and Education*. New York: Collier Books.

Engeströ, Y., Miettinen, R., & Punamaki, R. L. (1999). *Perspectives on Activity Theory*. Cambridge, UK: Cambridge University Press. doi:10.1017/CBO9780511812774

Fox, S. (2000). Communities of practice, Foucault and actor-network theory. *Journal of Management Studies*, *37*(6), 853–867. doi:10.1111/1467-6486.00207

Gergen, K. J. (1994). *Realities and Relationships*. Cambridge, MA: Harvard University Press.

Gibbons, M., Limoges, C., Nowotny, H., Schwartzman, S., Scott, P., & Trow, M. (1994). *The New Production of Knowledge: The Dynamic of Science and Research in Contemporary Societies*. London: Sage Publications.

Guilford, J. P. (1950). Creativity. *The American Psychologist*, *5*(9), 444–454. doi:10.1037/h0063487 PMID:14771441

Gwee, M. C. (2008). Globalisation of problem-based learning (PBL): Cross-cultural implications. *The Kaohsiung Journal of Medical Sciences*, *3*(3Suppl), 14–22. doi:10.1016/S1607-551X(08)70089-5 PMID:18364282

Haggis, T. (2007). Conceptualizing the case in adult and higher education research: a dynamic system view. In J. Bogg & R. Geyer (Eds.), *Complexity, Science, and Society*. Oxford, UK: Radcliff.

Hmelo-Silver, C. E. (2004). Problem-Based Learning: What and how do student learn? *Educational Psychology Review*, *16*(3), 235–266. doi:10.1023/B:EDPR.0000034022.16470.f3

Illers, K. (2007). *How We Learn: Learning and Non-Learning in School and Beyond*. London: Routledge. doi:10.4324/9780203939895

Jackson, N. (2006). Imagining a different world. In N. Jackson, M. Oliver, M. Shaw, & J. Wisdom (Eds.), *Developing Creativity in Higher Education: an Imaginative Curriculum* (pp. 1–9). London: Routledge. doi:10.4324/9780203016503

Jing, Y., & Osborne, S. P. (2017). *Public Service Innovation in China*. Singapore: Palgrave. doi:10.1007/978-981-10-1762-9

Jørgensen, P. S. (1999). Hva er kompetence [What is competence]? *Uddannelse (Copenhagen, Denmark)*, *9*, 4–13.

Khoo, H. E. (2003). Implementation of problem-based learning in Asian medical schools and students' perceptions of their experience. *Medical Education*, *37*(5), 401–409. doi:10.1046/j.1365-2923.2003.01489.x PMID:12709180

Kolmos, A. (2002). Facilitating change to a problem-based learning model. *The International Journal for Academic Development*, *7*(1), 63–74. doi:10.1080/13601440210156484

Kolmos, A. (2013). Problem- and project-based learning in a global perspective: community building or certification? In L. Krogh & A. A. Jensen (Eds.), *Visions, Challenges, and Strategies: PBL Principles and Methodologies in a Danish and Global Perspective* (pp. 47–66). Aalborg: Aalborg University Press.

Kolmos, A., Fink, F. K., & Krogh, L. (2004). The Aalborg Model- Problem-Based and Project-organized learning. In A. Kolmos, F. K. Fink, & L. Krogh (Eds.), *The Aalborg PBL Model-Progress, Diversity and Challenges* (pp. 9–18). Aalborg: Aalborg University Press.

Lam, T. P., Wan, X. H., & Ip, M. S. (2006). Current perspectives on medical education in China. *Medical Education*, *40*(10), 940–949. doi:10.1111/j.1365-2929.2006.02552.x PMID:16987183

Lattura, L. R. (2002). Learning interdisciplinarity: Sociocultural perspectives on academic work. *The Journal of Higher Education*, *73*(6), 711–739.

Li, W. (2011). How Creativity is Changing China (M. Keane, Ed.; H. Li & M. Guo, Trans.). Bloomsbury Academic.

Mezirow, J. (2000). Learning to think like an adult: core conceptions of transformation theory. In J. Mezirow & ... (Eds.), *Learning as Transformation: Critical Perspectives on a Theory in Progress*. San Francisco: Jossey-Bass.

Mullen, C. A. (2017). *Creativity and Education in China: Paradox and Possibilities for an Era of Accountability*. New York: Routledge. doi:10.4324/9781315665856

Nandi, P. L., Chan, J. N. F., & Chan, C. P. K. (2000). Undergraduate medical education: Comparison of problem-based learning and conventional teaching. *Hong Kong Medical Journal*, *6*, 301–306. PMID:11025850

Olesen, H. S. (1989). *Adult Education and Everyday Life*. Roskilde: The Adult Education Group, Roskilde University.

Pucciarelli, F., & Kaplan, A. (2016). Competition and strategy in higher education: Managing complexity and uncertainty. *Business Horizons*, *59*(3), 311–320. doi:10.1016/j.bushor.2016.01.003

Purushothaman, A., & Zhou, C. (2014). Change toward a creative society in developing contexts: Women's barriers to learning by Information and Communication Technology. *Gender, Technology and Development*, *18*(3), 363–386. doi:10.1177/0971852414544008

Ramaswamy, V., & Ozcan, K. (2014). *The Co-creation Paradigm*. Stanford, CA: Stanford University Press.

Reimeris, R. (2016). Theoretical features of the creative society. *Creativity Studies*, *9*(1), 15–24. doi:10.3846/23450479.2015.1088902

Resnick, M. (2007, December). Sowing the seeds for a more creative society. *Learning and Leading with Technology*, 18–22.

Sáenz, C. (2009). The role of contextual, conceptual and procedural knowledge in activating mathematical competencies (PISA). *Educational Studies in Mathematics*, *71*(2), 123–143. doi:10.100710649-008-9167-8

Savery, J. R. (2006). Overview of problem-based learning: Definitions and distinctions. *Interdisciplinary Journal of Problem-Based Learning*, *1*(1), 9–20. doi:10.7771/1541-5015.1002

Sawyer, R. K. (2005). *Social Emergence: Societies As Complex Systems*. New York: Cambridge University Press. doi:10.1017/CBO9780511734892

Tan, O. S. (2009). *Problem-Based Learning and Creativity*. Singapore: Cengage Learning Asia Pte Ltd.

The World Bank. (2013). *China 2030: Building A Modern, Harmonious, and Creative Society*. Washington, DC: The World Bank.

Verstegen, D. M. L., de Jong, N., van Berlo, J., Camp, A., Könings, K. D., van Merriöenboer, J. J. G., & Donkers, J. (2016). How e-learning can support PBL groups: a literature review. In S. Bridges, L. K. Chan, & C. E. Hmelo-Silver (Eds.), *Educational Technologies in Medical and Health Sciences Education* (pp. 9–33). Springer International Publishing. doi:10.1007/978-3-319-08275-2_2

Wang, J., Zhang, W., & Qin, L. (2010). Problem-based learning in regional anatomy education at Peking University. *Anatomical Sciences Education*, *3*, 121–126. PMID:20496433

Weber, M. (1922). Die protestantische Ethik und der Geist des Kapitalismus. In M. Weber (Ed.), Gesammelte Aufsätze zur Religionssoziologie. Tübingen: Mohr Siebeck.

Wenger, E. (1998). *Communities of Practice, Learning, Meaning and Identity*. New York: Cambridge University Press. doi:10.1017/CBO9780511803932

Zhang, G. (2002, October). Using problem based learning and cooperative group learning in teaching instrumental analysis. *The China Papers*, 4-8.

Zhou, C. (2012). *Group Creativity Development in Engineering Education in Problem and Project-Based Learning (PBL) Environment*. Aalborg: akprint.

Zhou, C. (2014). Student Project as an 'Extra Group Member': A Metaphor for Creativity Development in Problem-Based Learning (PBL). *Academic Quarter*, *9*, 223–235.

Zhou, C. (2016a). Fostering creative problem solvers in higher education: a response to complexity of society. In C. Zhou (Ed.), *Creative Problem-Solving Skill Development in Higher Education* (pp. 1–24). Hershey, PA: IGI Global.

Zhou, C. (2016b). Going towards adaption, integration and co-creation: a conclusion of research on creative problem solving skills development in higher education. In C. Zhou (Ed.), *A Handbook Research on Creative Problem Solving Skills Development in Higher Education*. IGI Global.

Zhou, C. (2017). How Ha-Ha Interplays with Aha! Supporting a playful approach to creative learning environments. In T. Chemi, S. G. Davy, & B. Lund (Eds.), Innovative Pedagogy: A Recognition of Emotions and Creativity in Education (pp. 107-124). Rotterdam: Brill.

Zhou, C. (2018). A Study on creative climate in Project-Organized Groups (POGs) in China and implications for sustainable pedagogy. *Sustainability*, *10*(114), 1–15. PMID:30607262

Zhou, C., & Luo, L. (2012). Group Creativity in Learning Context: Understanding in a Social-Cultural Framework and Methodology. *Creative Education*, *3*(4), 392–399. doi:10.4236/ce.2012.34062

Zhou, C., Otrel-Cass, K., & Børsen, T. (2015). Integrating Ethics into Engineering Education. In S. S. Sethy (Ed.), *Contemporary Ethical Issues in Engineering* (pp. 159–173). IGI Global. doi:10.4018/978-1-4666-8130-9.ch012

Zhou, C., & Purushothaman, A. (2017). Developing creativity and learning design by Information and Communication Technology (ICT) in developing contexts. In The Encyclopedia of Information Science and Technology (4th ed.; pp. 4178 - 4188). IGI Global.

Zhou, C., Rasmussen, P., Chemi, T., & Luo, L. (2017). An investigation of creative climate of university R&D centers and policy implications for innovation in China. In Y. Jing & S. Osborne (Eds.), Public Service Innovations in China (pp. 185-205). Singapore: Palgrave Macmillan. doi:10.1007/978-981-10-1762-9_9

Zhou, C., & Shi, J. (2015). A Cross-Cultural Perspective to Creativity in Engineering Education in Problem-Based Learning (PBL) between Denmark and China. *International Journal of Engineering Education*, *31*(1A), 12–22.

ADDITIONAL READING

Baillie, C., & Catalano, G. (2008). *Engineering and society, working toward social justice*. Canada: Morgan & Claypool Publishers.

Broad, C. D. (1925). *The Mind and Its Place in Nature*. New York: Basic Books.

Calvano, C. N., & John, P. (2004). System engineering in an age of complexity. *Systems Engineering*, *7*(1), 25–34. doi:10.1002ys.10054

Chen, H., Tao, T., & Zhou, C. (2018). A three-dimension analysis of fostering creative engineers in China. *International Journal of Engineering Education, 34*(2A), 1–11.

Christense, J. (2004). Reflections on Problem-Based Learning. In A. Kolmos, F. K. Fink, & L. Krogh (Eds.), *The Aalborg PBL Model: Progress, Diversity and Challenges* (pp. 93–108). Aalborg: Aalborg University Press.

Claxton, G., Edwards, L., & Scale-Constantinou, V. (2009). Cultivating creative mentalities: A framework for education. *Thinking Skills and Creativity, 1*(1), 57–61. doi:10.1016/j.tsc.2005.11.001

Cropley, A. J. (1999). Education. In M. A. Runco & S. R. Pritzker (Eds.), *Encyclopedia of Creativity* (Vol. 1, pp. 629–638). USA: Academic Press.

De Graaff, E., & Kolmos, A. (2007). History of Problem-Based Learning and Project-Based Learning. In E. De Graaff & A. Kolmos (Eds.), *Management of Change, Implementation of Problem-Based and Project-Based Learning in Engineering* (pp. 1–8). Rotterdam: Sense Publishers.

Dolmans, D., Wolfhagen, I. H. A. P., van der Vleuten, C. P. M., & Wijnen, W. H. F. W. (2001). Solving problems with group work in Problem-based Learning: Hold on to the philosophy. *Medical Education, 35*(9), 884–889. doi:10.1046/j.1365-2923.2001.00915.x PMID:11555227

Grossen, M. (2000). Institutional framing in thinking, learning and teaching, In Cowie, H., Aalsvoot, & G.vander (Eds.) Social Interaction in Learning and Instruction, the Meaning of Discourse for the Construction of Knowledge (pp.21-34). Amsterdam: Elsevier Science.

Haggis, T. (2004). Theories of dynamic systems and emergence: new possiblities from an espistemology of the 'close up'? *Paper presented at SCUTREA 34*[th] *Annual Conference*. University of Sheffield, UK, 6th-8th, July.

Jackson, N., & Sinclair, C. (2006). Developing students' creativity, searching for an appropriate pedagogy. In N. Jackson, M. Oliver, M. Shaw, & J. Wisdom (Eds.), *Developing Creativity in Higher Education: an Imaginative Curriculum* (pp. 118–141). London: Routledge. doi:10.4324/9780203016503

Leighton, R. (2011). sociology of education. In Arthur, J., & Peterson, A. (Eds.) The Routledge Companion to Education (pp.58-65). London: Routledge.

Lissack, M. (1999). Complexity: the science, its vocabulary, and its relation to organizations. *Emergence: A Journal of Complexity Issues in Organizations and Management, 1*(1), 110-126.

Lohman, M. C., & Finkelstein, M. (2000). Designing groups in problem-based learning to promote problem-solving skill and self-directedness. *Instructional Science, 28*(4), 291–307. doi:10.1023/A:1003927228005

Loveless, A. M. (2007). Creativity, technology and learning – a review of recent literature (No. 4 update). Last retrieved May 2009, from www. futurlab.org.dk/ litereviews

Loveness, A., Burton, J., & Turvey, K. (2006). Developing conceptual frameworks for creativity, ICT and teacher education. *Thinking Skills and Creativity, 1*(1), 3–13. doi:10.1016/j.tsc.2005.07.001

Mumford, M. D., Reiter-Palmon, R., & Redmond, M. R. (1994). Problem construction and cognition: applying problem representations in ill-defined domains. In M. A. Runco (Ed.), *Problem Finding, Problem Solving, and Creativity* (pp. 3–39). New Jersey: Ablex Publishing Coorperation Norwood.

Newman, M. J. (2005). Problem based learning: An introduction and overview of the key features of the approach. *JVME, 32*, 12–20. PMID:15834816

Ng, A. K. (2003). A cultural model of creative and conforming behavior. *Creativity Research Journal, 15*(2-3), 223–233. doi:10.1080/10400419.2003.9651414

Oancea, A. (2011). Philosophy of education. In J. Arthur & A. Peterson (Eds.), *The Routledge Companion to Education* (pp. 66–74). London: Routledge.

Purushothaman, A. (2013). *Empowering Women Through Learning To Use The Internet - An Ethnographic Action Research Project To Address The Second Order Digital Divide*. Denmark, Denmark: Aalborg University.

Qvist, P. (2004). Defining the problem in Problem-Based Learning. In A. Kolmos, F. K. Fink, & L. Krogh (Eds.), *The Aalborg PBL Model: Progress, Diversity and Challenges* (pp. 77–92). Aalborg: Aalborg University Press.

Rubinstein, M. F. (1974). *Patterns of Problem Solving*. New Jersey: Prentice-Hal.

Runco, M. A. (2007). *Creativity, Theories and Themes: Research, Development, and Practice*. London: Elsvier Academic Press.

Schloemer, S., & Tomaschek, N. (2010). *Leading in Complexity: New Ways of Management*. Germany: Carl-Auer Verlag GmbH.

Smith, G. F. (2005). Problem-Based Learning: Can it improve managerial thinking? *Journal of Management Education, 29*(2), 357–376. doi:10.1177/1052562904269642

Smith-Bingham, R. (2006). Public policy, innovation and the need for creativity. In N. Jackson, M. Oliver, M. Shaw, & J. Wisdom (Eds.), *Developing Creativity in Higher Education: An Imaginative Curriculum* (pp. 10–18). London: Routledge.

Stacey, R. D. (2001). *Complex Response Process in Organizations: Learning and Knowledge Creation*. London: Routledge.

Sternberg, R. J. (1999). *Handbook of creativity*. New York: Cambridge University Press.

Sternberg, R. J., & Lubart, T. I. (1996). *Defying the Crowd: Cultivating Creativity in a Culture of Conformity*. New York: Free Press.

Tanggaard, L. (2014). A situated model of creative learning. *European Educational Research Journal, 15*(1), 107–116. doi:10.2304/eerj.2014.13.1.107

Tongia, R., Subrahmanian, E., & Arunachalam, V. (2005). *Information and Communications Technology for Sustainable Development: Defining a Global Research Agenda*. Bangalore, India: Allied Publishers.

Vignoles, A. (2011). Economics of education. In J. In Arthur & A. Peterson (Eds.), *The Routledge Companion to Education* (pp. 86–94). London: Routledge.

Wang, F., & Zhou, C. (2013). A Theoretical Study on Development of Information and Communication Technology (ICT)-Supported Education Systems. In J. Chen, X. Wang, L. Wang, J. Sun, & X. Meng (Eds.), *The Proceedings of 2013 10th International Conference on Fuzzy Systems and Knowledge Discovery (FSKD).* (1 ed., Vol. 1, pp. 1080-1084). Red Hook, NY: IEEE Press.

Wisdom, J. (2006). Developing higher education teachers to teach creatively. In N. Jackson, M. Oliver, M. Shaw, & J. Wisdom (Eds.), *Developing Creativity in Higher Education: An Imaginative Curriculum* (pp. 183–196). London: Routledge.

Zhou, C. (2015). Bridging creativity and group by elements of Problem-Based Learning (PBL). In A. Abraham, A. K. Muda, & Y.-H. Choo (Eds.), *Pattern Analysis, Intelligent Security and the Internet of Things* (pp. 1–10). London: Springer. doi:10.1007/978-3-319-17398-6_1

Zhou, C., Kolmos, A., & Nielsen, D. (2012). A Problem and Project-Based Learning (PBL) approach to motivate group creativity in engineering education. *International Journal of Engineering Education, 28*(1), 3–16.

KEY TERMS AND DEFINITIONS

Co-Creation: From an organizational management perspective, co-creation is a joint creation and evaluation of value with stakeholding individuals, intensified and enacted through platforms of engagements, virtualized and emergent from ecosystems of capabilities, and actualized and embodied in domains of experiences, expanding wealth-welfare-wellbeing. Introducing the concept of co-creation to an educational context, it means to design a curriculum by involving the following elements: 1) students' active and reflective participation, 2) changes of teachers' roles towards becoming facilitators of learning, 3) a dynamic and interactive process of teaching and learning, 4) multiple channels of resources of teaching and learning, and 5) increased levels of individual and collective students' responsibility for their learning.

Creative Society: It is an expansion or evolution of information and knowledge society. It has been defined both in a narrow sense and a broad sense. From a narrow sense, the creative society labels the society as being creative or interchangeably inventive; creativity is just the one of possible features, likely the most important one, which can be attributed to the contemporary society. From a broad sense, the creative society should be understood as a phenomenon; it is a name of the contemporary society, not limited only to one attribute as being creative, but emphasizing the creativity as state of the society, affecting all other attributes. Creativity and new technology are key enablers in developing a creative society.

Creativity: Etymologically speaking, the term "creativity" means to generate new and useful ideas. The field of creativity was practically started from psychological studies. Today the field has seen an explosion of interest: creativity has been discussed much by the theories such as psychology, social psychology, cultural psychology, social culture, and even philosophy.

Information and Communication Technology (ICT): ICT can be seen as a set of information technological tools that can be chosen as supporting educational environment. The technological resources can support the creation and development of ideas by stimulating the learners to engage into deeper learning process and activities.

Learning: Learning involves any process that in living organisms leads to permanent capacity change. Learning develops knowledge, abilities, understandings, emotions, attitudes, and sociality, which are important elements of the conditions and raw material of society.

Problem-Based Learning (PBL): As an innovative educational model, problem-based learning (PBL) has been widely used in diverse disciplines and cultures throughout the world. In PBL, students' learning centers on complex problems that do not have a single answer or solving real-life projects. Students work in collaborative groups to identify what they need to learn in order to solve the problems. The teacher acts to facilitate the learning process rather than to provide knowledge. So "student-centered learning" is the core philosophy of PBL.

Transformative Learning: It refers to the process by which we transform our take-for-granted frames of reference (meaning perspectives, habits of mind, mind-sets), to make them more inclusive, discriminating, open, emotionally capable of change, and reflective so that they may generate beliefs and opinions that will prove more true or justified to guide action. Through transformative learning, personality-integrated knowledge is developed on the basis of which associations can be freely made in all subjectively relevant contexts.

Chapter 2

Design of Crowd Creative Collaborative Education Model Based on PBL:
Background, Reflection, and Teaching Practice in Northeastern University in China

Xinbo Sun
Northeastern University, China

ABSTRACT

The global information technology revolution puts forward the following requirements for higher education: education mode transforms from experience education to overall education; education mechanism transforms from traditional management to comprehensive governance; the educational goal transfers from the traditional knowledge to the ability training. In such a macro educational background, the structural contradictions in China's higher education have triggered the supply-side reform of education. The implementation of this reform to Northeastern University requires us to vigorously promote the excellent education action plan in view of the current teaching reality and local difficulties in Northeastern University to change the logic of unilateral teaching into the logic of co-creating education. Based on comprehensive learning of PBL education paradigm, the author of this chapter, based on his own teaching practice and reflection of educational philosophy, puts forward the collaborative education mode of crowd innovation and gives the basic framework of this model. On this basis, specific cases and suggestions are given.

DOI: 10.4018/978-1-5225-9961-6.ch002

INTRODUCTION

Problem-Based Learning (PBL) is a student-centered education method based on the real world. It was initiated by American neurology professor Borrows in McMaster University in Canada in 1969 and has become a popular teaching method in the world.

Different from the traditional subject-based teaching method, PBL emphasizes students' active learning rather than teachers' teaching in traditional teaching. PBL links learning to larger tasks or problems to engage learners in the problem; it designs realistic tasks, emphasizes setting learning in complex and meaningful problem situations, and solves problems through learners' independent exploration and cooperation, to learn the scientific knowledge hidden behind the problems and develop problem-solving skills and independent learning ability.

Problem-oriented teaching method, problem-based, student-centered, teacher-oriented heuristic education, to cultivate students' ability as the teaching goal. The essence of PBL teaching method lies in giving full play to the guiding role of problems in the learning process and arousing students' initiative and enthusiasm.

BACKGROUND

The Global Information Technology Revolution Puts New Demands on Chinses Higher Education

As so far, human society has experienced the pre-agricultural society, agricultural society, industrial society, and information society. Today's human beings are in the early stage of the information age. Under this circumstance, the global reality of informatization poses new challenges to Chinese higher education, and the challenges mainly include the following three aspects:

First, the education model has transformed from traditional experience education to integrated education. The traditional higher education model is a segmented, single-field empirical education. The teachers engaged in higher education mainly come from a certain major or a certain subject in a university. The basic logic of educational activities is from books to books, and research to the research. Such a logic lacks experience and test of the practical process. In other words, this single-experienced education model has already not adapted to the needs of the cross-disciplinary integration of higher education in the context of big data in the information age. The age of information network asks for the integration of the natural and social science education models to cope with the challenges of digital civilization. The integrated education concept, based on humanity's destiny community and world citizenship and lifelong education, is increasingly important. So, based on the requirements of the global information network, higher education has emerged as an interdisciplinary, cross-regional and cross-cultural integration of "teaching, learning, and education". At the same time, information technology elements are more quickly integrated into education, schools, and classrooms which enrich the selectivity, diversity and inclusiveness of learning resources. Thus, learners can choose their own learning style more freely. Besides, the development of artificial intelligence (AI) has shown a great impact on education and teaching, and also teachers and students. Nowadays, the classes selection model is being gradually promoted. Personalized learning that can meet the individual needs of learners has also become an important form of learning. All these are the reality under technical logic that the integrated education concept must face in the future.

Second, the educational mechanism has changed from traditional management to comprehensive governance. Managerial education is often top-down, passively accepted which based on control logic. Its efficiency, effectiveness, and utility come from the controllers. The trend of cross-border integration in the age of information network requires the transformation of the educational mechanism from management to governance, which involves innovations in teaching mode, resource service, and educational governance. As for teaching mode, education should, under the overall design of "Internet + Teaching", make full use of information technology to develop new formal teaching methods such as MOOC, creative and hybrid teaching to make up for the shortcomings of traditional formal classroom teaching. Then to establish an education and teaching model that sets learners as the center. At the same time, there should be a supportive educational environment. Education should strive to build classrooms that meet the needs of learning in the 21st century, making it a learning space full of creativity. Teachers should guide more students to participate in the construction of classes so to make the classes more open, more temperate and richer in humanity, full of personality and vitality. As for resource service, education should, under the overall requirements of the "education supply-side reform", make full use of the Internet's quality educational resources to form a new pool of large educational resources and cooperate with parties to build a smart, research-oriented, application-driven educational supply-side. Education can build immersive and experienced learning methods and immediate feedback mechanisms for students by using information technology. Thus, learners can become the masters of classes by returning rights of learning choices and decision-making back to them. Therefore, learners can have both healthy bodies and perfect personalities which can promote the development of sustainable innovation under the guidance of advanced thinking. As for educational governance, education should, under the advantage of the preciseness of "educational information big data", improve and perfect the world-wide education quality monitoring, evaluation, and feedback system as to realize the scientific, normalized, personalized and accurate evaluation of education and teaching quality. Furthermore, education should develop a multi-agent open educational ecosystem that fully respects the development of teachers and students' personality based on Chinese traditional cultural characteristics, big data analysis. The ecosystem will realize: (1) the transformation that from result-based evaluation to process-based evaluation with the help of big data analysis tools and information advantages. (2) greater importance to the construction of higher education governance capacity. (3) a new collaborative, multi-participating, co-constructed and shared governance mechanism.

Third, the educational goal shifts from traditional knowledge transferring to abilities development. The educational goal that based on knowledge transferring is often satisfied with classes indoctrination, which forms the main teaching mode of higher education in China. It is test-oriented, indoctrinated, one-dimensional which lacks two-way and even multi-directional communication. It has not adapted to the requirements both of quality education and information age. The requirements for innovation are getting higher and higher in the information age, which forced the learners to transition from the original staged learning to lifelong learning while also from the original knowledge learning to ability improvement. For students, this requires them to have theoretical and practical interactivity to analyze and solve practical problems. For teachers, this requires them to enhance their digital competencies based on the future and adhere to the traditional local cultural literacy. For all the public, this requires us to change the role of our own laborers, then to enhance lifelong learning. That is, it is better to teach one how to fish rather than give he/her fishes. Driven by informatization, education must be transformed into a holistic, guided, and multi-dimensional learning unit. It is impossible to improve literacy without the influence of culture. Therefore, it is imperative to promote Chinese traditional culture and the world's excellent culture, so that teachers and students can be qualified for the requirements of the information age.

The technological revolution of informatization is an empowerment for higher education. The realization of empowerment through information, data etc. can enable teachers and students of colleges and universities and related supporting organizations to obtain the capabilities that are not available or cannot be achieved in the past. This is a complete reform of educational and ideological baptism and education paradigm for the 270 million students and 16 million in-school teachers from primary school to university in China. It will also reconstruct the future of Chinese higher education. In this report, I call it the external technical logic and technical basis of PBL implementation in Northeastern University of China.

The Structural Contradiction of China's Higher Education Leads to the Reform of the Supply-Side of Education

The informatization of education promotes the modernization of education, and the modernization of education has brought about the modernization of China. The modernization of China asks for modern talents, and the cultivation of modern talents will inevitably ask for modern education. As we all know, China's development is a hybrid modernization model. It is different from the United Kingdom and Germany that uses the endogenous power to explore and advance. It is also different from the United States and Singapore that uses external power to imitate the advancement. It achieves spiral advance and transformation under the dual effects of endogenous power and external power. We must understand China's educational modernization in this context. It contains three main aspects:

Firstly, the higher education development strategy of typical national (Gao, 2018). The development of China's educational modernization should be recognized in the perspective of world education. Then, what are the strategic planning of higher education in the United Kingdom, Germany, the United States, Japan, India, and other countries? Table 1 gives a partial ranking of QS Universities in 2018. It shows that the monopoly of the top ten universities of England and America has been broken. Tsinghua University in China has entered 25, and there are 6 Chinese universities in the top 100. Under this circumstance, we will understand the higher education plans of the above five countries.

- **The United Kingdom:** The 2030 education development goal is based on the goals of British science and innovation. In order to continue to maintain the overall scientific research strength behind the United States and the leading position in productivity, the United Kingdom will establish a world-class research center, which relies on the world-class universities and complete education systems in the UK to attract international R&D investment and high-tech talents. In this way, the UK will be established as a world-class innovation center.

Table 1. Partial ranking of QS universities in 2018

#	University	Country	China	Ranking
1	MIT	US	Tsinghua University	25
2	Harford University	US	Peking University	30
3	Cambridge University	UK	Fudan University	40
4	Stanford University	US	Shanghai Jiao Tong University	62
5	California University of Technology	US	Zhejiang University	87
6	Oxford University	UK	University of Science and Technology of China	97
7	University College London	UK	Nanjing University	114
8	Imperial University, London	UK	Beijing Normal University	256
9	Swiss Federal Institute of Technology	Switzerland	Wuhan University	282
10	Chicago University	US	Tongji University	316

- **Germany:** The path of the education powerhouse originated in 1807. Germany first put forward the idea of "returning education, saving the country, strengthening the country". By the middle of the 19th century, Germany had become an important center of education, academic and knowledge innovation in the world. In the 1870s, Germany took the lead in proposing and implementing free compulsory education and founded the modern university -Universität Zu Berlin. After 1950, Germany has become a European industrial power.

- **The United States:** The country which is founded before the appearance of college. From the president of Harvard University studied in German universities in 1815, the number of Americans studying in Germany is increasing. By 1880, the Americans in Germany had reached their peak. In 1860, Yale University was the first to set up the philosophy doctor. Cambridge established the one in 1882 while Oxford made it in 1990. It is 1890-1920 that was a crucial period for the United States to become a world power. In 1900, the United States' GDP was the highest in the world. And from this year, American education entered the first 40 years of leaping development in history. In 1941 and 1971, the United States became the first country to realize the popularization and popularization of higher education. Doctoral education is a success of American universities.

- **Japan:** A competitive country in education. In 1930, the level of education in Japan almost completely exceeded that in European countries. In 2002, Japan formulated the "Strategic Outlook as a Human", which clearly stated that it is necessary to train students into "Japanese who can think and act on their own, and who have a self-cultivation." In July 2008, the Japanese government issued a medium-and-long term education development plan for the Basic Plan for Education Revitalization. The plan proposes that the development goal of Japanese education in the next 10 years is to strive to cultivate the basic ability of all students in the compulsory education stage, improve the quality of public education, establish a sense of social trust, and jointly train the next generation with the strength of society. In the higher education stage, Japan achieves the goal of cultivating outstanding talents by cultivating leaders who preside over social activities, promoting social development, and leading international trends.

- **India:** The strategy of higher education in 2030 is to establish "a higher education for the future new world and build a fair, low-cost, high-quality development model for higher education in the 21st century. Indian higher education must not only become the best education system in the world, but also the best example of world higher education. Graduates of higher education need global skills to smoothly pass on knowledge and skills in countries where labor is scarce, and to make students entrepreneurs." At least 100 Indian universities are currently among the world's most competitive universities. India is a regional center of higher education that attracts global learners from around the world.

Through the above comparison, it will be found that Germany and the United Kingdom are world education centers in the 18th and 19th centuries, and the United States is the world education center in the 20th century. Gao Shuguo believes that Tokyo, Japan, and Beijing, China will become one of the world education centers in the 21st century. It is expected that by 2030, the 21st Century World Education Center will jointly lead and drive the development of world education, which is dominated by Germany (Berlin), the United Kingdom (London), the United States (New York-Washington), Japan (Tokyo) and China (Beijing). It is in this perception that we explain the difference between Chinese tradition and the new type of education.

Secondly, the comparison between traditional education and new education. Nicholas Kristof believes that the strategic challenge to the United States is not China's stealth fighters, but the Chinese public's determination to improve the education system and the passion to learn from the outside world. He holds the idea that the emphasis on education in Confucianism has been deeply infiltrated by Chinese culture, and thus has derived the greatest strength of the Chinese school system.

The education of China has gone through four stages, including extending education under poor and wide circumstances as well as strengthening education under great and powerful circumstances. It is currently undergoing a transition to the fourth stage, which is an overall understanding of the transformation of China's educational strategic planning. The traditional education is based on the definition of "Where am I? Where to go? How to get there?" This kind of logic cultivates "I" based on others' judgment and standards and pursues self-realization. As has been analyzed above, it is impossible to modernize education without human modernization. It is impossible for human modernization to be self-fulfilling without self-awareness. New education needs to be transformed into human self-realization. New education must be designed around the uncertain, active logic of "Who am I? Whom do I want to be? How to be me?" Only in this way can the educated person become self-conscious, free and self-sufficient to me. This is the basic premise for realizing a strong country to strengthen education, and it is possible to realize the strategy of "two steps" for the education power. China's "Educational Planning Outline" proposes that the first step is to achieve the educational goal of achieving or over-building a well-off society in an all-around way by 2020, basically realizing the modernization of education and forming a learning society. The second step is to achieve the comprehensive improvement of education quality and educational competitiveness and influence by 2035. The strategic transformation from catching up to surpassing will be carried out, and the ranks of countries with high human development index will be built into a modern education power. Then, what is the current state of higher education? This issue needs to be further understood in China's current major social conflicts. The 19th National Congress has clearly pointed out that the main contradiction in the current Chinese society is 'the contradiction between the people's growing needs for a better life and the development of inadequate imbalances.' In the field of education, the development of educational imbalance is not only the main structural contradiction but also the stage characteristic of the process. The main contradiction of education is the contradiction between the people's growing demand for quality education and the uneven development of education (Gao, 2018). This is also a direct expression of the structural contradiction between supply side and demand side of higher education in China. Improving the quality of higher education to meet demand is the main contradiction of higher education that must be solved at present.

Thirdly, the specific manifestation of the contradiction between supply and demand of education development. At present, the strategy, policy, management and resource allocation of China's higher education still do not form a management system and governance method that enhances and promotes the comprehensive and individual development of human beings. It has not yet reached the realm of "teaching without class" proposed by Confucius. It should be said that China is working hard in this direction. The imbalance of education is mainly manifested as regional, hierarchical, school and interpersonal development; The inadequacy of education mainly manifests as inadequate basic conditions of education, resource preparation, institutional system, quality mechanism, and confidence level. Therefore, there is still a huge space for the road, theory, system and cultural construction of China's higher education. As far as development space is concerned, there is the universal value of the higher education China program, sustainable communication, and reproduction, quality connotative development, comprehensive openness to the world and the future, etc.. In terms of theoretical space, there is a complete scientific system, universities, education, teaching theory, and interdisciplinary construction, etc. Considering the institutional space, there are lifelong learning systems, various legal systems, higher education standards, governance and management levels, etc.; As far as cultural space is concerned, there is a connection with traditional culture, a connection with world culture, and a successful practice of localization, etc.. These are all problems that must be gradually solved under the contradiction between basic supply and demand in the future.

In this context, Northeastern University needs to re-innovate education and teaching. Next, we will discuss the needs of the reform of Northeastern University under the new engineering background.

The Realistic Needs of Education and Teaching Reform in Northeastern University Under the Background of New Engineering

The "Articles of Association of the Northeastern University" closely links the mission of building a high-level research university in Northeastern University with the historical process of China's new industrialization road and condenses the construction of a high-level research university that plays a leading role in China's new industrialization process. Furthermore, the Northeastern University has developed the "Northeastern University Undergraduate Education Excellence Action Plan" around this goal, and this section begins to analyze as follows.

Firstly, the analysis of "Northeastern University Undergraduate Education Excellence Action Plan". "Northeastern University Undergraduate Education Excellence Action Plan" is a programmatic document developed by Northeastern University to create a first-class undergraduate course. It is also a guide to deepening the reform of undergraduate teaching and comprehensively launching a new journey of quality improvement and character development. Northeastern University actively advocates the theme of improving the quality of personnel training and taking high moral values establishment and people cultivation as the fundamental task of education. It is guided by innovation, coordination, green, open, and shared development concepts, as well as the guidance of the strategy of supporting innovation-driven development to deepen the reform of undergraduate talent training mode.

As a breakthrough, we will use information technology and education and teaching as a means to enhance students' social competitiveness as a foothold, deepen reform, and cooperate with innovation to give full play to the construction benefits of discipline construction, scientific research and teacher team construction, and promote scientific research advantages and "the double transformation" of teaching and industry to form a good ecological environment for educating people, promotes the construction of first-class universities as a whole, and continuously improves the quality of undergraduate education.

Therefore, six major education's should be implemented: general knowledge and quality education, field and professional education, innovation and entrepreneurship education; perfect four combinations: professional construction and subject development, intramural teaching and extracurricular practice, teaching content and scientific research results, common requirements and personality development; promote three kinds of training: strengthen Sino-foreign cooperation, school-enterprise cooperation, colleges and universities to run schools, and cultivate top-notch innovative, cross-compositing, application-oriented, collaborative and innovative talents. To truly achieve excellence, we must move from a traditional teacher-centered, classroom-centered to the student-centered, learning-centered track, which requires revolutionary changes in educational models and thinking, teaching logic and methods.

Secondly, teaching and learning unilateral logic to create a logical transformation. We start with a question, is the vase in Figure 1 or the face? Is it a vase with two faces? what is this else? And the answer depends on what?

The answer depends on the teaching and learning thinking and the teaching and learning logic under the guidance of the thinking. The answer also depends on the teaching and learning methods provided by the education supply side (educators) to the educational needs side (learners). Then we will analyze it in depth.

Figure 1. A vase or two faces?

At present, the teaching and learning thinking behind the higher education model is linear thinking. The specific process is first of all the traditional classroom communication type of informed learning, then the internship, practical application learning, and finally the design-style forced innovation learning. The three practical learning processes constitute the linear relationship between the current teaching and learning logic of higher education. As we all known, the course teaching, course examination and course practice of most colleges are arranged in this way, and the inertia of thinking has been formed. This is the main learning logic that Northeast University provides as a learner on the demand side as a supply side of higher education. It is a one-way linear, non-continuous, intuitive one-sided, unilateralism. It cannot grasp the essence and laws behind the current and future natural and artificial world complex phenomena. It is not applicable to the current society and the development of the times. It is also the most important and direct cause of insufficient innovation in higher education.

I refer to the above logic as unilateral logic, and this corresponds to co-creation logic. The specific teaching and learning methods and processes of creating logic are the coexistence of knowledge, application and innovative, teaching and learning co-existence in this process. The thinking is not a linear relationship, but a non-linear thinking of coexistence and symbiotic relationship. It is a nonlinear, continuous dynamic, abstract, all-dimensional, non-central and borderless network structure, creating logic requires educators and learners to learn, apply, and innovate at the same.

Co-creation logic is at least trilaterally and even multilateralism. It is not unilateralism, it must be a community of educational collaboration. Co-creation logic is the product of non-linear thinking. The establishment and cultivation of non-linear thinking is the key to learners' innovation and application of science and technology. The reflection of non-linear thinking in the process and mode of teaching and learning is the process of multi-dimensional juxtaposition thinking, linear thinking. It helps to deep thinking to explore the true face of things. Non-linear thinking focuses on horizontally expanding thinking to obtain the universal connection of things. In a narrow sense, nonlinear thinking is to use width to obtain depth, macroscopically, the width of Chinese traditional culture can be developed in tandem with the deep development of Western science and technology, complementing yin and yang, and dynamically balancing, and jointly creating a future-oriented 'co-learning and co-teaching', thus forming a global-based, global-oriented collaborative education paradigm, this educational paradigm behind it is the overall education concept, which is in complete agreement with the previous discussion.

Thirdly, the current predicament of undergraduate education teaching in Northeastern University. Under the influence of traditional teaching and research relationship, the following major problems exist in the training of undergraduate talents in Northeastern University: The first is that some teachers pay insufficient attention to teaching, the teaching energy is insufficient, the updated teaching content and the teaching methods are not enough, and the education quality monitoring and protection system remains to be improved. The second is the insufficient number of teaching-related personnel. The teaching tasks of some departments are too heavy, and there is a serious shortage of full-time teachers in some majors and disciplines. What's more, there is no teacher input mechanism that is oriented to social needs. The third is that some teachers' teaching ability needs to be improved. Teachers are lack of international vision and foreign communication skills, teachers' practical experience need to be strengthened, and there is no mechanism to improve teachers' teaching ability. At the same time, teachers' teaching ability is not improved with their promotion and appointment. The fourth is that the school is not enough to invest resources in undergraduate talent training. The absolute value of undergraduate teaching funding is not high. The experimental funding for students is significantly lower than that of other top colleges and universities. The fifth is that the undergraduate training program needs to be further optimized, students' independent choice is not strong enough to meet the standard of international high-level universities. Sixth, northeast university students' international vision training measures need to be improved, and the international joint talent training program is lacking.

Based on the above-mentioned new requirements of the macro-informatization technology revolution for higher education, the structural contradiction of China's higher education triggered the supply-side reform, and the analysis of the actual needs of education and teaching reform under the background of the new engineering, we think it is very necessary for Northeast University to introduce the PBL education model.

CURRENT TEACHING PRACTICES, BELIEFS AND VALUES

Current Teaching Practice

There are two main ways about my teaching practice. One way which I used in Management Philosophy and the other way I used in Enterprise Innovation and Entrepreneurship Management.

Firstly, I will give the details about how I can teach the course of Management Philosophy. At present, I give the Management Philosophy curriculums through four steps:

The first step, Preparing: Before each class, I would spend 2-3 hours to prepare this course again. According to different teaching objects, I usually update about 30% of the lecture content.

The second step, Dialogue: In my class, I usually teach the course by asking questions or problems and then talking with the students. In China, the duration of a course is 100 minutes every time, the knowledge points are generally taught for 50 minutes, and the conversation with the students for another 50 minutes.

The third step, Assignment: In class, besides having dialogue with students, I will arrange three assignments for the Management Philosophy course. The form of assignment includes: case discussion, enterprise investigation, brainstorming and some more creative activities, etc. Such as once, I let the students designed "a dance of management", They must design a dance include plan, organizing, command, coordination, lead and others management functions, they must submit video homework. It's a very interesting activity, and the students complained at the beginning and were grateful at the end. All assignments must be done in their spare time and in groups, which is conductive to developing student's teamwork sprit and problem-solving ability.

The fourth step, Test: There are some test forms for Management Philosophy course. The usual form is that, there are three questions on the test. The first question is the student's own questions; The second question is the students answer questions; The third questions is the students give their own scores. Finally, I reviews the test papers and gives the final grades based on the scores given by the students themselves and ordinary performance.

Secondly, I will introduce the way that how I can teach the course of Enterprise Innovation and Entrepreneurship Management. It's a very interesting way in the School of Business and Administration in NEU.

The first step is to set up a teaching team. We have built a teaching team of 50 people, including Chinese and overseas teachers. The members of this teaching team come from both enterprises and universities. Half of them come from businesses and the other half from universities. As the course leader, I will issue an appointment letter of part-time professor to each participant of the enterprise side, which is used to prove their identity.

The second step is to start designing the teaching content for the teaching team. The course is designed into eight chapters, including innovation and entrepreneurship situation analysis, innovation thinking and innovation strategy, entrepreneurs and entrepreneurship, innovation and entrepreneurship opportunities mining, business model innovation, business plan, venture financing and venture risk, the establishment and management of new enterprises and eight components.

The third step is the division of teaching tasks for each member of the teaching team. According to the specific situation that students choose the course Enterprise Innovation and Entrepreneurship Management, we will divide it into different teaching units. Each teaching unit is taught by 8 teachers in the teaching team, 4 of whom are from enterprises and 4 from universities. The eight teachers will coordinate their teaching.

The fourth step is the assessment and evaluation after the teaching. The assessment of the course Enterprise Innovation and Entrepreneurship Management is divided into two parts. One part is the classroom random assessment, including attendance. The score of each teacher is 5 points, and the total score of 8 teachers is 40 points. This part of the assessment by 8 teachers alone, more flexible, direct sum is the total score. The second part is to evaluate the "business plan" submitted by students. Eight teachers independently give the score according to the percentage system, and then calculate the score of this part with the formula of 'total score of eight people /8*60%". The sum of the two is the student's score in the course.'

Current Teaching Philosophy

In NEU, I always insist on the education belief is "Student-Based" I think in the classroom, students have three roles and teachers have four roles.

Let's talk about the three roles of students: The first role, Students are the receivers of classroom content knowledge. The second role, Students are the producers of classroom innovation knowledge. The third role, Students are the owners of curiosity, they are looking at the world with untainted wonder.

Then let's talk about the four roles of teachers: The first role, Teacher are the disseminators of classroom content knowledge. The second role, Teacher are the facilitators and guide for the generation of classroom innovation knowledge. The Third role, Teacher are the producers of classroom innovation knowledge. The fourth role, Teacher are the makers of classroom ambience for innovation.

In the future, I think the relationship between teachers and students is equal, Teachers are students and students are teachers, Because of the Internet Era.

In my education career, I have successively put forward such iterative education ideas and teaching methods as "Crowd Creative Collaborative Teaching Mode" and "Crowd Creative Collaborative Education Mode". Later, I will compare " Crowd Creative Collaborative Education Mode " with Problem-Based Learning (PBL). This part only introduces the basic concepts of these two modes. The "Crowd Creative Collaborative Teaching Mode", means in the context of the Internet, several teachers from the universities and enterprises as knowledge both senders to jointly develop course, each teacher to choose personal best knowledge through class or Internet platform (MOOC) is transmitted to more knowledge demand of two-way interactive new teaching pattern. Crowd Creative Collaborative Education Mode, means in the technology and humanities background such as the globalization, Community of shared future for mankind, Internet, big data, artificial intelligence, " The Belt and Road ", integrating education resources at home and abroad, in the study of global education, promoting professional categories of training mode, professional project design characteristics, strengthen the comprehensive training and the introduction of social evaluation and promotion and so on to build learner centered panoramic collaborative teaching network platform of ecological system.

Teaching and Learning Challenges

I think there are four kinds of challenges in my teaching practice.

The first is new technology, such as AI, 5G, Blockchain, Biotechnology, New energy, Electromobile, Space technology, Marine technology and so on. These new technologies have changed the produced way of productivity, the social and economic structure. Fast speed, technical integration, mathematization, formal logic is the performance.

The second is the needs of students and teachers have changed. On the student's hand, with the advent of online courses, students can learn knowledge at any time. So, they need more new contents in the classroom. On the teacher's hand, Naomi Schaefer Riley points out that research shows that the more time a college professor spends teaching, the lower his income. This conclusion applies to both large research universities and small liberal arts colleges.

The third is uncertainty caused by an uncertain environment. Before the internet era, the environment of education is deterministic. Now, it's changing. Volatility, uncertainty, complexity, ambiguity is the greatest feature of the era. All of these are the new challenges for education and teaching.

The fourth challenge mainly comes from education management system and mechanism. At present, Chinese universities emphasize the construction of first-class universities and disciplines, and only on this basis can they further emphasize the construction of first-class undergraduate courses. This pattern is more suitable for the overall situation of China's development, but it will also bring some negative effects. For example, the problem of "attaching importance to scientific research and ignoring teaching" is still prominent, and teachers who have been struggling in the forefront of teaching for a long time can hardly get happiness under the system.

I think there are two challenges about PBL.

The first challenge is to adapt different cultures and systems, such as China. In 2013, Bertel Harder, Denmark's education minister said: "Our exams must reflect the daily learning in the classroom, and the daily learning in the classroom must reflect the real life in society." You know, the slogan of the Finnish education system "profession deliver trust." I fully agree this.

The second challenge is the practical dilemma caused by the long-term division of disciplines and majors. University is based on the development and promotion of high school "arts and sciences". At present, despite the trend of integration between disciplines and majors, the major contradiction of differentiation still exists, which leads to the lack of effective communication and in-depth integration between disciplines and majors. In my opinion, this is also the main reason for the lack of innovation. Problem-Based Learning (PBL) exactly advocates cross-border cooperation, but it takes time to gradually promote it and cannot be accomplished overnight.

Teaching Motivations

The first condition to be a good teacher is to have love, which is especially important for teachers. Teachers should first love themselves, it is difficult to imagine that a person who does not love themselves will love others; Then love and protect students, especially good at protecting and mining students' nature, based on the nature of students gradually achieve the goal of "teaching students according to their aptitude", so as to integrate students' nature into the needs of disciplines and majors; Finally, teachers should take good care of the environment, including the natural environment and social environment, and create an atmosphere conducive to innovation.

The second condition to be a good teacher is to have a sense of responsibility. Teachers face students every day, and the sense of responsibility is extremely important. Charles Handy believed that a good teacher only wanted to tell stories and ask questions, and that it was the students' duty to find the answers themselves, and that a teacher could only give directions and advice. I think this is the best expression of teachers' sense of responsibility in the Internet era. The most important thing for teachers' sense of responsibility is to know who they are and help students know who they are.

The third condition to be a good teacher is to have empathy. James G. March thinks that I think I am a teacher. The happiness of a teacher lies in that students understand and possess our thoughts and regard them as their own. The students are gems, and my role is just to polish them up a little bit. In the end, I will be forgotten while they are still there. This is the Chinese ancient said "wax torch ashes tears before dry". Teachers should understand students from the perspective of students, so as to constantly promote the development of education career.

The fourth condition to be a good teacher is to have more learning. The current era is the era of lifelong learning. Changes in the external environment put forward higher requirements for teachers. As a university teacher, on the one hand, one should learn new ideas, new theories and new knowledge; on the other hand, we should learn new techniques, tools and methods. Only in this way can we take on the challenges from home and abroad in the information age and cultivate more outstanding talents.

I think that to be able to make a student who he or she is the best that an educator can do. In fact, we should learn the process of grasping the object: the original state of "one" before the object becomes the object; In the process of object becoming object, "one" + "person" become "two" after the counselor's cultivation; After the object becomes the object: gradually conscience is divided into "three"; We should grasp the object rather than simply look at it, which is not a given object but a human structure.

REFLECTIONS ON THE AALBORG UNESCO CENTRE CERTIFICATE COURSE AND FUTURE PLANS FOR DEVELOPMENT

Impact of the Course on My Teaching Philosophy, Competences and Skills

There is one detail in the last class: the material for each exercise (no matter how long if takes), and how messy it looks, is left intact. I suddenly realized, in fact, the real work is often incomplete at first, although the form is imperfect, but the content is true; Later present works of the "real" already "recognition", it is only a "perfect" form, it has deviated from the nature. PBL have to do is to help find nature. This is the same as Harvard University education purpose "Let students become themselves". This is also consistent with "Ben-oriented" in China.

Based on the "crowd-created collaborative education mode" and considering the core points of PBL, the theoretical guidance and implementation framework of integrity were designed (figure 2). The framework consists of an inverted triangle and four concentric circles: the inverted triangle subverts the traditional teacher-centered design. "PBL-based mass innovation collaborative education mode" pursues the symmetry between students and teachers, and truly establishes the relationship between students and teachers, which is reflected in the process of teaching and learning. In this process, students can ask any questions, and teachers should dare to admit their ignorance of students' questions. The four concentric circles are teachers on the supply side, students on the demand side, projects on the action side and related parties on the evaluation side.

L is the abbreviation of the learner, represents the concept of learners in a broad sense. In the contemporary era of the fourth industrial revolution, students, teachers and even all people must position themselves as learners, to keep pace with The Times and lead social development. In figure 2, L is the center of the overall framework and represents the concept and action of "learner-centered", so that we can change ourselves through education and be based on the future.

Figure 2. Schematic diagram of the overall mode of PBL-based mass innovation collaborative education

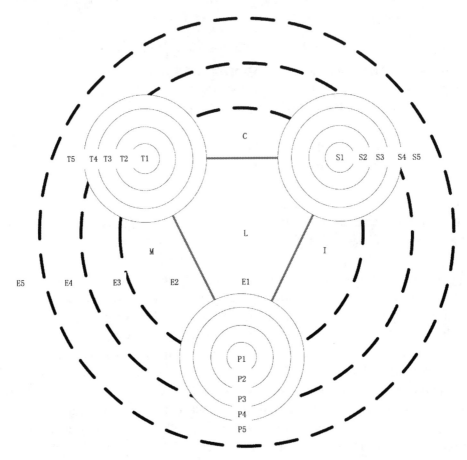

C is the abbreviation of the course, the narrow sense and the closed sense are the corresponding courses of the class, the broad sense and the open sense are all available courses (such as MOOC on the network platform, etc.), and the implementation of PBL corresponds to one or more courses.

M is the abbreviation of major. At present, the higher education in the world, no matter in China which adopts the training mode of large categories, or in Europe and the United States which advocate the education mode of liberal arts, or even in universities such as the integration education recently proposed by Xi'an Jiaotong University in China and Liverpool University, basically takes the professional setting as the starting point to train talents.

I is short for implementation, human creation VUCA era gave the chance of higher education remodeling, colleges and universities should not only stay in the stage of knowledge, knowledge integration capability is more urgent than ever, the a type of collaborative education based on PBL mode must be in such a premise to carry out the implementation of activities, creating a favorable education environment, students participate in the consolidation process, ability is the key to the implementation of cross-border integration of culture.

E is short for evaluation and includes five levels of evaluation in figure 2. E1 is the evaluation of learners themselves. It evaluates whether learners have formed themselves in the learning process rather than being shaped by teachers. Therefore, Harvard University has been pursuing to "let students become their own appearance". E2 is the evaluation of professional ability, which evaluates the interest orientation of major selection and the influence of specialty construction.E3 is the evaluation provided by the school, as a comprehensive evaluation provided by the supply-side university to the demand-side students;E4 is the evaluation of the demand side, especially the enterprise and other social demand side. The demand side can participate in the design of the whole education process and help the supply side provide learners with the ability to solve complex problems. E5 is a global evaluation to evaluate whether learners have a sense of world citizenship, cross-cultural leadership and the ability to solve complex global social problems.

T is short for teacher, S is short for student, and P is short for project.

Future for Further Development

First, Learn according to AAU's study plan.

Second, Select a major for the pilot in NEU.

Third, Promote in all majors of NEU.

The figure 3 shows 'Sun Taxonomy' developed by this reflection based on my own plan.

Learning Outcome:

LO1: Becoming Oneself

LO2: Competence

LO3: Can/Be able to Oneself

LO4: Knowledge

Figure 3. Sun Taxonomy

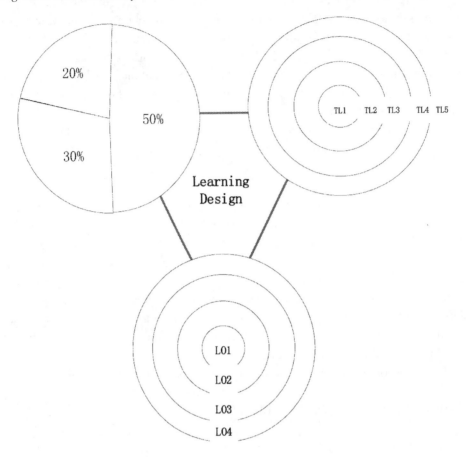

Teaching & Learning Methods:

TL1: Lecture: Teachers and some CEO
TL2: Video: Some little video about case and story
TL3: Q&A + Interactive
TL4: Dialogue
TL5: Presentation

Three parts of Assessment:

20%: Quiz in class
30%: Project & Case

50%: Examinations: First step, students must give themselves three questions; Second step, students must give themselves the answer of the three questions; Third step, students must give themselves the score about the questions. At the end of, I will give the total score.

Suggestions and Recommendations for Teaching Improvement

In my opinion, the core features of PBL include six aspects:(1) the problem is the starting point of all the learning content of students;(2) the problem must be an unstructured problem in the real world without fixed solutions and processes;(3) students undertake the responsibility of learning, independent discussion, decision-making and reporting through question-based project practice activities;(4) teachers play the role of coaches in guiding students' cognitive skills in the interdisciplinary learning process;(5) promote students' competence in solving complex problems through self-evaluation and group evaluation;(6) develop the ability and skills of social learning in a project-based independent learning group.

Next, I want to ask three questions. The first question is what is the relationship between PBL and innovation? The second question is which abilities have been significantly improved? The third question is how to holistic the different culture.

Finally, as the vice dean in charge of undergraduate teaching in the school of business administration of Northeastern University, I have invited professor Anette and Zhou of the PBL planning center of Aalborg university to teach PBL in our school.

ACKNOWLEDGMENT

This chapter is funded by the 2018 Liaoning province undergraduate teaching reform research project of general higher education (Project Name: PBL-Based Research and Practice of Crowd Innovation Collaborative Teaching Model, Project Number: 2-7).

This chapter is funded by the second batch of industry-university collaborative education project of the higher education department of the ministry of education of China in 2017 (Project Name: Research and Practice of Crowd Innovation Collaborative Teaching Model, Project Number: 201702077001).

This chapter is funded by the 2018 second batch of industry-university collaborative education project of the higher education department of the ministry of education of China (Project Name: PBL-Based Crowd Innovation <Enterprise Innovation and Entrepreneurship Management> Textbook Compilation and MOOC Recording).

This chapter is funded by Special Fund for Teacher Development of Northeastern University (NEU), China, 2019.

REFERENCES

Gao, S. (2018). *China Program for Higher Education Powers - Analysis of Basic Contradictions in New Era Education*. Tianjin University of Finance and Economics Higher Education Conference.

Pan, S., & Cui, L. (2016). *SPS Case Study Method: Process, Modeling and Examples*. Beijing: Peking University Press.

Chapter 3

Fostering Practical Developers in Computer Science Classrooms:
A PBL Approach

Yin Zhang
Northeastern University, China

ABSTRACT

Real-life software development requires practical developers. This chapter discusses the challenges put by real-life software development on computer science education of modern universities, and how to face these challenges by changing traditional teaching and learning to a PBL-based approach. Based on a literature review on PBL theories, methods and tools, and observations made in classrooms and group rooms at Aalborg University, this chapter discusses possible aspects to consider when changing traditional computer science classrooms. A case is then used to demonstrate the process of changing traditional teaching and learning of a computer science course named Visual Programming and Applications to a PBL-based approach.

DOI: 10.4018/978-1-5225-9961-6.ch003

INTRODUCTION

Software development is a fast-developing domain. It is developing new techniques, frameworks, and platforms every day, and expanding its territory into other industrial domains every year. Projects in such a territory can always require new knowledge and may be very complex involving lots of people from different areas. Real-life software development is calling for practical developers that can adapt to the expanding body of knowledge in software development, and have skills and competencies beyond technical ones such as problem-solving, collaboration, project management and critical thinking (Dolog, Thomsen, & Thomsen, 2016).

However, the teaching and learning in today's Computer Science classrooms are still somewhat traditional. Computer Science courses often consist of teacher-centered long lectures and written-based exams. These traditional learning and assessment methods may be effective at low-level learning outcomes in Bloom's taxonomy such as remembering but may have trouble at high-level learning outcomes such as evaluating and creating (Anderson & Krathwohl, 2001). Meanwhile, such non-practical ways of learning may also have trouble in fostering non-technical transferable skills such as collaboration and project management, as these skills are highly situated and require lots of practice and participation (Kolmos & de Graaff, 2014). Fostering practical skills of developers requires changes in the teaching and learning in today's Computer Science classrooms.

Problem-Based Learning (PBL) is a potential solution towards nurturing practical developers. PBL is a student-centered methodology in that learning takes place in the process of students solving problems. PBL is a complex training and closely related to a large bunch of pedagogical concepts (Kolmos & de Graaff, 2014). Typical learning principles involved in PBL include problem organized learning, interdisciplinary learning, team-based learning, self-directed learning, etc. Thus, PBL learning principles highly coincide with the industry's requirements on practical developers. Meanwhile, PBL provides a concrete set of methodologies, methods, and tools to realize the social requirements.

This chapter discusses the challenges posed by real-life software development on Computer Science education of modern universities, and how to face these challenges by changing traditional teaching and learning to a PBL based approach. This chapter reviewed the literature on PBL and related learning theories and observations made in Aalborg University classrooms and group rooms to discuss possible ways to change the traditional teaching and learning of Computer Science courses. This chapter also introduces a case of reforming a traditional Computer Science course named Visual Programming and Applications to demonstrate a possible process of changing traditional Computer Science courses.

CHALLENGES IN TEACHING AND LEARNING OF TRADITIONAL COMPUTER SCIENCE COURSES

A bunch of challenges could be identified in the teaching and learning of traditional Computer Science courses, from perspectives of teaching visions and school policies on education.

For challenges related to teaching visions, a question that bothers teachers could be: What exactly is "ability". Many descriptions are used to define abilities. For example, "being able to program" may be an ambiguous description of ability, as "being able to program a 'for' loop" could be a more specific requirement toward ability. On a broader level, "being able to program according to some coding conventions", "being able to program in an Object-Oriented way", "being able to program collaboratively using GitHub", "being able to program in a team" are all descriptions for abilities. These abilities are different from one another, for some abilities are not even in the same conceptual layer and demonstrated in very different fields.

Meanwhile, some of these abilities are closely related. One example is "being able to program according to some coding conventions", which is very important to "being able to program in a team" in the condition that each team member should easily understand codes from others. The word "ability", therefore, enunciates general meanings. One challenge for teachers is to clarify and understand what the "ability" is, and what are the differences between different abilities.

Another challenge related teaching visions is how to equip students with a specific set of abilities. As mentioned before, some abilities are closely interrelated. However, to achieve abilities are not merely like to transfer knowledge. Teachers cannot specifically stress different abilities one by one and hopefully make students understand how to combine those abilities. Students should practice different ways to achieve the necessary abilities separately and then integrate them in a systemetic approach. The requirement of integrated learning evokes a series of questions, i.e. what should be taught in the lectures, what should be practiced in activities, and how to design assignments.

A third challenge is how to assess learning outcomes, primarily how to assess the performance of a student in group work. Ability assessment is nowhere near as theoretical knowledge, which is concrete and can be tested in the form of written examinations. What's more, in group work, different students need to work on different parts of the project, and thus may gain different abilities. It leads to questions like "What are the mandatory abilities that all students should have", and "What other optional abilities can a student learn if he decides to ignore a certain ability".

The school policies on education may also bring about some problems. One major problem could be that, for specific reasons, school policies tend to encourage individual competitions strongly. Although a case can be made that competitions have half a point to promote individual research, it is a disservice to teaching. A good strategy for teaching requires strong group work, as individual teacher directed teaching often is ineffective. If a teacher in the group is not allowed to share their teaching results, or only the first author of a paper or a project can take advantage of the fruits and other team members cannot gain benefits, there may not exist collaboration in group work, which compromises the good willings of teaching.

Some universities value academic research much more than teaching, partly due to national policies in education. Moreover, there is a misunderstanding in teaching with the opinion that "Teaching is much easier than research" or "Once you get used to a course, you will not need to work on it for the following several years". These statements may be right in the fact that some teachers tend to organize extended, dull lecture-centered classrooms, to assess students by purely written exams and to test only at the level of remembering knowledge by using same questions, barely change for years. However, this will result in severe consequences and rote learning. If a teacher is forced to organize student-centered classrooms and the exams are required to test various abilities, moreover, the content of a course is mandatory to be updated yearly, then teaching will take at least as much time as researching. Good teaching is never easy. It is erroneous to get used to mechanic teaching, especially at a policy level, no matter in a school or a country.

According to the above discussions, specific questions should be answered to improve traditional teaching in Computer Science courses:

- What abilities should be the focus?
- Why do these abilities matter?
- How do these abilities relate to each other?
- How to deliver these abilities to the students?
- How to assess the students?
- How to build a sustainable environment to insist on good teaching?
- How to make continuous improvements to my teaching?

To answer these questions requires a set of theoretical tools:

- A comprehensive model defining what exactly is knowledge, skill, ability, etc. and the relations between them

- A system of pedological methodologies, methods, and techniques to deliver the abilities to the students
- An applicable set of evaluation methods and tools

THEORIES

PBL is a potential solution towards the challenges in the previous section. PBL is a student-centered pedagogy in which learning happens when students solve problems. PBL is a complex pedagogy and is closely related to a large bunch of pedagogical concepts. This section discusses PBL theories and related concepts.

What Is PBL

PBL is Problem/Project Based Learning. However, it is not just "students learning something based on a project" but refers to a complicated and consistent pedagogical system. Understanding PBL requires inspecting the concept from three perspectives: principles, objectives, and the environment.

Kolmos and Graaff defined PBL as a set of learning principles following learning approach, social approach and contents approach (Kolmos & de Graaff, 2014). The learning approach concerns how the learning process is organized. In PBL, the learning process is problem-based. Thus, the learning approach is about how students learn and solve problems. It firstly includes the source and the ownership of the problems, which have a substantial impact on the learning motivations, especially intrinsic motivations (Chin & Chia, 2004). However, the PBL curriculum might increase students' stress thereby de-motivate students (Bedard, Lison, Dalle, & Boutin, 2010). It also refers to the organization of the learning process of the problem: case-based or project-based (Barrows, 1986), and how to mix and balance lectures and projects (Dolog, Thomsen, & Thomsen, 2016).

The social approach states that learning in PBL happens in a team-based environment. This statement is closely related to constructivism (Piaget, 1977). Constructivism suggests that knowledge is constructed via interactions with the environment (Jonassen, 1991). In PBL, a team forms the direct social environment for learning to happen. It is of course about students learning from each other (Kolmos & de Graaff, 2014), but it is also about students experiencing how to integrate professional skills, interdisciplinary skills, and transferable skills all together in a problem and social context. The social approach also refers to participant-directed learning, especially the identification of the problem (Kolmos & de Graaff, 2014). Here, forming a common understanding of the problem and sharing the same goal is also critical to successful teamwork as well as proper social context for effective learning (Spliid, Bøgelund, & Dahl, 2017).

The contents approach refers to the learning outcomes of students. In different learning practices, teachers have different methods to control the learning outcomes. In a more teacher-centered environment, it may be easier to control the learning objectives, although it may lead to passive and inefficient learning (Barrows, 1986). While in a more student-centered approach, teachers would have to pay more attention to supervising to make sure that students do learn the necessary knowledge and skills (Kolmos & de Graaff, 2014).

As a summarization, PBL could relate to the following learning principles:

- Problem approach
  - Learning is organized around problems
  - Experience learning
  - Formulation: complexity, structuredness, etc.
  - Practical or purely theoretical problems (Learning approach)
  - Ownership of the problem (Learning approach)
- Content approach
  - Interdisciplinary learning
  - Exemplary practice (Content approach)
- Team-based
  - Social learning/Team-based learning (Social approach)
  - Student-centered
  - Participant-directed learning (Social approach)
  - Self-Directed
  - Self-Reflective
- Constructive
  - Constructed via interactions with the environment
  - Meaning and thinking are distributed among the culture and community
  - Knowledge is anchored in the context
  - Stimulated by a question or need or desire to know
- Situated learning
- Metacognitive learning
- Cases as demonstrations
- Outside evaluation

- Stimulus
  - Problems as a stimulus for learning
  - Group work as a stimulus for interaction
- Facilitative

These learning principles quickly lead to a set of problems such as "Why these principles?", "Why does PBL work like this?" and "What are these for?". These questions are closely related to the learning objectives associated with PBL. The quick changing world expects students to master specific professional and interdisciplinary skills as well as transferable skills. Expected learning objectives of professional and interdisciplinary skills can be modeled as the revised Bloom's taxonomy (Anderson & Krathwohl, 2001). While transferable skills could refer to a set of skills that could be easily transferred between different professional domains, including critical thinking, creative problem solving, interpersonal, and project management skills (Barrow, 1987; Spliid et al., 2017; Zhou, 2017). It is necessary to notice that the professional, interdisciplinary and transferable skills are not separated from each other but are tightly interwoven. These skills cannot be learned separately but need to be learned and used integrally. PBL provides a methodology and a practical framework to enable integrated learning of professional, interdisciplinary and transferable skills.

Enabling the learning objectives requires a PBL learning environment. Marra et al. proposed that a PBL environment should be: problem-focused, student-centered, self-directed, self-reflective and facilitative (Marra, Jonassen, Palmer, & Luft, 2014). The key to the learning environment of PBL is, from the perspective of constructivism, to provide a context to gives meaning and values to knowledge. The problem to be solved gives meanings to the knowledge to be learned. Students decide how they solve the problem, as well as the necessary knowledge, giving context to the knowledge. Students also decide their learning process and evaluate their learning results, fostering lifelong learning skills. Meanwhile, teachers help students to construct knowledge by probing students' knowledge deeply, but not to construct knowledge for them by lecturing (Marra et al., 2014). The PBL learning principles, objectives, and environment work together to make students learn in the problem and social context, fostering students with the necessary knowledge, skills, and competencies to meet the challenges in the quick changing world.

PBL Models

Different universities can take PBL in really different forms, such as the "One day, one problem" process at Republic Polytechnic (O'Grady, Yew, Goh, & Schmidt,

2012), and the PBL Aalborg model (Kolomos, Fink, & Krogh, 2004). As a summary, Kolmos et al. introduced a PBL curriculum model concerning seven dimensions: outcomes; type of problems and projects; progression, size, and duration; students' learning; academic staff and facilitation; space and organization; assessment and evaluation (Anette, Graaff, & Du, 2009).

Another factor to be considered in PBL is cost. As pointed out by Barrows (Barrows, 1986), a lecture-based method is the least expensive regarding cost, time and effort for teachers. The designing, teaching, and assessing of lecture-based method require the least effort from teachers and administrations. While for PBL, depending on the different choices made on the dimensions in the last paragraph, lots of effort could be required in the course and curriculum designing, preparing, and evaluating.

Kolmos et al. proposed a curriculum change model to PBL (Kolmos & Graaff, 2007). The model consists of 2 layers. The inner layer is the curriculum layer covering elements directly connected to curriculum change. The outer layer is the organizational layer, forming an environment for curriculum change as well as providing context for knowledge construction.

Problem Design

In PBL, learning is about working to solve problems. Learning starts when students are presented with the problems. If students are asked to design their questions, learning start even before the formulation of the questions. Making learning meaningful requires a PBL problem to have specific characteristics. Dolmans et al. described that problems should (1) simulate real life, (2) lead to elaboration, (3) encourage integration of knowledge, (4) encourage self-directed learning, (5) fit in with students' prior knowledge, (6) interest students, and (7) reflect the faculty member's learning objectives (Dolmans, Diana H J, Snellen-Balendong, & van der Vleuten, 1997). Sockalingam et al. stated that problems should (1) lead to learning, (2) trigger interest, (3) be of suitable format, (4) stimulate critical reasoning, (5) promote self-directed learning, (6) be of suitable clarity, (7) be of appropriate difficulty, (8) enable application, or use, (9) relate to prior knowledge, (10) stimulate elaboration, and (11) promote teamwork (Sockalingam & Schmidt, 2011). Such identifies some characteristics of so-called "good" problems including engaging students, requiring students to make a decision, be sophisticated enough to foster collaboration, connect previous knowledge with new knowledge; and furthermore, it is stressed that the first stage of a problem should be open-ended (Duch, 2001; Holgaard, Guerra, Kolmos, & Petersen, 2017).

Another characteristic to be considered is problem difficulty, which could be characterized by problem complexity and problem structuredness. Problem complexity refers to the breadth, difficulty level, intricacy, and interrelatedness of problem space, while problem structuredness represents the intransparency, variety of interpretations, interdisciplinary, and interdisciplinary nature of problems (Jonassen & Hung, 2008; Marra et al., 2014). Teachers have the responsibility to control the difficulties of the problems. By controlling the difficulties, one problem can be used to reflect different learning objectives, and be applied to students from different semesters. In 2010, Jonassen further distinguished five characteristics of problems: structuredness, context, complexity, dynamicity, and domain specificity (Holgaard et al., 2017; Jonassen, 2010).

The problem design process can be entirely teacher driven, such as the 3C3R model and the five-step model introduced by Hung (Duch, 2001; Hung, 2006), or be student-driven, such as the five-step model proposed by Holgaard (Holgaard et al., 2017), or be a hybrid approach.

Although some simple problems can be readily formulated and understood, there are also complex and ill-defined problems that could only be formulated or understood by learning new knowledge continuously. In this case, students will need an iterated process to learn new knowledge and to formulate or understand a problem (Holgaard et al., 2017). Thus, the problem analysis process could be as crucial as the problem-solving process of learning.

Kolmos pointed out the importance of proper analyses of problems in PBL. As she specified (Kolmos, 2017), Engineering students are especially keen to jump directly to solution phases and to try out solutions. In teaching practices, an essential reason for failures in projects could be that students started to work on problems that had not been adequately specified. It is normal that students do not know how to clearly define problems when they are used to work on well-defined problems given by teachers. Thus, it is necessary for students to learn about how to define problems accurately in PBL. The paper written by Holgaard et al. provides a useful tool for students to clarify problems (Holgaard et al., 2017).

Collaboration

In PBL, students work in groups to solve problems. Katzenbach et al. identified 5 different types of teams (Katzenbach & Smith, 2015; Spliid et al., 2017): 1) A working group and 2) a pseudo-team are not really teams, but either a group of individual people collaborating on a shared issue or a group of individual people, who speak and act as if they are committed to the same goals without being truly united on the performance goals. 3) A potential team is a group of individual people who are on the cusp of having a common purpose and goal. They also recognize the need for collective activities and achievements and acknowledge and accept the collective need for mutual accountability, conflict resolution, and negotiation from a shared point of view. That is, they are following the conviction "we are all in this together". Katzenbach et al. identified 5 + 2 characteristics that identify 4) real and 5) high-performance teams: (1) Real teams have a common purpose and goal; (2) apply collective activities; (3) produce collective products; (4) hold each other mutually accountable; and (5) dare to go into conflicts. High-performance teams, also, also have (1) an explicit focus on continuous learning and (2) mutual trust and respect.

The 5 types of teams could also be summarized as (Spliid et al., 2017): 1) The working group: No performance need, no common purpose, and an individualistic approach; 2) The pseudo team: A performance need paired with the lack of common purpose or goals; 3) The potential team: Acknowledging the risks - taking the first steps towards teamwork; 4) Real teams: Common purpose, performance goals, and approach; accountability and courage; and 5) High-Performance Teams: Mutual trust and respect along with a focus on explicit learning.

Effective collaboration requires a large set of different interpersonal skills. There are many ways to train every single interpersonal skill. For example, a team charter can be used to help identify goals, roles and rules in team working. Process analysis can be used to help teams analyze how they are doing in teamwork. Another important skill is how to listen to people. The Active Listening practice can be an excellent way to train interpersonal skills. People should also know that they need to give other people time, for example, 5 minutes, before letting them talk.

Collaboration is also cultural. Just like some Chinese teachers would argue, "Chinese people do not know how to collaborate." It is false, and it is true. It is false because Chinese people do work together, but they may usually work in a tree structure. Everyone may talk only to their leaders, but not to each other. When they work together, e.g., writing a report, Chinese people may tend to do their jobs and may pay few attentions to what the other people are doing. It is not surprising to see that even teachers from Computer Science have no experience of collaboration tools such as GitHub. According to (Katzenbach & Smith, 2015), these teachers form teams that are far from "real teams". So, it may be a problem that how do teachers who do not even know how to collaborate with their coworkers teach students how to collaborate effectively.

The fact that teachers do not collaborate a lot may reflect some systemic problems in an institution. An institution's current policies may encourage individual competitions in an extraordinary way. Generally, the first author of a result (e.g., a published paper or an accepted proposal) may take all the essential credits of the result (such as the credits to get promoted, and the profits). The other authors may usually get nothing important in return. As a result, most teachers will become very demotivated in group work since they cannot get what they expect. This may also lead to illicit competitions that people may start to steal and race to publish other people's ideas, which will lead to even less group work since people start to suspect each other. Promoting individual competitions may be right in scientific researches since scientific researchers are individual to a large extent. However, in education, this is not the case. PBL, especially at a programme-level and beyond, requires lots of seamless group work. It is essential to motivate teachers to work with each other to achieve the same goal. Moreover, to do that, it is vital to give teachers chances to share their results, instead of having the first authors take advantage of the others.

Course and Curriculum Design

The first thing to consider when design a course or a curriculum is what students are expected to learn, or the learning goals. Bloom's taxonomy is an excellent tool to analyze learning goals. Besides learning goals, knowledge also has different levels. Anderson and Krathwohl summarized four levels of knowledge: factual knowledge, conceptual knowledge, procedural knowledge, and metacognitive knowledge (Anderson & Krathwohl, 2001). Thus, a learning goal can be analyzed according to a combination of Bloom's taxonomy and Anderson and Krathwohl's levels of knowledge.

One thing to be pointed out is that a learning outcome can be at different levels of Bloom's taxonomy, and different levels of knowledge. For example, a learning outcome A can be both factual and procedural and be applying and analyzing. Most importantly, learning outcomes, teaching and learning methods, and assessment should be aligned.

To design a PBL course or curriculum, several strategies could be considered (Kolmos, 2017): 1) an add-on and course strategy change to more active learning within the existing courses, 2) an integration strategy consisting of a merger of existing courses and integration of skills and competencies like project management and collaboration, and 3) a re-building strategy which involves re-thinking of the role of the university in society and re-thinking the curriculum towards much more flexibility.

Changes of a course may involve a single staff member, but changes of an institution may involve many staff members. Staff members may encounter many problems in changes. If they cannot receive help on changes, they may go back to traditions. Thousand and Villa summarized factors in complex changes as vision, consensus, skill, incentives, resources, and action plan (Thousand & Villa, 1995). Staff members may need help in covering all these factors.

However, even with help on different factors in change, staff members may still face challenges. Woods pointed out that before staff members change to reach a new level of performance, their actual performance may drop down. The descent of performance relates to detrimental factors such as depression, panic, and resistance (Woods, 1994). Experiencing such descent, staff members may have strong willing to return to routine. Support is needed to help them overcome frustrations.

An interesting fact pointed by Graham in curriculum change is that the number of courses changed may not be a good indicator of successful reform, but the change needs to be curriculum-wide (Graham & Royal Academy of Engineering (Great Britain), 2012). Successful and sustainable changes are embedded into a re-designed, coherent and interconnected curriculum.

OBSERVATIONS FROM AALBORG UNIVERSITY CLASSROOMS AND GROUP ROOMS

Problem-based learning has been the pedagogy of Aalborg University since it was inaugurated in 1974. There were two PBL models, the old Aalborg model and the new Aalborg model (Dolog, Thomsen, & Thomsen, 2016), used at Aalborg University. In the new Aalborg model, PBL activities take up to 50% of students' learning time.

The Workload of Students and Teachers

In Aalborg University, each semester is credited 30 European Credit Transfer System (ECTS) points (Dolog, Thomsen, & Thomsen, 2016). That means a student needs to spend 900 hours on learning activities per semester, as 1 ECTS point corresponds to 30 learning hours. However, students quantified that to deliver high-quality results, they may work more than 900 hours per semester.

While for teachers' workload, a teacher can work as a group work coordinator or a lecturer. For lecturers, a course corresponds to 195 working hours, including

11-12 times of teaching. The working hours also include the time for teachers to prepare themselves and the time for exams which is 20 minutes for each student. For group work coordinators, one student corresponds to 14.5 facilitation hours. For a group of 6 students, it is 14.5 x 6 = 87 facilitation hours. These hours include time for report reading, facilitation meeting and project exam.

In a semester, there can be three courses, each of which corresponds to 5 ECTS points, and one project corresponding to 15 ECTS points. Learning of a course per week at Aalborg University can consist of 2 parts, and each part can last for 4 hours. The first part of the learning of a course per week may consist of 2 hours of lectures, and 2 hours of exercises. The second part may be a 4-hour self-study.

Lectures in Aalborg University can be active learning based or in a more traditional way. The university puts efforts to make lectures more attractive to students. Teaching instructors may sit in classrooms to observe how teachers lecture. There can be two instructors in a classroom: an instructor from the same department as the lecture as a professional instructor, and an instructor from the learning department as a pedagogical instructor. The instructors may observe a whole 2-hour lecture. Teachers and instructors will discuss how to improve lectures. They can make detailed discussions on different teaching activities to involve active learning methods to improve lectures.

Exams for courses at Aalborg University can be oral exams or written exams. Oral exams can assess high-level learning goals such as evaluating and creating but are more expensive. Considering a course of 70 students, the lecturer will need 1400 minutes or 23 hours 20 minutes to assess all the students when adopting a 20-minutes oral exam for each student. Written exams are much cheaper, especially for large classrooms. A written exam may take 3-5 hours. Questions from previous years' exams are given to students to help students prepare for this year's exams. However, written exams can only assess low-level learning goals such as remembering. Thus, it is a realistic consideration to decide whether an exam should be written or oral.

Exams for projects are all in oral. A project exam can take 3-6 hours. A 45-minute project presentation is conducted firstly, and then each student needs to take a 45-minute exam. The coordinator of the team and an external examiner will host a project exam. The external examiner may be from the apartment of the coordinator, or another institution. The external examiner system of Denmark makes sure that the scores given in exams can be compared among different schools. However, the external examiner system is expensive. For a department in Aalborg University, 200 million kroner may be used each year for inviting external examiners from different institutions.

Since coordinators are also examiners, it is facilitators' responsibility to balance between facilitation and exams. From such a perspective, an exam can be seen as long facilitation. Facilitators can also point out possible problems before exams so that students can prepare for them. There are also many written exams.

Projects and Group Rooms

In each semester, students are asked to form groups to work on semester projects. Some students would like to work on projects individually, but it will be difficult for them to finish the projects. Thus, most students would work in groups. Meanwhile, if some students always work together every semester, they may not develop interpersonal skills to work with different personalities. Thus, in some programme, coordinators will make sure that students can work with different partners in different semesters.

An interesting fact about how to group students in Aalborg University is that, in the 7th semester (i.e., the first semester for graduate students), there are master students with PBL experiences as they might graduate from Aalborg University and some students without PBL experiences such as international students. Different strategies can be used to group students with different PBL backgrounds. In some programme, coordinators may try to make sure that students without PBL backgrounds can group with students with PBL backgrounds. In some other programme, students with and without PBL experience may be separated into different groups. However, no matter which strategy it is, students without PBL backgrounds have to take a PBL training course to learn about PBL.

In a semester, students spend most of their time in their group rooms. Students consider a group room as an essential part of PBL. In a group room, students can always work together, sharing and discussing their ideas. Aalborg University also provides discussion tools such as whiteboards so that students can write down their ideas or schedule their development activities. Coordinators also facilitate students in their group rooms, as shown in Figure 1.

Learning

AAU updates its education frequently to adapt to the quick changing world. Educational programmes may be updated every year, and there can be a significant revision of educational programmes every five years[1]. Administrators who design educational programmes keep contacts with graduated students and companies to know what the outside world needs. When introducing new courses, they may be

Figure 1. A coordinator is facilitating a group of students in their group room

put into later semesters, and old courses may be pushed to earlier semesters. The reason for pushing old courses to earlier semesters is that as techniques develop, students start to use new techniques in earlier semesters.

Two lines of learning can be identified from the learning at Aalborg University. The first line is about the learning of the profession. This line is about what knowledge, skills, and competencies should be developed for high school students to become engineers. The second line is about the transfer of students' thinking to become engineers. Following the two lines of learning, the end products of the learning at Aalborg University are educated professionals in different domains. However, some students will fail in exams and may drop out of school. 10% of students may drop out of school during the first semester.

Students are very proud of their PBL experiences at Aalborg University. Students understand that the way they work on projects are simulations of what they need to do when they graduate and go to companies. Students seem to have chances to develop sophisticated transferable skills, such as communication and project management skills. The development of various skills is due to that projects of different semesters can be entirely different. In some semesters, projects may be more well-formed and involve larger groups. In some other semesters, projects may be more open-ended and involve smaller groups. By working on different projects with different people, students can develop various transferable skills to help them face different challenges in the future. When they go to work, they may already be quite familiar with how people work in companies. Thus, engineering students from Aalborg University are very competitive and employable.

Group work at Aalborg University is motivated by project problems. Coordinators need to get a hold on the complexities of problems. Different instances of a problem with different complexities can be given to students at different semesters. Students are expected to give new solutions to new problems, not known solutions to known problems. Solving new problems is related to the concept of small Creativity, and also helps to ensure student ownership of solutions to problems.

During facilitation, coordinators do not answer questions from students directly but may ask more questions to push students to think. That is, coordinators do not lead students but push them. For example, facilitators need to let students understand that if a solution cannot be realized in real life, or a problem barely occurs, then it may be a wrong solution or problem. Facilitation usually costs less than an hour. In facilitation of high-performance teams, students talk much more than facilitators. Students control discussions. Facilitators only give pieces of advice. The facilitation at Aalborg University are good examples of PBL learning principles such as facilitative and student-centered learning.

A CASE OF REFORMING A TRADITIONAL COMPUTER SCIENCE COURSE

In this section, a case is introduced to demonstrate the reforming of a traditional Computer Science course. The course used as the case in this section is named "Visual Programming and Applications". The course introduces how to build Universal Windows Platform apps for Windows 10.

Teaching Visions

The reformation starts with a change in teachers' teaching visions. The teaching visions draw a picture of what a good student looks like after he finished Visual Programming and Applications. The teaching visions of Visual Programming and Applications is summarized as:

1. Understanding critical concepts of Graphical User Interface designing and programming, being able to scale these concepts to Graphical User Interface platforms other than Universal Windows Platform (such as Windows Presentation Foundation, Android and iOS)

2. Being able to integrate various techniques such as Web Services, Audios, Videos, Cameras, Sensors, Maps, Calendars, etc. to build a Universal Windows Platform app

3. Being able to specify user needs on apps clearly

4. Being able to design and program in an Objective-Oriented manner leveraging modern design and architecture patterns

5. Knowing how to ensure software quality by for example testing, debugging and performance profiling

Some of these teaching visions are about professional knowledge and skills on Universal Windows Platform development, such a 1 and 2. Some other visions are about general development principles in Computer Science, such as 3 and 4. These principles may have very different forms in different kinds of projects and are very important to the success of the projects. Students need to practice these principles many times to be able to seamlessly integrate these principles with professional techniques to form necessary development competencies.

People may argue that Teaching Vision 3, 4 and 5 are very Software Engineering, and since Visual Programming and Applications is not Software Engineering, it may be improper to include Teaching Vision 3. We would argue that, since the projects in Visual Programming and Applications will be much more complicated than the projects in traditional elective courses, it will become tough for students to handle the projects without following certain Software Engineering principles. Software Engineering principles are fundamental if students want to succeed in the complex projects in Visual Programming and Applications. Visual Programming and Applications also provides a playground for students to try out Software Engineering on projects that are even more complex than the projects in the Software Engineering course. This is an example showing the potential that PBL could help integrate knowledge from different courses, even when being applied only at a course level. Meanwhile, since Software Engineering provides lots of methodologies, methods, and tools to help students deal with various challenges they may meet in complex projects, Software Engineering serves as an excellent toolkit to help students develop various transferable skills such as creative problem solving, project management, communication, and writing, etc.

Learning Goals

Learning goals can be extracted based on the five teaching visions in the previous sections. There can be several different approaches to extract learning goals, e.g., Bloom's taxonomy, Anderson and Krathwohl's level of knowledge (Anderson & Krathwohl, 2001), and the knowledge, skills, and competencies used in Aalborg University. In this section, we firstly adopt the knowledge, skills and competencies perspective used in Aalborg University to analyze teaching visions and extract learning goals. The five teaching visions in the previous section would lead to a set of learning goals shown as Table 1.

Based on the learning goals in Table 1, we further use Anderson and Krathwohl's level of knowledge (Anderson & Krathwohl, 2001) to understand learning goals as Table 2.

Table 1. Learning goals of visual programming and applications

Knowledge	• Know how to use common controls and layout controls • Know how to use various techniques such as Web Services, Audios, Videos, Cameras, Sensors, Maps, Calendars, etc. • Know how to use data binding • Understand what is and why we need Dependency Injection, Model-View-ViewModel and services to propose Objective-Oriented Design • Know how to use Entity Framework Core to access data • Know how to unit test, debug and profile on performance both on client side and server side
Skills	• Be able to design and implement complex Graphical User Interface with various controls • Be able to integrate various techniques into Graphical User Interface apps • Be able to use data binding, Dependency Injection, Model-View-ViewModel and services to propose and implement Object-Oriented Design • Be able to use Entity Framework Core to manage data • Be able to test, debug and profile on performance effectively both on the client side and server side • Be able to specify user need on apps clearly
Competencies	• Be able to provide integrated solutions to meet complex user needs on modern apps

Table 2. Detailed learning goals of visual programming and applications

Knowledge
Know how to use common controls and layout controls • Remembering o Conceptual & Factual: Students do not need to remember exactly how to use each control since they can always check them on the Internet. Instead, students should remember the fact that they can use common controls to implement specific functions, and use layouts controls to layout common controls • Understanding o Conceptual & Factual: There are certain ways to control the properties and behaviors of controls and how to do it.
Know how to use various techniques such as Web Services, Audios, Videos, Cameras, Sensors, Maps, Calendars, etc. • Remembering o Conceptual & Factual: Various functions can be implemented using various techniques.
Know how to use data binding • Remembering o Factual: Data binding is an alternative and effective way to interact data with controls. • Understanding o Conceptual & Procedural: How to use data binding
Understand what is and why we need Dependency Injection, Model-View-ViewModel and services to propose Objective-Oriented Design on the client side • Remembering o Factual: Objective-Oriented Design is an elegant solution to complex software design, and Dependency Injection, Model-View-ViewModel are excellent methods to realize Objective-Oriented Design. • Understanding: o Conceptual: What is Dependency Injection, Model-View-ViewModel, and Objective-Oriented Design, and why we need Dependency Injection and Model-View-ViewModel to realize Objective-Oriented Design o Procedural: How to use Dependency Injection and implement Model-View-ViewModel
Know how to use Entity Framework Core to access data • Remembering: o Factual: Entity Framework Core is an Object-Oriented and more natural way to access databases. • Understanding: o Conceptual & Procedural: How to use Entity Framework Core to access databases.

continued on following page

Table 2. Continued

Know how to unit test, debug and profile on performance both on client side and server side • Remembering: o Factual: Unit test is a necessary and useful way to ensure the quality of software. Debugging is a standard and effective way to figure out what is going wrong with codes, and is much more potent than printf. Performance profiling is a powerful way to understand which codes are slowing down an app. • Understanding: o Conceptual & Procedural: How to unit test, debug and profile on performance.

Skills
Be able to design and implement complex Graphical User Interface with various controls • Applying: o Conceptual & Procedural: Use various controls to design and build complex Graphical User Interface. • Analyzing: o Conceptual & Procedural: Analyze the functions of Graphical User Interface and the relations between controls. o Meta-cognition: Policies on how to understand the complex relations between controls and when to use these policies.
Be able to integrate various techniques into Graphical User Interface apps • Applying: o Conceptual & Procedural: Use various techniques and integrate them into apps. • Analyzing: o Conceptual & Procedural: Analyze the relations between techniques and the business logic of an app. o Meta-cognition: Policies on how to understand the complex relations between different parts of an app and when to use these policies.
Be able to use data binding, Dependency Injection, Model-View-ViewModel and services to propose and implement Objective-Oriented Design • Applying: o Conceptual & Procedural: Implement Objective-Oriented Design with data binding, Dependency Injection, Model-View-ViewModel, and services. • Analyzing: o Conceptual & Procedural: Analyze what Objective-Oriented Design should be used for given business logic. o Meta-cognition: Policies on how to propose Objective-Oriented Design and when to use them.

continued on following page

Table 2. Continued

Be able to use Entity Framework Core to manage data • Applying: o Conceptual & Procedural: Use Entity Framework Core to design and access databases. • Analyzing: o Conceptual & Procedural: What design should be used for a specific set of data. o Meta-cognition: Policies on proposing database designs and when to use them.
Be able to test, debug and profile on performance effectively both on the client side and server side • Applying: o Conceptual & Procedural: Propose unit test, debug and profile on performance on a given set of codes • Analyzing: o Conceptual & Procedural: What design should be used to unit test a set of codes, what debugging and profiling tools should be used to a set of codes and where to use them. o Meta-cognition: Policies on proposing unit test designs, choosing debugging and profiling tools and when to use them.
Be able to specify user need on apps clearly • Applying: o Conceptual & Procedural: Specify user needs using Software Engineering principles and methods. • Analyzing: o Conceptual & Procedural: What methods and tools should be used to specify user needs.
Competencies
Be able to provide integrated solutions to complex user needs on modern apps • Evaluating: o Conceptual & Procedural: Evaluate a solution and its components concerning aspects such user needs, difficulty, costs, etc. o Meta-cognitive: Policies on understanding and evaluating complex systems and when to use them. • Creating: o Conceptual & Procedural: Propose comprehensive designs and implementations of modern apps to solve authentic, complex problems o Meta-cognitive: Policies on creative problem solving and when to use them.

Teaching and Learning Methods

Both lectures and projects will be used in Visual Programming and Applications. All the lectures are Active Learning based to maximize the delivery of knowledge, skills, and competence. Meanwhile, projects are used to help students to practice knowledge and develop skills and competencies. There are 40 teaching hours in Visual Programming and Applications. According to the knowledge of learning objectives, lectures will take 22 hours. The other 18 hours will be used as facilitation hours. Visual Programming and Applications will be given during week 1-8. There could be four lectures, each with two teaching hours, during week 1-8. A detailed plan of the lectures is shown as Table 3. Each of the lectures will last for 110 minutes (with a 10-minute break).

The Active Learning methods are explained as follows:

1. **Follow-Me Coding:** Ask students to follow teachers to code right in the class. Check if all students can follow up.
2. **One Answer to Sit Down:** Ask a set of students to stand up and propose one or a series of questions. Each student has to give at least one answer to sit down.
3. **Figure it Out:** Teams of students are asked to figure out instances of given concepts.
4. **Good to Agree:** Pairs of teams share their answers and figure out common answers.
5. **Good to Disagree:** Pairs of teams share their answers and figure out different answers.
6. **Prove it:** Read materials, make sense of them and prove your understanding is right.

From the lecture plan we could see that, at the beginning of Visual Programming and Applications, small pieces of knowledge are introduced in lectures. It is easy to separate these pieces of knowledge and design Active Learning activities for each piece of knowledge so that students can follow the lectures for a little while and then do some activities. Changing teaching methods can help students maintain their attention and motivate their learning. As the topics of the lectures become complex, it would be hard and even impossible to separate a lecture into several pieces. The increasing complexity brings challenges to the design of Activity Learning lectures. Visual Programming and Applications uses follow-me coding all alone the lectures to

Table 3. Lecture plan of visual programming and applications

#	Contents (Including Estimated Time and Active Learning Methods)
1	1) The HelloWorld app (30 minutes, follow-me coding); 2) Layout controls: Grid, Stack Panel (80 minutes including 10 minutes break with activities, follow-me coding, one answer to sit down)
2	1) Layout controls: Relative Panel, Variable Sized Wrap Grid (45 minutes, follow-me coding, one answer to sit down); 2) Page Patterns (20 minutes with 10 minutes break with activities, figure it out (Any Universal Windows Platform apps)); 3) Common controls: List Box, Flip View (15 minutes, follow-me coding); 4) Common controls: Check Box, Radio Button, Combo Box, Toggle Button, Toggle Switch, Time Picker, Calendar Date Picker, Flyout, Menu Flyout, Progress Ring (20 minutes, figure it out (Microsoft Store)); 5) Common controls: Calendar View (10 minutes, follow-me coding)
3	1) Common controls: Auto Suggest Box, Slider, Progress Bar (20 minutes, follow-me coding); 2) Split View and Hamburger Navigation Menu (45 minutes with 10 minutes break with activities, follow-me coding, one answer to sit down); 3) Visual State Manager (45 minutes, one answer to sit down)
4	1) NavigationView (15 minutes, follow-me coding); 2) Navigation (45 minutes including 10 minutes break with activities, follow-me coding, figure it out + good to disagree (navigations in Cloud Music)); 3) Connected animations and page transitions (30 minutes, follow-me coding, figure it out + good to agree (transitions in XAML Controls Gallery)); 4) ScrollViewer (20 minutes, follow-me coding)
5	1) Manipulating Web service data (110 minutes including 10 minutes break with activities, follow-me coding, prove it): Get, Post, Put, Delete
6	1) Manipulating Web service data on the client side using services (50 minutes, follow-me coding); 2) Data binding (50 minutes, follow-me coding, figure it out)
7	1) Model-View-ViewModel (110 minutes with 10 minutes break, follow-me coding, figure it out)
8	1) IServices, Dependency Injection, library and project organization (110 minutes with 10 minutes break, follow-me coding, figure it out)
9	1) Adaptive data binding (110 minutes with 10 minutes break, follow-me coding, figure it out)
10	1) Entity Framework Core (110 minutes with 10 minutes break, follow-me coding, figure it out)
11	1) Unit testing, Debugging and Performance Profiling (110 minutes with 10 minutes break, follow-me coding, figure it out)

make students code with teachers. Follow-me coding itself can be seen as an Active Learning activity. The fact that it is hard to change teaching methods in lectures of complex topics may become a problem because students may become demotivated and lose their attention. However, the desire for solving complex problems itself is a source of intrinsic motivation, especially when students are facing the problems by themselves, e.g., in their projects. Thus, it is necessary for teachers to motivate students in earlier lectures and projects to help them focus on the complex, long lectures coming latter.

The lectures cover almost all the learning objectives of knowledge and skills, except for the following:

- **Knowledge - Know how to use Various Techniques such as Web Services, Audios, Videos, Cameras, Sensors, Maps, Calendars, etc.:** Only some of the techniques are introduced
- **Skills - Be Able to Specify User Need on Apps Clearly:** Not covered

Projects, as well as assignments, are used to help students practice the knowledge and develop skills and competencies, including the open ones in lectures. The design of the project is introduced first.

Students will be asked to propose a solution to an app. The requirements on projects are shown as Table 4.

The projects and the lectures cover most of the learning objectives of Visual Programming and Applications, but the competence of "Be able to provide integrated solutions to complex user needs on modern apps" needs to be considered in more details. Students are asked to integrate various techniques into the final project but may limit the possibilities that they explore techniques other than their need. Such possibilities are expanded in assignments of Visual Programming and Applications.

Assessment

Assessment is a significant part of Visual Programming and Applications. The Assessments in Visual Programming and Applications follow the principle saying "assessments are for learning". Such an "assessment for learning" perspective interacts with various aspects of Visual Programming and Applications.

The assessment of Visual Programming and Applications interacts with teachers of Visual Programming and Applications by changing and expanding their teaching

Table 4. Requirements of the projects of visual programming and applications

Technical Requirements
1. Use the Universal Windows Platform or any equivalent platform
2. Use at least one technique besides Web Service and database, such as GPS, Audios, etc.
3. Use data binding or any equivalent or more advanced technique
4. Use Dependency Injection, Model-View-ViewModel (or any equivalent or more advanced technique) and services to propose Objective-Oriented Design on the client side
5. Use Entity Framework Core or any equivalent or more advanced Object Relation Mapping tool to access data
6. Propose unit tests or any more advanced testing methods to ensure quality on software
Non-Technical Requirements
1. Solve authentic problems that make sense. Problems can be from you or people you know
2. Document user needs according to Software Engineering principles
3. Document to explain your design, e.g., functional modules, Graphical User Interface elements, software architectures, techniques used, in detail

and knowledge. Visual Programming and Applications, as well as many other topics, is a vast domain that it is impossible to cover all the necessary knowledge using a minimal set of lectures. Assessments can be designed to push students to look outside of the lectures to learn essential knowledge that cannot be covered in lectures. Such an idea can go even further. In a big, complicated and innovative, fast-changing field like Visual Programming and Applications, only the very few and most talented and experienced professionals may know everything, and it is very reasonable that the Visual Programming and Applications teachers are not those very best professionals. However, just like that a good coach is not necessary to be one of the best athletes, good teachers are not necessary to know everything to facilitate students to explore and learn unknown or unfamiliar knowledge. Assessments can be designed to encourage students to step outside the field of a course into unknown knowledge, and teachers can still facilitate students with their professional experiences. Teachers can also learn from students to expand their knowledge. The assessment of Visual Programming and Applications overcomes the problem that teachers cannot know everything by expanding both the teaching and the knowledge of teachers.

The assessments of Visual Programming and Applications interact with students by personalized and contextualized learning. Although the general goals of learning and assessment in Visual Programming and Applications are predefined, the processes of learning and assessment are still highly personalize. Students can choose to work on their favorite platforms, techniques, and problems both in the assignments and the projects. The freedom of choosing their platforms enables students to learn their favorite knowledge in their way. The learning and assessments are also highly contextualized by not just the problems proposed by students, but also the learning goals. For example, assignment 2 in Table 6 are contextualized by the problems of students' projects, and the learning goals of learning about controls and adapting to different platforms. Such contextualization does not just give meaning to students' learning, but also help students to hold a focus and prevent them from learning too much blindly which may lead to inefficient learning.

The assessments complete the learning objectives of Visual Programming and Applications. As discussed in the previous paragraphs and sections, lectures cannot cover all the knowledge in Visual Programming and Applications, and specific learning objectives can be tough to achieve even with active learning lectures. Transferable skills such as creativity, project management, and interpersonal skills need extra practice to develop. The assessments are designed not just to expand the coverage of knowledge, but also to guide and help students to develop transferable skills in solving complex Visual Programming and Applications problems. The assessments are also used to make tacit knowledge of transferable skills and metacognition skills explicit so that students can reflect on and share it. Making these skills explicit is the other perspective of "assessment for learning" and socialized learning beside the perspective of domain-specific professional knowledge.

The design of the assessment in Visual Programming and Applications also considers how to challenge and motivate students. In lectures, it is usually teachers who own the challenges. Students are challenged by teachers to do activities. While in the projects of Visual Programming and Applications, it is students who own the problems. Students solve the problems proposed by themselves and are free to use the techniques they like. They can also do the same in the assignments. Some assignments are based on the problems of the projects. These assignments are to help students discover possible techniques and solutions to their problems, and thus are part of their problem-solving processes. The other assignments are to push the student to look beyond the domain of the Visual Programming and Applications lectures. Students are challenged and motivated by their potentials to adapt to different domains they selected by themselves and do the same things in different ways. In these assignments, students and teachers own the challenges together.

There are three types of assessments in Visual Programming and Applications: assignments, milestones, and the final exam, as shown in Table 5. The list of assignments is shown as Table 6.

The alignment of learning objectives, methods and assignments are shown as Table 7.

Space and Resources

Visual Programming and Applications may be the first step towards PBL in a traditional institution. Thus, there may be no group rooms for students to do group work as in Aalborg University. Instead, classrooms are used as group rooms. There are 18 facilitation hours in Visual Programming and Applications. These facilitation hours are also used as group work time. During the facilitation hours, teachers facilitate groups of students right in the classroom. The other groups that are not in facilitation may use the classroom as group rooms. However, it is necessary to use classrooms with movable desks and chairs so that students can adjust the positions of desks and chairs to form islands. Students may encounter problems in classrooms with fixed desks and chairs, as they can only sit in a straight line, making them hard to communicate with each other.

Table 5. Types of assessment in visual programming and applications

	Assignments	**Milestones**	**The Final Exam**
Who	Individual students	Groups	Individual students in groups
What	Technical knowledge	Project status	Learning goals
When	Weekly	Alpha release (around week 4) & beta release (around week 6)	Week 9
Where	Online	Booked classrooms	Booked classrooms
How	1. The students are asked to work on open-ended assignments and document how they solve the problems. 2. The teachers comment and score on the assignments online using streaming videos.	1. Groups present their software for 10 minutes. 2. After one groups' presentation, another chosen group and the teachers comment on the software for 15 minutes.	1. Groups present their software for 15 minutes. 2. Each group member takes a 15-minutes oral exam, covering the learning objectives of Visual Programming and Applications.

Table 6. List of assignments for Visual Programming and Applications

#	Assignment
1	Know your weapons, Part 1 Install XAML Controls Gallery from Microsoft Store. Figure out five controls that may contribute to your project and impress you the most. Explain how they may contribute to your project and why they impress you.
2	Know your weapons, Part 2 Install Windows Community Toolkit from Microsoft Store. Figure out five controls that may contribute to your project and impress you the most. Explain how they may contribute to your project and why they impress you.
3	Know your weapons, Part 3 Browse the list of available techniques in Universal Windows Platform. Figure out five techniques that may contribute to your project and three limitations that Universal Windows Platform may prohibit you from realizing your ideas. Explain how they may contribute to your project and prohibit you.

Table 7. Alignment of learning objectives, methods, and assessments of visual programming and applications

Knowledge
Know how to use common controls and layout controls • Learning methods: Lecture 1, 2, 3, 4 • Assessment: Technical Requirement 1, Assignment 1, 2
Know how to use various techniques such as Web Services, Audios, Videos, Cameras, Sensors, Maps, Calendars, etc. • Learning methods: Lecture 5, 6 • Assessment: Technical Requirement 2, Assignment 3
Know how to use data binding • Learning methods: Lecture 6, 9 • Assessment: Technical Requirement 3
Understand what is and why we need Dependency Injection, Model-View-ViewModel and services to propose Objective-Oriented Design on the client side • Learning methods: Lecture 7, 8 • Assessment: Technical Requirement 4
Know how to use Entity Framework Core to access data • Learning methods: Lecture 10 • Assessment: Technical Requirement 5
Know how to unit test, debug and profile on performance both on client side and server side • Learning methods: Lecture 11 • Assessment: Technical Requirement 6

continued on following page

Table 7. Continued

Skills
Be able to design and implement complex Graphical User Interface with various controls • Learning methods: Lecture 1, 2, 3, 4 • Assessment: Technical Requirement 1, Assignment 1, 2
Be able to integrate various techniques into Graphical User Interface apps • Learning methods: Lecture 5, 6 • Assessment: Technical Requirement 2, Assignment 3
Be able to use data binding, Dependency Injection, Model-View-ViewModel and services to propose and implement Objective-Oriented Design • Learning methods: Lecture 6, 7, 8, 9 • Assessment: Technical Requirement 3, 4
Be able to use Entity Framework Core to manage data • Learning methods: Lecture 10 • Assessment: Technical Requirement 5
Be able to test, debug and profile on performance effectively both on the client side and server side • Learning methods: Lecture 11 • Assessment: Technical Requirement 6
Be able to specify user need on apps clearly • Assessment: Technical Requirement 1, 2
Competencies
Be able to provide integrated solutions to complex user needs on modern apps • Assessment: Technical Requirement 2, 3

Students would need to bring their laptops to classrooms for group work. Power sockets should be provided to students so that they can have enough power during group working. It is also necessary to educate students how to share public space so that several groups can share a large classroom. Noise meters can be used to help students keep their sound low.

CONCLUSION

PBL is a potential solution towards fostering practical developers who can adapt to the expanding body of knowledge and have skills and competencies beyond technical ones. This chapter discussed the possible challenges in today's traditional

Computer Science classrooms, and the possible ways of facing these challenges by changing towards PBL. A case was used to demonstrate how to change the teaching visions, learning goals, learning and assessment methods of a Computer Science course named Visual Programming and Applications. This chapter may be used as a template to implement PBL in Computer Science classrooms at a course level, which can be a start point to push PBL to higher levels.

ACKNOWLEDGMENT

This paper is funded by the 2018 undergraduate teaching reform research project of the School of Computer Science and Engineering, Northeastern University, the 2018 undergraduate teaching reform research project of Northeastern University, and the 2018 Liaoning province undergraduate teaching reform research project of general higher education (Project Name: PBL-Based Research and Practice of Crowd Innovation Collaborative Teaching Model, Project Number: 2-7).

REFERENCES

Anderson, L. W., & Krathwohl, D. R. (2001). *A Taxonomy for Learning, Teaching, and Assessing: A Revision of Bloom's Taxonomy of Educational Objectives.* New York: Longman.

Anette, K., de Graaff, E., & Du, X. (2009). Diversity of PBL-PBL learning principles and models. In *Research on PBL practice in engineering* (pp. 9–21). Rotterdam: Sense.

Barrow, R. (1987). Skill Talk. *Journal of Philosophy of Education, 21*(2), 187–195. doi:10.1111/j.1467-9752.1987.tb00158.x

Barrows, H. S. (1986). A taxonomy of problem-based learning methods. *Medical Education, 20*(6), 481–486. doi:10.1111/j.1365-2923.1986.tb01386.x PMID:3796328

Bedard, D., Lison, C., Dalle, D., & Boutin, N. (2010). Predictors of student's engagement and persistence in an innovative PBL curriculum: Applications for engineering education. *International Journal of Engineering Education, 26*(3), 511–522.

Chin, C., & Chia, L.-G. (2004). Problem-based learning: Using students' questions to drive knowledge construction. *Science Education, 88*(5), 707–727. doi:10.1002ce.10144

Dolmans, D. H. J. M., Diana, H. J., Snellen-Balendong, H., & van der Vleuten, C. P. M. (1997). Seven principles of effective case design for a problem-based curriculum. *Medical Teacher, 19*(3), 185–189. doi:10.3109/01421599709019379

Dolog, P., Thomsen, L. L., & Thomsen, B. (2016). Assessing Problem-Based Learning in a Software Engineering Curriculum Using Bloom's Taxonomy and the IEEE Software Engineering Body of Knowledge. *ACM Transactions on Computing Education, 16*(3), 1–41. doi:10.1145/2845091

Duch, B. J. (2001). Writing problems for deeper understanding. In *The power of problem-based learning* (pp. 47–58). Stylus Publishing.

Graham, R. H., & Royal Academy of Engineering (Great Britain). (2012). *Achieving Excellence in Engineering Education: The Ingredients of Successful Change.* Anchor Books.

Holgaard, J. E., Guerra, A., Kolmos, A., & Petersen, L. S. (2017). Getting a Hold on the Problem in a Problem-Based Learning Environment. *International Journal of Engineering Education, 33*(3), 1070–1085.

Hung, W. (2006). The 3C3R Model: A Conceptual Framework for Designing Problems in PBL. *Interdisciplinary Journal of Problem-Based Learning*, *1*(1). doi:10.7771/1541-5015.1006

Jonassen, D. H. (1991). Objectivism versus constructivism: Do we need a new philosophical paradigm? *Educational Technology Research and Development. ETR & D*, *39*(3), 5–14. doi:10.1007/BF02296434

Jonassen, D. H. (2010). *Learning to Solve Problems: A Handbook for Designing Problem-Solving Learning Environments*. Routledge. doi:10.4324/9780203847527

Jonassen, D. H., & Hung, W. (2008). All Problems are Not Equal: Implications for Problem-Based Learning. *Interdisciplinary Journal of Problem-Based Learning*, *2*(2). doi:10.7771/1541-5015.1080

Katzenbach, J. R., & Smith, D. K. (2015). *The Wisdom of Teams: Creating the High-Performance Organization*. Harvard Business Review Press.

Kolmos, A. (2017). PBL Curriculum Strategies. In PBL in Engineering Education (pp. 1–12). Academic Press. doi:10.1007/978-94-6300-905-8_1

Kolmos, A., & de Graaff, E. (2014). Problem-Based and Project-Based Learning in Engineering Education. In Cambridge Handbook of Engineering Education Research (pp. 141–160). Academic Press.

Kolmos, A., & Graaff, E. D. (2007). Process of changing to PBL. In *Management of change: Implementation of problem-based and project-based learning in engineering* (pp. 31–44). Rotterdam: Sense Publishers.

Kolomos, A., Fink, F. K., & Krogh, L. (2004). *The Aalborg PBL Model: Progress, Diversity and Challenges*. Aalborg Universitetsforlag.

Marra, R. M., Jonassen, D. H., Palmer, B., & Luft, S. (2014). Why Problem-Based Learning Works: Theoretical Foundations. *Journal on Excellence in College Teaching*, *25*(3&4), 221–238.

O'Grady, G., Yew, E., Goh, K. P. L., & Schmidt, H. (2012). *One-Day, One-Problem: An Approach to Problem-based Learning*. Springer Science & Business Media. doi:10.1007/978-981-4021-75-3

Piaget, J. (1977). *Psychology and Epistemology: Towards a Theory of Knowledge*. Academic Press.

Sockalingam, N., & Schmidt, H. G. (2011). Characteristics of Problems for Problem-Based Learning: The Students' Perspective. *Interdisciplinary Journal of Problem-Based Learning*, 5(1). doi:10.7771/1541-5015.1135

Spliid, C. C. M., Bøgelund, P., & Dahl, B. (2017). Student challenges when learning to become a real team in a PBL curriculum: Experiences from first year science, engineering and mathematics students. *International Research Symposium on Problem-Based Learning 2017*.

Thousand, J. S., & Villa, R. A. (1995). Managing Complex Change Towards Inclusive Schooling. In Creating an inclusive school (pp. 51–79). Academic Press.

Woods, D. R. (1994). *Problem-based learning: how to gain the most from PBL*. Academic Press.

Zhou, C. (2017). Fostering Creative Problem Solvers in Higher Education. In Advances in Higher Education and Professional Development (pp. 1–23). Academic Press. doi:10.4018/978-1-5225-0643-0.ch001

KEY TERMS AND DEFINITIONS

Assessment for Learning: Assessment activities that are designed to provide feedbacks to improve learning.

Assessment of Learning: Assessment activities that are designed to assess the end results of learning.

Learning Activity: A recreation of organized learning.

Learning Goal: An end to which learning effort is directed.

Professional Knowledge: Knowledge about how to conduct professional activities.

Teaching Vision: A thought formed by imaging the results of teaching.

Transferable Skills: Skills that can be applied to different professional domains.

ENDNOTE

[1]   http://sict.aau.dk/computer-science/curricula/

Chapter 4

Rethinking Environmental Education:
Reflections on AAU UNESCO Center Certificate Course of Problem-Based Learning

Fenghua Li
Northeastern University, China

ABSTRACT

This chapter brings a participatory learning experience on PBL at Aalborg University in Denmark. Based on the inherent wholeness of the human-nature ecosystem, interdisciplinary, sustainability-oriented teaching philosophies in environmental education endeavor for the appeal of more concern the value of life, aiming at promoting greater sensitivity to critical thinking, individual happiness, and social responsibility. Problem-based learning may be an effective way to realize the action competence of students by solving real problems and adjusting their behavior and finally to compass transformative learning and lifelong learning.

DOI: 10.4018/978-1-5225-9961-6.ch004

INTRODUCTION

The Ministry of Education initiated the "Undergraduate Teaching Quality and Teaching Reform Project" to take the construction of Teaching Demonstration Courses as one of the critical measures for the majors of biotechnology, information technology, finance and law in the fields of high and new technology. To meet the needs of informatization, participants should take steps and strive to achieve the global vision of the courses. With the rapid development of the world economy, environmental pollution and environmental safety have gradually moved from locals to regions and the globe. From Japan's earthquake nuclear safety incidents to the trend of global warming, all countries in the world are faced with the problem of initiative or forced to cooperate to prevent and control environmental pollution. The field of Environment involves not only basic theoretical knowledge but also many international, regional conventions, agreements or treaties between two or more countries. Therefore, China urgently needs to cultivate high-end talents with environmental specialty, who must be familiar with the rules of international activities and try their best to protect China's international interests and create a favorable environment for the development of the country.

Initiatively, the idea of establishing environmental science and engineering specialty in universities is to meet the needs of the development of environmental protection in China. In order to further broaden the scope of environmental specialty, equip with high and new technology, continuously improve the academic level and the ability to participate in mega projects, China has established branch disciplines such as environmental system engineering, air pollution control, water pollution control, solid waste disposal and management, environmental planning and management, environmental engineering chemistry and monitoring. Scientific research provides the scientific basis for relevant departments' decision-making, or applicable national laws and regulations. In the other side, it promotes the improvement of teaching quality. Teachers have increased their talents through their practice and compiled high-level textbooks. Higher environmental education in China started late, but it is "borderless" on environmental issues, which requires us to learn from the experiences of developed countries and strengthen international academic exchanges and cooperation.

However, pragmatism-based ideology tends to emphasize skills and professionalism in environmental education in China. In addition to the field of humanities and social sciences, most universities have arranged massive professional and technical courses for teachers and students of engineering institutes, which results in the inconsistency between the integrity of human-environment ecosystem and the proportion of liberal-professional knowledge, and triggers many teachers' reflection on the essence of environmental education.

TEACHING PHILOSOPHIES IN ENVIRONMENTAL EDUCATION

In China, teachers are expected to be able to "propagate the doctrine, impart professional knowledge, and resolve doubts". The supposed objective of teaching in universities is to improve the scientific literacy of students. The approach to teaching is to put a good deal of effort into preparation before class. For each class, responsible teachers always collect far more materials than they can present. What they concerned most is whether they have delivered all they had known to the students.

Modern teaching philosophy is that teaching should help both academic and lifelong learning, attend students more concern for the value of life, promote greater sensitivity to individual happiness and social responsibility, finally escort humanistic learning. The followings present advanced approaches to teaching philosophies in environmental education.

Interdisciplinary Teaching

The prominent feature of contemporary scientific development is to strengthen cross-disciplinary linkages and mutual penetration and intersection, resulting in many emerging comprehensive interdisciplinary sciences. The development of environmental science embodies this characteristic, and a series of integrated environmental science and departmental environmental science, which are transiting to adjacent science, have been produced accordingly. Environmental problems arising from human activities are not only natural science problems related to biology, physics, and chemistry, but also involve the specific contents of sociology, economics, ethics, politics, and other social disciplines. Because human beings are organized into complex societies, environmental science also must deal with politics, social organization, economics, ethics, and philosophy. Understanding environmental justice, addressing global issues such as biodiversity, climate change, and ozone hole inevitably lead to the interdisciplinarity, which is derived from the nature of connectivity of environmental science. Scientific principles, societal values, economic factors, and political awareness are essential in solving environmental problems. Interdisciplinarity connects various cognitive aspects of science in the way of combining knowledge and skills and attaches importance to mutual comprehension in collaboration.

From a holistic point of view, environmental education, based on the basic principles of human-ecosystem and the principles of universal connection and development, involves diversified environmental problems and issues, such as environmental ethics, environmental risks, population, fossil energy, renewable energy, biodiversity, soil and its application, water management, air quality, global response and other related themes. It systematically expounds the principle of interaction between human beings and the environment from various aspects, levels, and perspectives. Environmental science presents the overall outline of the human and environmental system. By introducing the basic theory and methodology of environmental science, students have a comprehensive understanding of the content of environmental research, task, and subject system of environmental science. The outcomes aim at stimulating students' interest in environmental issues and a sense of social responsibility and laying a foundation for subsequent professional courses.

Sustainability-Oriented Learning

Despite the increased popularity of the use of the term "sustainability", the possibility that human societies will achieve environmental sustainability has been, and continues to be, questioned—in light of environmental degradation, climate change, overconsumption, population growth and societies' pursuit of unlimited economic growth in a closed system. (Parker, 2017)

China has contributed much to help the world realize the UN's 17 Sustainable Development Goals (UN, 2017). The target of environmental courses in Chinese universities is to provide more "future-oriented" methodology to bridge the gap between environmental education and future research. It involves individuals' perceptions of the future, how their ideas affect their behavior today, and how their current actions affect the future. Core concepts and attitudes include respect for life, respect for animals as creatures, and understanding and concern for all life that preserves the safety and nature of the environment, and being a "responsible global citizen." The target also is to help students develop a more positive attitude towards people in other countries, thus promoting international understanding. It deals with worldwide violence, poverty, and injustice issues. It also includes research on conflicts and resolution between individuals, groups, and countries, and explores the relationship between humans and the environment.

Also, there is a profound metaphor to "sustainability" from the individual aspect of the way to success. Although the world is volatile, pushing us to reorganize our knowledge structure incessantly, fundamental understandings should be realized. Important levers of success that will lead to a life of primary greatness include contribution, sacrifice, service, responsibility, loyalty, reciprocity, diversity, learning, teaching, and renewal. It is concerned with every level and type of learning and the provision of quality education for all (Covey, 2016).

Aiming at Improving Systems Thinking

The core of environmental education is to take the human and environmental system as a whole and make a comprehensive study of the human and environmental system utilizing systemic analysis and combination. On the whole, the development, prediction, regulation, transformation, and benefit of the human and environmental system are comprehensively studied from the aspects of many contradictions of different natures and levels and the particularity of their interconnection. For a long time, modern science has made significant achievements in the study of "segmented parts" of the objective world. At the same time, it has also resulted in the limitation and one-sidedness of people's understanding of the world to trigger many problems in practice to make use of and reform the unified and holistic "human and the environment" system. The core position of Environmental Science in environmental education is determined due to, on one hand, the cognitive root of people's misunderstanding of the human-environment system separately and unilaterally; on the other hand, to the fact that the segmented form of environmental science in its initial development stage is becoming more and more incompatible with the integration of its research object, which contributes to the overall converge of environmental science.

Aiming at Improving Critical Thinking

Western universities emphasized the importance of critical thinking to stimulate students to evaluate information and recognize bias. "Learning to learn" is what actual reflections on taking critical thinking as an important learning outcome

(Cunningham & Cunningham, 2014). It can be seen that critical thinking has become the core educational concept of American universities. Moreover, Richard C Levin, the former president of Yale University, evoked us to rethink the essence of university spirit. His report on the 4th Asia-Foreign University Presidents Forum in April 2010, entitled "The Rise of Asia's Universities" (R. Levin, 2010), pointed out the fact that the leaders of China, in particular, have been very explicit in recognizing that two elements are missing in their universities – multidisciplinary breadth and the cultivation of critical thinking. His interpretation of liberal education in *The Work of the University* (R. C. Levin, 2008) states an inspiring view of the challenges and responsibilities of a great university:

...the essence of liberal education is to develop the freedom to think critically and independently, to cultivate one's mind to its fullest potential, to liberate oneself from prejudice, superstition, and dogma.

The core curriculum of Harvard University also puts efforts on empowering individuals with broad knowledge and transferable skills, and a stronger sense of values, ethics, and civic engagement ... characterized by challenging encounters with important issues ("The Core Curriculum Requirement," 2008).

The philosophy of the Core Curriculum rests on the conviction that every Harvard graduate should be broadly educated, as well as trained in a particular academic specialty or concentration. It assumes that students need some guidance in achieving this goal, and that the faculty has an obligation to direct them toward the knowledge, intellectual skills, and habits of thought that are the hallmarks of educated men and women.

Hence, it is creative and crucial of introducing the concept of critical thinking into environmental classes. Case analysis and debate in groups are two ways to implement critical thinking in the teaching process, which require students to characterize the assumptions behind arguments and organize information. The special series-- Taking Sides: Clashing Views on Environmental Issues (Easton, 2017) are excellent debate resources selected from various journals, with the sequence of presenting literature of YES and No sides first, then listing learning outcomes, implementing debate and finally giving a topic summary. Because appropriate or right decisions are often made based on ethically effective negotiation and dialogue, argumentation is not only a means for one party to persuade the other, but more importantly, a tool for the party to find common aspirations and goals and resolve differences and conflicts. Besides, with all differing opinions, compromise is the only way to address environmental disputes.

In today's society, informatization enables human beings to acquire and transmit all the civilization achievements created by humankind in a faster and more convenient way, to promote close exchanges and dialogues between people all over the world, and to enhance mutual understanding. However, at the same time, we will hear a lot of different voices, talk shows and anti-comments on social media. Some are well-informed opinions, some are gullible misunderstandings, and some is even deliberate to mislead. How do we critically evaluate the information we get? (Smith & Enger, 2015)

Critical thinking involves a set of skills to identify premises and conclusions in an argument, to clarify equivocation and contradictions, to distinguish between facts and values, and to understand conceptual frameworks systematically and thoughtfully. Critical thinking also can help us better understand our own opinions as well as the points of view of others. It can help us evaluate the quality of evidence, recognize bias, and avoid jumping to conclusions. Students with excellent critical thinking ability also show dispositions of skepticism, independence, open-mindedness, flexibility, accuracy, orderliness, decisiveness, courage, and humility.

CHALLENGES IN SUSTAINABLE EDUCATION

Transformative Learning

Transformative learning theory, as Jack Mezirow interprets it, is a metacognitive epistemology of evidential (instrumental) and dialogical (communicative) reasoning (Mezirow, 2009). The distinction between instrumental learning and communicative learning lies in the learning process of which instrumental learning is hypothetical-deductive, arriving at improving performance or prediction, and communicative learning is analogically-abductive, pertaining to intellectual and empathetic understanding and judging the context of the assumptions or contradictions. Transformative learning can make students or adults more inclusive, critical thinking, open, reflective and emotionally able to change.

Environmental education should direct in the orientation of transferring the professional knowledge to address environmental issues, but in the long run, in cultivating students the capability of negotiation to seek common ground with the wide range of relevant participants in the social context, where dialogue and compromise play the crucial roles in problem-solving.

Understanding an Ecological Approach

An ecological approach to environmental education is with the view of the earth as wholeness, emphasizing the interconnection. It is more concerned with the dynamic process crossing borders in an integrated way. Addressing environmental issues like a tropical rainforest, global warming, emerging economies, sustainable agriculture, needs the reorientation of education towards the sustainability of "The One". Ecological thinking offers the potential both to critique current educational theory and practice and to provide a basis by which it may be both transformed and transcended (Sterling, 2001).

Towards Lifelong Learning and Globalization

Lifelong learning is more than instrumental as it occurs whenever we experience social situations and integrate the perceived content into the individual's biography (Jarvis, 2009). The essence of cultivation requires educators to deal with the learning process of students more prudently, with the aim at shaping the knowledge structure and students' mindset to connect with the broader society, especially in the trend of digital information-driven globalization. However, globalization tends to emphasize certain forms of scientific knowledge risen in western countries and omit others, i.e., forms of traditional and indigenous knowledge. One main danger of globalization is that of homogenization (Jarvis, 2009). It is a social ambiguity in the issues of lifelong learning.

LEARNING IN THE AALBORG UNIVERSITY UNESCO CENTER OF PBL

Problem-based learning in Aalborg University (AAU-PBL) was initiated with the foundation of this young university in 1974 as an innovation in educational models.

AAU developed the notions of Knud Illeris, a professor in Roskilde University, Denmark, who formulated principles as problem-orientation, project work, interdisciplinarity, participant-directed learning, and the exemplary principle and teamwork (Knud Illeris, 1976)(Kolomos, Fink, & Krogh, 2004). PBL is implemented at an institutional level in AAU through the strong interplay between staff and students and intense collaboration with public and private sectors, with expectation in new insights, new solutions to societal challenges and knowledge that changes the world ("AALBORG UNIVERSITY – KNOWLEDGE FOR THE WORLD," 2018).

The PBL training course in the AAU UNESCO Center provides basic knowledge of PBL, premises and implementing suggestions of a change to PBL. The whole course schedule includes four modules: 1) Introduction and preparation, 2) Thematic workshops, 3) Experimentation and evaluation, 4) Examination (ucpbl.moodle.aau. dk). Among the four modules, the central part "Thematic workshops" go through the learning process, companying with interval group discussion and project report writing. The following will present the primary learning outcomes and reflections during the learning journey.

Literature Reading About PBL

On the Theories for PBL

AAU-PBL seeks theoretical foundation from ideologies of Experiential Learning, the reflective practitioner, constructivism and social learning (De Graaff & Kolmos, 2009a)(de Graaff and A. Kolmos, 2003). The book *Contemporary Theories of Learning: Learning Theorists——in Their Own Words*, edited by Knud Illeris introduces modern learning theories of most famous educators, which are also instructive to PBL. Knud Illeris is acknowledged as an innovative contributor to learning theory and adult education. He presented his idea of *The Three Dimensions of Learning*, i.e., the content dimension, the incentive dimension, and the interaction dimension. The three dimensions form a triangle which depicts the field of learning in general and related development of functionality, sensibility, and sociality, which are the general components as competencies. In a school situation, both the content and the incentive are crucially dependent on the interaction process between the learner and the social, societal, cultural and material environment. He also mentioned that the barriers to learning must be taken into account, for example, one's defense mechanisms, mental resistance, would be activated if external elements in the influences do not correspond to their pre-understandings. This implies that the question of relevant learning types must be included, that possible defense or resistance must be considered and that internal, as well as external learning conditions, must also be dealt with (K. Illeris, 2009).

John Dewey emphasizes education must start with the experience that learners already have; where the ability developed in the learning process provides a starting point for all future learning. Dewey's experience was different from the Kolb's experience which is the common sense of experience. John Dewey worked all his life on refining his notion of experience and defined it first as interactional (resting on a principle of causal relations between subject and worlds) and later as a transactional concept (resting on a principle of mutual relations between subject and worlds) (Dewey & Bentley, 1949). Experience is the concept Dewey used to interpret the relation between subject and worlds as well as between action and thinking, between subject existence and becoming conversant about selves and the object. Learning based on Dewey's notion of experience is closely connected to his notion of inquiry and knowledge (Elkjaer, 2009). Dewey's pragmatism theory specifies the way to understand learning as an experimental approachability to change and creation. In 1984, David Kolb published his book Experiential Learning (Kolb, 1984), in which the term 'experiential learning' refers to participants' learning progress from 'experiences' derived from physical actions and memory as tacit knowledge. However, Kolb's experience is traditionally understood as an epistemological concept in which the purpose is production and acquisitions of knowledge through reflection on action. In contrast to this, Dewey's concept of experience is ontological and based upon the transactional relationship between subject and worlds(K. Illeris, 2009).

Donald Schön's book *The Reflective Practitioner* attaches importance to reflective practice, which brings insight to the practical reflection procedure and the perception of standing outside of ordinary professional understandings which may lead to blind faith and bias (Schön, 2017). His notion has become guidance to practice-based learning settings which differs from formal learning or didactic knowledge transfer. Jerome Bruner believes that knowledge learning includes three almost simultaneous processes: acquiring new knowledge, transforming old knowledge, and checking whether knowledge is appropriate which involves reflective thinking and more or less creative action. He also illustrates the relationship between culture, mind, and education. He believes that knowing and communicating are in their nature highly interdependent, indeed virtually inseparable; that learning and thinking are always situated in a cultural setting and always dependent upon the utilization of cultural resources (Bruner, 2009).

Howard Gardner published the book *Frames of Mind: the Multiple Intelligences*, based on his documenting how different parts of the brain are dominant for various cognitive functions(Gardner, 1983). Gardner's theory also inspires teachers, school administrators, and special educators to seek other ways, such as active learning, to develop an ordinary student's intellect rather than traditional teaching approaches. These contemporary theories of learning as some supportive ideologies, enable the practice of PBL rest on the theoretical basis for the method to achieve academic and social competences in learning outcomes.

On Principles of AAU-PBL

Kolmos (De Graaff & Kolmos, 2009a) differentiated the principles of problem-based learning in AAU and Roskilde University by comparing with the principles of the project-based learning in McMaster and Maastricht University. Five elements were categorized for PBL in Aalborg University—problem orientation, interdisciplinary, exemplary learning, participant-directed, and teams or group work. Among these principles, interdisciplinary and exemplary learning are more distinctive by presenting the striking characteristics of AAU-PBL. Moreover, Kolmos concluded three approaches to these principles: 1) the cognitive learning approach; 2) the content approach; and 3) the collaborative learning or social approach. The cognitive learning approach is illustrated by the elements which can help students reach deep learning by reflection-in-action when solving a problem and reflection-on-action, by writing project analysis, after completing a project-based task. The problem or project offers students' vivid experience in a particular context which connects the experience they already have and rebuilds their knowledge system. The content approach includes interdisciplinary, exemplary, theory and practice including research methodologies. An authentic social problem which may be ill-structured gives opportunities for students touching on unfamiliar but interrelated disciplines. They broaden their different disciplinary knowledge by exploring the theories and methodologies of unknown segments within the problem. Interdisciplinary, which may stimulate the curiosity of students, acts as an incentive or driving force of seeking solutions to a real problem. The social approach refers to teams or participant-directed activities, which comprises discussion, debates, communication, collaboration, leadership, facilitation, and compromise, etc. Teamwork involves transformative learning which always, to some extent, leads to an epistemological change rather than merely behavior adjustment or an increase in the quantity or fund of knowledge (Kegan,

2009). These experiences are probing the attitudes towards loyalties and devotions of students that are required by the foundation of teamwork, which will affect their future development in the long run.

On Interdisciplinarity of AAU-PBL

'Interdisciplinarity' as One Characteristic of AAU-PBL Model

Kolmos (Kolmos & de Graaff, 2014) differentiated Problem-based learning in Aalborg university from project-based learning in Mcmaster university with its distinct of interdisciplinary context and authentic exemplary problems, as table 1 shows. Most emerging engineering innovation projects or mega-projects are based on collaborative and interdisciplinary knowledge, which requires a systemic vision on the project from the institutional level in designing curriculum. This dominant character is quite an accord with the eccentric element of environmental science. The practice of AAU-PBL exemplifies the prospective orientation for environmental education.

'Interdisciplinarity' in Modes of Knowledge Production

The US National Academies defined interdisciplinarity as: 'Interdisciplinary research (IDR) is a mode of research by teams of individuals that integrates information, data, techniques, tools, perspectives, concepts, and/or theories from two or more

Table 1. Original learning principles at the pbl universities

McMaster and Maastricht Universities Problem-Based Learning	Aalborg and Roskilde Universities Problem-Based and Project Organized Learning
Problems form the focus and stimulus for learning.	Problem orientation
Problems are the vehicle for development of problem-solving skills.	Interdisciplinary
New information is acquired through self-directed learning	Exemplary learning
Student-centered	Participant-directed
Small student groups	Teams or group work
Teachers are facilitators/guides	(Knud Illeris, 1976)
(Howard S. Barrows, 1996)	

disciplines or bodies of specialized knowledge to advance fundamental understanding or to solve problems whose solutions are beyond the scope of a single discipline or area of research practice' (Harper, 1969).

There are two goals for interdisciplinary research: (1) to advance fundamental understanding and (2) to solve problems. Researchers differentiate 'Mode 1 interdisciplinarity' with 'Mode 2 interdisciplinarity' as 'Mode 1' is described as an older mode of knowledge production that is characterized by being hierarchical, homogeneous, and with discipline-based work(Boden, Cox, Nedeva, & Barker, 2004). While the attributes of Mode 2 include non-linearity, intricacy, mixing, and interdisciplinarity (Frodeman, 2010). In other words, 'interdisciplinarity' in Mode 2 arises from the need of problem-based, characterized by the interaction and feedback between the theoretical and the practical in the authentic social context.

Finding a solution to a problem demands that different skills have to be integrated in a framework of action. The degree to which this framework fits the requirements set by the specific context of application, however, determines how long consensus on the framework will be sustained. In general, consensus will be temporary. Moreover, the solution that is produced will normally involve contributions from several disciplines. It will, in other words, be transdisciplinary. (Gibbons, 2003)

The three most widely 'multidisciplinary', 'interdisciplinary', and 'transdisciplinary' are included in the taxonomy of interdisciplinarity for understanding individual species within the general classification. Multidisciplinarity was defined as an approach that juxtaposes disciplines. Juxtaposition fosters broader knowledge, information, and methods. Yet, disciplines remain separate (Frodeman, 2010). A critical characteristic of transdisciplinary research is that beyond an academic or disciplinary collaboration level, through active collaboration with people involved the research sphere and community-based stakeholders. Collaboration becomes a way of exploring the unknown area, producing new knowledge, and helping stakeholders incorporate the research results (Wickson, Carew, & Russell, 2006). The practical common interest in a project to solve complex problems will reinforce the collaboration of teamwork, especially in domains of industry, government, or society more generally.

System-Based Thinking for Interdisciplinarity

AAU-PBL Model embraces interdisciplinarity in educational innovation, much more than other curriculum reformation. It not only reflects the dichotomous strategy of knowledge production but represents its expansion to include holistic, integrative, system-based thinking. Specifically, from a curriculum design perspective, AAU-PBL model facilitators pay attention to lead students to identify, analyze and formulate a problem with an iterative delimiting process, with the learning objective of adapting students to work in a more holistic system. Jette (Jette Egelund Holgaard, 2017) proposed a five-step model for project design, initiating students to (1) relate to the theme, (2) map the problem field, (3) narrow down the problem, (4) analyze the problem in context and (5) formulate the problem. The model stressed a system-based view to exploring the processes of solving ill-structured real-life problems.

Systems-based thinking takes a contextual problem as the wholeness, emphasizing that the problem has many academic and social dimensions, each of which is interwoven in the complex, dynamic, interconnected world. Thus, cross-discipline of integration and implementation is necessary. Bammer (Bammer, 2013) (Bammer & Smithson, 2012) lays out five core concepts for describing and planning interdisciplinary integration. As shown in Figure 1, the five core concepts are: 1) system-based thinking, 2) attention to problem framing and boundary setting, 3) attention to values, 4) a sophisticated understanding of ignorance and uncertainty, and 5) understanding collaborations. According to Bammer, the five core concepts are linked that commonly contribute to developing strategies for carrying out interdisciplinary integration research.

Among the five core concepts, systems-based thinking provides a view to research a real-life problem in a broad scope, in particular to the interplays between different

Figure 1. Five core concepts for integration
(Shani, Mohrman, Pasmore, Stymne, & Adler, 2007).

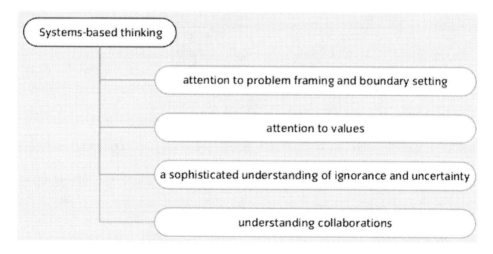

elements or issues in practice that usually involves multiple dimensions from social, environmental, organizational, technological, and cultural understandings. Moreover, whole systems thinking extends, connects and integrates the three aspects of paradigm: ethos(the distinctive spirit of a culture), eidos(culture connotation), and praxis (reality) to reflect wholeness (Sterling, 2001). This further indicates the critical trait of the wholeness of the human-nature environment. When to address environmental problems in a specific social and cultural context, culture differences and strategies on how to overcome cultural value barriers should be considered. For example, when to discuss the incident of Japan's withdrawal from the International Whaling Commission (IWC), the ecological, historical, social and economic attention should be paid. We also should understand it is often tough to force other countries to comply with global environmental, ethical commitments, which is the central predicament in environmental conservation and ethical education.

Thematic Workshops

For the AAU UNESCO PBL training course, all learning materials and schedule were presented on the Moodle system of AAU. It was convenient for students to prepare the classes and communicate with teachers. The course included eight thematic workshops. Participants can watch videos for an online course and read related references, also can pose questions for reading and discussion in the forum.

Thematic Workshop 1: Teaching Portfolio as an Instrument for Reflection

Teaching portfolio was introduced as a tool for reflection and career development. The Kolb cycle for reflective practice, which leads to self-learning and lifelong learning, is the theoretical basis for a teaching portfolio. Group discussion was exercised in workshops outside of the classroom. Practitioners felt more inclined to talk and concentrated on the task because it became much more comfortable to communicate with classmates. Listening to others and cooperation with colleagues was an exciting and active experience. Teaching portfolio templates were designed for individual reflection and teaching professionalism, by identifying relevant topics for reflection throughout the course. As far as the template sharing is concerned, the atmosphere presented in the discussion between group members showed they were much serious and contributed to the homework. Participants deeply reflected their teaching experience as practitioners in the procedure of cultivation, as Chinese education stressed.

Thematic Workshop 2: Active Learning and PBL

In this thematic workshop, different theories of learning were introduced, such as Piaget (Piaget, 1964), Vygotsky(Daniels, 2016), and Dewey(Dewey, 2007), etc. Constructivism was comprehended as one of the crucial foundations of active learning and PBL. From Chinese teachers' perspective, the educational system of Denmark is much more attractive and referential as a future-oriented national shared welfare compared other countries. Higher education in Denmark adopts the European Credit System (ECTS), which is 60 ECTS per academic year. Higher education institutions in Denmark are divided into the following categories: 1) Academy profession programs: They provide professional-oriented short-term education, mainly for business, technology and IT professionals, about 90-150 ECTS. These courses mainly help students solve practical problems and analyze career tasks so that graduates can be competent for middle-level management positions. The teaching method is based on a combination of theoretical research and practice orientation. The degree holder can use the credits to offset for his major study if he continues to study in Professional Bachelor's programmes. 2) Professional bachelor's programs: They are similar to traditional undergraduate education, mainly for business, education, nursing, engineering and shipping professionals training, about 180-240 ECTS. These courses focus on developing the theoretical knowledge and practice of the bachelor's degree in the professional field, which requires at least 30 ECTS internships. Most schools provide opportunities for undergraduates to further study in their major. 3) University level programs: The courses are offered by Danish universities, which are research-intensive institutions offering project-based learning courses. It can be divided into three degrees: the bachelor's degree, the master's degree, and the doctor's degree. Most students will continue to study for a master's degree, that is, to complete 120 ECTS of bachelor program, and 30 ECTS of master's thesis independently. Students with master's degrees may engage in professional work or scientific research. After completing 180 ECTS, one can get a doctor's degree, participating in joint research projects.

PBL is implemented at an institutional level in Aalborg University. The faculties and study boards in each department play an essential role in planning programmes and inspecting the teaching and learning process. Each program of Aalborg university includes general courses and the hierarchy in the teaching-learning system is as figure 2 shows. In each semester, students need to complete the required European Union Credits and carry out parallel project work at the same time. The teaching group sets a theme and a framework for the relevant curriculum system. Within this

Figure 2. The teaching-learning system in AAU-PBL

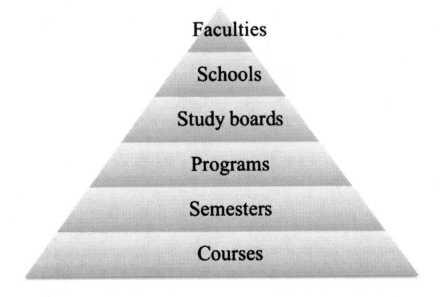

scope, students can follow the advice of their facilitators and external enterprises. Course learning accounts for a coincidence of credits, usually given after the first month of the lectures, and project credits at the end of the semester. The project work is organized in teams, with the number of people in each group ranging from the first grade to fourth grade. The principle of grouping is that students can combine freely according to their interest in the project.

Active learning is emphasized as an essential approach in student-oriented learning, which is differentiated from didactic teaching and rote learning. It reminds teachers that students as the subject of learning, experiencing and thinking, should be taken care of when designing class activities and lectures. The experience of liberal teachers implied that teacher should create a relax environment and be aware of the attention span of students.

Thematic Workshop 3: PBL Principles, Practices and Models

As the literature indicates (H. S. Barrows, 1986), problem-based learning methods can be categorized into different types, as figure 3 shows: complete case or case vignette, partial problem simulation, full problem simulation (free inquiry), teacher-directed learning, student-directed learning, and partial student and partial teacher

Figure 3. Variables in problem-based learning methods
(H. S. Barrows, 1986)

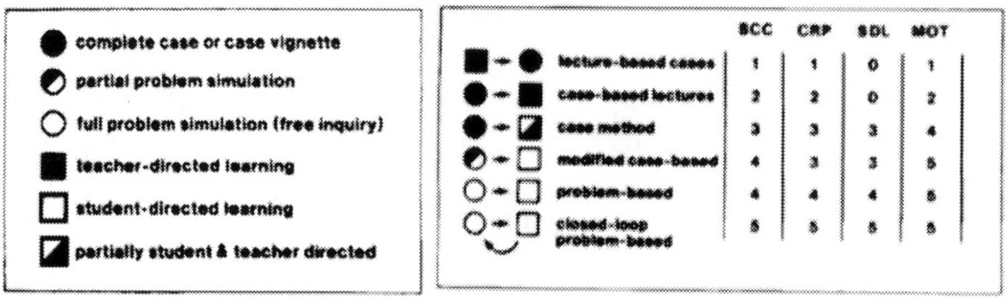

			SCC	CRP	SDL	MOT
■→●	lecture-based cases		1	1	0	1
●→■	case-based lectures		2	2	0	2
●→☑	case method		3	3	3	4
◐→□	modified case-based		4	3	3	5
○→□	problem-based		4	4	4	5
○→□	closed-loop problem-based		5	5	5	5

- ● complete case or case vignette
- ◐ partial problem simulation
- ○ full problem simulation (free inquiry)
- ■ teacher-directed learning
- □ student-directed learning
- ☑ partially student & teacher directed

directed. The taxonomy is based on possible educational objectives: 1) Structuring of knowledge for use in clinical contexts (SCC); 2) The developing of an effective clinical reasoning process (CRP); 3) The development of effective self-directed learning skills (SDL); 4) Increased motivation for learning (MOT). He suggested that planned variables in course design have a potent effect on the quality of PBL, which also is the understanding and skills of the teacher or tutor. He also indicated that the methods with the highest educational potential are also the more difficult and expensive to mount.

This thematic workshop introduced the basic knowledge of PBL. When concerning the literature of PBL principles (De Graaff & Kolmos, 2009a)(De Graaff & Kolmos, 2009b), there was active participation in the post of the Moodle forum. When asked about "What qualities should PBL teachers have to avoid novices teaching novices, especially in the disciplinary field where a teacher cannot master all the knowledge?", and "In Chinese traditional education regime, teachers used to be didactic, it is tough for them to let the thing go out of control. How can practitioners be convinced to change our rooted mind?" the trainer emphasized the role of a teacher as a facilitator, not traditional knowledge transferors and encouraged teachers should be PBL practitioners to try and change boldly. As far as the question "With what criteria teachers decide exemplary authentic problems to achieve overall objectives? " concerned, the history, philosophy, the learning principles of PBL, and methods for designing and planning of a specific curriculum and problem were introduced.

The mini exercise of selecting one word to define PBL went between two people in a group. The results showed that it was hard to define PBL with only one word and hard to reach consensus when a disagreement took place, even just two people involved. Varied curriculum models of PBL were also presented with the exercise to compare specific elements in those models and chose one model as a sample to design a PBL curriculum. Practitioners were divided into groups and gave short lectures to explain our choice and curriculum design after peer discussion. It was exactly the practice of active learning and small-scale problem-based learning. As each form of PBL in the world has its strengths and limitations, participants should consider the cultural context when introducing PBL into China.

Thematic Workshop 4: Problem Design

Jette (Jette Egelund Holgaard, 2017) proposes that learning outcomes should be explicated or formulated in different stages of the problem design. An overview of the five steps, i.e.1) Relating to a theme, 2) Mapping the problem field, 3) Narrowing down the problems, 4) Problem analysis and contextualization, 5) Problem formulation, is presented to frame the process as well as exemplify implementation of the problem design in a sequential systemic manner. Guerra (Holgaard, 2013) outlined two different approaches to problem design: bottom-up and top-down. In a bottom-up approach, students raise questions by exploring social-context-based discrepancy for potential problem seeking. In the top-down approach, students start with a solution in search of problems.

The exercise was assigned as for formulating a problem, taking adapting to a PBL environment as an example. Groups were required to list elements for the three aspects in the triangle in figure 4. Participants also practiced bottom-up problem

Figure 4. The exercise for formulating a problem

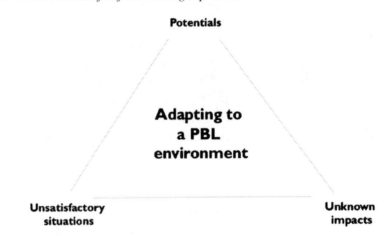

analysis by answering 5W1H (what-why-who-when-where-how) questions. After this workshop, participants are capable of outlining and formulating a problem in group work, relating potentials, unsatisfactory situations to unknown impacts from teachers' perspectives. Participants think the possibilities of adapting to a PBL environment are the possible learning outcomes, i.e., self-directed learning, logic and analysis, solutions to authentic problems, critical thinking, creativity, social responsibility, collaboration, etc. The unsatisfactory situations are improper evaluation system and curriculum setting, lack of virtual classrooms and shared digital resources. The unknown impacts of adapting to a PBL environment are market needs, learning objectives, reaction, and acceptance of students, to what extent Chinese universities can change to support PBL.

Thematic Workshop 5: Collaboration and Project Management

This workshop listed several references and the small inspirational YouTube on Time Management by Steven Covey for preparation and warm-up. Two sample reports of problem analysis of international master students and junior students group were shown as examples, respectively, with apparent differences of cognition to their collaboration in project work. During the workshop participants exercised the art of listening in communication. It was a fantastic experiment which proved few people could listen to others with patience, or without misleading or interruption. It indicates the social difficulties that lie in communication, collaboration, and project management. As for project management, the schedule and time management are essential for fulfilling the project in a semester. As group members, participants tried to fill in a team charter to identify their roles in the community and to pilot the project work as a group contract.

Thematic Workshop 6: Course and Curriculum Design

Recently, Bloom's taxonomy for learning objectives has been served as the pillar for teaching practitioners, in particular, those that rest more on skills rather than content, involving school and department administrators, curriculum planners, and classroom teachers at all levels of education. In an earlier model, Bloom's taxonomy classified educational learning objectives into levels of complexity and specificity: Knowledge, Comprehension, Application, Analysis, Synthesis, Evaluation (Bloom, Krathwohl, & Masia, 1984). In 2001, Anderson (Krathwohl & Anderson, 2010) revised the Bloom's taxonomy by slightly changing the levels into verb forms:

Remembering, Understanding, Applying, Analyzing, Evaluating, Creating (rather than Synthesize). Additionally, the lowest level of the original, 'knowledge' was renamed and became 'remembering'. Comprehension and synthesis were retitled to understanding and creating (Forehand, 2010).

According to Biggs (J. Biggs, 1996), it is essential for teachers to recognize the paralleling logic of matching instructing with student performance with accepted standards. Matching learning outcomes with the original intentions of learning should be done in such terms that teaching activities provided corresponding and valuable information for both teacher and students. This workshop trained participants how to create course and curriculum alignment with learning outcomes, teaching and learning methods, and assessment, based on Bloom's taxonomy. The preparation for the course were pieces of literature of Bloom's taxonomy and its application case. Participants also exercised to propose a curriculum integration strategy, by connecting interrelated courses, as the example in table 2 shows. An ill-designed course would not cover all learning outcomes, or further fulfill the teaching task, as it would finally lead to unintentional knowledge missing and confusing.

Thematic Workshop 7: Facilitation

This thematic workshop presented an exciting exemplary class of active learning. The lecture was given in the way of telling a story. The exercises of "Who is the killer" and "Lego assembling" were impressive, which tested the capacity of collaboration and working roles in our group. It diagnosed the facilitation and current group situation. Understanding, role determination, and collaboration are critical in the

Table 2. Curriculum integration strategy – how could this look

Semester	Courses	Courses	Courses	Courses
Semester 4	Traditional active class	Traditional active class	PBL	coordinated
Semester 3	PBL	Traditional active class	PBL	Traditional active class
Semester 2	PBL	coordinated	Traditional active class	Traditional active class
Semester 1	Traditional active class	Traditional active class	Traditional active class	PBL

project work and facilitation. According to the schemed circle of guiding facilitation in figure 5, there are 6 phases (starting in the anti-clockwise direction) involved: situation clarifying, linear questions, circular reflections, generating possibilities, evaluative action and finalizing. The first stage is to probe the situation by raising linear questions? For example, the question "what do you want to achieve through this meeting?" is to set a contract for this facilitation meeting. The second stage is to reflect the results, methods, and theories by asking investigative questions, which is circular based on the Kolb's reflection concept. The next stage is to explore the possibilities for further research by raising challenging questions. For example, what do you think will happen if you......? The last stage is to finalize the facilitation by asking clarifying questions, as the decision that should make, like "What should be done? By whom? Through which......?"

Figure 5. Facilitation guide from the workshop

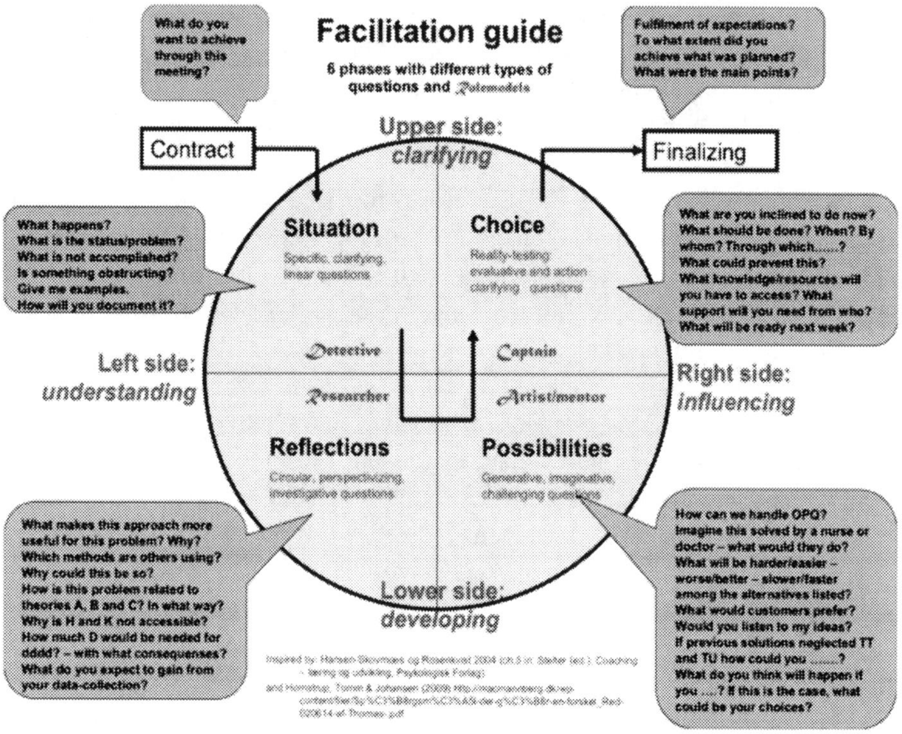

Thematic Workshop 8: Assessment of and for Learning

As Biggs criticized (J. Biggs, 1982), present models of instruction and evaluation are mostly restricted to quantitative definitions of the criteria of learning. There is an urgent need for qualitative criteria of learning that have formative as well as summative value. Biggs (J. Biggs, 1982) posed two questions to Bloom's taxonomy as he concerned about the assessment based on the taxonomy might frame in the conceptual knowledge: the one was about the need for modes of assessment which can value unintended learning outcomes, and the another was how participants could change our current modes of assessment to enable and encourage that to happen. He (J. Biggs, 1982) introduced the SOLO terminology (the Structure of the Observed Learning Outcome) in which four main dimensions are used to categorize responses: working memory capacity, operations relating task content with cue or question and response, consistency within a response and relative necessity for closure in making that response, and general overall structure, which results from the interaction between the previous dimensions. "The levels of prestructural, unistructural, multistructural, relational, and extended abstract are isomorphic to, but logically distinct from, the stages of preoperational, early concrete, middle concrete, concrete generalization, and formal operational, respectively". It systematically provides a structure to help the teacher make judgments about the quality of learning that takes place in his classroom.

Biggs (John Biggs & Tang, 2011) stresses the need for alignment – to ensure the intended learning outcomes match up with the assessment, and the teaching and learning activities, as shown in Figure 6. It is a good starting point to take with Biggs the first step in improving teaching, which is "to avoid those factors that encourage a surface approach".

As Biggs clarifies, there are two types of assessment: formative assessment for learning and summative assessment of learning. Summative assessment is what most people understand as final evaluation: grading. Formative and peer assessment have an impact on motivation. Active learning is shifting from assessing to learn "what students do not know" to assessing to learn "what students understand", from judgemental feedback that may harm student motivation to descriptive feedback that empowers and motivates students.

Formative evaluation is an ongoing process which acts as an instruction for following teaching and learning. If the student did not meet the initial requirements or objectives, it gave the right directions and led to reflection on the prior learning

Figure 6. Constructive alignment for a course
(J. Biggs, 1996)

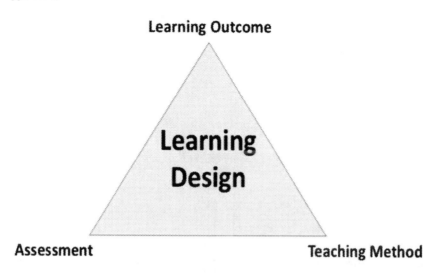

process. It also reveals what is intended to be taught by providing analysis to the teacher and an appreciation of what steps might be taken to improve things. There are many innovative ways of informative assessment teachers can employ, like "Rubrics and Portfolios", "Strategic Questioning", "Most confusing area of the topic", "Creative Extension Projects", etc. Without formative assessments, the first indication that a student doesn't grasp the knowledge is when they fail a quiz or a test. An innovative formative assessment strategy like the above can take failure out of the classroom. It is also an effective alternative way of employing active learning.

Thematic Workshop 9: Management of Change

The last workshop is managing change to PBL. Introducing PBL to China encounters the challenges of different culture and educational ideologies derived from the combined influences of Confucianism, Marxism, Maoism, Dengism, etc. In top-down and bottom-up change strategies, diverse education change leaders are included in the change to PBL for faculty development strategies: rectors/dean, head of departments, teachers at different levels in the organizations. The Knoster model proposes that six aspects, i.e., vision, consensus, skills, incentives, resources, action plan, are involved in the process of change, as figure 7 shows. When lacking

Figure 7. The Knoster model for leading and managing complex change

Leading and Managing Complex Change

Vision +	Consensus +	Skills +	Incentives +	Resources +	Action Plan	= Change
	Consensus +	Skills +	Incentives +	Resources +	Action Plan	= Confusion
Vision +		Skills +	Incentives +	Resources +	Action Plan	= Sabotage
Vision +	Consensus +		Incentives +	Resources +	Action Plan	= Anxiety
Vision +	Consensus +	Skills +		Resources +	Action Plan	= Resistance
Vision +	Consensus +	Skills +	Incentives +		Action Plan	= Frustration
Vision +	Consensus +	Skills +	Incentives +	Resources +		= Treadmill

Adapted from Knoster, T. (1991) Presentation in TASH Conference. Washington, D.C.
Adapted by Knoster from Enterprise Group, Ltd.

a vision, the change will confuse staff in the faculty. If there is no consensus, the change will sabotage. Without necessary skills, staff will arouse anxiety. If there are no incentives, the change will encounter resistance. Without supportive resources, change agents will feel frustrated. And if there is no action plan, the change process is a treadmill. Ruth Graham (Graham & Royal Academy of Engineering (Great Britain), 2012) illustrates that successful and sustainable changes are embedded into a re-designed, coherent and interconnected curriculum.

In this thematic workshop, participants were required to propose a 4-day PBL training plan in China for the initiative of change to PBL. They were divided into two groups. One group designed for a top-down strategy for the compulsory training course and another for a bottom-up strategy of PBL training for attentive students and teachers. The principal suggestion from the trainer was that the design should pay attention to course alignment, i.e., the accordance between activities and learning outcomes. As a result of this, many elements, such as topics, materials, time management, places, audience, exercises, etc., should be seriously considered.

Ruth Graham (Graham & Royal Academy of Engineering (Great Britain), 2012) analysed the change implemented by an individual faculty member or small groups of individuals, was triggered by persuasive evidence of the efficacy of new pedagogies and/ or broader national/international drivers such as the changing needs of industry or the role of engineering in solving the 'grand challenges'. However, the drivers of change at an institutional level often derived from a critical social problem with universities' "position in the marketplace", often declining student intake quality/ quantity, increasingly fierce competition or abysmal student satisfaction scores, resulting in significant pressure to change from the university senior management.

Project Work

The topic of the project was discussed in the group and decided as "Exploring Strategies of Employing Problem-based Learning at Northeastern University in China". The main contents, methods, and strategies were discussed. In the following group discussion, each member shared the ideas for different strategies by sticking notes to categories. Participants agreed that they should seek strategies of employing PBL to varying levels for changing approaches. The change will initiate from individual course-level PBL. Then with the consensus of liberal teachers on a change to PBL, intercourse-level PBL can take place inside a department or between different departments. In a larger scale, the institutional-level PBL can be introduced if the policies are supportive to the related sources, such as evaluation criteria, teaching hours, payment for external lecturers, etc. In the following group discussion, the tasks for each member were assigned to specific chapters and sections. As far as a research project is concerned, participants reached a consensus that an innovative idea was necessary, which also was the incentive for further discussion and report writing. As introducing PBL into NEU should consider the social context, participants focused on the possibility of linking PBL to traditional Chinese culture. It is necessary to induct the practice-based learning ideas of traditional philosophies and compare them with the principles of PBL.

Tracking A Student Group of the Master's Programme in Water and Environmental Engineering

During the learning process, the writer sat on several classes of "Environmental Soil Science", a course for the master's programme in Water and Environmental Engineering, and the mini-project and main project discussions within a 5-master-student group in the programme project "Soil and Groundwater". To deepen understanding the implementation of AAU-PBL, the writer enrolled in the 1st-semester courses in the curriculum for the Master's Programme in Water and Environmental Engineering. Figure 8 is the module of the 1st semester and Figure 9 is the overview of the Master's programme.

The module of the 1st semester includes three courses: Hydrogeology and Groundwater Modeling, Environmental Soil Science and Geostatistic, and Experimental Hydrology. Fieldwork and soil experiments in the laboratory started from the course beginning. There is a mini-project after one-month course study and laboratory experiments. The left picture in Figure 10 shows the result of a group discussion about the mini-project and the structure of the mini-project report was listed. The exam followed the study guidelines from the respective study boards. The right picture in Figure 10 shows the exam. Teachers internally discussed group mini-projects typically following the list of contents in group mini-project reports. Each person should prepare well to engage in the discussion and raise hand whenever one wants to answer/join the conversation. The duration was around 2 hours per group. Grading was individual.

The writer followed one mini-project group with five students. Three of them were international students. Usually, the 4-hour class was divided into two parts. The former part was lecture and the next 2 hours were for group discussion and doing exercises together. Some students felt confident in their exercises and project work. They could handle preparation for classes and were familiar with group work.

Figure 8. The module of the 1st semester

Courses (15ECTS)   **Project (15ECTS)**

Hydrogeology and Groundwater Modeling

Environmental Soil Science and Geostatistic

Experimental Hydrology

Mini-project

Soil and Groundwater Pollution

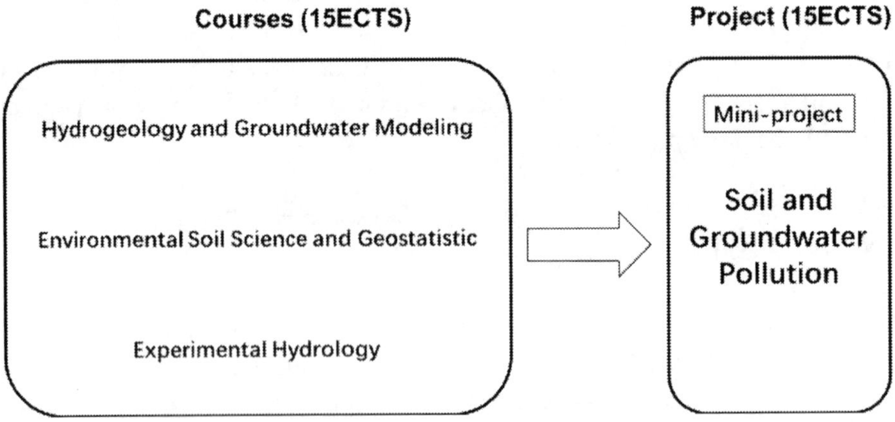

Figure 9. The overview of the master's programme in water and environmental engineering

Semester		Module	ECTS	Assessment	Exam
1st		Soil and Groundwater Pollution[3]	15	7-point scale	Internal
		Hydrogeology and Groundwater Modelling	5	Pass/no-pass	Internal
		Environmental Soil Science and Geostatistics	5	Pass/no-pass	Internal
		Experimental Hydrology	5	7-point scale	Internal
2nd	A	Marine and Freshwater Pollution[1,3] (optional for international students)	15	7-point scale	External
	B	Wastewater Treatment Systems[1,3] (optional for international students)	15	7-point scale	External
		Hydrodynamics and Time Series Analysis of Environmental Flows	5	7-point scale	Internal
		Marine Pollution	5	7-point scale	Internal
	C	Limnology[2] (optional for international students)	5	7-point scale	Internal
	D	Fundamental Wastewater Treatment[2]	5	7-point scale	Internal
3rd	A	Numerical Modelling and Experimental Methods[3]	15	7-point scale	Internal
	B	Advanced Urban Drainage[3]	15	7-point scale	Internal
		Advanced Hydrodynamic Modelling (CFD) and Visualisation.	5	Pass/no-pass	Internal
	A/B	Urban Hydroinformatics	5	Pass/no-pass	Internal
		Measurement Technology,Data Acquisition, Test and Validation	5	Pass/no-pass	Internal
	C	Study at another university	15-30	See below	-
	D	Academic Internship	30	7-point scale	Internal
3rd - 4th		Long Master's Thesis	45/50/60	7-point scale	External
4th		Master's Thesis	30	7-point scale	External
Total			120		

Figure 10. Mini-project of environmental soil science and hydrogeology

Few international students felt frustrated at first as computer skills and software simulation were involved in exercises. After the accomplish of mini-project, students reorganized freely into new groups for the project "Soil and Groundwater". In the mini-project group the writer followed, two students turned to other groups, and three new ones joined in. Two of the new ones were friends and schoolfellow of one international student in the old group. They were happy to work together. Figure 11 shows the new group is planning for the field work of the project. The topic of the project was decided on their own after guiding by the teacher and the external expert from a company who also was the lecturer of Hydrogeology course.

Visiting Aalborg University Hospital and Technical High School

The writer visited Aalborg University Hospital & Science and Innovation Centre with the students of the programme for Anthropology and Technology. The receptionist introduced the program of innovation in this hospital. The innovation center got most of the inspiration from nurses submitting ideas. The project screening follows the procedure as project meeting, evaluation, validation phase, and development phase. There have been many successful innovation cases, such as the transportable bed lift, washing beds locally, intelligent transportation, robot-assisted ultrasound,

Figure 11. Group discussion for "soil and groundwater" project planning

and fetal ultrasound. Specifically, one stuff introduced her ongoing project "Height Adjustable Platform" for surgeons. Problem-based learning is attested by the fact that emerging new ideas is the pride and source for students' deep learning and continuous exploration.

Participants also visited Aalborg Technical High School with the opportunities of being introduced how PBL was organized in the range of Dansk high school. The Danish technical high school HTX (Higher Technical Examination Program) was established to provide opportunities in engineering studies as an apprentice, furthermore, an admission to the technical colleges. Ordinary high schools in Denmark are divided into four academic directions (in China, high school is universal only divided into liberal arts and science at sophomore year.): Three years of general high school (STX), 3-year Business High School (HHX), 3-year Engineering High School (HTX), 2-year preparatory high school (HF). The primary purpose of the sub-disciplines is to prepare students for further study and to cultivate their individual and comprehensive abilities. Denmark's high school education aims at improving students' independent and analytical abilities, equipping them with a global vision and social consciousness. Each type of high school has its compulsory courses. STX is more comprehensive, HHT has some financial courses, HTX has some engineering courses. Each school will also have some elective courses for you to choose from. However, the criteria for graduation examinations are unified by the state. STX graduates enter ordinary universities, HHT graduates enter business schools or business universities, HTX graduates enter technical universities, and HF graduates enter social science universities.

As the practice of HTX demonstrates, PBL is rooted in Danish learning culture and educational system. The HTX technical high school prepares Danish students for a future as engineering, science or technology students. For many organizations, even though in Denmark, any changes take time and efforts to overcome the various barriers from different aspects.

REFLECTIONS ON NEU-AAU UNESCO CENTER CERTIFICATE COURSE

Reflection on the PBL Method as a PBL Student

There was a 20-year period of being a student in much of the writer's life, most of which utilize rote and didactic learning by repetitive exercises. But as a student in the

Figure 12. Pictures of tours (left: Aalborg University Hospital; right: project report of Technical High School)

 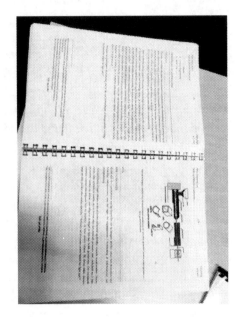

UNESCO PBL training course, the writer was involved in group work. The different feeling came from the intimate discussion with the partners and critical thinking on a particular issue. Maybe we are adept at managing a project by own or instructing undergraduates or master students carrying out projects. But collaboration and conversation are seldom engaged in the range of several classmates or colleagues. Listen to others' opinions need open-mindedness, modesty, and flexibility. From the experience of the project, the writer realizes a group is a complex ecosystem with the characteristic of diversity. Participants can't force anyone to comply with, but if there is a task to finish, compromise is the ultimate solution to conflicting minds. Time-Planning and group contract are essential to handle the collaboration and manage the project from the start of the teamwork. The role of each member should be identified first, or he/she is confused about what to do. Facilitator takes the responsibility of boosting the collaboration. Critical thinking is crucial and contributed to innovative ideas. Conversation is indispensable for the wholeness and accordance of the report writing, at the same time, collectivism should be stressed in the group.

Reflection on the PBL Process as a Witness

On Individual Challenges for International Students

As the writer followed courses taught in English, international students were met and interviewed. If they have no experience of PBL before, they will take PBL training classes in the cross semester - Problem Based Learning and Project Management. The objective is to make newly started Master students coming from institutions other than AAU prepared to enter the problem-based learning environment at AAU and manage study projects in close collaboration with peers (moodle.aau.dk).

The students discussed and reflected their challenges/curiosities in a peer learning group. The following lists some of the problems they met:

- Fall behind the group, try to catch up;
- Hope to be helpful in the group/get used to the learning system/fit the role;
- Danish communication problem: what did they do? What can I do?
- Danish students find a solution after a few meetings. I feel ignored.

However, they reflected, discussed and strived to find solutions to encounter the challenges, as the following may address:

- Learning Danish, positive attitude;
- Change group when all members are international students;
- Show your strength and weakness;
- Figure out your role;
- Do finish your homework.

One interesting thing the writer found out is that the international student who said he felt behind others showed his leadership in the new group, in which all members were international. He is trying hard to learn computer skills such as Excel, programming, GIS, simulation and modeling that he didn't learn in the bachelor's period, and to spend time finishing his homework. In this sense, teachers can discover the fact there is an implicit leadership disposition in many seemed lag-off students.

On Steering Group Meeting

The writer witnessed the steering group meeting, where representative students sit with the teacher face to face, stating their requirements and challenges. The content of the meeting includes: 1) Who writes the minutes; 2) Comments to courses; 3) Comments to project; 4) Comments to facilities; and 5) Miscellaneous. In the steering meeting, students complained a particular teacher's lecture form, or some of them couldn't catch up with the modeling. About the project, students wanted more explicit information about roles and obligations and to find out how the system worked. They needed information about new group email, materials, distribution, experimental services and project for real life. When asked about their project job, some students said they enjoyed it and used to lab work. They were optimistic in searching for specific instructions. However, they also said some members missed group meetings, and the group needed more time to reset lab work. The frustrations they met was the time; it was emergent for project planning. Some students who lived far away had to seek a balance between commute and doing useful things. Finally, the facilitator assured the arrangement of field work, guidelines for the exam, and offering help with booking cars, drivers, etc.

Above observations on the activities of PBL students, it seems that there is a vast gap between bachelor and master learning. Students are frank of what the gap is. Their challenge comes from the time-consuming self-learning on tool use and models. However, the fact that three or more group workshops share a big seminar room made students feel crowded and noisy. It indicates the importance of the shared physical environment to the workshops.

On Environmental Education in Denmark

The fifteenth Conference of the Parties on Climate Change (COP15) was held in Copenhagen in December 2009, demonstrating the efforts and consequences of Danish environmental education and decisive countermeasures. Denmark maintains a political attitude of high social responsibility, particularly emphasizing on social justice, reallocation, involvement, and parity. It is known for public social welfare with a substantial subsidy of health care and education based on a high tax drain. "The most important and innovative educational research related to environmental education has taken place in close cooperation with explicitly democratic school development processes and projects."(Breiting & Wickenberg, 2010)

But the intention of conserving the nature did not intrinsically exit in history. In Denmark, the impacts of human activities posed on the urban, terrestrial environment and marine ecosystem were serious because there were no available rural areas as a buffer, nor available new land to replace degraded land. The Danish Ministry of Pollution Control was established in 1971 and renamed as the Ministry of the Environment in 1973. Media and teachers with environmental consciousness mostly initiated public movement in environmental protection. Environmental education was linked to in-service teacher training. The dominant progress of environmental education in Denmark was the paradigmatic shift from morally preaching to developing students' "action competence" in finding solutions to local environmental issues(F. Mogensen, 1997)(Finn Mogensen & Schnack, 2010)(Barrett, 2006). The concept of "action competence" was proposed by skepticism in the current educational paradigm. "The concept of action competence, it is argued, should occupy a central position in the theory of environmental education as many of the crucial educational problems concerning a political liberal education are united in this concept." At the same time, it was viewed as a progressive approach compared to the traditional, science-oriented environmental education. As the concept involves not only scientific analysis of the nature of environmental problems but also an assumption of education as behavior modification(Jensen & Schnack, 1997).

Environmental consciousness presents in the educational idea of Aalborg University by the widely used concept of "sustainable" in programmes that are in the periscope of traditional environmental related disciplines, for example, "Sustainable Biotechnology", "Sustainable Energy Engineering", "Sustainable Design", "Sustainable Cities", etc. Moreover, the concept of action competence towards learning outcomes is commonly yielded via the practice of problem-based learning in addressing local social issues. Students are encouraged to seek problems arising from public concerns in the sphere of democracy and social responsibility oriented.

Implication and Guidance on Teaching

On Active Learning

Although most teachers give lectures in the traditional way, however, great efforts were taken for an active class. Most PBL training teachers are good at active learning and well-control in the progress of the course. They can combine exercises, group discussion with presentations and lectures, taking care of the spiritual response of the audience, which make the classes more active and enjoyable. Another example, the teacher of Environmental Soil Science, Professor Per Møldrup fascinatingly started his class. He showed students some bottles of soil samples from Toyoura, Ziban, Lunar and Mars Space station, etc. The real soil samples aroused the curiosity of students. Per did not directly tell students the composition of soil, but he asked for responses via questions. Students actively participated in raising hands. Then some specialized terms were introduced in the way student could easily understand. With the interplay between teacher and students, 2-hour lecture seemed too short. But the exercise Per left to students was somewhat tricky, for data sieving, excel simulation, and model comparison were needed. Hence preview and reading related materials were indispensable. If students didn't read the documents, they couldn't figure out how to finish the exercise in the next 2 hours.

On this point, teachers of Chinese universities might do quite differently. Because most of them don't assign too much homework to students. The evaluation criteria for students is relatively lower than foreign universities. Lower criteria result in lower quality graduates. Eventually, it may lead to the dissatisfaction of social enterprises and institutions, also may disappoint those students with high self-expectations.

On Change of Teaching and Learning

According to Ruth Graham's interview to successful reform efforts (Graham & Royal Academy of Engineering (Great Britain), 2012), the driving force for single course level change comes from persuasive evidence of the efficacy of new pedagogies and/or broader national/international influence. However, successful School/department-wide change or strategic reforms across curriculums were triggered by either a very significant threat that required urgent action or an externally-imposed requirement for fundamental structural change.

As an ordinary faculty member, what we can do is to start from own courses, furthermore, to combine with friend teachers who are willing to change. The preparatory work for change will include: 1) gathering local evidence, such as student

Figure 13. Soil samples exhibited in the class

real employment rates and feedback from employers on employability, compared to peer competitor institutions; 2) introducing excellence of PBL approach; 3) presenting the early vision to senior management; 4) presenting the need for change to faculty (Graham & Royal Academy of Engineering (Great Britain), 2012). From a single course aspect, we will more carefully observe the reaction of students and try to cut down tedious lecture hours with interval exercises or formative assessment. Evaluation approaches can be changed through student questionnaires and employing exemplary, innovative assessment methods. Groups who actively participate in class can be encouraged with spiritual or material awards. The task distributed "Design a four-day workshop for your colleagues" may be helpful to start the implementation and the proposal of problem-based learning.

On Sustainable Education at Chinese University

Influenced by the United Nations Conference on the Human Environment in Stockholm in 1972, China has always attached great importance to environmental

Table 3. A four-day workshop for PBL training

Day	Learning Outcomes	Lectures			Project / Seminar	
		Workshop	Activities	Hours	Topic	Hours
1a	Understand Analyze	Lecture 1: What is PBL?	Exercises	4		
1p	Understand Analyze	Lecture 2: Principles of PBL	Exercises	1	Theme introduction	1
2a	Remember Understand Apply	Lecture 3: Course alignment	Exercises	4		
2p	Understand Analyse Apply	Lecture 4: Formative assessment	Exercises	1	Group discussion	1
3a	Remember Understand Apply	Lecture 5: Change to PBL	Exercises	4		
3p	Analyze Apply				Project	2
4	Evaluate	Peer review	Presentation	8		

protection and public education. In 2009, the Ministry of Environmental Protection, the Ministry of Publicity and the Ministry of Education jointly issued the Opinions on Environmental Publicity and Education under the New Situation, which closely linked environmental education with the construction of ecological civilization and the cultivation of ecological awareness of the whole people. Chairman Xi Jinping pointed out that "Ecological environment protection is an undertaking that benefits the present and the future", "A good ecological environment is the most equitable common resource and the most shared benefits for livelihood"(Zhang, 2016).

However, environmental education has always been an ambiguous area: although few people doubt the urgency and importance of learning to live sustainably, environmental education is not a priority in formal education all over China or broadly the world. This is because most people want the environment to be cleaned up, but do not want to change their way of life, with the assumption that environmental problems will ultimately have technical fixes. Adolescents in today's society generally suffer from natural-deficit disorder --the reduction and isolation of contact with the nature leads to their lack of understanding of nature. That is, the action competence as called in Denmark is dearth in Chinese practical and universal environmental education.

Environmental education in Colleges and universities should take up the responsibility to make the youth profoundly realize that most of the current ecological crises originate from the widening gap between the rich and the poor. We must care for the disadvantaged groups, protect the natural ecosystem, take responsibility for the whole society, and minimize the harm to our fellow human beings. All in all, the liberal, political and democratic ideas should bear in mind. Environmental education in universities should spans and integrates all significant fields of study, involving economic development, peace, humanities, future, sustainable development and global concerns on the basis of existing curriculum, and emphasizes the cultivation of students' inclusiveness and pluralistic value orientation.

CONCLUSION

PBL model is very suitable for implementing in engineering and interdisciplinary fields. Its interdisciplinarity can cooperate institutes with enterprises to obtain real problems, industry development trends, practical opportunities, and project resources. Environmental education based on real problems can guide students to integrate the existing knowledge of different disciplines in their minds and make a comparative evaluation of the relationship between various elements of inherent knowledge, so that students can learn to manage problems, to improve their cognitive ability, and to cultivate their professional and critical thinking abilities. Case analysis, group discussion, and project can be combined into courses, which highlights the cultivation of students' critical thinking, collaborative and self-learning abilities. Teachers can seek external experts from local environmental agencies who appeal to cooperation with the university and willing to provide real problems and supportive resources. The social activities and group communication provide the way into transformative learning. The multiple project-based and problem-solving training shed light on lifelong learning and addressing globalization. An ecological approach to environmental education rests chiefly on the content of the problem, and is holistic as much as systems thinking, if not more so.

ACKNOWLEDGMENT

This research is under the support of the project *Research and Practice of Collaborative Teaching Mode with Common Creation based on PBL* (Project No. 2-7) on the Undergraduate Teaching Reform Research of General Higher Education in Liaoning Province, China in 2018.

Special thanks to Aalborg Center for Problem Based Learning in Engineering Science and Sustainability under the auspices of UNESCO for understanding in PBL and many supports from the facilitator Zhou Chunfang and my group members Sun Xinbo, Zhang Yin, Song Xiu, Song Jingping, Wang Fei, and Zhang Xufang.

REFERENCES

Aalborg University – Knowledge for the World. (2018). Retrieved 2018, from https://www.en.aau.dk/about-aau

Bammer, G. (2013). *Disciplining Interdisciplinarity: Integration and Implementation Sciences for Researching Complex Real-World Problems.* ANU E Press.

Bammer, G., & Smithson, M. (2012). *Uncertainty and Risk: Multidisciplinary Perspectives.* Routledge. doi:10.4324/9781849773607

Barrett, M. J. (2006). Education for the environment: Action competence, becoming, and story. *Environmental Education Research*, *12*(3-4), 503–511. doi:10.1080/13504620600799273

Barrows, H. S. (1986). A taxonomy of problem-based learning methods. *Medical Education*, *20*(6), 481–486. doi:10.1111/j.1365-2923.1986.tb01386.x PMID:3796328

Barrows, H. S. (1996). Problem-based learning in medicine and beyond: A brief overview. *New Directions for Teaching and Learning*, *1996*(68), 3–12. doi:10.1002/tl.37219966804

Biggs, J. (1982). *Evaluating The Quality of Learning:The SOLO Taxonomy.* Academic Press.

Biggs, J. (1996). Enhancing teaching through constructive alignment. *Higher Education*, *32*(3), 347–364. doi:10.1007/BF00138871

Biggs, J., & Tang, C. (2011). *Teaching For Quality Learning At University.* McGraw-Hill Education.

Bloom, B. S., Krathwohl, D. R., & Masia, B. B. (1984). *Taxonomy of educational objectives: the classification of educational goals.* Academic Press.

Boden, R., Cox, D., Nedeva, M., & Barker, K. (2004). Scientific Knowledge Production Processes. In Scrutinising Science (pp. 136–156). Academic Press. doi:10.1057/9781403943934_6

Breiting, S., & Wickenberg, P. (2010). The progressive development of environmental education in Sweden and Denmark. *Environmental Education Research*, *16*(1), 9–37. doi:10.1080/13504620903533221

Bruner, J. (2009). Culture, mind and education. In *Contemporary Theories of Learning* (pp. 179–188). Academic Press.

Covey, S. R. (2016). *Primary Greatness: The 12 Levers of Success*. Simon and Schuster.

Cunningham, W., & Cunningham, M. (2014). *Cunningham, Environmental Science: A Global Concern*. McGraw-Hill Education.

Daniels, H. (2016). *Vygotsky and Pedagogy*. Routledge. doi:10.4324/9781315617602

De Graaff, E., & Kolmos, A. (2009). *Management of Change: Implementation of Problem-Based and Project-Based Learning in Engineering*. Sense Publishers.

de Graaff, A., & Kolmos, E. (2003). Characteristics of Problem-Based Learning. *Int. J. Engng Ed., 19*(5), 657-662.

Dewey, J. (2007). *Experience And Education*. Simon and Schuster.

Dewey, J., & Bentley, A. F. (1949). *Knowing and the Known*. Boston: Beacon Press.

Easton, T. A. (2017). *Taking Sides: Clashing Views on Environmental Issues*. McGraw-Hill Education.

Elkjaer, B. (2009). Pragmatism: A learning theory for the future. In K. Illeris (Ed.), *Contemporary Theories of Learning* (Vol. 5, pp. 66–82). Taylor & Francis Routledge.

Forehand, M. (2010). Bloom's taxonomy. In M. Orey (Ed.), Emerging perspectives on learning, teaching, and technology (pp. 41–47). Academic Press.

Frodeman, R. (2010). *The Oxford Handbook of Interdisciplinarity*. Oxford University Press.

Gardner, H. (1983). *Frames of Mind: the Multiple Intelligences*. New York: Basic Books.

Gibbons, M. (2003). A new mode of knowledge production. In Routledge Studies in Business Organizations and Networks. Academic Press. doi:10.4324/9780203422793.pt4

Graham, R. H., & Royal Academy of Engineering (Great Britain). (2012). *Achieving Excellence in Engineering Education: The Ingredients of Successful Change*. Anchor Books.

Harper, W. (1969). The Oxford Handbook of Interdisciplinarity. *Theological Librarianship, 5*(2), 88–89.

Holgaard, J. E. (2013). Information technology for sustainable development: A problem based and project oriented approach. In *Proceedings for Engineering Education for Sustainable Development 2013*. University of Cambridge.

Illeris, K. (1976). *Problemorienterad och deltagarstyrd undervisning: förutsättningar, planering och genomförande*. Academic Press.

Illeris, K. (2009). A comprehensive understanding of human learning. In K. Illeris (Ed.), *Contemporary Theories of Learning: Learning Theorists -- in Their Own Words* (pp. 7–20). Taylor & Francis Routledge. doi:10.4324/9780203870426

Jarvis, P. (2009). The Routledge International Handbook of Lifelong Learning. Academic Press. doi:10.4324/9780203870549

Jensen, B. B., & Schnack, K. (1997). The Action Competence Approach in Environmental Education. *Environmental Education Research*, *3*(2), 163–178. doi:10.1080/1350462970030205

Jette Egelund Holgaard, A. G. A. A. K. (2017). Getting a Hold on the Problem in a Problem-Based Learning Environment. *International Journal of Engineering Education*, *33*(3), 1070–1085.

Kegan, R. (2009). What "form" transforms? In K. Illeris (Ed.), *Contemporary Theories of Learning: Learning Theorists In Their Own Words*. Taylor & Francis Routledge.

Kolb, D. A. (1984). *Experiential learning: Experience as the source of learning and development*. Prentice-Hall.

Kolmos, A., & de Graaff, E. (2014). Problem-Based and Project-Based Learning in Engineering Education. In Cambridge Handbook of Engineering Education Research (Vol. 8, pp. 141–160). Cambridge University Press.

Kolomos, A., Fink, F. K., & Krogh, L. (2004). *The Aalborg PBL Model: Progress, Diversity and Challenges*. Aalborg Universitetsforlag.

Krathwohl, D. R., & Anderson, L. W. (2010). Merlin C. Wittrock and the Revision of Bloom's Taxonomy. *Educational Psychologist*, *45*(1), 64–65. doi:10.1080/00461520903433562

Levin, R. (2010). The Rise of Asia's Universities. *The New York Times*.

Levin, R. C. (2008). *The Work of the University*. Yale University Press.

Mezirow, J. (2009). Transformative learning theory. In K. Illeris (Ed.), Contemporary Theories of Learning (pp. 114–128). Academic Press.

Mogensen, F. (1997). Critical thinking: A central element in developing action competence in health and environmental education. *Health Education Research*, *12*(4), 429–436. doi:10.1093/her/12.4.429 PMID:10176372

Mogensen, F., & Schnack, K. (2010). The action competence approach and the "new" discourses of education for sustainable development, competence and quality criteria. *Environmental Education Research*, *16*(1), 59–74. doi:10.1080/13504620903504032

Parker, R. (2017). Essentials of Environmental Science (2nd ed.). Lulu.com.

Piaget, J. (1964). Part I: Cognitive development in children: Piaget development and learning. *Journal of Research in Science Teaching*, *2*(3), 176–186. doi:10.1002/tea.3660020306

Schön, D. A. (2017). *The Reflective Practitioner: How Professionals Think in Action*. Routledge. doi:10.4324/9781315237473

Shani, A. B., Mohrman, S. A., Pasmore, W. A., Stymne, B., & Adler, N. (2007). *Handbook of Collaborative Management Research*. SAGE Publications.

Smith, B., & Enger, E. (2015). *Environmental Science*. McGraw-Hill Education.

Sterling, S. R. (2001). *Sustainable Education: Re-visioning Learning and Change*. Green Books.

The Core Curriculum Requirement. (2008). Retrieved from http://static.fas.harvard.edu/registrar/ugrad_handbook/2009_2010/chapter2/core02.html

UN. (2017). The 17 Sustainable Development Goals as one indivisible system. In Integrated Approaches for Sustainable Development Goals Planning (pp. 10–12). UN.

Wickson, F., Carew, A. L., & Russell, A. W. (2006). Transdisciplinary research: Characteristics, quandaries and quality. *Futures*, *38*(9), 1046–1059. doi:10.1016/j.futures.2006.02.011

Zhang, J. (2016). Striking a Balance Between Environmental Protection and Rapid Development. In *China in the Xi Jinping Era* (pp. 151–185). Academic Press. doi:10.1007/978-3-319-29549-7_7

Chapter 5

PBL Implementation in Material Science and Engineering Education at Chinese Universities

Xiu Song
Northeastern University, China

ABSTRACT

Traditional university education with ordinary lectures is changing to more practical and actively student-centered learning systems. Materials science and engineering is originally the study of actual engineering materials but now becomes more interdisciplinary and sophisticated in the rapidly advancing industrial society. It is very necessary to cultivate the practical materials engineers and it also becomes a big challenge for Chinese universities to make a change. PBL is one of the potential approaches for Chinese universities. This chapter describes PBL theories, discusses PBL principles, PBL models, and also some PBL experiences at Aalborg University. In addition, this chapter exposes how PBL could be applied to materials science and engineering education in Chinese universities, and a case of PBL implementation has been given to show the process of transformation from traditional education at Chinese universities to PBL in the materials science and engineering field.

DOI: 10.4018/978-1-5225-9961-6.ch005

INTRODUCTION

Higher education reforming has become one of the human concerns all over the world recently since education in University gives the main priority direction for the development of economic society and humanities in all developed and developing countries. The trend towards globalization with technological developments requires more practical and innovative experts who have professional skills and even much creativity in every field of the industry.

Under above educational environment of the world, how to speed up the reform and innovation of engineering education in Chinese Universities is also an issue of concern. Nowadays, the concept of "Emerging Engineering Education, 3E", which has been put forward (http://www.moe.gov.cn/s78/A08/moe_745/201702/t20170223_297121.html) by Chinese Ministry of Education in 2017 has provided us the new sight for reform in engineering education. 3E is a national strategic action in China, which actively responds to a new round of worldwide Science and Technologies revolution and industrial transformation. It is characterized by new technologies, new industries, new situations, and new models. It involves a new idea of engineering education, a new structure of the programme, a new model of student cultivation, a new quality of education and teaching, and a new system of hierarchical development. In addition, the upgraded traditional engineering programmes also belong to this category.

Materials Science and Engineering is one of the traditional engineering programmes but now it should be upgraded and changed to be interdisciplinary with other new technologies and new industries with the development of the industry. That is because materials are one of the bases of many fields of industries, thus materials are every necessary to be used especially in new industries. Thus the Materials Science and Engineering education in Chinese Universities should be necessarily to be reformed at present. That is well coordinated with the essence of the political efforts calling 3E construction, which is to build up the ability of the students to learn new things based on the background of the new economy, new industry and so on. In other words, it aims to cultivate innovative graduates for China society. For example, Materials Science and Engineering graduates are not only required to know and understand about the actual materials used in the industry, but also they could create new materials in order to meet the demand for new industries. Accordingly, students are required to study in learning environments facilitated by curriculum designs with the integration of professional skills, scientific and engineering knowledge, as well as humanities thinking. Therefore, the educational reform in Materials Science and Engineering programme will be coincident with the development of new economy represented by new technologies, new formats, new models and new industries in order to foster young engineers who are expected to master comprehensive skills, interdisciplinary thinking, and innovative capabilities.

Although there are recent changes and reform in some Chinese Universities, lecture-centered teaching and paper written examination are still the main ways of organizing teaching and learning activities, especially for some Chinese Universities which has a long tradition of education and the curriculum design has been deeply influenced by traditional Chinese educational culture. So, there are still some barriers to developing active and creative learning environments at Chinese Universities. For example, the Materials Science and Engineering graduates can't obtain practical skill without practical training in the traditional lecture classrooms, and also transferable skills such as collaboration and team-work are hardly to be obtained. Furthermore, Materials Science and Engineering cannot easily have the innovation abilities to create new materials or invent new technologies about the Materials Science to adapt to the development of new industries, if almost all the traditional Chinese teachers always play roles of being "knowledge authority" that enlarges "power distance" between teaching and learning. Briefly, particular attention on how to fostering innovative Materials Science and Engineering graduates under the traditional Chinese educational environment should be paid and it is still essential to make a change in the Materials Science and Engineering education under the new 3E strategic in China.

Problem-based learning (PBL) is one of the potential solutions to for Chinese traditional Universities to cultivate practical and creative Materials Science Engineers. Under the impact of new values and ideas from some western universities, one of the main aims of curriculum change with implement of PBL is to enforce intrinsic motivation through engaging the learners in the real problem and project situations in order to find the solution by themselves, and fill their knowledge gaps (Morales Bueno, Bueno, & Rodas, 2018). Since the 1950s, there has been growing and sustained interests in developing PBL in diverse in particular to medical educations (Kolmos & de Graaff, 2014). Rather than learning basic knowledge through via textbooks and lectures by teachers, students could learn how to solve the realistic clinical problems by giving a task. Accordingly, the theory of "learning by doing" was formed. Furthermore, the primary characteristics of a PBL learning environment are not only problem-focused but also student-centered, which means the teachers are facilitators serving in a supportive role rather than dominate the main lecture and other learning activities (Borhan, 2014). That is the basic ideas to develop the model for core changing concepts from Chinese traditional education to a new module using PBL. In addition, students are self-directed and self-reflective through PBL(Ulseth, 2016), and students individually and collaboratively assume responsibility for generating learning issues and processes through self-assessment and peer assessment, and the students monitor their understanding and learn to adjust strategies for learning.

Therefore, PBL will be introduced to change the traditional Chinese education at Universities. The aim of this chapter is to try to make a change of the Materials Science and Engineering education system at Chinese Universities form the traditional ones by introducing PBL. By literature review on PBL theories, discussing PBL principles, PBL models and also some PBL experiences at Aalborg University, this chapter exposes how PBL could be applied to Materials Science and Engineering education in Chinese Universities, and a case of one course in Materials Science and Engineering programme with PBL implementation has been given to show the process of transformation from traditional education at Chinese Universities to PBL.

BACKGROUND

As well known, Materials are one of the bases of industries, transport, communication, construction, agriculture and even global economy and society in the world, thus the development of Materials Science and Engineering has become one of the fundamental factors to measure the technology development level of one country. So, Materials Science and Engineering education at Universities is so crucial that the nature of Materials Science and Engineering today nearly covers all the fields of industries. The traditional objective of Materials Science and Engineering education is to let the students to master the basic principles and theories of materials science, including the composition, structural defects, phase diagram of the alloy and the basic laws and principles of diffusion of the metals and ceramic materials, based on the theory of the electron and atom aggregation structure of the materials, and also have an ability of combining the materials principles with the Engineering in their own field, such as applying the phase diagram to analyze the relationship between the microstructure and the properties of the alloy and applying the materials treatment process in the realistic applications for metals and design and create a new materials production or some treatment processes.

In order to meet today's societal challenges, a need arises to cultivate the specialists in Materials Science and Engineering who not only have knowledge of Materials technology, but also the engineers who have the ability to solve the actual problems in the companies and the creative competence to innovate new materials to promote the development of other industries and changing the world. That means, the learning goals of Materials Science and Engineering education at Universities not only contain the fundamental conceptual knowledge to let the students to understand the principles and behavior of materials, but also cultivate the students to have the abilities to solve the practical problems about the materials through an introduction to the industrial and engineering context of the companies where the materials are manufactured and processed. In addition, some transferable skills such as collaboration, communication, and group work should also be considered in the University education, because the manufacture of making materials and process treatment on the materials is a complicated system, combing with other parts of industries. Finally, it is important to give students motivation and pleasure to have the ability of creativity in new discovery, and an ambition to initiate a new field through synthesizing a new material or a new process of materials treatment.

Another recent remarkable trend in Materials Science and Engineering is that it has a vigorous interaction with Mathematics, Physics, Chemical, crystallography, Mechanics, Medicine, and other technologies. So we can also consider that the basic nature of new science and technology in Materials Science and Engineering field is interdisciplinary and sophisticated with the rapid development of advancing industrial society. In turn, the synthesis of new materials can also effectively affect other science and technology in other fields of the industries through the discovery of novel and exotic phenomena and new physical or chemical concepts, and new devices of the materials.

Anyway, it becomes a challenge to fostering Materials Science and Engineering experts and Engineers at Chinese Universes.

MAIN PROBLEMS AND CHANLLENGES OF MATERIAL SCIECE AND ENGINEERING EDUCATION

Since Materials Science and Engineering education system as one of the important elements of social, political and economic has become a prerequisite for the development of all the sectors of the industries in one country, and it is significant to be the basis of innovation of the technology. Considering the demands emerging in the Materials Science and Engineering experts and Engineers in companies and market of the industrial society, the traditional educations can't catch up with the rapid developments in the business world. With the rapid development of high and new technology, new breakthroughs have been made in the field of Materials Science and Engineering, promoting the complete transformation of the mode of production in human society, and constantly crossing and merging with other disciplines. Thus, the education changing and reforming have become more visible due to the globalization. There are still some problems and challenges in Materials Science and Engineering at Chinese Universities which has been described in the following aspects:

Firstly, the traditional Materials Science and Engineering education system inherit the traditional education paradigm, which means, the objectives, teaching contents, learning principles, and the teaching method even the assessment are totally determined by the teachers. That means the students performed their passive response as the "receivers" of knowledge in the traditional education lecture classrooms. Thus the students have less motivation to learn actively. However, as mentioned above in the background of the Materials Science and Engineering filed, it is a complicated and interdisciplinary system, requiring the experts and engineers with a wider perspective, an ability to see the whole vision in materials and other related industries filed and have the ability of making proper decisions and solutions in order to keep up with the world's pace. That needs the students to have the ability of self-developing and self-learning rather than relying on the knowledge given by the teachers. The teacher-centered traditional educations restrict the enthusiasm and motivation of students for active learning.

Secondly, the teaching and learning method in traditional Materials Science and Engineering education is still monotonous. It is hard to cultivate the diverse skilled and intelligent graduates with special professional competences just by giving the lecture as nearly the main teaching method, thus leads to the suppression of the students' personality and character to the develop the potential of the students to be adapted to the real society. Actually, the advanced purpose of the education is to motivate different types of students to have diverse abilities by active learning, providing as many as opportunities to students for "learning by thinking, doing and reflection" rather than delivering lectures to them and giving direct answers and solutions to the students. Other teaching activities and diversified teaching methods could be used in the teaching contexts in accordance with the rapid change and transformation taking place in the world.

Thirdly, the educational system at its current state at Universities is oriented at equipping the student with the knowledge and training the students' abilities, but it hardly cultivates the students to have the abilities to solve the real-world problems and practical training just through the lectures. The experts needed in the companies in Materials Science and Engineering field is closely linked to the reality industry. And there is close contact between the theory of the Materials Science and Engineering in the lecture and the application of materials in the engineering application in the world, some cases should be shown to the students to make the students learn more about how to apply the basic theory in the textbook.

Finally, many Chinese Universities has a long tradition of engineering education history, and the Chinese educational system including curriculum design and assessment has been deeply influenced by traditional Chinese educational culture, policy, values, and organizations. So, it is difficult to make a change of education under the traditional environments affected by the above factors especially the policy and organizations. For example, how to evaluate the learning effects of the students is one of the important parts of higher education. However, the traditional exam is usually strictly to the paper exam which is easy to test the received knowledge if the students have the master and professional skills but it is hard to evaluate the creative skills including the ability to apply the received knowledge as well as finding new ways to create new knowledge. Because the main content of the exam is limited to the designated by textbooks but not cover the additional knowledge to exciting students' active thinking and imagination. Also, the students only focus their attention on reviewing the teaching content and make exercises only related to the fixed content of the paper exams. Considering the exam or the curriculum design is closely connected with a number of issues, it is a more substantial process for the Chinese organization to create a social and cultural environment by changing the policy.

Therefore, there are still some teaching challenges for the traditional Materials Science and Engineering education system to make a change, and the challenges are for the teachers, students and also the origination of the education system.

For the teachers, they should have the some new sight of teaching. The teachers should think about how to motivate Materials Science and Engineering students to learn the knowledge actively? How to facilitate the student to fill the gap between the theories of Materials in the textbook and innovation/creation in practice? How to make the Materials Science and Engineering students to be innovative and creative?

Diverse teaching method should be considered. The teachers not only just design the curriculum and give the whole sum of knowledge, but also teach students the methods of thinking including some theoretical and systematic approach to analyze and solve the problem and even have the ability of critical thinking and metacognition about the knowledge and then create new knowledge. Learners should not only passively accept the knowledge taught by teachers, but also to actively think about the knowledge. The famous educator John Dewey have suggested that the functions of the teacher should be limited to individual observation and directing the student's activity into an established "trajectory" of development within the module educational process (Dewey, 1900). That means the teacher should change their teaching sight to cultivate the creative skills of the students, by applying the received knowledge to establish the task himself and finding the solution to accomplish the task. In addition, some realistic case in the factory about the Materials Science and Engineering filed should also be considered, even some processes and videos by the work members in the factory to show students how to solve the real problems about the materials.

For students, the transformation from the teacher-directed learning to student-initiated integration of learning and reasoning is still a challenge. The student himself should have the motivation to choose what to study and how to study. The students should have a skill of self-consciousness and autonomy in learning, and be good at asking questions and finding problems on their own. The education should focus on the student himself, on his wishes and aspirations. Furthermore, for the origination of the education system, a new model of the curriculum including the way of assessment should be changed from the traditional ways.

Therefore, it is a complex and difficult task to constitute the education system with new structure, new model, new quality, and new system form traditional education system. And it is urgently required to continuously strengthen the innovation and exploration of teaching modes and teaching methods in the teaching of Materials Science and Engineering at Chinese universities. Since the 1960s, PBL arises in the western countries there are many researches, practices, and implementations of PBL at engineering education, indicating that PBL has obvious advantages in cultivating the student's practical ability, collaboration ability, and self-developing ability, and so on (Zhiyu, 2012). Nowadays, PBL teaching mode has been widely applied to the medical course. And in some Universities such as Aalborg University, all the programme are using PBL model, but there are few practices of PBL implementation in Materials Science and Engineering at Chinese universities

THEORIES AYALYSES, EXPERIENCES AT AALBORG UNIVERSITYS AND REFLECTIONS

What Is PBL?

PBL means "problem-based learning", and it is one of "active learning" pedagogical approaches in higher education at Universities using complex authentic problems in real-world. Recently, PBL has attracted more attention by the educators. Compared with the traditional teaching approach such as lectures, PBL places the student at the center of the learning process, to promote students' learning motivation and cultivate innovative competence and skills of commutations and team-work by presenting scenarios and problems in groups for students to research and find suitable solutions. In PBL curriculum, Students are divided to several groups with several people in each group, to get the solution of the problems under the main guidance and directions through the collaborations with the members in the group. Because higher education at Universities today can no longer address only the cognitive part; it is necessary to think in broader terms. PBL approach is more positive than the traditional one which is more passive, and spoon-feeding rote learning based on teacher-directed lectures and instructions at Chinese Universities. PBL encourage the students to think critically and finally obtain collaborative skills and as wells an ability to solve the problems and the self-directed learning.

Prince and Felder (Prince & Felder, 2006) defined Problem-based learning (PBL) as follows: "PBL begins when students are confronted with an open-ended, ill-structured, authentic (real-world) problem and work in teams to identify learning needs and develop a viable solution, with instructors acting as facilitators rather than primary sources of information". So, the distinguish of PBL with other student-centered learning methods, such as inquiry-based, and case-based learning, is that PBL encourages the students to identify their own knowledge and skills and apply them to novel situations through the process of dealing with the authentic problems by combining previous knowledge or principles and then achieve specific leaning goals (Schmidt, 1995). The intent of the case-based learning is just to give the students printed data from actual situations, and let the students study and analyze these cases, in order to consider in every detail the differential diagnosis in medical teaching system. It seems like that case-based learning also use the problem for a case, and it is similar with PBL which use a problem as the trigger for learning, but the term "cases" in case-based learning is used to denote a case where the decision is stated and already has a decision, while "problem" in PBL is used to denote a case which ends with a question rather than a statement of decision (Servant-Miklos, 2018). Dewey expressed the essence of the "problem": "whatever-no matter how slight and common place in character - perplexes and challenges the mind so that it makes belief at all uncertain" (Dewey 2012). Based on the definition of the "problem", the key point of PBL is that the inclusion of a problem in PBL curriculum is an unknown problem that students conversed in group work prior to their self-study, guided by the teachers as the facilitator who could encourage them to think deeper about the unknown problems.

Furthermore, some researchers have given a critical overview of PBL and obtained some research data compared with traditional learning at Universities. The meta-analysis found that PBL had a positive effect on gaining higher theoretical scores assessed through examinations, and the results of questionnaires for students' feedback showed that PBL is superior to conventional teaching methods in improving students' outcomes of self-study, learning interest, team spirit, problem solving, analyzing, scope of knowledge, communication, and expression (Liu et al., 2019). Wyness L and Dalton F present evidence that students perceive the value of employing PBL in order to develop their research and problem-solving skills, build knowledge of various accounting, auditing, and reporting procedures, and motivating them to learn the subject matter to solve problems (Wyness & Dalton, 2018).

In all, PBL is a very comprehensive system of organizing the content in a new way through the real-problems or the authentic projects in the industries and students' collaborative learning by group works, enabling them to achieve diverse sets of knowledge, skills, and competence. PBL has been developed with the increasing demand for competence that goes beyond the technical field and reaches into process competence and integrative personal competences such as collaborative and creative knowledge processes.

How Does PBL Develop?

Since the 1950s, there has been growing and sustained interests in developing higher education in diverse in particular to medical educations (Kolmos & de Graaff, 2014). Rather than learning basic knowledge through via textbooks and lectures by teachers, students could learn how to solve the realistic clinical problems by giving a task. The higher education starts to attract more attention in the 1960s, because of the increasing of the students' numbers at Universities. PBL was originally coined by the famous educator named Don Woods in McMaster's University in Canada. PBL was firstly used for the Chemistry students in McMaster's University, the number of lectures and other top-down modes is therefore necessarily limited, at the same time a completely new medical curriculum consisted of a series unrelated discipline-related courses and specialty courses preparing for a series of practical training periods in the hospital was designed (Neufeld & Barrows, 1974). The learning of these curriculums begins with a realistic problem tackled by a small group of students. The early PBL curriculum at McMaster's University was fluid and variable, and there are no summative assessment and formal examinations in the PBL curriculum, only formative evaluations basis evaluated by the group's tutor (Servant-Miklos, 2018). The main characteristic of PBL at McMaster's University is that the application in practical medicine area is acted as more important factors in the teaching.

After that, PBL has been subsequently worldwide spread to more than 500 higher education institutions in west Universities with the introduction of this educational method at the medical school of McMaster University (Hillen, Scherpbier, & Wijnen, 2010). PBL has been applied to medical schools of Maastricht in the Netherlands and Newcastle in Australia (Gijselaers et al. 1995). In New Mexico, a newly established programme using PBL in health sciences was started (Kaufman, 1985). Since then, PBL has spread to other fields of University education such as architecture, economics and so on, not only limited to the medicine and health educations (Albanese and Mitchell, 1992). The development of PBL through the 1970s and 1980s has been characterized by small adjustments for pragmatic reasons. The theoretical roots of PBL began to receive serious consideration in the 1990s.

In Denmark, project-oriented PBL models were developed during the early 1970'ties. And the history of project-oriented PBL started at Roskilde University (RU) in 1972 and was followed up at Aalborg University (AAU) in 1974 (Schmidt, 2012). The occurrence of PBL in the Universities in Denmark arises from the strong student movement and the requirement for engineers with practical skills and creative competence in industries that wanted new profiles for engineers. In PBL models at above two Universities, interdisciplinarity has been considered in the design of the curriculum, thus the problem design is not limited to the traditional professional boundaries, and the problem analysis let the students to self-study learning cross the programmes at the Universities.

PBL Principles and Characteristics

There are two main theories that support PBL in higher education at Universities, which are social constructivism (Detel, 2001) and cognitivist constructivism (Bruner,

1965). From the main theory of social constructivism, the students can easily build their prior knowledge and understand and create the new knowledge through the social and collaboration work under PBL curriculum, in which the challenging problem and collaborative activities are given by PBL. Form the main theory of cognitivist constructivism, individual and critical thinking about the problem and experience during the process of the project is a core part of the learning under the PBL curriculum. Thus, the professional skills and innovation abilities can be obtained for students under the PBL curriculum through team-work, communication, report writing, and reflections during the process of the project.

Different institutions utilize the many different types of PBL principles which are formed based on the history of learning theories and some pedagogic experiences during the late 1960s and early 1970s with the reforming and changing of the education at some Universities, such as McMaster, Maastricht, Aalborg, Roskilde, Newcastle and so on. There are several typical theoretical learning principles of PBL in the following aspects (Sockalingam & Schmidt, 2011):

Firstly, the primary characteristics of a PBL learning environment are "problem-focused". In addition, the problems are based on real-life problems which have been selected and edited to meet educational objectives and criteria. The project for every group of five to eight students each semester usually starts with a problem. The content of the problems is what they normally defined by themselves within a thematic framework. After analyzing and solving the problem, they write a project report at the end of the semester.

Secondly, students are "self-directed" and "self-reflective" through PBL (Ulseth, 2016), and students individually and collaboratively assume responsibility for generating learning issues and processes. In the vast majority of cases, students have the opportunity to determine their own problem formulation within the given subject area guidelines. In other cases, the teacher defines the problem and the student uses this as a starting point.

Thirdly, "inter-disciplinary learning" is easy to be achieved through PBL. Usually, the problem in the real word is combined with different fields of the industry. The students not only need to understand the knowledge but also inter-disciplinary skills In order to solve the problem in real life, because the problems in real life are usually complex in society combing many skills in different fields.

Fourthly, "experience learning" is also an implicit part of the participant-directed learning process, where the student builds from his/her own experiences and interests. At that time, as the student must gain a deeper understanding of the selected complex problem through the "exemplary practice".

Fifthly, "Group-based learning" is also one of the main principles of PBL, because the majority of the learning process takes place in groups or teams under the PBL curriculum. The students can obtain some transferable skills such as collaborative abilities through group work.

At last, PBL is "student-centered learning", which means the teachers are facilitators serving in a supportive role rather than dominate the main lecture and other learning activities (Borhan, 2014). The learning ways have been changed from teacher-centered learning in traditional education. That is also the basic ideas to develop the model for core changing concepts from traditional education to a new module using PBL.

Of course, the Learning Principles at PBL used in different Universities may be different because of the tiny differences in PBL models at different Universities. Table 1 shows the Original Learning Principles at PBL Universities (Kolmos and de Graaff, 2014).

PBL Models and Curriculum Design

There are many different models of PBL which have been developed during these years, such as A PBL Model at McMaster, Chemical engineering, A PBL Model at AAU, A PBL Model at Delaware University, and A PBL Model at Republic Polytechnic, in Singapore. The four models are all based on the problems or projects or cases. But there still some differences. Here, the PBL Model at Aalborg University is introduced for example.

Table 1. Original learning principles at PBL universities

McMaster and Maastricht Universities Problem-Based Learning	Aalborg and Roskilde Universities Problem-Based and Project Organized Learning
• Problems form the focus and stimulus for learning. • Problems are the vehicle for development of problem-solving skills • New information is acquired through self-directed learning • Student-centered • Small student groups • Teachers are facilitators/guides • (Barrows,1996)	• Problems orientation • interdisciplinary • Exemplary learning • Participant-directed • Teams or group work • (Illeris,1976)

The AAU model is employed as a university-wide pedagogical approach. The problem-based project work is an integrated part of every educational programme at AAU. There are six principles of the AAU PBL model: 1) primary characteristic of problem-based learning: The problem is the point of departure for and directs the learning processes of the students; 2) A project is characterized by being a unique task that for its execution requires a range of complex activities and therefore a group of people with different skills; 3) The AAU PBL model is a hybrid PBL model where the students use half of their time working on their semester projects; 4) both collaboration in the project group, cooperation with facilitators and working together with external partners; 5) The problem-based project work has to be exemplary with regard to both the academic content and the methodological approach; 6) The students are responsible for achieving the project goal and for organizing the work processes that lead to the achievement of that goal, i.e. to the solution of the project problem.

As Kolmos (Kolmos, 2002) figured out, for analyzing the process of changing to PBL, we need to design a curriculum model that is more comprehensive and coves not only institutional procedures but also the relation to society, organization, culture, and values. Figure 1 shows the curriculum model for design. The model

Figure 1. The curriculum model for PBL design

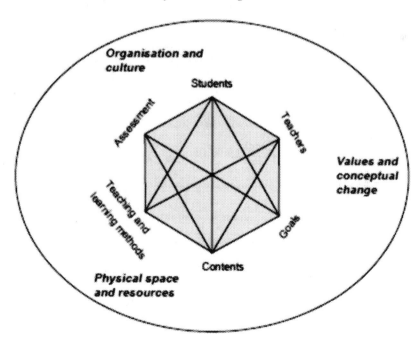

features two layers, the curriculum layer, and the organization and values layer. The curriculum layer covers six elements: 1) students, 2) teachers, 3) goals, 4) selection of contents, 5) teaching and learning methods, and 6) assessment. Changing over to PBL also entails changes in all six elements: students' prerequisites concerning their previous PBL experience have to be reconsidered. Teachers' qualifications have to be developed. New types of objectives, new competence will emerge. The contents will be reselected in a new manner. The teaching and learning methods will be based on PBL methods and new forms of assessment methods will arise.

Problem Design

The main focus of the PBL curriculum is the problem, because PBL emphasizes putting teaching actives into the real-world problems and students can learn the knowledge implied in the problems through solving these problems. So, problem design is one of the cores of PBL implantation and it can play a significant role in the teaching process. As the problems increase in complexity and even urgency with the development of the society, it is very difficult for students to identify the topic of problems and thereby more attention is needed to the problem design in PBL curriculum.

Especially, the approach to find the problems varies in various engineering institutions, so the ability to identify, analyze and formulate problems themselves have become one of the achievements for students besides the ability to solve pre-defined problems. Jette et al, has proposed five-step model in a systematic way for engineering students to identify, analyze and formulate problems:1) Relating to a theme; 2) Mapping the problem field; 3) Narrowing down the problems; 4) Problem analysis; 5) Problem formulation (Jette Egelund Holgaard et al, 2017).

Bloom's Taxonomy for PBL Design

Bloom's taxonomy is being considered and used by more and more educators for PBL design because it contemplates the nature of thinking, and provide a powerful tool for innovative thinking and fit educators' needs. Bloom's taxonomy is a multi-tiered model of classifying thinking according to six levels of learning, which are remembering, understanding, applying, analyzing evaluating and creating, from bottom to top in turns (revised Bloom's taxonomy) (Barrows, 1986).

According to this taxonomy, there are four different types of knowledge: (a) factual knowledge, (b) conceptual knowledge, (c) procedural knowledge, and (d) metacognitive knowledge. Unlike the levels of cognitive processing, these four types of knowledge are not a hierarchy (Forehand, 2010). So, we consider these four types of knowledge when we design a PBL curriculum and outline the teaching content, teaching method as well as the assessment. This means that alignment is required by developing consistency among all of the core parts of the course including 1) the learning objectives, 2) the teaching and learning activities, and 3) the assessment exercises. For example, instructors need to plan how students will practice engaging with content that requires different types of knowledge and not assumes that they will learn the conceptual or procedural knowledge by attending lectures or demonstrations. When instructors ask students to reflect on their own learning processes and to assess their learning progress, thus using metacognitive knowledge, students will learn the content of the course better.

Assessment

Assessment in a PBL learning environment can be aligned with the learning outcomes and the learning methods. In order to be coordinated with the learning goals and teaching method of a model, formative and summative assessment should be also included. And oral assessment is the best way to evaluate the students' report instead of written assessment.

Formative assessment is very much in alignment with the principles of PBL, supporting the metacognitive reflection of the students' learning process. And the summative assessment should mainly judge the group performance. So the oral assessment is the main way to measure the performance of the students, combined with many types of written work such as portfolios, projects, and so on, for assessing the learning process of the students in the teamwork as well as individual outcomes. Usually, the oral assessment is very often a group based assessment with individual judgment and grading of an individual's performance (Kolmos, Holgaard, & Du, 2009). Furthermore, other types of oral assessment are conducted, for instance, peer review among the groups, in order to motivate the students to perform better in a team and have better collaboration with the other members in the group.

APPLYING PBL TO MATERIALS SCIENCE AND ENGINEERING EDUCATION AT CHINESE UNIVERSITIES

Any changes cannot happen over one night, so there are multiple opportunities of changes at Chinese Universities that further implies other traditional universities in China even in Asian countries for improving learning and teaching in the future. Although there are a wide variety of educational models in PBL, a curriculum change could be regarded as a social construction in the Chinese context, between different elements, such as Chinese culture, Chinese regulations, and institutional policies, and so on. So, the characteristics of the traditional course at Chinese Universities should be considered firstly in order to introduce PBL to one course. The Materials Science and Engineering in Chinese Universities also have a long history for many years. That also means the changes seem more difficult and complex, and all the new proposals of curriculum designs in Materials Science and Engineering indicate that educational reforms at Chinese Universities should be an incremental innovation process.

A New Model Design in Materials Science and Engineering at Chinese University

In order to introduce PBL to Chinese traditional courses under the Chinese context, a design for introducing PBL to a single course in Materials Science and Engineering is designed as shown in Figure 2, compared with the traditional course at Chinese Universities. We divide the whole course into three parts, including 1) traditional

Figure 2. A model designed for material science and engineering education at Chinese universities compared with the traditional course

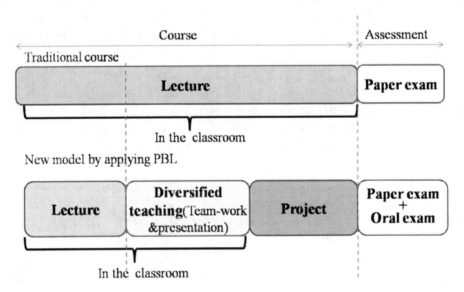

lecture (given by teachers), 2) diversified teaching process and 3) project activities. The former two parts educational activities are in the classroom, but the most important change is the last one, project activities.

Firstly, the lecture part of the course has been reduced. As well as, diverse learning methods should be used in the teaching contexts in order to provide as many as opportunities to students for "learning by thinking, doing and reflection" rather than delivering lectures to and giving direct answers the students. Diversified multimedia is a good choice in the lecture part, although it is just the change in form, which can motivate the students to learn the knowledge from diverse perspectives and different ways, to facilitate them to think and reflect about the knowledge about the Materials Science they have learned from the lecture. Instead of just giving the knowledge and conclusion to the students directly, many other teaching methods could be considered, such as the heuristic method. This concept of education drives the teachers to give the problems and questions rather than give the solutions and answers. Of course, the above methods are mainly dominated by teachers, and the problem and questions are provided by teachers. Students just think the questions passively.

Secondly, some teaching activities such as"5W1H-ask and answer", "group discussion" and "students presentation" should be considered in order to improve active learning among students.

"5W1H type asking" have drawn much attention by the researchers, which means the students should try to ask questions by themselves, including 5 W "who, what, when, where, and why", and 1H "who" (Ikeda, Okumura, & Muraki, 1998). Using above "5W1H" model, the students are driven to ask questions actively. That accords well with the principles of PBL. The students can find the problems by themselves through group discussions. And also, that reflects the education concept of "student-centered learning". Of course, there are various types of group discussions in the lectures. Students can behave as self-learners on the internet by "Massive Open Online Courses, MOOC". It is a typical new type of online learning in China; teachers give lectures on the internet, students search for the lecture videos and read references by themselves, students also propose and discuss problems and findings they have learned from the lectures and the references. Students may have discussions in groups in the classroom for pointing out problems, sharing literature reviews, and seeking the solutions.

The "group discussion" may be encouraged and organized in the classroom facilitated by the teachers. It is due to a consideration that most of the Chinese university students do not have rich group work experience required by PBL. When students start a PBL course for the first time, it is important to give the students some tools for project management and collaboration and to orchestrate the development of the students' learning of PBL skills by reflections. So, it is just a practice for Chinese students to learn how to criticize the context in the lecture and have the experience of group discussions against the problems within one course by the teacher's facilitating in the classroom. The case in Materials Science and Engineering can be given by teachers, for example, "who invented the phase diagram of the metals?", "what can we learn from the line and region in the phase diagram of the metals", "how to draw the phase diagram of the metals?", and so on. Then, group discussion is around the above questions, and after the group discussions, the students can give a presentation to state the answers to the questions.

After the group discussion, a process should be facilitated which the students are given opportunities to clarify their understanding and share their metacognition about how they meet knowledge gaps between the theory and practice. This is inspired by the revelation of relationship between four types of knowledge in Baumard's mode. The Baumard's mode show that the first type of knowledge is explicit and individual; second, the collective and profound knowledge of a terrain, environment, rules and laws we achieve; Third, a body of knowledge that is tacit and collective, which is of the unspoken, of the invisible structure of a practice. Fourth and last, a body of knowledge that is tacit and individual (Chunfang Zhou, 2012). Tacit expertise is complemented by "hard" technical knowledge-a sort of inimitable technical skills. These four forms of knowledge are indissociable. That means learning not only needs to listening they heard and remembering they saw, but also needs the discussions involving tacit knowledge and explicit knowledge in social practice. The students need a learning environment that provides conditions of both individual reflection and common engagement to support interactions between individual creativity and group creativity, through the group discussion. But after the group discussion, the tacit and individual knowledge forms by expressing their own cognition and metacognitive. Through this process which students make a presentation to share their experience during the group discussion, the students can make creative knowledge system.

The most important thing we should concern that as to the limit of organization and the policy of Chinese universities, the teamwork can also be conducted in the classroom. On one hand, the students are no longer passively to receive the knowledge through the lecture by the teachers. On the other hand, the student can actively learn the knowledge and be metacognitive to the knowledge through diversified team-work. Due to most of the Chinese university students have very poor PBL experience which could be one of the barriers to developing excellent team-work, it is necessary that teachers should pay active roles to facilitate group dynamics and overcome the barriers with students together.

Thirdly, we design the part of project activities within one course which is the most important changes during the model design. The theme of the project about the Materials Science and Engineering should be carefully considered by the teachers. Three types of the project should be suggested, and the students can select anyone from the two. One type is well-structured by the teachers. For example, to design a proper heat treatment process for a steel (e.g. No.40). The second type of project comes from a company, which is "How to enhance the strength and ductility of one steel (e.g. 45Mn) since this steel has cracked after serving for a while". The other type of project can be designed by the students, which is mostly encouraged by the teachers, and the teachers can help the students to find the topic of the project.

The last part of the new module is the change of assessment. Because PBL is a student-centered learning methodology, so the traditional paper exam cannot evaluate correctly the real skills, knowledge and the competence that the students have obtained by the project. So a new type of assessment should be designed by using PBL, and the mandatory paper exam will be changed to diversified types of assessment methods including formative assessment, self-assessment, oral assessment, peer assessment, and summative assessment, and so on (Dalrymple et al., 2007). However, the percentage of the paper exam should be cut down, and the assessment is mainly oral exam relating to the report submitted by the students according to the project. During the oral exam, the teacher can ask the questions to the students about the report of the project. Furthermore, the students in one group can also give scores to the other group, and through this peer evaluation, the students can be motivated to engage in active learning process. And the left part of the assessment is students' learning portfolio which reflects the learning process of the course.

Furthermore, the teaching method will also be changed after integration of PBL to Materials Science and Engineering education at Chinese Universities and it will be coincided to the changes of the curriculum. While diversified teaching methods should be considered to match the diversified form of the teaching model in single course. The teachers are no longer to just give lectures to the students which provide the knowledge directly on the textbooks, explanation to the subjects, and the solution to the problems; they acts more likely as facilitators to let the students to find the question and the solution by themselves, especially in diversified teaching context and project activities. Besides this, more other teaching methods should be considered, for instance, heuristic teaching, systemic teaching, and so on.

Learning Goals of Materials Science and Engineering

As Kolmos (Kolmos, 2002) figured out, in an organizational change process towards PBL, the curriculum layer covers six elements: 1) students, 2) teachers, 3) goals, 4) selection of contents, 5) teaching and learning methods, and 6) assessment. Changing over to PBL also entails changes in all six elements: students' prerequisites concerning their previous PBL experience have to be reconsidered. Teachers' qualifications have to be developed. New types of objectives, new competences will emerge. The contents will be reselected in a new manner. The teaching and learning methods will be based on PBL methods and new forms of assessment methods will arise. All these points drive us to discuss the following.

As we mentioned above, the new model for Materials Science and Engineering education includes three parts, which are traditional lecture (given by teachers), diversified learning(including group discussion, students presentation, and students self-learning by MOOC and other diversified multimedia through the internet) and the project. We design this new type of a course related to the learning goals of Materials Science and Engineering education. To follow such ideas, the relationship between the learning goals and revised taxonomy through the design for Materials Science and Engineering education has been discussed.

The learning goals of the course in Materials Science and Engineering are included in Table 2. The students not only should know and understand some principles and the mechanism of the metals but also have an ability to apply the Materials principles to analyze the relationship between the microstructure and the properties of the alloys. In the lecture, the knowledge is easy to be shown through the diversified media. And the skills of applying and analyzing the real problem about the Materials in the industry could be achieved by the teamwork in the classroom, through some cases in the real factories discussed by the students. Furthermore, the students should have the ability to design and create a new material or invent a new treatment process for real metals. This kind of competence should be achieved through the project subjected to real problems, and the students can have an ability of communication and collaboration.

There are relationship between the learning goals and revised taxonomy through the design for single course in Materials Science and Engineering at Chinese Universities. Students can easily get the knowledge through the lectures; this is well corresponded with the "remembering and understanding" in the revised Bloom's taxonomy, which is the lowest learning goals. Of course, the other learning goals such as "the innovative competence and technical skills" can also be obtained through the

Table 2. Learning goals of materials science and engineering education

Learning goals 1 (LO1) Knowledge	• Understand the typical structure of the metals • Know the crystallization process of the metals • Remember the phase diagram of binary metal • Understand the binary alloy phase diagram • Know the heat treatment process of the general metals • Know the microstructure changes during the plastic deformation • Understand the recrystallization process during the annealing • Know the mechanism and principle of recrystallization • Understand the plastic deformation and elastic deformation process • Know the main defect in microstructure of the metals • Know the characteristic of different types of materials • Know the mechanical properties of different types of materials Understand the typical structure of the metals • Know the application of the materials
Learning goals 2 (LO2) Skill	• Analyze the microstructure evolution of Fe-C alloy during the equilibrium cooling • Analyze the microstructure evolution of Fe-C alloy during the non-equilibrium cooling • Be able to explain the relationship between the properties using the phase diagram • Evaluate the heat process of general metals Evaluate the heat process of general metals • Be able to choose a proper process of a material • Analyze the main crack reasons for a material
Learning goals 3 (LO3) competence	• Design a appropriate process for a metal • Solve some actual problem during the heat treatment in the factory • Have an ability of collaboration and communication

lectures, but it can hardly to be achieved except the students could actively learn the knowledge through the lectures. However, it is easy to encourage students to master the transferable skills, in particular to the communication and collaboration skills, by the activities in teamwork and solving project solutions. Furthermore, diversified learning in the classroom is designed in order to obtain the learning goals of technical and management skills. Through the small group discussion, students can try their best to apply and analyze the problems teacher and students think out by themselves.

The students can also evaluate the knowledge they have learned through students' presentation. So, that is well corresponded with the "applying, analyzing, and the evaluating" in the revised Bloom's taxonomy. At last, the project activities are complex processes combining students' basic knowledge and theories, the teamwork ability, and creative thinking. So, the students could "understanding" deeply the knowledge in the textbook through the authentic problem, and "analyzing" the real problems in Materials Science and Engineering, in order to solve this problem. During the process of solving problem, the technical and transferable skills will be obtained by the collaboration of the group members. After solving the problem, the students have the potential to have the creative and innovative competence to create a new material or invent a new process for the metals.

Teachers and Students

The teachers should change their attitude and education concept according to the new model in one course in Materials Science and Engineering at Chinese Universities. Here, teachers are actually acted as facilitators. So, the teachers are not able to teach the students with the attitude of standing tall. Instead, the teachers should learn together with the students, and let the students solve the problem by themselves. Only in that way, the students can be motivated to have the potential to create a new material or a new process. That also means the teacher and student relationship is so important to be considered in the new model, and it is believed to be at the heart of the endeavor of the reform. Because if the researchers manipulate the learning environment so that students feel it is more accepting of risky behavior, students' creativity increases. And the students are more excited about the potential to excel and less worried by the possibility of failure. However, when the environment reinforces the penalties for failure, students become more prevention-focused and, therefore, less creative in their work. The teachers' role in the new model is obviously different from the traditional ones, which is, the teacher acts to facilitate rather than to provide knowledge directly (Chunfang Zhou, 2012).

In addition, the teachers should provide as many as opportunities to the students for encouraging the students to seek for research problems bout the materials and propose the projects by themselves, providing guidance in time, and giving supportive references or guidelines for developing teamwork abilities required by PBL.

The students in the new module should learn a lot of skills by using PBL in the single class. They should communicate with the other members in the group. They learn by doing not just reading the books and listening to the lectures and remembering the knowledge. For students, the key issue is in the process of performing a new PBL model including the project and teamwork is one of their challenges. So there are many strategies for helping students to adopt the new model. For example, firstly, the well-defined problem will be provided for the students to select from, which will not so complicated that the students can easily solve it. Secondly, a case with the project content and the report of the project will be provided to the students. Thirdly, the number of members in one group should be optional. If one student insists in doing the individual project, it is acceptable. However, this situation is not allowed always for one student. That means the student should take part in the groups in other semesters, in order to learn collaborative skills and other abilities by teamwork.

Teaching Method

In order to facilitate students to reach to learning goals, as discussed in last section, teaching methods are accordingly required to be designed. There are various teaching methods according to the new model design for one course in Materials Science and Engineering at Chinese Universities.

Firstly, Systemic teaching and holistic teaching method will be combined to be considered when the teacher give the lecture and combine the knowledge to that of other courses, giving the systemic looking on the technologies combining different kinds of discipline. That is good for students to have a whole concept to combine each kind of knowledge in the real world. Secondly, heuristic teaching means that the teachers could only give the problems and questions rather than give the solutions and answers. And the heuristic teaching method could be used in the lecture, giving the knowledge in the sentence instead of. Actually, the problem and questions are provided by teachers. Students just think the questions passively. But also, it can be important to be used in the teamwork and the project. And at that time, the teachers can approach the route for students to find the questions and the problems by themselves. It is effectively to motivate students to develop creative and innovative competence through this method. Thirdly, the group work is the main core in a PBL environment, and it is well core corresponded with the spirit of teamwork. That means students could obtain the communication and collaboration skills through the teamwork and the project. The various teaching methods discussed here will cooperate with each other that commonly forms a new PBL teaching culture.

Teaching Content in Materials Science and Engineering

The lecture content of Materials Science and Engineering should be changed compared with the traditional course just presenting the knowledge to the students. As mentioned above, diversified multimedia is a good choice in the lecture part, so the teachers should collect other resources to students, including the advanced knowledge, theories and research, even interesting doubt about the knowledge of the materials. Meanwhile, the teachers should encourage the students to find the explanations and the questions by themselves, which can attract student to learn the knowledge from diverse perspectives and ways, to motivate them to think about the knowledge they have learned.

For the project part, the theme of the project is so important, because problems are the vehicle for the development of problem-solving skills. Here, the project theme can be decided by the students to show the student-centered spirit of PBL principles. Of course, it is difficult for students to find the problem if they have poor PBL experience. In that case, the teachers can provide the well-structured problems for the students. Some other projects are provided by the companies for the students to choose. At last, the students are encouraged to identify the projects by themselves. Any of the above suggestions are acceptable at Chinese Universities.

Organization and Policy Support

In addition, the changes of the model need the supports of the organizations of the Chinese universities. And then the changes of the organization provide the resources for the changes of the model. Finally, the changes of the model can affect the culture reversely.

Based on the above theoretical discussion focusing on how to introduce PBL to one courses in Material Science and Engineering at Chinese Universities, the organizational policies need to be changed accordingly. For the single course, although the changes can be moved on by the teachers, but the support of diversified teaching is encourage and motivation for the teachers to change the model. For instance, the project part of the course should be supported after the class. So the extra teaching hours could be counted in the whole hours the students spend in one course. Secondly, the mandatory paper exam will be changed, and diversified type of assessment will be allowed according to the new mode.

CONCLUSION

How to fostering innovative Materials Science and Engineering graduates under the traditional Chinese educational environment has been paid attention and it is still essential to make a change in the Materials Science and Engineering education under the new 3E strategic in China. With the rapid development of high and new technology, new breakthroughs have been made in the field of Materials Science and Engineering, thus the education changing and reforming have become more visible due to the globalization. There are still some problems and challenges in Materials Science and Engineering at Chinese Universities. Therefore, this chapter described PBL history, PBL principles and characteristics, PBL models and curriculum design, and share some PBL experiences and reflections at Aalborg University. At last, a model for one course in Materials Science and Engineering at Chinese Universities has been designed in this chapter, indicating how PBL could be applied to Materials Science and Engineering education in Chinese Universities, and a case of PBL implementation has been given to show the process of transformation from traditional education at Chinese Universities to PBL in a Materials Science and Engineering field.

REFERENCES

Albanese, M. A., & Mitchell, S. (1993). Problem-Based Learning: A Review of Literature on Its Outcomes and Implementation Issues. *Academic Medicine: Journal of the Association of American Medical Colleges, 68*(1), 52–81. doi:10.1097/00001888-199301000-00012 PMID:8447896

Barrows, H. S. (1986). A taxonomy of problem-based learning methods. *Medical Education, 20*(6), 481–486. doi:10.1111/j.1365-2923.1986.tb01386.x PMID:3796328

Borhan, M. T. (2014). Problem based learning (PBL) in teacher education: A review of the effect of PBL on pre-service teachers' knowledge and skills. *European Journal of Educational Sciences, 01*(01), 76–87. doi:10.19044/ejes.v1no1a9

Bruner, J. S. (1965). EDITORIAL: The Process of Education. *The Physics Teacher, 3*(8), 369–370. doi:10.1119/1.2349211

Chunfang Zhou, A. K. A. J. D. N. (2012). A Problem and Project-Based Learning (PBL) Approach to Motivate Group Creativity in Engineering Education. *International Journal of Engineering Education, 28*(1), 3–16.

Dalrymple, K. R., Wong, S., Rosenblum, A., Wuenschell, C., Paine, M., & Shuler, C. F. (2007). PBL Core Skills Faculty Development Workshop 3: Understanding PBL process assessment and feedback via scenario-based discussions, observation, and role-play. *Journal of Dental Education, 71*(12), 1561–1573. PMID:18096882

Detel, W. (2001). Social Constructivism. In *International Encyclopedia of the Social & Behavioral Science* (pp. 14264–14267). Academic Press.

Dewey, J. (1900). *The School and Society*. University of Chicago Press.

Forehand, M. (2010). Bloom's taxonomy. In M. Orey (Ed.), Emerging perspectives on learning, teaching, and technology (pp. 41–47). Academic Press.

Gijselaers, W. H., Tempelaar, D. T., Keizer, P. K., Blommaert, J. M., Bernard, E. M., & Kasper, H. (1995). *Educational Innovation in Economics and Business Administration: The Case of Problem-Based Learning*. Springer Science & Business. doi:10.1007/978-94-015-8545-3

Hiim, H., & Hippe, E. (2004). *Learning through experience, understanding and action*. Gyldendal Uddannelse.

Hillen, H., Scherpbier, A., & Wijnen, W. (2010). History of problem-based learning in medical education. Lessons from Problem-based Learning, 5–12. doi:10.1093/acprof:oso/9780199583447.003.0002

Holgaard, J. E., Guerra, A., & Kolmos, A. (2017). Getting a Hold on the Problem in a Problem-Based Learning Environment. *International Journal of Engineering Education*, *33*(3), 1070–1085.

Ikeda, T., Okumura, A., & Muraki, K. (1998). Information classification and navigation based on 5W1H of the target information. *Proceedings of the 17th international conference on Computational linguistics*, 571–577.

Kaufman, A. (1985). *Implementing Problem-Based Medical Education: Lessons from Successful Innovations*. Springer Publishing Company. doi:10.1891/9780826146618

Kolmos, A. (2002). Facilitating change to a problem-based model. *The International Journal for Academic Development*, *7*(1), 63–74. doi:10.1080/13601440210156484

Kolmos, A., & de Graaff, E. (2014). Problem-Based and Project-Based Learning in Engineering Education. In Cambridge Handbook of Engineering Education Research (pp. 141–160). Cambridge University Press.

Kolmos, A., Holgaard, J., & Du, X. (2009). Transformation du curriculum: vers un apprentissage par problèmes et par projets. Innover dans l'enseignement supérieur, 151.

Liu, L., Du, X., Zhang, Z., & Zhou, J. (2019). Effect of Problem-Based Learning in Pharmacology Education: A Meta-Analysis. *Studies in Educational Evaluation*, *60*, 43–58. doi:10.1016/j.stueduc.2018.11.004

Mencius, B. I., & Ivanhoe, P. J. (2011). Mencius. Columbia University Press.

Morales Bueno, P., Bueno, P. M., & Rodas, R. S. (2018). Metacogntion and motivation relationship in a hybrid PBL approach. *ICERI2018 Proceedings*.

Prince, M. J., & Felder, R. M. (2006). Inductive Teaching and Learning Methods: Definitions, Comparisons, and Research Bases. *Journal of Engineering Education*, *95*(2), 123–138. doi:10.1002/j.2168-9830.2006.tb00884.x

Schmidt, H. G. (1995). Problem-Based Learning: An Introduction. *Instructional Science*, *22*(4), 247–250. doi:10.1007/BF00891778

Schmidt, H. G. (2012). A Brief History of Problem-based Learning. In *One-Day* (pp. 21–40). One-Problem. doi:10.1007/978-981-4021-75-3_2

Servant-Miklos, V. F. C. (2018). *Fifty Years on: A Retrospective on the World's First Problem-Based Learning Programme at McMaster University Medical School.* Health Professions Education.

Servant-Miklos, V. F. C. (2018). *The Harvard Connection: How the Case Method Spawned Problem-Based Learning at McMaster University.* Health Professions Education.

Sockalingam, N., & Schmidt, H. G. (2011). Characteristics of Problems for Problem-Based Learning: The Students' Perspective. *Interdisciplinary Journal of Problem-Based Learning, 5*(1).

Ulseth, R. (2016). Development of PBL Students as Self-Directed Learners. *2016 ASEE Annual Conference & Exposition Proceedings.* 10.18260/p.26823

Wyness, L., & Dalton, F. (2018). The Value of Problem-Based Learning in Learning for Sustainability: Undergraduate Accounting Student Perspectives. *Journal of Accounting Education, 45*, 1–19. doi:10.1016/j.jaccedu.2018.09.001

Zhiyu, L. (2012). Study on the Cultivation of College Students' Science and Technology Innovative Ability in Electrotechnics Teaching Based on PBL Mode. *IERI Procedia, 2*, 287–292. doi:10.1016/j.ieri.2012.06.090

Chapter 6

The Change Towards PBL:
Designing and Applying PBL
at a Program Level

Fei Wang
Northeastern University, China

ABSTRACT

This chapter proposes the design of course groups PBL at program level for students from the BSc. programs of Robot Engineering (RE) at Northeastern University (NEU), China. The overall courses are divided into four groups throughout Grades 1 to 4. In this chapter, the authors provide background information about student cultivation and discipline construction in RE, and then they discuss correlation of characteristics between PBL and RE program, which indicates the reasons for applying PBL in RE. Finally, they introduce the detailed design of course groups.

DOI: 10.4018/978-1-5225-9961-6.ch006

INTRODUCTION

Chang to PBL

The institutions, such as McMaster, Maastricht, Aalborg, Roskilde, Linköping, and Newcastle, started PBL with a blank slate. These are young universities that were able to develop an entire curriculum without the burden of traditions and habits. This book addresses the much more complicated transformation process from traditional teaching and learning systems with ordinary lectures to PBL systems based on PBL learning principles including problem-based, team-based, interdisciplinary, and contextual learning.

The transformation from traditional to more student-centered learning is a widespread global process caused by new demands for process and lifelong learning skills. But even if this is a global process, each programme utilizing PBL principles has its history. In many cases, the shift to PBL was caused by more or less similar wishes:

- To decrease drop-out rates
- To stimulate motivation for learning
- To accentuate institutional profile
- To support the development of new competences

Change can be observed from many different angles. Some changes manifest at an institutional level when a faculty, a department, or a programme opts for a total curriculum change. In other cases, the subject is a single course sought infused with innovation by a teacher. This article deals primarily with the institutional change – the more holistic transformation of a system. These types of transformation processes are complex, and each institution that has undergone such a transformation process has a unique story to tell. However, these stories also share a lot of similarities, revealing a pattern for transformation processes in Higher Education.

Relating these terms to Higher Education, the product is not a tangible, material product, but the students' knowledge and competencies. In other words, it is about changing students' learning.

Fullan (2001) is one of the few educational researchers working with change in education at a practical level and at the same time contributing to the theoretical knowledge within the field. Fullan emphasizes that the outcome of an educational change process is not only a change in student learning but also the organizational capacity. Students leave the education – the sustainable factor is that the staff has changed to constantly develop students' learning and the learning outcomes. Fullan stresses that change is a process, not an event (Fullan, 2001), entailing that change does not occur overnight. It takes time, and it has a deep impact.

Henriksen et al. (2004) maintain that to understand organizational change, we need to understand the concept of reality – since the change in organizations is a change of reality. He emphasizes that to obtain an understanding of reality. It is necessary to look into at least four elements; fact (documentation), logic (a core part of the constitution process), values (to describe the importance), and communication (as being a member of society and interpretation).

So change should be analyzed and interpreted in a broader context, and values are an important part of the educational change as change processes entail both a systemic and value-oriented change if the superficial change is to be avoided. Henriksen makes another important point, namely that change happens in contexts – and that it might be difficult to develop one overall model for analyzing these very complex processes as there is always a story to tell - like the stories that are told in this book. Some of the changes occur within a course, whereas others address the overall systemic level.

Applying this to a curriculum perspective requires a concept of a more holistic and systemic approach to curriculum development. Biggs (1999) has developed the 3P model describing presage (students' prior knowledge and teaching contexts such as objectives, assessment, climate, and institutional procedures), process (learning-focused activates), and product (learning outcome). This 3P model describes a balanced system where the components are aligned with each other. Consequently, the principles of holism and alignment are key to this approach.

The principles of alignment entail the existence of consistency and logic among all the elements and mutual support between the elements:

- The curriculum that we teach.
- The teaching methods that we use.
- The assessment procedures that we use, and the methods of reporting results.
- The climate that we create in interaction with the students.
- The institutional climate, the rules, and procedures we have to follow (Biggs, 2003:26).

The model is not developed to analyze the change in an organization, but for analyzing curricula. Any change in the teaching context will affect the student factors, the learning activities, and the outcomes and one has to consider the entire curriculum as an aligned system.

However, for analyzing the processes of changing to PBL, we need a model that is more comprehensive and covers not only institutional procedures but also the relation to society, organization, culture, and values. The Scandinavian approach to curriculum development (in continental Europe called didactics) covers these elements. The interrelation between educational politics and curriculum development has been emphasized, so to understand curriculum change, the understanding of the societal framework is crucial. Him and Hippe (1997) have developed a model for relationship didactics, the aim of which is to critically analyze and understand teaching and learning. They operate with six factors, which make up the most important elements in teaching and learning analysis:

- The student's social, cultural, psychological, and physical prerequisites for learning.
- Cultural, social, and physical factors of the frame (including the prerequisites of the teacher).
- Goals for learning.
- Contents.
- The process of learning.
- Assessment.

According to this model shown in Figure 1, all of the educational elements must be included in the curriculum change processes to achieve change. Thus, the model helps explain why changes in teaching methods within a traditional educational framework would not result in a changed educational model if the way of assessment and/or the principles for material selection were not changed concurrently.

The model features two layers – the curriculum layer, and the organizational and values layer. The first layer is the curriculum covering six elements: students, teachers, goals, selection of contents, teaching and learning methods, and assessment. Changing over to PBL also entails changes in all six elements: students' prerequisites concerning their previous PBL experience have to be reconsidered. Teachers' qualifications have to be developed. New types of objectives, new competencies will emerge. The contents will be reselected in a new manner. The teaching and learning methods will be based on PBL methods, and new forms of assessment methods will arise.

Figure 1. A curriculum model for change

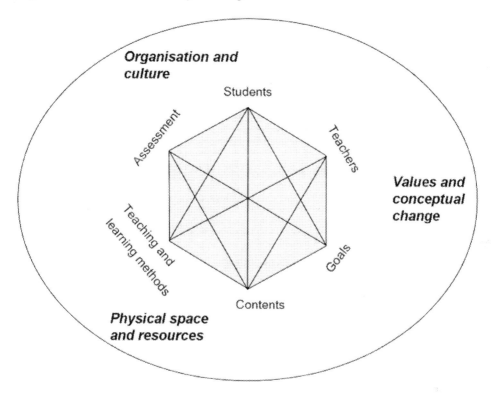

The second layer is the organizational aspect, which is crucial as the contents layer is not sufficient to explain curriculum change. All these elements form the frame for curriculum development – and beyond these elements and their interrelation is the very core change of knowledge construction consisting of values, conceptual change, and the use of new learning principles.

The operation of changing an organization involves strategic planning, with short-term and long-term goals. Chin and Benne (1985) distinguish three types of strategies that can be applied when changing an organization:

- Empirical-rational strategies.
- Normative-re-educative strategies.
- Power-coercive strategies.

Each strategy rests on implicit beliefs about human nature. The first strategy treats man as a rational being. In the end, everyone is interested in personal gain, so to effect change, the advantages should be pointed out. The second strategy recognizes that man is conservative. This strategy also emphasizes the social aspects of human behavior and the ability to learn new behavior.

Consequently, to change an organization, you will have to change the value system of the people within the organization - what we call cultural change today. Power-coercive strategies depart from the assumption that man primarily identifies with his profit, and that most men do not care for the advantages or risks of the organization as a whole. Top-down management is, therefore, necessary to protect the larger interest at stake.

To change to PBL, it is necessary to constitute a bridge between different strategies of organizational change and, not at least, a bridge between organizational learning and education.

Moesby (2004) has developed a model for implementation of change to PBL in higher education covering four phases:

- **Investigation Phase:** Pre-action activities.
- **Adoption Phase:** Formulation of Vision; Defining criteria of success; Communication of the results.
- **Implementation Phase:** Staff development programme, Evaluation programme.
- Institutional state which is the final state of the change process.

Table 1. Eight steps to transforming your organization

Phase	
1	Establishing a Sense of Urgency
2	Forming a Powerful Guiding Coalition
3	Creating a Vision
4	Communicating the Vision
5	Empowering Others to Act on the Vision
6	Planning for and Creating Short-Term Wins
7	Consolidating Improvements and Producing Still More Change
8	Institutionalizing New Approaches

Regardless of appointed or elected leaders, Kolmos, Gynnild and Roxå (2004) point to the fact that all organizational levels become involved if the organization enters a change process. Bottom-up strategies are not efficient since the change at a system level requires a decision at top-level. Top-down strategies are not as efficient as they create much resistance in the system. So the optimal situation is to establish change by using both top-down and bottom-up strategies. Top-down strategies are comparable to empirical-rational and normative-re-educative strategies whereas bottom-up is comparable to the power-coercive strategy.

The different models can help explain elements of the occurring change processes, and, not least, point out the areas that definitely should be taken into consideration previous to the implementation of the change processes, such as:

- Including all curriculum elements.
- Thinking of coherence between curriculum and organization/culture.
- Employing a range of strategies for change.
- Creating a general view of the total change process.
- Creating visions.
- Motivating staff and colleagues.
- Developing visions for long-term goals without compromising short-term goals.
- Planning development of staff qualifications.
- Raising resources.
- Developing a specific plan of action.
- Establishing networks.
- Including and developing a staff development unit responsible for recurring energizers.
- Providing evidence of the development of students' learning outcome.
- Providing evidence of the development of faculty' s capacity.

The success of curriculum innovation, in the long run, depends on the ability of the faculty to adapt the educational method to suit its own specific needs – and on the ability to constantly renew itself. An important advantage of the introduction of PBL is that it entails a new way of thinking about education and learning. In traditional organizations in higher education, little reflection on the task of teaching exists. The introduction of a PBL curriculum can help to break down these traditional boundaries. In the course of the introduction process, the staff has to be trained and re-educated to learn to function effectively in the new situation. Finally, successful educational leadership assumes the responsibility of making decisions, including those decisions that will not be embraced by all parties involved, but that is necessary for the organization to survive in a competitive world.

The Necessity of Applying PBL to BSc. Programme in RE

Establishment of BSc. Programme in Robot Engineering in China

Today, some structural contradictions (e.g., professional surplus in traditional industries and shortage in emerging industries) in the field of engineering manufacturing promote people to explore new models of engineering education. The concept of "Emerging Engineering Education, 3E" is to a large extent an embodiment of the current education trend in engineering. Developing new engineering is to solve the urgent problem of professionals' shortage in emerging industries (Zhong, 2017).

As China has entered a new era, the overall productive forces have significantly improved, and in many areas, the production capacity leads the world. The more prominent problem is that the development is unbalanced and inadequate. This has become the main constraining factor in meeting people's increasing needs for a better life. In emerging industries, especially in the robot industry, structural contradiction is still serious. According to "Analysis Report on Robot Industry in China 2018", there is a huge professional shortage in Chinese robot industries in the future decade, as shown in Figure 2.

Figure 2. Installed capacity of industrial robots and demand of robot engineering professionals in China

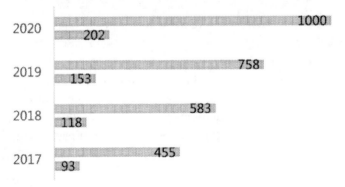

To meet the huge demand of professionals for a new revolution in manufacturing industries, a new BSc. programme in Robot Engineering (RE) was established by the Ministry of Education (MoE) of China in 2015. It was reported there are nearly one hundred universities and colleges setting up BSc. programme in RE to recruit undergraduate students in China until 2018. Northeastern University (NEU) was the first "985 Project" university establishing Robot College in China. Figure 3 shows that the college was a new type of engineering education co-constructed by NEU, Shenyang Institute of Automation (SIA) in Chinese Academy of Science (CAS), and Shenyang SIASUN Robot & Automation Co., LTD.

SIA's research focuses on robotics, industrial automation, and photoelectric information processing. As the cradle of China's robotics technology, the institute has had more than 20 "firsts" in robotics development in China, making it the national leader. SIA is home to 10 national and provincial key laboratories and engineering centers, including the National Engineering Research Center on Robotics, the State Key Laboratory of Robotics, and the CAS Key Laboratory for Networked Control Systems.

SIASUN is a high-tech listed enterprise belonging to CAS, which takes robotic technology as the core and focuses on providing intelligent products & services. It is TOP 10 leading enterprise in Chinese robotic industry, who has the most comprehensive robotic products line in the world. At present, SIASUN market value is the 3rd in the robotic industry globally, which has the fastest rate of growth.

Figure 3. Tripartite Robot College of NEU

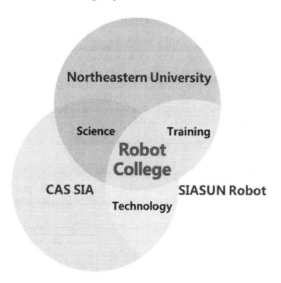

Based on the development trend and demand of China's intelligent robot industry, the college aims to cultivate intelligent robot technology, the intelligent, intellectual property industry with independent intellectual property rights as the core, and high-quality, intelligent application professionals for the high-end intelligent robot industry for national economic construction. The robot college adopts a new engineering education model that teachers and researchers from the three parties carry out cooperative teaching and student cultivation jointly, which can promote the integration of robotics and related disciplines.

Demands of New Pedagogical Mode for Robot Engineering

For robotics education, Plymouth University of the United Kingdom is the first to provide robotics undergraduate education programmes all over the world in 2004. The teaching philosophy of PU is to provide students with a quasi-true learning experience, to train students' practical and analytical skills in the field of electronics, embedded and advanced programming, artificial intelligence and so on, and to track the recent advances in robotics research.

During 2006 to 2011, several universities in the US established BSc. Programme in RE based on different disciplines, such as The Worcester Polytechnic Institute (WPI), the University of California, Santa Cruz (CUSC), Lawrence Technological University (LTU). Though there are no BSc. programme in RE, several universities are famous for their remarkable achievement in robotics education. In Massachusetts Institute of Technology (MIT), the Robotics courses are highly valued in combination with scientific and technological practice and have a flexible period of independent activity. There are no regular classroom arrangements for the courses offered during the period, which gives students more autonomy and selective participation in the classroom learning to gain the supplement knowledge. All robotics courses require substantial results. Carnegie Mellon University (CMU) / (Robotics Institute, RI) is the world's largest and most advanced robotics research institute. It has several laboratories and research centers covering research fields, such as robotics, imaging processing, artificial intelligence and so on. In the U.S., only CMU has physical robotics college, including undergraduate and graduate programmes. For undergraduates, RI offers a dual degree (major), minor (minor), and a 5-year undergraduate + master's programme. RI also has internships and outreach programs to develop high school and undergraduate interest in robotics research and development. Undergraduate students firstly have a basic understanding of the robotics field through the introductory course, while mastering some basic skills. Then, through the study of the core modules of cognition, perception and execution, they can deeply understand all aspects involved in intelligent robots. Secondly, choose a hands-on course to enhance hands-on ability, choose two elective courses, and increase the breadth of knowledge. Finally, through the systematic study and the study and practice of the culmination course, the above-mentioned content will be integrated to lay a foundation for future study and work. The mode of CMU has great reference value in the field of robotic degree setting, programme scheme, student cultivation and curriculum design. The evaluation of robotics engineering teaching in U.S. universities focuses on students' self-reflection in the course of activities. The diversified evaluation methods help to fully reflect the knowledge acquired by students in the course and the flexible use of knowledge. The evaluation can be based on the completion of the student's experiment and design project, or on the student's substantive outcome.

However, due to different social needs, educational environment and development level in China and abroad, it is difficult to copy the beneficial experience of foreign countries to China directly. Compared with the actual demand of professionals in innovative countries, the cultivation of students' initiative, creativity and practical ability in knowledge learning is insufficient in China's colleges and universities. A survey of college students' evaluations shows that the level of competence in applying professional knowledge, ability to analyze problems, creative thinking ability, independent work ability, and hands-on ability is related to the quality of innovation. More than 50% of university graduates are at the "general" level.

In general, there are several shortcomings in the cultivation of students under the existing teaching-learning system in China: 1) Knowledge: weak foundation, loose structure, narrow scope, poor practicality; 2) Practical aspects: poor self-learning ability and hands-on ability, lack of ability to use knowledge flexibly; 3) Consciousness: narrow vision, rigid thinking, lack of challenge and innovation awareness; 4) Humanistic quality: lack of team awareness and management skills, lack of communication skills, poor emotional control and self-regulation.

In November 2017, Minister of Education Chen Baosheng wrote in the Guangming Daily that it is necessary to "make a good fight to improve the quality of student cultivation in colleges and universities, promote the intensive development of higher education, and deepen the reform of innovation and entrepreneurship education in colleges and universities." The BSc. programme in RE has just started in China, and there is an extremely lack of reference cultivation modes and programmes in subject connotation construction and innovative student cultivation. Due to the comprehensiveness of robotics and the extensive application of robot technology, the student cultivation of robotics has obvious interdisciplinary, cross-cutting and practical characteristics.

As an emerging undergraduate major, the BSc program in RE of China's universities began to be established in 2015, so they are all in the early stage of construction. Most of them are only undergraduates of the first grade. Only a few colleges have sophomores through major changing or streaming.

Since the graduates have not yet been trained, the BSc program of RE in China has not formed a reference case in terms of curriculum system, teaching methods, practical teaching setup, innovation activity organization, and comprehensive quality cultivation of students, and they are all at the stage of exploration. NEU established the Robot College firstly in China, and it aims to construct a throughout comprehensive cultivation system from BSc, MSc to Ph.D. It has the responsibility and obligation to accelerate the development of targeted research, explore reasonable models and steps to achieve the connotation construction of the RE programme. The student cultivation and curriculum design have played a leading role in the construction of the RE program in China and has taken the lead in the rapid development of Northeastern University in the field of robot engineering education in China.

Connotation Consistency Between Robot Engineering and PBL

The cultivation of undergraduate students' innovative ability has always been an important issue facing the education community all over the world. According to different national conditions and cultural characteristics, countries around the world have proposed innovative student cultivation ideas in terms of student teams, active learning, innovative thinking, and project activities.

Traditional engineering education at programme level has many limitations which have prompted the growth of newer approaches. As diverse pedagogical models have been in use at many higher education institutions, it may be difficult to find a standard method that fits for all. In general, the classical pedagogical models are classified as deductive and inductive. While the former derives theories and applications based on the basics such as particular observations or measurement data, the latter is considered to be a discovery style. Problem-based learning (PBL) is an inductive learning method and considered to be the "best" method for engineering students (Elamvazuthi, et al., 2015).

The origins for PBL does not come from one source or organization but emerge from a societal period with experimentations in the educational systems. The pedagogy behind the PBL practices that were established has developed into a sound theory of learning and is today well documented in all aspects of curriculum development, learning and competence development. Since the establishment of the

PBL universities, PBL models have been implemented all over the world. Especially the McMaster and the Maastricht models are utilized in health and law, whereas the Aalborg model with the problem based and project based/organized is most often used in variations in engineering and science.

PBL is an innovative initiative, which offers an alternative educational framework for producing better-prepared and highly skilled engineering graduates. The students learn to solve problems and complete projects. To improve the teaching and learning of engineering students, the PBL initiative aims to make four important improvements; increases active and hands-on learning, emphasizes problem formulation and solution, explores the underlying concepts of the tools and techniques of engineering, and institute innovative and exciting ways of gathering feedback.

PBL is an educational concept that organizes learning content through problem-based inquiry. Is a teaching method that encourages learners to use critical thinking, problem-solving skills, and content knowledge to solve real-world problems and controversies. It has four characteristics: student-centered self-directed learning, group learning, stimulating learning with problem-focused points, and teacher as inducer and facilitator. Different from traditional classroom teaching, PBL advocates students as the main body of learning and information acquisition and is the participants, coordinators and responsible persons of the project, rather than passive recipients and objects that are instilled with knowledge. The traditional learning method is simple and rude, and the knowledge is broken up and instilled. PBL encourages mistakes, learns from mistakes, discovers problems, and integrates knowledge through project operations. Find "pleasure" in self-directed learning.

It can be said that there is a strong internal relationship with PBL in terms of student cultivation mode, curriculum system, knowledge content, and practical process.

1. The essential similarity between PBL and student cultivating mode in Robot Engineering
   a. Core knowledge, conceptual understanding, and success skills: the project focuses on the student's learning goals, including knowledge and skills based on standards in the field of robotics.
   b. **Challenging Problems:** The entire project is based on meaningful core issues that need to be addressed, and with a certain degree of challenge.
   c. **Continuous Inquiry:** Students can participate in a series of rigorous and continuous questions, access to and use of information in the process of inquiry.

d. **Practicality:** It involves a real background, covering tasks, tools, and quality standards in the real world.

e. **Student's Voices and Choices:** Students can make decisions about the project, including what they are prepared to do and what they are going to create.

f. **Reflection:** Students and teachers reflect on the effectiveness of the inquiry, the project activities, the quality of the work, the difficulties encountered, and the process of overcoming.

g. **Criticism and Modification:** Students use the feedback given and received to improve the process and the outcome.

h. **Public Display:** Students explain and present their projects to people outside the class.

2. PBL is deeply related to robotics knowledge system and contents. Interdisciplinary learning, interdisciplinary cooperation, to achieve the integration of disciplines as much as possible, so that students acquire more comprehensive knowledge, more positive and more active in the search for knowledge.

3. PBL is similar to student cultivation process in Robot Engineering. Open, more than one reasonable answer. It is easy to understand and illuminating, consistent with the learning objectives of core knowledge, conceptual understanding and successful skills. The process of answering or solving this problem will inevitably touch and learn these knowledge, concepts and skills.

MODEL DESIGN OF PBL IN PROGRAMME LEVEL

Issues, Controversies, Problems

Till now, in addition to 180 undergraduate students from grade 1 to 3 in BSc. programme, there are also 168 graduate students in MS and Ph.D. programmes in Robot College of NEU. The main objective of student cultivation of BSc. programme in RE is to makes the students gain up-to-date knowledge within science and engineering in the field robotics and develop skills in the use of advanced tools and techniques in multidisciplinary robot engineering environment after graduation. The BSc programme in RE is a 4-year, research-based, full-time study program. The program is set to 159 credits, in which the percent of practical courses is more than 25%.

RE is a classical interdisciplinary major involving material, mechanics, electronics, computer science, automation, philosophy and neuroscience as shown in Figure 4 Considering the characteristics and trend of robotics and artificial intelligence, the overall courses are divided into 4 groups, named general courses group, automation courses group, robotics courses group and Artificial Intelligence course group as shown in Figure 5.

In general knowledge courses group, it includes some fundamental principles of mathematics, mechanics, electronics and computer system, also includes some basic skills of mechanical drawing and programming. Hands-On and programming exercises including laboratory work.

In Automation courses group, it consists of some common specified courses for automation large class including fundamental technology of analog &digital electronics, embedded system, the principle of circuit, the principle of automatic control and so on.

Figure 4. Knowledge and skill structure of BSc. Programme in RE

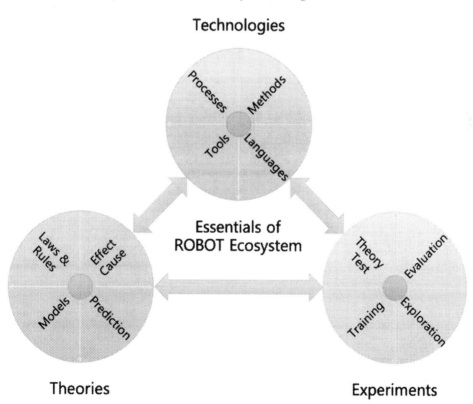

Figure 5. Courses group in programme of RE

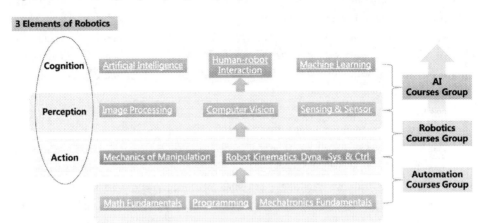

In Robotics courses group, courses involving kinematics, kinetics, control and human-robot interaction make-up of the knowledge system in robotics field including basic principle in robotics, mechatronics of robot system, robot operation system, robot perception & human-machine interaction and robot dynamics control.

With intelligent robot as the main study object, the cultivation direction of RE focuses on intelligent decision-making theory and engineering realization of the robot. In Artificial Intelligence courses group, courses related to intelligent robots such as introduction to artificial intelligence, cloud computing, image processing, object-oriented programming (C++), Python programming (bilingual), introduction to machine learning and so on are set, accounting for more than 30% of the total credits of the basic courses and specified courses.

The programme is structured in course groups throughout eight semesters and organized as a problem-based study. It aims to give students a set of professional skills within a fixed time frame and concluding with one or more examinations within specific exam periods. The programme is based on a combination of academic, problem-oriented and interdisciplinary approaches and organized based on the following work and evaluation methods that combine skills and reflection:

- Lectures
- Classroom instruction
- Project work
- Workshops
- Exercises (individually and in groups)

- Teacher feedback
- Reflection
- Portfolio work

All courses are assessed by external examination (external grading) or internal examination (internal grading or assessment by the supervisor only). Figure 6 shows an overview of the programme.

In the traditional programme, the curriculum system usually consists of public courses, specified compulsory courses and specified elective courses, showing a pyramid structure. Among them, the bottom level is a public class. The main purpose is to carry out basic education for students, to develop students' basic knowledge and skills, to prepare for specified study. In the upper grades, professional education is the focus, and the curriculum gradually becomes more refined and specialized. Once a student cultivation scheme is determined, the curriculum structure and teaching process of the programme will have the desired stability. The characteristics of the teacher center and the subject center of the traditional education model are obvious. The former means that the teacher decides the choice of teaching content and the arrangement of teaching progress, while the latter means that the educational process is based on professional knowledge and fewer relations with society and life. This,

Figure 6. Progressive PBL curriculums design of robot engineering at NEU

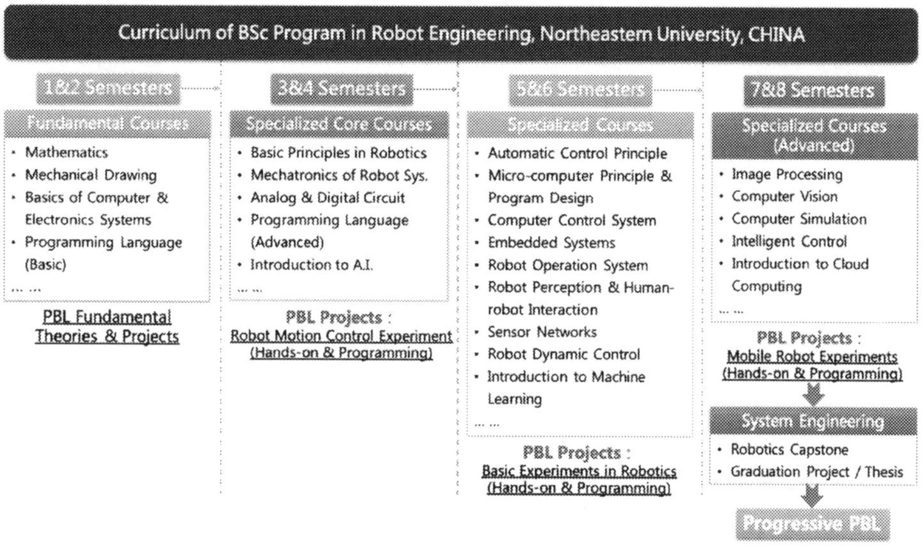

to a certain extent, leads to the disconnection between theory and time in teaching, affecting students' interest and enthusiasm for learning (Li & Du, 2018).

Based on the practical application of the robot engineering, the students focus on the problems in the process of innovation practices, and organize the learning content through the project, which is carried out in groups to maximize the subjective initiative of students to participate in learning, to improve the ability to find, analyze, and solve problems in practice. Based on this route, we carry out the program connotation construction and student cultivation mode construction of Robot Engineering.

This course model breaks the pyramidal structure and adopts a very different curriculum design strategy. In the course group design, the courses and teaching contents of each semester are centered on a larger theme, including the two parts of the lecture and project. This design classifies courses into two categories: one is a general lecture designed to provide students with more basic theories acting as a scaffolding. The other is a hands-on practice that revolves around the semester theme and requires knowledge that is directly relevant to the project.

Students

Though BSc. Programme in RE has more practical courses than traditional ones in NEU. The PBL mode is fresh and unfamiliar for the students. They have no idea of basic principles of PBL and experience on PBL implementation.

After elementary, secondary education in the traditional mode, most Chinese students are used to passive learning and obtaining the knowledge from lectures in large-scale classrooms.

Also, in the current stage of Chinese higher education, students are more concerned about scores beyond the cultivation of self-innovative practical ability. It's important to give a clear and measurable evaluation criteria to them.

Teachers

Course groups are designed to introduce intelligent robotics involving knowledge and skills. The course groups cover required and elective courses in different levels from different disciplines. In one semester, several courses that contents are related closely (project-orientated) can be aligned and share the same PBL project.

For the limited teachers and expectable expanded enrollment of undergraduate students of BSc. Programme in RE in the near future, researchers and engineers from SIA and SIASUN Robot with latest technologies and rich practical experiences can be selected as facilitators, which is an alternative way to solve the shortage of teachers.

Learning Goals

Robotics is a typical multidisciplinary and cutting-edge high-tech emerging engineering discipline covering cutting-edge fields such as mechanics, electronics, computers, automation, artificial intelligence, biomedicine, and cognitive science. The goal of robot engineering is to adapt to the international science and technology frontier and national intelligent manufacturing strategy development needs, to teach the basic theories and practical knowledge of robot engineering, pay attention to humanities and social science quality cultivation, social responsibility and

Table 2. The learning goals of the course groups in BSc. Programme in RE

Knowledge	• Get knowledge of and insight into fundamental theories, methods, tools and practical subjects within the fields of robot engineering • Master the mathematical and programming technical foundations related to robot engineering • Get knowledge of the electrical and electronics, mechanical systems, electromechanical systems, software and robotic manipulators, automation and artificial intelligence. • Get knowledge of sensors and actuators relevant for robotics
Skills	• Be able to utilize the latest scientific methods, tools, and techniques to analyze and solve complex problems in the fields of robotics • Be able to evaluate and compare theoretical and practical problems, furthermore, describe and select relevant solution strategies • Can implement such solution strategies and evaluate their success in a systematic manner • Can present problems and solution strategies within the fields of robotics both in writing and orally, to specialists as well as non-specialists in the fields, including external parties, users, and so on.
Competencies	• Can handle complex situations that arise in research and/or development-related environments, such as university studies and/or engineering workplaces. • Can develop and test robotics hardware and software and integrate them into a broader systems-oriented context • Can work independently as well as in collaboration with others, both within and across technical fields, in an efficient and professional manner • Can identify own learning needs and structure own learning in a various learning environment

engineering professional ethics education, training in the field of robotics practice skills, cultivate innovative spirit and practical ability, and cultivate high-quality compound professionals with international vision.

Contents

A set of different learning contents are necessary to support the learning goals of RE. For technical knowledge, teachers can provide learning materials (references and courseware) to students in the classroom. Meanwhile, authoritative websites such as MOOC provide qualified resources for students to conduce self-directed learning. To learn about methodologies, methods, and tools in the robotics field, students can refer to reference books of the corresponding course.

For different courses, teachers will ask the students to submit different kinds of reports concerning metacognition, methodologies, skills, technical details and so on. The teachers could also summarize these reports to help future students develop their metacognitive skills.

Teaching and Learning Methods

Both lectures and projects will be used in most of the courses in RE. In one semester, several courses with content closely related are aligned and share a common project. For example, in semester 4, the project theme is "Robot Motion Control". The lectures under this theme include: digital circuits, analog circuits, programming language and so on. In semester 5, the project theme is "Basic Principles in Robotics", the lecturer under this theme include: fundamental robot principle, robot mechatronics and so on.

Another important component of the PBL model of robot engineering is the project, which is placed in the fourth, fifth, sixth and seventh semesters, requiring students to choose a question independently, to carry out problem-based learning and inquiry, in groups (usually 4~6 students) discuss and exercise for the unit and complete the project report. The first three semesters of the title mini-project are designed to give students an initial experience of trying and conducting project work, and another project called robotics capstone at the end of the specified course before the graduation design begins.

The design of multiple lectures combining with one project can cover most of the learning goals of RE. The most important thing for this design is to find out the internal connections between courses and make a systematic arrangement of the whole courses in RE programme according to the learning goal and assessment.

Assessment

The assessment of robot engineering completes the learning goals. The assessment is divided into process assessment and content assessment (Tai & Yuen, 2007).

Process assessment which contains Self Reflection, Peer's Evaluation and Task Completion Reports allowed the students in identifying one's progress and deficiencies, making them independent learners. Content assessment served as a measuring tool to evaluate students' knowledge gain, together with the ability to understand and apply knowledge learned from this PBL setting. And lastly, portfolio assessment enabled students to not only see the final learning outcome but to track their learning progress, achievement, and growth with the documentation done in various forms.

REFERENCES

Albanese, M. A., & Mitchell, S. (1992). Problem-based learning: A review of the literature on its outcomes and implementation issues. *Academic Medicine*, *68*(1), 52–81. doi:10.1097/00001888-199301000-00012 PMID:8447896

Algreen-Ussing, H., & Fruensgaard, N. O. (1990). *Metode i Projektarbejde*. Aalborg University Press.

Barrows, H. S. (1986). A taxonomy of problem-based learning methods. *Medical Education*, *20*(6), 481486. doi:10.1111/j.1365-2923.1986.tb01386.x PMID:3796328

Barrows, H. S., & Tamblyn, R. M. (1980). *Problem-Based Learning: An Approach to Medical Education*. New York: Springer.

Berthelsen, J., Illeris, K., & Poulsen, S. C. (1977). *Projektarbejde*. København: Borgen.

Boud, D., & Feletti, G. (1991). *The Challenge of Problem-based Learning*. London: Kogan Page. Fraenkel, G. J. (1978). *McMaster Revisited. British Medical Journal*, *2*, 1072–1076.

Elamvazuthi, I., Lee, H. J., Ng, J. C., Song, H. L., Tiong, Y. X., Parimi, A. M., & Swain, A. K. (2015). Implementation of a New Engineering Approach for Undergraduate Control System Curriculum using a Robotic System. *Procedia Computer Science*, *76*, 34–39. doi:10.1016/j.procs.2015.12.272

Graaff, E. de, & Bouhuijs, P. A. J. (Eds.). (1993). *Implementation of problem-based learning in higher education*. Amsterdam: Thesis Publishers.

Graaff, E. de, & Kolmos, A. (2003). Characteristics of problem-based learning. *International Journal of Engineering Education*, *5*(19), 657–662.

Heitmann, G. (1993). Project study and project organised curricula: a historical review of its intentions. *Project-organized curricula in engineering education, Proceedings of a SEFI-seminar held 5th*.

Holten-Andersen, C., Schnack, K., & Wahlgren, B. (1983). *Invitation til projektarbejde*. Gyldendals pædagogiske bibliotek.

Jansen, T., & van Kammen, A.-R. (1976). *Projektonderwijs: afleren en aanleren* [Project education: un-learning and re-learning]. Purmerend: Muusses.

Kaufman, A. (Ed.). (1985). *Implementing Problem-based Medical Education. Lessons from Successful Innovations.* New York: Springer Publishing.

Kolb, D. A. (1984). *Experiental Learning. Experience as the source of learning and development.* Prentice Hall.

Kolmos, A. (1996). Reflections on Project Work and Problem-based Learning. *European Journal of Engineering Education, 2*(21).

Kolmos, A., Fink, F. K., & Krogh, L. (Eds.). (2004). The Aalborg PBL Model – Progress, Diversity and Challenges. Aalborg: Aalborg University Press.

Kolmos, A., & de Graaff, E. (2007). Process of changing to PBL. In E. de Graaff & A. Kolmos (Eds.), *Management of change: implementation of problem-based and project-based learning in engineering* (pp. 31–43). Rotterdam: Sense Publishers.

Li, H., & Du, X. (2018). *Educational Design for Future: Analysis of the Curriculum Model and Education Idea of Problem Based Learning at Aalborg University in Denmark. Chongqing Higher Education Research.*

Little, P., Ostwald, M., & Ryan, G. (Eds.). (1995). Research & Development in Problem Based Learning (Vol. 3). PROBLARC, University of Newcastle.

Negt, O. (1968). *Soziologische Phantasie und exemplarisches Lernen.* Frankfurt am Main: Zur Theorie der Arbeiterbildung.

Negt, O., & Kluge, A. (1972). Öffentlichkeit und Erfahrung: Zur Organisationsanalyse von bürgerlicher und proletarischer Öffentlichkeit. Frankfurt am Main: Academic Press.

Neufeld, V., & Barrows, H. S. (1974). The McMaster Philosophy: An approach to medical education. *Journal of Medical Education, 49*, 1040–1050. PMID:4444006

Norman, G., & Schmidt, H. G. (1992). The psychological basis of problem-based learning: A review of the evidence. *Academic Medicine, 67*(9), 557–565. doi:10.1097/00001888-199209000-00002 PMID:1520409

Norman, G. R. (1986). Problem-solving skills, Solving problems and problem-based learning. *Medical Education, 22*(4), 279–286. doi:10.1111/j.1365-2923.1988.tb00754.x PMID:3050382

Ostwald, M., & Kingsland, A. (Eds.). (1994). Research & Development in Problem Based Learning (Vol. 2). PROBLARC, University of Newcastle.

Post, G. J., & Graaff, E. de, & Drop, M. J. (1988). Efficiency of a Primary-Care Curriculum. *Annals of Community-Oriented Medical Education*, *1*, 25–31.

Prince, M., & Felder, R. (2006). Inductive Teaching and Learning Methods: Definitions, Comparisons, and Research Bases. *Journal of Engineering Education*, *2*(95).

Rogers, C. (1961). *On becoming a person*. Boston: Houghton Mifflin.

Ryan, G. (Ed.). (1993). Research & Development in Problem Based Learning (Vol. 1). PROBLARC, University of Newcastle.

Savin-Baden, M. (2000). *Problem-based Learning in Higher Education: Untold Stories*. Buckingham, UK: SRHE and Open University Press.

Schmidt, H. G. (1983). Problem-based learning: Rationale and description. *Medical Education*, *17*(1), 1116. doi:10.1111/j.1365-2923.1983.tb01086.x PMID:6823214

Schmidt, H. G. (1993). Foundations of problem-based learning: Some explanatory notes. *Medical Education*, *27*(5), 422–432. doi:10.1111/j.1365-2923.1993.tb00296.x PMID:8208146

Spaulding, W. P. (1969). The Undergraduate Medical Curriculum Model: McMaster University. *Canadian Medical Association Journal*, *100*, 659–664. PMID:5776441

Tai, G. X.-L., & Yuen, M. C. (2007). Authentic assessment strategies in problem based learning. Proceedings of Ascilite Singapore, 983-993.

Van Woerden, W. M. (1991). *Het Projectonderwijs onderzocht* [Research into the project method of teaching] (Thesis). Enschede: University of Technology Twente.

Wilkerson, L., & Gijselaers, W. H. (Eds.). (1996). *Bringing Problem-Based Learning to Higher Education: Theory and Practice*. San Francisco: Jossey-Bass Publishers.

Zhong, D. (2017). *Connotations and Actions for Establishing the Emerging Engineering Education*. Research in Higher Education of Engineering.

Chapter 7

An Elective Course–Based Model for the Change of Traditional Engineering Curriculum Towards PBL in a Chinese University

Xufang Zhang
Northeastern University, China

ABSTRACT

The chapter presents two PBL models for the change of traditional engineering curriculum based on traditional courses across colleges at the Northeastern University in China. A particular focus of the PBL model design is about interdisciplinarity. In this regard, the E2-iPBL model is developed based on general and major elective courses offered across many disciplines, whereas the JD-iPBL model is considered to develop PBL courses by further introducing compulsory major courses for a joint-degree training program. For practical implementations within the traditional engineering curriculum background, the change of the teacher's role for student-centered constructive learning is briefly summarized. Possible realizations and simple cases are illustrated. Finally, a comparative study of the E2-iPBL and JD-iPBL models is outlined.

DOI: 10.4018/978-1-5225-9961-6.ch007

BASIC THEORIES ABOUT THE PBL

This PBL course at AUU is organized with nine thematic workshops and many observational activities of lectures and examinations in the Civil Engineering department of the Aalborg University. At first, the PBL theory courses mainly focus on PBL model, approaches, the design of PBL problem, collaboration and project management techniques, the course and curriculum design, facilitation and teacher roles in the PBL, assessment for different learning goals, and the management of change at course and institutional levels. Therefore, by providing basic knowledge and understand of student-centered learning methodologies and PBL related theories, techniques and required skills, learning goals of the PBL course are to: (a) Understand active learning methodologies, in particular problem- and project-based learning; (b) Understand curriculum design and management; (c) Understand and experience PBL as a learning process and the learning of PBL skills; (d) plan an implementation of the designed curriculum/course change.

A teaching portfolio is a tool for personal reflection and development for professional teaching skills. The reflection is normally following the Kolb's cycle "experience- reflect - generalize - actively experiment – new experience". Materials within the teaching portfolio are based on personal teaching practices and experiences that are towards teaching professional development. Especially, key elements in the Kolb's cycle can be realized as (a) Experience: what have been experiencing in teaching. Related materials are the teaching philosophy, teaching material, and teaching strategies; (b) Reflect is used to answer the questions of what is good about your teaching, what the main challenges, which teaching strategies work and don't work; (c) Generalize refers to why things go as they did, and why challenges are challenges, why did the strategies work and did not work; (d) In the stage of the active experiment, you need to answer questions of: what you can use to improve your teaching, what can you use to design your teaching implementation, and how can it be used and when.

Generally, basic theories about learning consist of the behaviorism, the cognitivism, and social constructivism learning theories. In the behaviorism leaning, all things that organisms do including acting, thinking and feeling are regarded as behaviors. To change behaviors, the environments are modified, or behavioral patterns are changed. In this regard, the behaviorism assumes that a learner is essentially passive, responding to environmental stimuli. Besides, a learner starts with a clean slate, and behavior is shaped by positive and negative reinforcement. Therefore, reinforcement, positive or negative, increases the possibility of an event happening again, whereas punishment, both positive and negative, decreases the possibility of an event happening again.

The constructivism is a philosophical position that views knowledge as the outcome of experience mediated by one's own prior knowledge and the experience of others. Under this theory, teachers must help the learner get to his or her understanding of content. As teachers, we must take on more of a facilitator's role than that of a teacher. A comparison for behaviorism, cognitivism and constructivism learning theories is listed in Table 1.

The PBL is shorted for problem-based learning and project-based learning. It is an active and student-centered learning method, and students learn by identifying and solving real problems. There are four stages that bridge instructor-centered and student-centered learnings: (a) Make the lecture active; (b) informal group activities; (c) structured team activities; (d) problem drive the learning. Each of them can be

Table 1. Comparative studies of behaviorism, cognitivism, and constructivism learning theories

	Behaviorism	**Cognitivism**	**Constructivism**
Focus	what the learner does; proper response to a given stimulus (observable)	how the learner organizes new information within the preexisting schema (internal)	how the learner interprets the new information and applies to their reality (meaning constantly evolves)
Learner	reactive	proactive	proactive
Type of learning	basic definitions and explanation of concepts; generalization, recall	higher-level reasoning and information processing; emphasis on memory, organization	higher-level problem solving and critical analysis; emphasis on real-word scenarios
Examples	pre-tests, comprehension checks; facilitate learning through assessments that allow practice, repetition	corrective feedback, learning strategies like analogy, metaphor, concept mapping; remove irrelevant information	apprenticeships, clinics, collaborative learning; encourage the application of new knowledge in a variety of contexts and perspectives

(From Prof. Chunfang Zhou and Aida Guerra slides on Workshop 2)

named as active learning, collaborative learning, cooperative learning and problem, and project-based learning. Besides, there are two ways to organize learning around problems: (a) Case-based learning (McMaster and Maastricht Models as examples), (b) Project-based learning (Aalborg Model as an example)

Then, through an exercise excises on comparing different PBL models, the duration of the PBL activities is one semester, and the type of activity is project organized. The degree of interdisciplinarity is high, and the degree of contextualization is variable. The size of a student's group is 4-7 students, and teachers should be expert on the PBL theme. Finally, the learning space is available for each PBL group. Besides, projects and problems of the AUU PBL model come from industry, non-profit organizations, teachers and students. Students select them, and its definitions are either well or ill-defined. The output of the PBL course is a written report that needs an oral and group-based exam for individual grades.

Also, from the reading material, I know that there are following seven important elements in a curriculum: objectives and knowledge, types of problems and projects, progression and size, students' learning, academic staff and facilitation, space and organization and, finally, assessment and evaluation. All these elements are elementary in a curriculum, and all elements must be aligned. The principle of alignment is based on a holistic understanding. If there is a change in one element it will effect change in all the other elements as well.

There is a five-step model to do problem design: (a) relating to a theme; (b) mapping the problem field; (c) narrowing down the problems; (d) problem analysis; (e) problem formulation. The problem can come from (a) a specified request from

Table 2. The McMaster and Aalborg PBL models

McMaster Model	Aalborg Model
Problems form the focus and stimulus for learning.	Problem orientation
Problems are the vehicle for the development of problem-solving skills.	Interdisciplinary.
New information is acquired through self-directed learning.	Exemplary learning
Student-centered	Participant-directed
Small student groups	Teams or group work
Teachers are facilitators/ guides (Barrows, 1996)	

(from Prof. Anette Kolmos slides)

a client; (b) a conclusion from a scientific study and a call for further research; (c) an observation of a problem that calls for problem analysis. And the problem can be something, as usual, the tension between the desired and actual state, paradox, and contradiction, i.e., statements/relations that mutually exclude each other. Variables of a problem included: structured vs. ill-structured, abstract vs. contextual, simple vs. complex, stable vs. dynamic, domain-specific vs. interdisciplinary. Additionally, different types of problems require different strategies for problem analysis. In this regard, the bottom-up analysis from practice to technology based on WHO and WHY questions can deal with a problem initiated by an unsatisfactory situation. The top-down analysis from technology to practice based on WHAT-IF questions might be useful to initiate un-utilized potentials. But the theoretical analysis is required to predict technology for some unknown Impacts. The analysis process can be gradually narrowed down form the subject area, the problem area and finally for problem formulation. For an evaluation of the problem design process, we can ask questions of: (a) what was challenging? (b) what caught your full attention? (c) How can we use this experience in our educational context? etc.

While a group member talks about an arbitrary subject of importance, the active listening suggests to focus on the other, be curious, be empathetic, let the other speak, and ask additional questions, but don't judge or evaluate, state your own opinion, give ideas or good advice, and talk about yourself. At some points, convey how we feel about the message on your behalf and on behalf of the other. This starts at an appropriate level for you. The starting words can be: It makes me curious…, I get excited about…, It makes me want to contribute…, I like it that…, I get puzzled…, I get kind of upset…, It annoys me that…, and how come…, etc. Besides, there are some techniques and training regarding time management, and how to use a tool to plan schedules.

In the PBL course design, Bloom's taxonomy for formulating learning objectives/outcomes which have to be combined with learning methodologies and assessment. At first, we discussed the John Biggs's constructive alignments among the learning outcome, teaching and learning methods, and the assessment. If we remain the learning outcome as "to become innovative engineers" based on "traditional lecturing system", and the assessment method is based on individual written exams. In the case, the learning outcome is not supported by the teaching and learning methods. Then the question would be what kind of teaching, learning and assessment methods can achieve the learning goal for innovative engineers. Here are the knowledge, skill and competence: Knowledge: "I know …"; Skills: "I do, I can …"; Competence: "I have the potential to do …" Here below are boom's taxonomy:

Table 3 summarizes the Bloom's taxonomy, and a revised taxonomy is also discussed in the workshop. In the revised taxonomy, the noun words have been revised as remembering, understanding, applying, analyzing, evaluating and creating, because verbs describe actions, nouns do not. Also, reorganized categories include: knowledge is the product/outcome of thinking (inappropriate to describe a category of thinking) now remembering, and comprehension now understanding; synthesis now creating to better reflect nature of thinking described by each category.

For a change to PBL, a single course strategy can be applied. In this regard, courses offered in each semester can be realized by a part of traditional lectures and some PBL/active learning course. Even though the PBL is easily for a change, but it is uncoordinated and nonstable. Then, one can resort to the integration strategy by mapping strategy of knowledge, skills, and competences, defining additional learning outcomes (employability and sustainability) and integration of company projects. Therefore, the integration strategy illustrated in Figure 1 is recommended. The learning goals on entrepreneurship, project management, oral communication, and sustainability can be gradually realized by several PBL courses through semesters.

The PBL model requires to the teacher can be effectively transformed from a course lecture to facilitator in the project stage because modern engineering problems are increasingly complex that cannot be defined and solved by knowledge and techniques in a single discipline. This makes the learning process is interdisciplinary in terms of context, methodology, and related knowledge. Many factors such as unclear communication, personal characteristics, uncertainty, and doubts, etc. cause barriers

Table 3. Bloom's taxonomy

Knowledge	Presentation of topics
Comprehension	Use what has been learned – but not relating to other domains or topics
Application	Use general ideas, theories, principles, procedures, and methods in concrete situations
Analysis	Breaking down relations between single topics and subjects in a complex problem
Synthesis	Bringing together a result of the analyses to a new pattern–new pattern
Evaluation	Judgment about the value of materials or methods for a given purpose

(from Prof. Anette Kolmos slides on Workshop 6)

Figure 1. Integration strategy for a change to PBL
(From Prof. Anette Kolmos slides on Workshop 6)

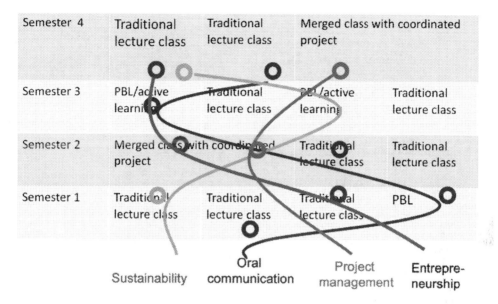

for sharing information within a student group. Also, no one has a global picture regarding the interdisciplinary project, and thus collaborative learning and effective communication are extremely essential in the interdisciplinary course. Therefore, in the interdisciplinary PBL project, teachers are required to be an effective facilitator to increase trust among group members and decrease disorder by encouraging dialogue between disagrees, encouraging positive emotional beliefs, and delivering high-quality feedbacks to students learning performance.

Through the workshop, I started to understand the formative and summative assessments in a PBL environment. Formative and peer assessment have an impact on motivation. The assessment is suggested to make some transfer, (a) from assessing to learn what students do not know to learn what students understand; (b) from using results to calculate grades to use assessment results to inform instruction; (c) from end-of-term assessments by teachers to students engaged in ongoing assessment of their work and others; (d) from judgmental feedback that may harm student motivation to descriptive feedback that empowers and motivates students. The formative assessment can initiate students in self-reflection and peer reflection by shared writing shared discussion and peer feedback. Therefore, the student-centered leaning approach focusing on interdisciplinary knowledge, PBL competences needs group-based formative assessment.

Table 4. Formative and Summative assessments

	Assessment for Learning	**Assessment of Learning**
Who	Teachers, students, and parents are the primary users	Teachers, principals, supervisors, program planners, and policy makers are the primary users
When	During learning	After learning
Use	Used to provide information on what and how to improve achievement	Used to certify student competence
Use	Used by teachers to identify and respond to student needs	Used to rank and sort students
Purpose	Improve learning	document achievement of standards
Motivation	Primary motivator: belief that success is achievable	Primary motivator: the threat of punishment, the promise of reward
Duration	Continuous	At the end
Examples	Peer assessment, using rubrics with students, descriptive feedback	final exams, placement tests, state assessments, unit tests

(from Prof. Anette Kolmos slides on Workshop 8)

The successful and sustainable changes are embedded into a redesigned, coherent and interconnected curriculum. And the change can be realized in various levels: (a) developing individual teachers, i.e., developing teachers' practice, thinking, motivation, and the ability to self-improve; (b) developing groups of teachers, i.e., developing communities of practices, the leadership of teaching, and the learning environment; (c) developing the institution, i.e. Change the flexibility teaching room booking system, developing facilities that support teaching, developing educational policies, an institutional learning and teaching strategy, aligning comments within the learning and teaching strategy, and developing an institutional pedagogy. To achieve, the topic of devising a PBL training workshop after returning to NEU was discussed in the workshop. The PBL workshop can be given at serval afternoons distributed across several weeks, which gives participants enough time within two workshops for self-reflection. Topics of the PBL workshop might cover the PBL model, the problem design, PBL curriculum development, facilitation, and assessment. Within each workshop, some assignments, group works, and case observations will be planned to achieve learning goals of the workshop on knowing and practicing the PBL at NEU.

REFLECTIONS ON THE PBL

My philosophy of teaching is entailed as following statements that provide fundamental structures of my beliefs on teaching and learning. At first, learning is a process through which we adapt to the world around us. It is not the result of something done for us but something we do for ourselves. The most crucial step in learning, therefore, is choosing to make an effort. I always have high expectations for students and insist on hard working. When students are putting their best efforts into class, I always give them all extra help and time. It follows that although as teachers we cannot make our students learn, we can make it possible and more comfortable for them to do so. We can either ignite or extinguish students' curiosity and readiness to learn, depending upon the attitudes we project in and out of our classrooms.

Secondly, teaching and learning are cooperative actions. Learner-Oriented teaching promotes learning is both purposeful and enduring. As a teacher, there is the responsibility to know who learners are, what kinds of knowledge and experience they bring to class, and what they want to achieve so that teacher can leave enough rooms to accommodate emerging topics. Teachers who demonstrate curiosity and passion about a subject area motivate students to learn. In this regard, student-centered learning strategies, e.g., case-based learning, the problem and project-based learning can stimulate intellectual argumentation and cooperation. I, therefore, consider training in critical thinking as an essential part of preparing students for personal and occupational challenges they would soon come to experience in society.

Finally, teaching and research can be integrated components. Research contributes to teaching by supplying up-to-date information and experiences to share with students. Reading discipline-specific journals and visiting classes of other instructors continuously produce new ideas. Teaching, in turn, provides contextual questions for researches. Research is, therefore, how I attain renewal and growth.

Therefore, the teacher's role is, or a good teacher should be able to: (1) Explain students the importance and benefit of learning some knowledge or skills to motivate their interests and reduce their uncertainty in the beginning, in the meantime it is also better to attract their curiosity to learn more. (2) Connect teaching to practice, development and tendencies in real life. Teaching related to research projects or real-life problems is much helpful for motivating students and explaining them the point of learning the subject, which needs experiences to do. At this moment, my performance of lecturing is limited by my experience of doing research projects and knowledge of practical issues. I will keep in mind to collect this kind of experience and materials so that I can freely link theory to practical problems during lectures.

(3) Use proper teaching method according to different knowledge, e.g., some math-related problems, teach students to understand by visualizing, relating the problem to practice. (4) Teach how to learn based on personal experience, e.g., tips and experiences about math and structural dynamic problems. (5) Share a better way of solving problems, and raise questions and discussions to encourage them to think and learn more. (3) Inspire thinking about possible future development, and teach students how to communicate with peers for new knowledge

First of all, it is important to build up a good cooperative relationship between PBL supervisor and students. Students feel free to discuss and express their own opinion, and able to argue for their choices and decisions. Use 'small talk' to start the supervision meeting is an efficient way to reduce the distance between students and supervisor, and to build a relaxed learning environment. The PBL supervisor is necessary to have a certain level of project management skills. I would like to clarify the responsibility of both parties and discuss the expectation to each other in the very beginning of the project. It is important to reach an agreement on: the frequency and duration of supervision meeting; what students need to prepare for the meeting; what written material to send to the supervisor and when to send; and how to document the meeting. This kind of agreement should serve as a guideline through the entire project procedure. In the early phase, both supervisor and students must be clear what the desired learning outcome is and why they choose such a method to promote the aims of the curriculum. It is also important to monitor regularly how well the project is achieving the learning outcomes during the project.

Secondly, I expect students to obtain not only the learning skill but also a kind of research skill, especially for the students doing their master thesis. In this regard, I am thinking to introduce them research techniques and methods and to build a link between learning and research. For example, to do a literature review is a critical step when preparing or conducting a master thesis. However, I could see a large group of students' regard literature review as a summary of articles. It is important to let them aware it is not only a process of searching for information and summarizing but also an evaluation and problem formulation process.

When students ask the question in the form of 'what do you think we should do?' My first reaction was to give advice or answer based on my own experience or opinion. However, there are four types of open questions: clarifying the question, examining the question, challenging question and evaluating the question. A very common question I have been asked in the structural dynamic course was 'how should we reduce daily vibrating noise?'. The supervision conversion starts in phase 1, which need to clarify students' need and expectation. For example, 'what expectation you would like to achieve by reducing noise?'. The second phase need to reach a deeper level to uncover the students' knowledge and understanding 'what principle you could implement in the system? How does a structural parameter characteristic the system vibration?'. The third phase is to create greater insight by asking challenging questions. For example, 'what is the consequence of using a passive absorber to reduce the noise?' The last phase is to ask student summarize what they have learned and what needs further work. For example, 'do you get a clear picture of how to design a vibration absorber? what should we follow-up in the next meeting?'

Although I have been involved in the PBL learning environment at AAU for six months, I still need to continuously adjust my 'inertia thinking' from the teacher-centered education approach to the student-centered one. Remember that students take control of most aspects of learning tasks in the PBL model for planning PBL meeting, sending agenda and planning the questions to discuss. Therefore, I am planned to improve my competences in many ways: (a) to know different teaching methods and how to use them properly in classes; (b) to show students the purpose of what they are going to learn and how it is related to the real world, which I think is very important to motivate students; (c) to structure lectures to make it easy to be understood; (d) to adjust the project topic based on students research interests, and (e) to guide the students without leading them and interfering their decision too much.

In general, there is a good correlation between my teaching activities and the research areas I work with. I finished my PhD study which I defended in 2013 with the topic of structural reliability. I am still working in the area and always find some interesting points from the literature and share them to students in teaching and supervision. I have already supervised several master students in the field, and I think I will continue doing that in the future. In the meantime, I have also been involved in several projects about design optimization under the uncertainty. It is a very good research topic for students to do as master thesis, and outcome of related projects will add more examples and materials to the course of Structural Dynamics and Numerical methods for structural reliability analysis.

Additionally, I am planning to develop a PBL course with hybrid topics on structural dynamics and reliability methods. Through the course, students will know and understand basic principles in structural dynamics and probability theory in engineering, and the ability to further applying numerical methods for vibration analysis and stochastic simulation in research. The basic theory and methods will

Figure 2. Basic elements for developing a PBL course

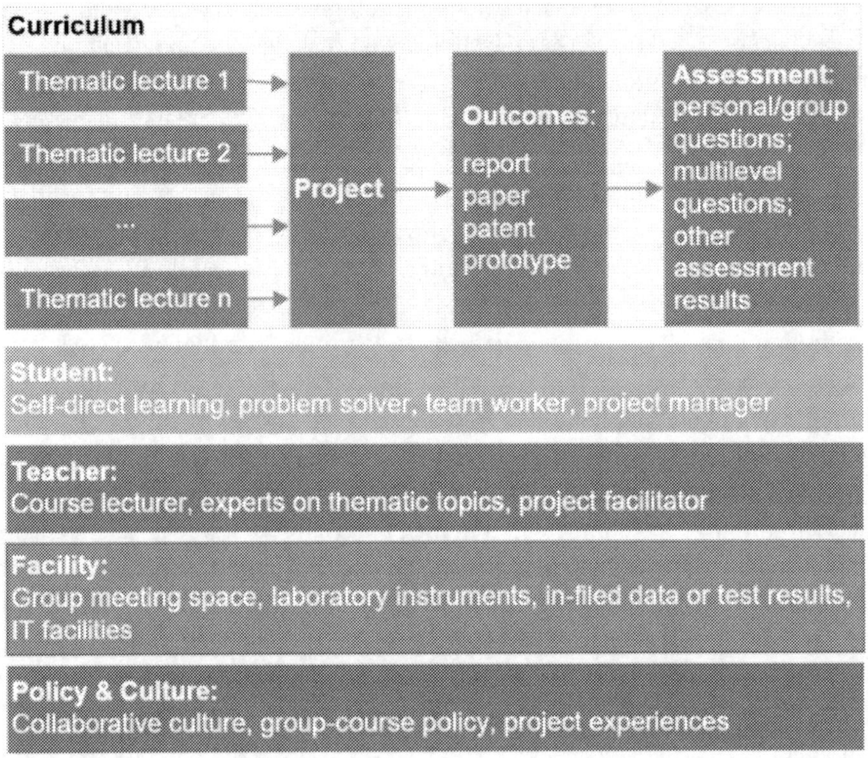

Curriculum

Thematic lecture 1				**Assessment:** personal/group questions; multilevel questions; other assessment results
Thematic lecture 2		**Project**	**Outcomes:** report paper patent prototype	
...				
Thematic lecture n				

Student:
Self-direct learning, problem solver, team worker, project manager

Teacher:
Course lecturer, experts on thematic topics, project facilitator

Facility:
Group meeting space, laboratory instruments, in-filed data or test results, IT facilities

Policy & Culture:
Collaborative culture, group-course policy, project experiences

be delivered in traditional lectures and followed by some assessments and one or two mini-projects. Especially, one mini-project is planned to reinforce the link of two topics, i.e., the structural dynamics and structural reliability methods. Applying course materials for real stochastic vibration problem can be achieved by a project, e.g., Extreme wind loads estimation for wind turbine blades, which can come from the industry or a research project that mimic real engineering problems. During the project stage, teachers will transform from course instructors to project facilitators. Students are grouped into several small groups, and regularly working together for the course project. It is possible that the knowledge provided by lectures cannot cover all aspects of the project. Students are motivated to be initiated as self-directed learners and problem solvers. In this regard, they are gradually trained for many core competencies in terms of group working, effective communication, project management, and lifelong learning.

INTRODUCING PBL TO INTERDISCIPLINARY COURSES ACROSS COLLEGES

As mentioned in previous sections, engineering education has been systemically extended from traditional science and technology to further combine with economic, morals, politics and arts in recent years. The concept of "Return to the real engineering world" and "Build up real engineering project" are becoming more and more popular in many top universities. With the background, general skills and competencies of problem analysis, critical thinking, coordinating, leadership and lifelong learning, etc. are particularly emphasized in modern engineering education, rather than merely focusing on transfer of basic knowledge and skills in the traditional manner. In this regard, the PBL is such a solution to make the transform by motivating group creativities (Zhou, Kolmos, & Nielsen, 2012). And, the concept of interdisciplinarity has become a crucial factor in meeting with the necessary of mega-project in the real engineering world (De Graaf & Kolmos, 2003). To this end, the objective of the section is to figure out applicable interdisciplinary course models for implementing PBL at NEU based on traditional curriculum across several colleges.

The Chinese word "跨学科 (Pronunciation: Kua Xue Ke)" has many translation results in English, e.g., interdisciplinarity, transdisciplinarity, and cross-discipline, etc. In this regard, the interdisciplinarity involves the combining of two or more academic disciplines into one research project. It, therefore, draws knowledge from several fields to create something by thinking across traditional boundaries of academic disciplines (Wikipedia, 2018). Large engineering projects are usually interdisciplinary, as a nuclear power station or mobile phone requires the melding of specialties in many working areas. However, the transdisciplinarity connotes a research strategy that crosses many disciplinary boundaries to create a holistic approach, whereas the cross-discipline refers to explains aspects of one discipline with the knowledge of another. Therefore, the term "interdisciplinarity" will be used in the section to refer to an interdisciplinary background that is emphasized while developing PBL courses across several colleges at NEU.

Indeed, the interdisciplinarity is one of the core characteristics of the PBL model that initiates a student-centered and problem-oriented learning process based on a project to mimic real engineering world (Kolmos & De Graaff, 2014). To achieve this, several thematic lectures are provided to address knowledge and techniques for the PBL project. For instance, a civil engineering PBL project on the design of wind energy structure requires backgrounds and knowledge in disciplines of business, marketing, environmental assessment, electrical engineering, etc. Even though core sections of the PBL project are rested in the civil engineering department, students are motived to learn those knowledge, skills, and technologies across many disciplines, and further coherently apply them for the problem-solving. In this regard, the interdisciplinarity has been originally emphasized in the PBL model at Aalborg University (Kolmos, Fink, & Krogh, 2004).

However, the traditional curriculum in Chinese universities has been deeply engaged in the Soviet model. Even though it was continuously undergone reformations in recent years, the fundamental structure still consists of basic, basic-disciplinary and professional courses that are implemented in a rigid order. In this regard, general basic courses, e.g., mathematics and mechanics will provide foundational knowledge to learn basic-disciplinary courses, which are further prerequisites of high-level professional courses. Besides, learning goals of the traditional curriculum model are related to knowledge and skills separately distributed in all courses provided within the discipline, rather than systemically cultivating communication, cooperation, lifelong learning, leadership and interdisciplinary competencies that are becoming increasingly significant in modern engineering projects.

For the sake of illustration, Figure 3 briefly illustrates course elements of a typical curriculum implemented at NEU, which includes six categorical course groups, e.g. mathematics and physics (MP), humanities and social sciences (HS), free elective courses (FE), specialty major elective courses (SME), specialty major compulsory courses (SMC), practice courses and thesis (PT). In general, those

Figure 3. A typical curriculum model at the Northeastern University in China

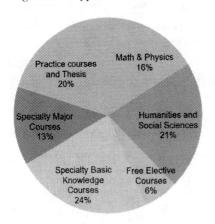

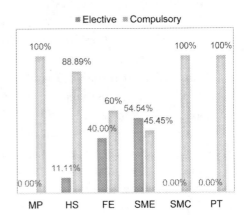

(a) The distribution of course credits   *(b) Elective and compulsory courses*

course groups are successively distributed in totally eight academic semesters at NEU. Figure 4 depicts a typical implementation order of those courses, and they are available to students in a relatively rigid order similar to that of in the conventional Soviet curriculum model. However, some flexibilities are also provided in the NEU curriculum regarding elective courses, i.e., the SME and FE categories as shown in Figure 3(b). Note that those elective courses are normally distributed in 2nd to 7th semesters. In this regard, students already have some knowledge and skills for a PBL project by taking MP, HS and SBK courses. In this regard, an FE and SME courses based interdisciplinary PBL (E2-iPBL) model is first proposed to emphasize the interdisciplinarity of PBL projects across many disciplines at NEU.

Besides the elective course-based model, another option to apply for the PBL at NEU with a particular emphasis on the interdisciplinarity across serval colleges can be realized by including SBK and PT courses. Since the general MP and HS courses are quite similar across most of the engineering disciplines at the Northeastern University, further inclusion of compulsory major courses allows initiating a joint degree program. In this regard, a joint degree-based interdisciplinary PBL (JD-iPBL) model is further presented. Students who interested in the JD-iPBL program can have an opportunity to have an engineering degree major in discipline A and secondarily major in discipline B based on several interdisciplinary PBL projects. Together with the E2-iPBL model, detailed depictions of the two PBL models that emphasize the interdisciplinarity are respectively given as follows.

The E2-iPBL Course Model

As summarized in the forgoing section, the E2-iPBL model initiates interdisciplinary PBL courses based on general, and major elective courses cross several disciplines. To achieve this, a schematic implementation procedure of the PBL model is depicted in Figure 5.

Figure 4. A typical implementation order for various course categories at NEU

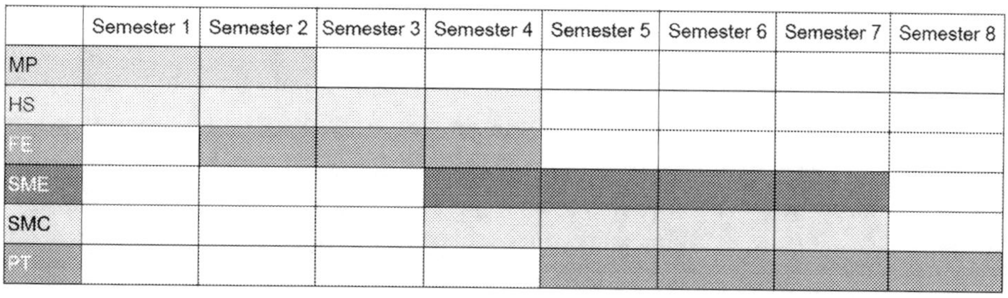

	Semester 1	Semester 2	Semester 3	Semester 4	Semester 5	Semester 6	Semester 7	Semester 8
MP								
HS								
FE								
SME								
SMC								
PT								

Figure 5. A schematic illustration of the E2-iPBL model

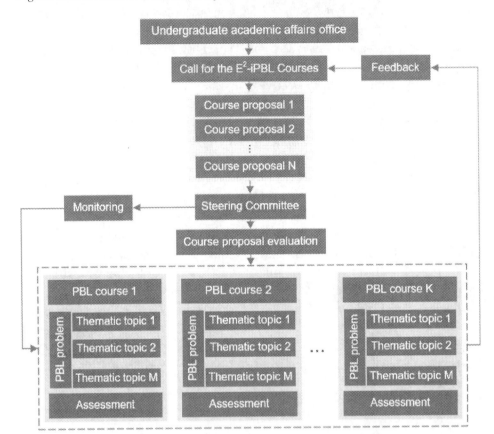

It is seen that the interdisciplinary PBL course development starts from "Call for E2-iPBL Courses" organized by the undergraduate academic affairs office. In the course description, the course objective, general learning goals, e.g., cooperation, interdisciplinary, self-direct learning, and among other skills and competences, the implementation and assessment criteria are provided. With personal or group course proposals, a steering committee (study board) will define the semester theme based on summited course proposals, and subsequently, all submitted courses are grouped into many PBL course groups. Each course group can contain three to five courses that are offered by different disciplines or colleges. Within each PBL course group, all lectures will be given as the traditional ones but with much fewer lecturing hours. Also, teachers within each such PBL course group need to work coherently in preparing for lecture materials to address the semester theme intensively, and about a half of original course hours are left for the final PBL project. Note that the steering committee will monitor all learning actives within each course group. Feedbacks from the committee, students, and teachers will be further to update and revise course objective, learning goals, implementation details of the E2-iPBL mode in the future.

Notably, an implementation of PBL actives within each course group is similar to that of an ordinary PBL model as shown in Figure 6, which starts from preparation and having of a series thematic lectures centering on the PBL course theme. Since the PBL course has been revised based on elective courses in the traditional curriculum, lecturing materials are highly suggested to focus on one topic of the semester theme, rather than superficially covering many topics in the ordinary elective course model. As a result, each course component will cover one or two aspects of the PBL theme,

Figure 6. A realization of each PBL course in the E2-iPBL model

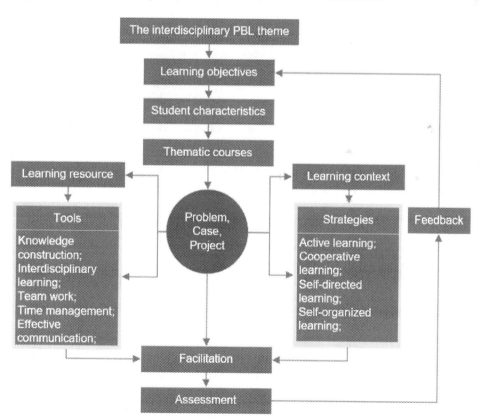

and their connections can be reinforced by some properly design assignments or mini-projects (Blumberg, 2009).

One challenging issue regarding course materials of the presented E2-iPBL model is regarding the laboratory and practice courses. Because all of the practice courses are compulsory in the traditional curriculum, and themes related to engineering disciplines, e.g., mechanical, civil, mining, material science, and automation, etc. require knowledge and skills on laboratory experiments and prototypes. In this regard, course proposals from laboratory technicians and industrial engineers are extremely encouraged to focus on practical sections and experimental topics. In this regard, the interdisciplinarity of the E2-iPBL model is also highlighted by multisource course teachers in terms of university faculties, laboratory technicians, and professional engineers in a company.

The E2-iPBL model is targeted for a student-centered learning process as shown in many other ordinary PBL practices at the Aalborg University (Kolmos & De Graaff, 2014). However, while implementing the model mainly based on traditional curriculum and teaching practices, an issue addressed herein is about teacher's roles, since the faculties normally involved in traditional courses and assessment models for many years might be difficult to be adaptive in the student-centered PBL model. The PBL course model requires teachers to act as different roles across the whole learning processes: (1) the interdisciplinary course designer; (2) thematic topic expert; (3) the provider of modern self-directed learning tools; (4) the creator of student-centered learning context; (5) an effective facilitator and examiner for students' multidimensional competencies.

Once the steering committee approved the PBL theme, teachers and technicians usually from different disciplines are working together to set up learning goals and related details for practical implementation of the interdisciplinary course. In the stage, related concerns for the course design might include: (1) how to select lecture materials to address the interdisciplinary theme; (2) how to organize thematic topics across many disciplines coherently with an equally focus of knowledge depth and their connections. Besides, PBL teachers are required to set up a self-directed learning context based on strategies and skills of active learning, cooperative learning, and self-organized learning, etc. This will further ensure the E2-iPBL course model is student-centered, rather than teacher-centered as traditional courses at NEU.

Even though teachers are also acting as course lecturers at the beginning stage, yet they will quickly transform to facilitators latterly in the project stage (Kolmos, Du, Holgaard, & Jensen, 2008). In this regard, basic tasks of PBL teachers are not limited to lecture providers as their traditional peers, but also responsible to create student-centered and self-directed learning context and provide basic tools for interdisciplinary learning and knowledge construction. This would be a great challenge for ones transformed from the original teacher-centered learning context. Therefore, some professional training on student-centered learning skills, e.g., coaching, questioning, communication, critical thinking, and teamwork, etc. might be required at the beginning of implementing the PBL course model at NEU.

As mentioned in forgoing sections, modern engineering problems are increasingly complex that cannot be defined and solved by knowledge and techniques in a single discipline. This makes the learning process is interdisciplinary in terms of context, methodology, and related knowledge. Especially with students from various disciplines of the university, many factors such as unclear communication, personal characteristics, uncertainty, and doubts, etc. cause barriers for sharing information within a student group. Also, no one has a global picture regarding the interdisciplinary project, and thus collaborative learning and effective communication are extremely essential in the interdisciplinary course. Therefore, in the interdisciplinary PBL project, teachers are required to be an effective facilitator to increase trust among group members and decrease disorder by encouraging dialogue between disagrees, encouraging positive emotional beliefs, and delivering high-quality feedbacks to students learning performance. More details regarding the facilitation in the PBL framework are directed to (Kolmos, Du, Holgaard, & Jensen, 2008).

As mentioned in forgoing sections, modern engineering problems are increasingly complex that cannot be defined and solved by knowledge and techniques in a single discipline. This makes the learning process is interdisciplinary in terms of context, methodology, and related knowledge. Especially with students from various disciplines of the university, many factors such as unclear communication, personal characteristics, uncertainty, and doubts, etc. cause barriers for sharing information within a student group. Also, no one has a global picture regarding the interdisciplinary project, and thus collaborative learning and effective communication are extremely essential in the interdisciplinary course. Therefore, in the interdisciplinary PBL project, teachers are required to be an effective facilitator to increase trust among group members and decrease disorder by encouraging dialogue between disagrees, encouraging positive emotional beliefs, and delivering high-quality feedbacks to students learning performance. More details regarding the facilitation in the PBL framework are directed to (Kolmos, Du, Holgaard, & Jensen, 2008).

In the proposed PBL course model, students acquire interdisciplinary knowledge in a constructive manner (Krathwohl, 2002). In this regard, teachers are responsible for creating a student-centered and problem-oriented learning context, whereas the

PBL problem mimics real engineering problems in reality. Such a scenario would be helpful to recall or simulate experienced knowledge and cases for reflection. On the other hand, the student-centered learning context also motives self-directed learning actives for new knowledge. Therefore, after the procedure of compiling, categorizing and assimilating by learner himself, it is possible to set up a connection between old and new knowledge. Note that the inner loop process depicted in Figure 7 can be automatically realized to produce procedure knowledge. The stage is also noted as meaningful construction. In the second stage, the self-directed learners will actively cooperate and communicate with peers or exchange learning results. During the process, personal knowledge can be updated for a new learning process. More importantly, students will acquire self-organized competences for new knowledge,

Figure 7. An illustration of a student's constructive learning process in the E2-iPBL model

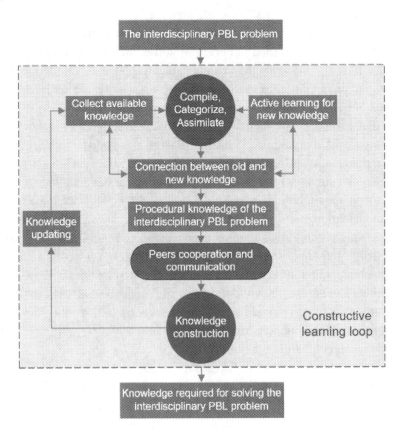

that is, assimilation, cooperation, and communication (Gibbs & Simpson, 2005). In this regard, students are not only having new knowledge and skills required to solve the interdisciplinary problem but also have competencies in terms of how to learn new knowledge by critical thinking, reflection, peer cooperation, and communication, which are also noted as learning goals of the PBL course model.

To summarize, the curriculum changing for PBL can be partially realized by the proposed E2-iPBL model, especially for a university that has implemented a traditional curriculum for many decades. This is because elective courses in the traditional curriculum have relatively large flexibilities in terms of course organization and student assessment. More importantly, each program at NEU has several free elective courses across disciplines. Teachers offering such courses require interdisciplinary experiences in terms of teaching and student assessment. In this regard, the student assessment is largely based on personal course project report in many elective courses. Therefore, from the perspectival of implementation complexity, faculties' teaching background, students, and assessment method, the elective course based interdisciplinary PBL model require minimum changes of the traditional curriculum at NEU. Once a steering committee is set up for course proposal evaluation and implementing process monitoring, the E2-iPBL interdisciplinary course can be realized by organizing of the undergraduate student learning affairs office, and student's assessment can refer to detailed learning goals of the PBL course (De Graaf & Kolmos, 2003).

However, the E2-iPBL interdisciplinary course model has some deficiencies. At first, the PBL course is realized based on elective courses across many disciplines. Backgrounds of students are highly inhomogeneous in terms of academic years and project experiences. It is quite possible to have both junior and senior students in a PBL course, which would be a challenge for thematic teachers to organize lecturing materials. The problem can be possibly extended to the evaluation process, which has to take into account of the factor of the academic year for student performance evaluation because there are divergent learning goals for students in the first and sixth semesters. Secondly, students involved in the E2-iPBL course model are much less than ordinary PBL participants, because the E2-iPBL course model is implemented based on elective courses and a semester at NEU, rather than covering most of the credits and all semesters at AAU. The skills and competences for critical learning, self-directed learning, and cooperative working required to be reinforced by continuously taking several PBL courses. Therefore, for those students are primary rested in traditional curriculum environment, it is highly possible to quickly reverse to conventional learning styles that focus on independent knowledge and skills

(Graham, 2012). To this end, a joint degree based interdisciplinary PBL model that further includes some of the compulsory major courses in two disciplines is further proposed as follows.

The JD-iPBL Course Model

Rather than simply develop an interdisciplinary PBL course based on the elective course categories in the traditional curriculum, the section is further proposing a joint degree-based interdisciplinary PBL (JD-iPBL) model to further include compulsory major courses in another discipline.

To begin with, we consider two engineering disciplines, e.g., mechanical and civil, course elements within the MP and HS categories are almost identical for the two engineering disciplines at NEU. Also, we have already developed a series of interdisciplinary courses based on the E2-iPBL model. In this regard, the common course within two engineering disciplines has been further extended to FE and SME categories. In another word, the course difference of two engineering disciplines at NEU is only limited to compulsory SBK and PT categories. Therefore, with interdisciplinary PBL courses developed based on some compulsory SBK and practical courses, it is possible to develop a joint degree program for a secondary major across the two disciplines.

Figure 8 presents the development of interdisciplinary PBL course models based on various course categories at the NEU. In this regard, the E2-iPBL model was implemented based on elective course categories, whereas the JD-iPBL model is designed to further include compulsory major courses. Besides, to be eligible for a double degree, students within the JD-iPBL model are required to satisfy with graduation requirements for the main Major A and a secondarily in Major B. To achieve this, several PBL courses based on various themes can be developed to bridge several courses cross colleges A and B.

For instance, a civil engineering student is interested in a secondary degree on computational fluid dynamics (CFD) in mechanical engineering, because analysis and design of modern wind turbines require knowledge and skills across of subjects structural engineering in civil and the CFD in mechanical engineering. It is possible to develop a joint degree program to help the student realize interdisciplinary learning interest. For implementation, two steering committees from both of civil and mechanical engineering disciplines are work together to determine which courses in CFD are necessary for the secondary degree. Note that courses considered here includes both of elective and compulsory courses in the FE, SME, SBM and PT

Figure 8. Interdisciplinary PBL course models based on various traditional course categories

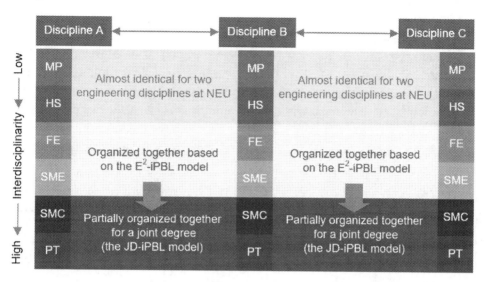

categories. Then, several PBL themes that cover structural engineering and CFD topics are systemically set up. Therefore, the JD-iPBL model offers an opportunity for students who are interested in a joint degree by finishing several properly designed PBL courses cross the two disciplines. Compared to the E2-iPBL model, the PBL theme, thematic courses, and the course organization have been clearly defined in the joint-degree training program, rather than temporally organized by steering and teaching committees in the E2-iPBL course model. Note teaching, and student learning characteristics in the JD-iPBL model are similar to those in the E2-iPBL model.

SUMMARY

To realize the interdisciplinarity based on the traditional curriculum at NEU, two PBL course models are presented in the section, i.e., the E2-iPBL course model and the JD-iPBL course model. The E2-iPBL model was developed based on elective courses across several colleges at NEU to emphasize the interdisciplinarity. In this regard, multidisciplinary teachers are working together to offer a PBL course for students across many disciplines. The JD-iPBL course model is further considered as a possibility to include compulsory courses as developing interdisciplinary PBL courses, and many such interdisciplinary PBL courses are systemized together for a joint-degree training program.

Table 5 compares the proposed E2-iPBL and JD-iPBL models for traditional curriculum change with the PBL concept from aspects of motivation, organizer, duration, related courses, PBL theme, teachers, students, implementation, and interdisciplinary breadth and depth. The E2-iPBL model can realize the interdisciplinarity and PBL with a minimum change of traditional curriculum.

Table 5. A comparative study of the E2-iPBL and JD-iPBL course models

	The E2-iPBL Model	The JD-iPBL Model
Motivation	Realizing the interdisciplinarity and PBL model at NEU with a minimum change of traditional curriculum	Realizing an interdisciplinary and PBL change based on various traditional courses
Organizer	Undergraduate academic affairs office	Colleges
Duration	One semester	The whole training program
Related courses	Elective courses in FE and SME categories	Elective and compulsory courses (FE, SME, SKB, PT)
PBL theme	Will be determined after having PBL courses proposals	Properly defined by study board for a joint-degree training program
Teachers	From various colleges	From two colleges
Students	Highly inhomogeneous (academic years, learning backgrounds, dynamic changes of students and teachers)	Similar backgrounds will have many experiences on PBL project
Implementation	Relatively easy, similar to the general elective or comprehensive course	Complex, need good knowledge on the design of a training program
Interdisciplinary breadth	Across many colleges	Two colleges
Interdisciplinary depth	Superficial or medium	Medium or deep

Besides, administrated by the undergraduate academic affairs office, the E2-iPBL course can be treated as a general elective or comprehensive course since the course is mainly developed based on elective courses, which have relatively large flexibilities in implementation within the current university administrative system. However, it also has some disadvantages. For instance, the E2-iPBL course might cover many university disciplines. It causes students backgrounds are highly inhomogeneous in terms of the academic year, learning goals and dynamic changes across different semesters. Besides, course teachers are normally forming various disciplines and without experiences of working together, which requires high coordination skills. In terms of the Interdisciplinary, the E2-iPBL course can be easily cover many disciplines, yet it might be difficult to go to very deep. In this regard, the JD-iPBL model will systemically have several PBL courses covers only two disciplines. Students in the PBL model can continuously deal with complex interdisciplinary projects.

To summarize, the section presents two PBL models based on traditional courses across colleges at NEU. A particular focus of the PBL model design is about the interdisciplinarity. In this regard, the E2-iPBL model is developed based on general and major elective courses offered across many disciplines, whereas the JD-iPBL model is considered to develop PBL courses by further introducing compulsory major courses for a joint-degree training program. For practical implementations within the traditional curriculum background, the change of teacher's role for student-centered constructive learning is briefly summarized. Possible realizations and simple cases are illustrated. Finally, a comparative study of the E2-iPBL and JD-iPBL models is outlined.

The PBL model proposals for a change of traditional curriculum at NEU are mainly based on six-month learning and observational activities at the Aalborg University. Additionally, the NEU has been deeply engaged in the traditional curriculum model for many decades. Even though some active-learning practices were tentatively realized in some single courses, the transformation from teacher-centered to the student-centered learning context requires continuous reformations at a course level, a program level, and finally for the institutional level. During the process, real teaching and learning data collected from faculties, students, administrative officers, employers and among others are significant for model assessment, validation, and improvement. Besides, many protentional problems in terms of students, teachers, project resources, and IT-based teaching and learning tools, etc. might arise during the learning context transformation process, which might finally devote to an organizational change of the traditional university system. Therefore, thoughtful discussions on how to deal with those changes in different stages of introducing the PBL to NEU are necessary, especially to elaborate on possible solutions and measures based on real data and cases.

FUTURE WORKS

The PBL is an advanced model for engineering education changes at NEU. It is unique characteristics of self-direct, and problem-oriented learning are critical to cultivating modern engineers and leaders. In this regard, a detailed analysis of characteristics of teaching and learning practices at NEU will be further carried out to clarify and justify many PBL course models proposed in the report. Priorities will also be given to practically implement those models within properly selected objectives, e.g., some courses, some classes, and some departments. These practical PBL activities at NEU allow collecting real teaching and learning data from facilities and students engaged in the transforming model. Besides, theoretical studies on course-based, program-based and institutional-based PBL models need further investigations by participially focusing on its combination with traditional teaching and learning practices at NEU. In this way, theoretical researches and teaching actives would joint together to gradually push forwards PBL practices at NEU.

Notably, the promotion and implementation of PBL practices need strong leadership at program and college levels. Besides, cooperation among teachers, technicians and teaching secretaries are necessary gradients for inter-course, inter-program, and inter-college PBL models. Therefore, how to motive many levels of teaching personnel are passionate for the PBL practices needs further investigations. Because a large scale and fundamental change to the PBL based on the traditional curriculum at NEU involves fundamental changes in syllabus, teaching plans, lecture organizations, and students' assessment methods. All those changes require approval of the teaching policy-maker at NEU. Therefore, how to amend related policies and rules to facilitate PBL practices at NEU needs further investigations.

REFERENCES

Blumberg, P. (2009). Maximizing learning through course alignment and experience with different types of knowledge. *Innovative Higher Education, 34*(2), 93–103. doi:10.100710755-009-9095-2

De Graaf, E., & Kolmos, A. (2003). Characteristics of problem-based learning. *International Journal of Engineering Education*, 657–662.

Gibbs, G., & Simpson, C. (2005). *Conditions under which assessment supports students' learning.* Learning and Teaching in Higher Education.

Graham, R. H. (2012). *Achieving excellence in engineering education: the ingredients of successful change.* London: Royal Academy of Engineering.

Kolmos, A., & De Graaff, E. (2014). Problem-based and project-based learning in engineering education. In A. Johri, & B. M. Olds (Eds.), Cambridge handbook of engineering education research (pp. 141-161). Cambridge University Press.

Kolmos, A., Du, X., Holgaard, J. E., & Jensen, L. P. (2008). *Facilitation in a PBL environment.* Aalborg: Center for Engineering Education Research and Development, Aalborg University.

Kolmos, A., Fink, F. K., & Krogh, L. (2004). *The Aalborg PBL model: progress, diversity and challenges.* Aalborg: Aalborg University Press.

Krathwohl, D. R. (2002). A revision of Bloom's taxonomy: An overview. *Theory into Practice, 41*(4), 212–218. doi:10.120715430421tip4104_2

Savin-Baden, M. (2004). Understanding the impact of assessment on students in problem-based learning. *Innovations in Education and Teaching International, 41*(2), 221–233. doi:10.1080/1470329042000208729

Wikipedia. (2018). Retrieved from Wikipedia: https://en.wikipedia.org/wiki/Interdisciplinarity

Zhou, C., Kolmos, A., & Nielsen, J. F. (2012). A problem and project-based learning (PBL) approach to motivate group creativity in engineering education. *International Journal of Engineering Education*, 3–16.

Chapter 8

Experience and Reflection on PBL and Implementation of Interdisciplinary– Level PBL Plan

Jingping Song
Northeastern University, China

ABSTRACT

This chapter introduces the author's own teaching practices, teaching philosophy, and teaching challenges by traditional ways in Northeastern University of China at first. Then it presents the author's experience by participatory learning of PBL in UNESCO center of Aalborg University in Denmark. And the impact and guidance of the course on author's teaching philosophy, challenges, and skills are also given in this chapter. To apply PBL teaching methods, the author proposes future teaching plans with PBL. Moreover, design and implementation of interdisciplinary-level PBL plan is presented. And the implementation plan is expounded by six aspects: students, teaching staff, learning goals, contents, teaching and learning methods, and assessment. Finally, a case is put forward by the implementation plan.

DOI: 10.4018/978-1-5225-9961-6.ch008

INTRODUCTION OF TEACHING PRACTICES, PHILOSOPHY AND CHALLENGES

As the author of this chapter, I have worked in Software College of Northeastern University (NEU) for a long time. There are three undergraduate majors named Software Engineering, Information Security and Digital Media Technology in Software College. Three departments are responsible for the corresponding three majors' teaching work. I used to work in department of Software Engineering and now I am working in department of Information Security. There are about 90 undergraduate students enrol in Information Security major. I am major in Communication and Information System, therefore, I taught courses in the field of communication.

Teaching Practices in NEU

I have taught three theoretical courses and a practical course in NEU. Three theoretical courses are Principle of Communication, Security Technologies of Data Communication and Interface and Communication Technologies. The practical course is Network Program Practice. Software college places great emphasis on practical teaching and students could have corporate training and graduation internship, and each major has five practical courses. But most courses in department of Information Security are theoretical courses. My teaching for a theoretical course usually includes three phases, preparation for teaching, lectures in the front of classroom and assessments. It is shown in figure 1.

Preparation for Teaching

According to teaching requirements of NEU, a teacher needs to prepare syllabus and teaching calendar on the basis of training programme of Information Security major. Syllabus usually includes course basic information, such as course number, course name, teaching hours, credits, evaluation and grading policy, textbooks, reference books, course description and so on. Syllabus also contains connections between

Figure 1. Three phases of my teaching for a course

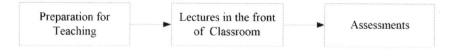

course objectives and graduation requirement, teaching methods and time allocation, course assessment and sustained improving mechanism and so on. Appendix 1 shows a syllabus example of Security Technologies of Data Communication. In other words, course objectives, teaching contents, teaching methods and assessments are required in syllabus. There are 12 graduation requirements in Information Security major and each course objectives in this major need to make connections between course objectives and graduation requirements. Table 1 describes an example of connections between course objectives and graduation requirements. H, M and L represent High, Medium and Low respectively. And they could indicate the extent to which the course objective support corresponding graduation requirement. The objectives of a course are unnecessary to meet all of the graduation requirements, and they only need to meet some of the graduation requirements.

Another required document need to prepare before a course begins is teaching calendar. Teaching calendar is the specific time schedule for teaching contents. In NEU, teachers need to make a teaching calendar for each course at the beginning of a term. An example of teaching calendar for Security Technologies of Data Communication is shown in table 2. From table 2 we can see that the start time of this course is from week 11 to week 13 according NEU calendar in May. And teaching hours for lectures are 32, while practice hours are 8.

Table 1. An example of connections between course objectives and graduation requirements

Graduation Requirements	Course Objectives
1. Knowledge of Engineering	H
2. Problem Analysis	M
3. Solution to Design/Development	
4. Research	
5. Using Modern Tools	L
6. Engineering and Society	
7.Environment and Sustained Development	
8. Professional Ethics	
9. People and Team	
10. Communication	
11. Project Management	
12. Lifelong Learning	

212

Table 2. An example of teaching calendar

Month	Week	Lectures		Homework, Experiment, Test	
		Chapter or Section Name According to Syllabus	**Teaching Hours**	**Teaching Contents**	**Practice Hours**
5	11	Chapter 1 Introduction Chapter 2 Business Information Chapter 3 Distributed Data Processing	8	Information and Communication, Data Communications and Networking for Today's Enterprise, The Nature of Business Information Requirements, Audio, Data, Image, Video, Centralized versus Distributed Processing, Forms of Distributed Data Processing, Distributed Data, Networking Implications of DDP.	4
	12	Chapter 4 Internet History and Architecture Chapter 5 TCP/IP and OSI Chapter 7 Internet-Based Applications Chapter 12 Circuit Switching and Packet Switching Chapter 13 Frame Relay and ATM	14	Internet History, Internet Architecture, Internet Domains, A Simple Protocol Architecture, The TCP/IP Protocol Architecture, Internetworking, The OSI Protocol Architecture, Virtual Private Networks and IP Security, Electronic Mail and SMTP, Web Access and HTTP, Web Security, Internet Telephony and SIP, Switching Techniques, Circuit-Switching Networks, Packet-Switching Networks, Wide Area Networking Alternatives, Frame Relay.	4
	13	Chapter 13 Frame Relay and ATM Chapter 14 Wireless WANs Chapter 18: Computer and Network Security Threats Chapter 19: Computer and Network Security Techniques	10	Asynchronous Transfer Mode (ATM), Cellular Wireless Networks, Cellular Wireless Networks, Multiple Access, Third-Generation Wireless Communication, Satellite Communication, Computer Security Concepts, Threats, Attacks, and Assets, Intruders, Malicious Software Overview, Viruses, Worms, and Bots, Virtual Private Networks and IPSec, SSL and TLS, Wi-Fi Protected Access, Intrusion Detection, Firewalls, Malware Defense	

Syllabus and teaching calendar are required to submit for each course every term in NEU. And teaching calendar could be submitted online now. Technologies of engineering, especially in IT area, update is developing very fast. Therefore, major training programs are usually adjusted slightly annual and a major adjustment will be made every five years in department of Information Security.

Lectures in Classroom

According to the requirements of syllabus and arrangement of teaching calendar, teachers could organize their own teaching contents by using teaching methods in NEU. Different courses have different teaching methods. For Principle of Communication I taught, classroom teaching is the only method since there is no practice in this course. Slices are the main teaching tool and I need mathematical derivation by using a blackboard. While for Security Technologies of Data Communication and Interface and Communication Technologies I taught, there are 8 teaching hours for practice respectively and students need to do experiments in laboratory. And 32 teaching hours are for theoretical lectures. In most of my lectures, I stood in the front of the classroom and gave a monologue by myself. I usually face to 90 to 100 students and the classroom in NEU is generally ladder classroom. A typical ladder classroom is shown in figure 2. Desk and chair could not be flexible placed since the classroom layout could not be changed. Therefore, there is almost none group discussion in my lectures duo to the students' number and classroom layouts.

My classroom teaching is usually combined with NEU's BB online platform. BB online platform is the abbreviation of Blackboard Online Platform. And it provides teachers and students with an online virtual environment for teaching and learning, and becomes a bridge for communication between teachers and students. I could use BB platform to help my classroom teaching. I could make an announcement, a schedule and a task by the platform. And I could also share my slices, send email and publish online tests by this platform. Moreover, I could get feedback from students by this platform. And I could get students' homework online and discuss with students online. Furthermore, I could organize virtual group by the platform and students could learn by group discussion. Finally, assessment and evaluation can also implemented by this platform.

Another teaching tool I used in my class teaching is Rain Class. Rain Class integrates complex information technology into PowerPoint and WeChat, and establishes a bridge between extracurricular preparation and classroom teaching. By using the Rain Class, I can push the pre-study courseware with MOOC videos,

Figure 2. A typical ladder classroom

exercises, and voices to the student's mobile phone, and I could communicate with students in time. In real-time answering and barrage interaction in the classroom, it provides interaction for me and students in traditional classroom teaching. The rain classroom covers every teaching session "before class - class - after class", providing complete three-dimensional data support for teachers and students, personalized reports, automatic task reminders, to help teaching and learning process.

Assessments

My courses assessments are usually include 3 parts, regular performance, in-class tests and final test. I use the hundred-mark system to evaluate the student's final grade. And final test is usually close book test, while in-class test is usually open book test. Figure 3 shows an example of the composition of the student's final grade in course Principle of Communication. Regular performance, in-class tests and final test are account for 10%, 20% and 70% respectively. For Security Technologies of Data Communication and Interface and Communication Technologies, practice score also account for a certain proportion.

Figure 3. An example of the composition of the student's final grade

All of my courses are used required course. In NEU, I need to prepare two different test papers and two standard answers for the final test of required course. Test questions in the two test papers should be different. Before the final test, the vice dean of my college selects one test paper to test. And after the final test, I need to do a test paper analysis report.

After the three phases which is shown in figure 1, a course teaching will go to the end. Students could query their final scores from the teaching achievement management system online. I could get feedback from the students and their comments and evaluation. Supervisor responsible for course evaluation also give the evaluation for a course and I could make some improvement for my course.

Teaching Philosophy

Cultivate Students to Become Useful to Society

One important goal of cultivate college students is make students become useful to the society after they finish studying in universities. When students enter the society, they can contribute to society and even change the world. Therefore, NEU has established 12 graduation requirements for Information Security students which are shown in table 1. My courses could not make my students meet all the 12 graduation requirements and corresponding abilities. But I tried my best to let my students to learn useful knowledges and technologies for society.

Firstly, Information Security major has its own particularity compare to other majors. We need to teach students to benefit to our society instead of do harm to society when they master information security knowledges and technologies. Information security is like a double-edged sword, attack and defence are the eternal theme in this field. I expect all my students to be Honkers, not Hackers. Although we have established legal-related courses, such as the Legal Basis of Information Security and Information Security Ethics, I still need to emphasize the importance of legal and moral in my class.

Moreover, we have already in the information age, science and technology are changing with each passing day, and the cycle of knowledge innovation is shortening. Therefore, as a college lecturer, I need to keep up with the development of the times. And I have to learn new knowledges and technologies day by day and update my teaching contents every year. Only in this way, I could let my students to learn useful knowledges and technologies for society.

Finally, there is an old Chinese saying "The teacher's job is everything for the students, for all the students, for the students' everything." It is means the teacher's job should be for the students, so everything the teacher does is for the students. Regardless whether the student is good or poor, teacher needs to be responsible for the students. And the teacher's job is to be responsible for the student's learning, life, and social aspects. Therefore, teaching should student-oriented, and I need to respect student's diversity and personality development.

Theory Combined With Practical Teaching

Practical teaching is very important in engineering education in NEU. Software College has formed a practical teaching system. Students in Software College have experimental teaching with course and practical courses in their first year and second year. In the third year, students are sent to enterprise to have corporate training lasts about 3 months. And in the last year, students will go to enterprise for graduation internship. But in my courses, most of teaching hours are for theoretical teaching. I could only find examples and cases in real life which could be related to theories I taught. For example, I could tell the concept of bandwidth both in time domain and frequency domain by using cases in real life. I instruct the concept of modulation and demodulation by using the mobile phones. And I could teach digital transmission of analogy signals by using the case of telephone transmission system in real life. Some of theoretical knowledges are not easy to apply in practical teaching. But it is could apply in some simulation software and system. I encouraged students to do simulation experiments after class to help understanding theoretical knowledges. In my opinion, only by combining practice, theoretical teaching can be deeply understood by students.

Research Work Feedback Teaching

Research and teaching are two parts works of college teachers. Research work is more important to teachers in NEU since annual assessment and promotion are closely related to the research work. Most teachers pay more attention to research work and ignoring teaching due to time is limited. If scientific research results could be used in teaching, it will be benefit both for teachers and students. Research work is usually new discoveries, new technologies developments in a certain field. If teachers could relate their research work to their teaching, students could gain the latest knowledges and technologies in a certain field in one hand. In the other hand, teachers could save time to prepare teaching contents.

Teaching Challenges

Strengthen Active Learning

Most students enroll in my courses only care of the final score, not knowledges and technologies. And it is due to the passive learning of students. These students have no interest in courses and they only want to pass the exam. I could not find an effective teaching method to stimulate students' active learning. And it also leads most students are lack of critical thinking. I think I need to learn how to organize, guide, help and promote students' learning. But it is still a challenge for me to let students to learn most effectively and achieve optimal teaching effect.

Enhance Teamwork

Teamwork in this section is not only for students, but also for teachers. Teachers who teach courses in related area could be grouped together for teaching in my department. And there are two groups in my department. One group is related network security courses and the other one is related content security courses. The teaching group should organize teachers to prepare lectures, conduct teaching reform research work, modify training plans and etc. But due to the poor organization and time management, teaching groups is unable to carry out effective work in practice. And teachers usually prepare lectures and conduct teaching reform research work by themselves. It has caused teachers to be unable to understand other teachers' teaching content of the same group or in the same department. It also leads to disconnect between a lecture and the other lectures. The cycle of knowledge innovation is shortening at present. Teachers in the same group could share update knowledges with each other and teamwork could help teachers to prepare lectures. But we could not organize an effective teaching group to face these challenges now.

In my courses, classroom teaching is the main teaching method for theoretical teaching. It is difficult to organize group discussion in classroom due to the students' number and classroom layouts. Therefore, students lack of discussion and teamwork in my classroom teaching. It leads students could not gain ideas from other students and share their own ideas. For this reason, students lack imagination and creativity. They could only learn what I taught to them. Although I use some tools to help my teaching, such as BB platform and Rain Class, the students are still could not have face to face discussion and group work. But teamwork is very important to students, especially after they graduate and work in society. So I should enhance teamwork for students in my teaching.

KNOW AND EXPERIENCE PBL IN AAU UNESCO CENTRE

Thematic Workshops

We have nine thematic workshops in the last four months and these workshops are very helpful to me to understand PBL and how it organizes and works. In workshop 1, I learned what teaching portfolio is and how it works for reflection and development. I understood theories of learning and what a teacher should do in classroom as a facilitator form workshop 2. And I have systematically studied Behaviourism, Cognitivism and Social Constructivism theories. In workshop 3, I learned history and philosophy of PBL, and its learning principles and methods. I also understood he underlying principles of problem based learning, project based learning and problem and project based learning as hybrid models. In workshop 4, I learned how to define a problem and the phases of problem design. In workshop 5, we did lots of excises and Pia tried to let us know core concepts on collaboration and time management. In workshop 6, I learned the concept of Constructive Alignment and curriculum Integration strategy. Anette taught us to how to create alignment in both course and curriculum design. In workshop 7, I learned what facilitation is and how to facilitate. Claus's lecture is impressive, not only vivid examples in slice, but also a teaching case by using LEGO. In workshop 8, I learned the difference between formative assessment and summative assessment. In workshop 9, I learned how to promote PBL in China and what activities need to change in a curriculum in Chinese universities.

Attend Lectures and Project Work

I have enrolled in three graduate students' course which related to my research and teaching area. They are Communication Networks and Ambient Intelligence,

Machine Learning and Wireless Communication Systems. The teaching contents of this course are similar to related courses in China. Some related courses in China are more difficult than the courses in AAU. By participating in these lectures, my deepest feeling is that all courses have a lot of time for students to discuss. The teacher can be interrupted in the lecture and discussed by the students at any time. And after the lecture, teacher could discuss students' project progress with group students. Compare to NEU, the number of students in the class is relatively small in AAU. Thus, teacher could look after every student in some lectures. The classroom layouts in AAU are more flexible than Chinese classroom, and it is easier for group discussion. And attending lectures experience help me understanding how to connect courses to students' project.

In fact, at the same time when I attend thematic workshops and lectures, our 7 teachers from NEU also formed a group to do a project. And we need to submit a research report as a result of the project. We try to use PBL method to do this project and we select research problem is "Exploring Strategies of Employing Problem-Based Learning at Northeastern University in China". We have serval group meetings to discuss our research contents and how to apply PBL in NEU. Then, we have an intra-group division of tasks and my task includes two aspects. One work is design interdisciplinary level PBL in a college of NEU. And another work is how NEU supports changes towards PBL. I realized the importance of group work when I do the project. And it also motivates me to learn more about PBL.

Tracked a Student Group

I have tracked a student group which compose by four undergraduate students in their 5th semester. They are major in Media Technology and the core issue for the 5th semester is Audio-Visual Experiments. The semester is comprised of a 15 ECTS group based project module and three 5 ECTS course modules. Projects will focus on the interplay between technology and some aspects of users and/or an application. Three courses are Computer Graphics Programming, Rendering and Animation Techniques, and Screen Media.

I started to contact with the student group in 13th of September 2018. Then I soon met the four students in the group, Agata Drozdek, Casper Østergaard Thomsen, Michelle Fly and Henrik Rohwer Dahl Gamborg. Their work flows for the project is shown in figure 4. At first, the four students have to go to class in the morning and they usually have group meeting in the afternoon. I have gone to have meeting with them during September and October. They read a lot of related materials at the start of September and developed a preliminary project plan. Then they divide

Figure 4. Work flows of the group students

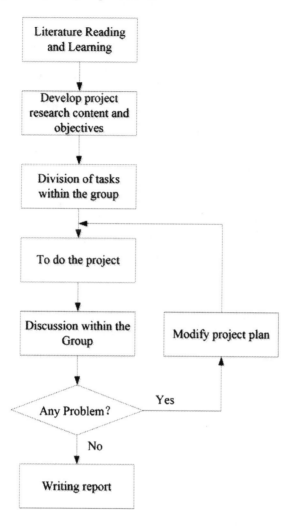

tasks within the group, one student is responsible for technologies, one student for the design of questionnaires and the other two students improve and refine project plan and write report. Moreover, they have group meeting every week and discuss the problem they encountered. During the group discussion, they could find where the project is not perfect and where the project is not possible to implement. And then, they modified the project plan together, so cycle back and forth until the project is implemented. At last, they will write the final report together by overleaf based on their work.

After reading, learning related knowledges and interviews, they decide their project to solve the problem "How is ViRZoom bike better compared to teleportation, for the urban design experience while moving over longer distance?". Due to a wide range of possibilities for moving over longer distances within VR, however their project will be focusing on teleportation using the hand held pointer controllers and the ViRZoom exercise bike. They have already design 5 types of questionnaires which included Simulator Sickness Questionnaire, Presence Questionnaire, Control method questionnaire, System Usability Questionnaire, and Comparing Control Methods Questionnaire. And they got 36 valid questionnaires for each type from the respondents. And they have done some statistics analysis work and finish some parts of the final report.

When I was tracking the student group, I was looking at PBL from the perspective of students. And I could feel students' problem, how they allocate tasks and work together, and how they manage time and project progress. And I think it is a good angle to understand PBL.

REFLECTIONS ON LEARNING PBL AND FUTURE PLANS FOR DEVELOPMENT

Reflection on Teaching Philosophy, Challenges and Skills

After learning from 9 thematic workshops, 3 selected lectures and tracking a student group, I have a certain understanding of PBL. These learned knowledges also have a profound impact on my teaching. The impact and guidance of the course on my teaching mainly includes the following aspects.

1. Discussion in class is very important teaching method which is lack in my teaching. There is no case in my classroom teaching, and even no vivid example. It leads some of my students could not interest in my teaching contents. And learn to be a good facilitator is also a big challenge for me. I will try to consider how to guide students to actively participate in discussions, active learning, and have critical thinking about the knowledge they have acquired.

2. If I go back to China to apply PBL teaching methods in NEU, I will face another challenge that how to design a good problem. Based on my learning in AAU UNESCO Centre, I think problem design is very important to my courses to apply PBL in NEU. One of my teaching philosophies is to cultivate students to become useful to society. Therefore, the problem should be designed be good for society.

3. Assessment is an important baton to students in Chinese universities. If I apply PBL teaching methods in NEU after I go back to China. How to design an assessment or evaluation architecture is a challenge for teachers. The assessment architecture should be combined with the actual situation of NEU. Formative assessment and summative assessment might need to combine.

4. Apply PBL should gain insight into the actual teaching situation of Chinese universities. And we could not apply the PBL models which are already exist in NEU directly. PBL applying needs to change many aspects related to teaching, such as teachers, students, learning goals, teaching contents, teaching and learning methods and assessments. We also need some resource and policies supports from NEU.

Future Teaching Plans With PBL

The main purpose of NEU to send our 7 teachers to Aalborg UNESCO Centre to learn is promote teaching reform by PBL and try to apply PBL methods in NEU. My future teaching plans with PBL as follows.

1. I will spread PBL teaching philosophy and PBL principles and methods in my department and college. If we want to promote the development of PBL method in NEU, we need to let other teachers know and understand of PBL. And I will organize workshops to spread PBL to teachers in software college as well as some teaching forums and seminars organized by department or college.

2. I plan to apply PBL on one of my course at first. It is easier for me to apply PBL method on my own course and it has no impact on other teachers' course. And I will summarize teaching experience after apply it on a single course. It could be seen as a preparation for applying PBL on interdisciplinary level.

3. I will try to apply PBL method on interdisciplinary level in Software College. After apply PBL on a single course, I could have experience on problem design, assessment, organization and so on. Then, I will apply PBL on 2 or 3 courses in Software College under the resource and policies supports from NEU.

DESIGN AND IMPLEMENTATION OF INTERDISCIPLINARY LEVEL PBL

Based on the theories I learned from UNESCO center in AAU. An interdisciplinary level of PBL plan is proposed in this section. In China, there are 13 subject categories for universities, which are including 110 first-level disciplines and over 600 subordinate disciplines. Northeastern University (NEU) has formed a multi-disciplinary system which covers philosophy, economics, law, pedagogy, literature, science, engineering, management, art disciplines. The university has 19 colleges and 68 undergraduate majors. Relevant majors under the same first-level discipline are in the same colleges in NEU. Interdisciplinary in this section means two or more subordinate disciplines in the same first-level disciplines. The plan of interdisciplinary level PBL reflects Chinese culture of "inclusiveness" and "harmonious".

Implementation Plan

In this section, we propose an implementation plan for interdisciplinary level of PBL. In NEU, students in the same college usually have study the same professional foundation courses in the first or second semester. Therefore, they could relatively easy to learn courses of other disciplines in the same college and it is provided foundation for this plan. And it is suitable for students in one college in NEU to apply this plan. Students in this plan could choose to learn one or two elective courses from other disciplines. As it is shown in figure 5, take 3 disciplines for example, students in

Figure 5. Course structure of the plan

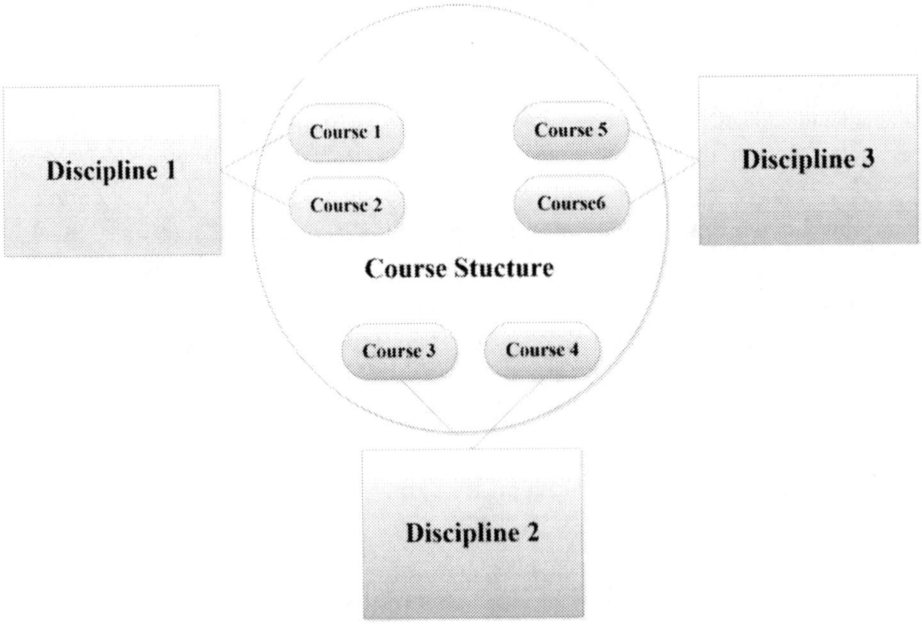

one discipline could select courses to learn from other 2 disciplines. And students need to do a project related to the courses of the 3 disciplines. We will elaborate the implementation plan on the following six aspects[1,2].

This plan is designed to minimize the impact on the original curriculum system. If a student enrolls in this plan and select courses from other disciplines, he or she will get double credits. The extra credits are for the project. The credit structure is shown in figure 6. If a student from discipline 1 selects N credits course of discipline 2 and N credits course of discipline 3, he or she will get extra 2N credits for project. Usually, 1 credit equals 16 teaching hours in NEU. That means, students could use 2N credits instead of taking other courses. PBL is a student-centered pedagogy in which learning happens when students solving problems. Therefore, students could propose problems by themselves as long as problem related the course they choose.

Students

This plan is suitable for the students who are in the sixth or seventh semester in NEU since they have relatively more elective courses than other semesters. And we encourage students from different disciplines to compose a group for PBL. Figure 7 describes suggested structure to compose groups. Take 3 disciplines for an example, three colors represent students from three disciplines. And the number of students in each discipline is the same. Thus, one group is composed by three students who are from three different disciplines.

In this plan, students need to learn how to cooperate with each other and they require team work with other team members. Chinese codes of teamwork have three aspects: personality, interpersonality and leadership. Every team member requires contribute to teamwork and respects to other member's contribution. As students in

Figure 6. Credit Structure

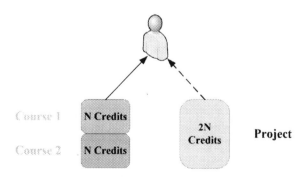

Figure 7. Group Work Structure

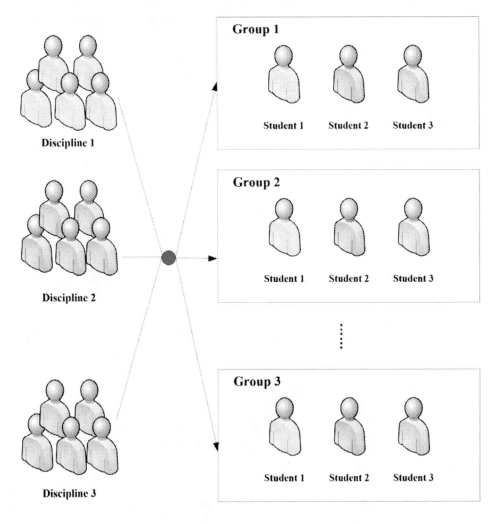

a team may from different disciplines, they need to know each other in short time and choose a leader who is the most suitable student in a team. The leader in a team needs to know each member's right and contribution. And the leader can be seen as facilitator and could deal with interpersonality in a team.

Most of the students in NEU do not have previous PBL experience. And their social, cultural, psychological, and physical prerequisites for learning are quite different from western students. Therefore, if we apply this PBL model to NEU, some lectures regarding PBL are required for students. And these lectures should tell students what is PBL and how to work with teammates.

Teaching Staff

Teacher's role will changed in this plan. In traditional way, teachers give lectures to students respectively in discipline, typically in classrooms. In interdisciplinary level PBL plan, teacher's role is not only a lecturer, but also a facilitator. And this change is shown in figure 8. We also take three disciplines as an example, three teachers will face students from three disciplines together. In one hand, teachers need to know other disciplines courses and what contents the students learned from

Figure 8. Change of teacher's role

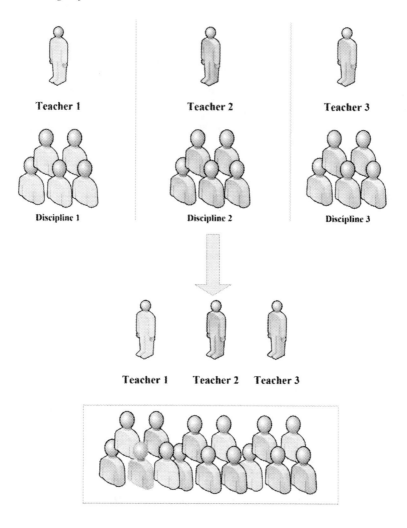

these courses. In the other hand, teachers need to know how to simulate and motivate students. Teachers should make use of students' face, rather than breaking their face.

As a facilitator, teaches also need to learn how to communicate with students and how to encourage students to contribute to their team. Compared to traditional lecture based teaching, the biggest difference is teachers have to supervise students to finish their projects. Teachers have to know each team's projects, what their problem is and solutions. In the process of guidance, there may be some knowledge which is new to the teachers. Therefore, teachers also need to constantly learn from projects.

With the change of teacher's role, the workload of teachers will also change a lot. In interdisciplinary level PBL plan, teachers need to spend more time on guiding students' projects. For example, if there are thirty students in a class and three students form a group, every teacher need to guide 10 groups on average. Teachers pay more time and energy for students' projects. As the number of groups increases, teachers' workload increases accordingly. Therefore, teachers' tuition fees allocation plan should also be adjusted accordingly. NEU should pay extra tuition fees to teachers which could encourage PBL teaching method to carry out. And the calculation of workload of teachers should be changed. In the final presentation assessment, teachers will act as internal examiners. External examiners are recommended to invite and it requires NEU to pay for external examiners. For example, in AAU mode, external examiners are invited from enterprise and universities and one AAU department will pay about two million for external examiners' fees per term. And to motivate teachers to work with each other to achieve the same goal, policy or institution of a traditional university should be changed accordingly. New remunerations allocation for teachers and promotion policy need to be established.

Learning Goals

In NEU, the goal of cultivating students is including four aspects: knowledge, technology, quality and competitiveness. Cultivate student plans should be consistent with the learning goals. Accordingly, when we design a new course in a discipline, the learning goals should be consistent with the four aspects. Thus, we divide learning goals into four aspects and table 3 shows some examples according to the four aspects in interdisciplinary level PBL plan. Different courses should have different learning goals. In this classification, knowledge includes theories, principles, predecessor's work and all knowledge from the textbook, lectures and so on. Technologies contain all the professional skills in the course. Quality should involve all transferable skills. And Competitiveness embodies the students' competence abilities compare to other students who do not enroll in the course, such as creative and innovative competence.

Table 3. Learning Goals

Learning Goals	**Knowledge**	Theories, Principles, Predecessor's work......
	Technologies	Professional Skills......
	Quality	Transferable skills......
	Competitiveness	Creative and Innovative Competence......

Professional skills are determined by the course itself. But transferable skills are generally not related to the specific course itself. Or in other words, transferable skills could be learned in all PBL courses. For example, transferable skills include teamwork ability, communication skills, leadership, project management, critical thinking, system thinking, and especially the Chinese codes of teamwork.

Learning goals also include the degree of mastery of knowledge and technologies, such as remembering, understanding, applying, analyzing, evaluating and creating abilities. But quality and competitiveness are different learning abilities and they are not easy for students to master. For example, transferable skills, creative and innovative competence are usually can't be taught through classroom teaching like knowledge and technology. They need more practice work and teamwork.

Contents

In interdisciplinary level PBL plan, teaching contents should include two aspects, lecture contents and project contents (see figure 9). For lecture content, discipline original courses can maintain most of the original teaching content, but need to make appropriate adjustments, such as interdisciplinary skills and relationships among courses in different discipline. Teachers from different disciplines require

Figure 9. Contents structure

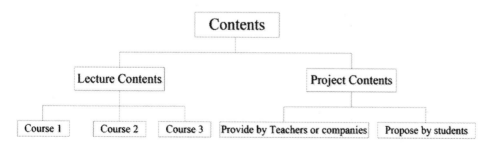

knowing other teachers' contents of different courses. Teachers from different disciplines should work together to discuss all courses' content adjustments every semester if possible.

For project contents, project work is problem-based by definition. Project based on problem which proposed by students should be encouraged. And problem itself arises from the problem-oriented theme and problem formulation should relate the choice of disciplines and methods. Projects also could be provided by teachers and companies, and teachers from different disciplines need to know all the lecture contents and discuss discipline related projects together. Projects design should consider personal achievements of students and contribution to society.

Teaching and Learning Methods

The teaching and learning methods include the two methods of teaching methods by teacher and student learning methods, which is the unification of teaching methods and learning methods. The teaching method must be based on the learning method. Otherwise it will not be able to effectively achieve the intended learning goals because of lack of pertinence and feasibility. However, in traditional teacher-centered learning, teachers are in a dominant position in the teaching process. Therefore, teaching method is in a dominant position in teaching and learning methods. The teacher-centered teaching methods mainly include methods of teaching, questioning, and argumentation. In interdisciplinary level PBL plan, teaching and learning methods are change to student-centered mode (see figure 10).

Figure 10. Teaching and learning method

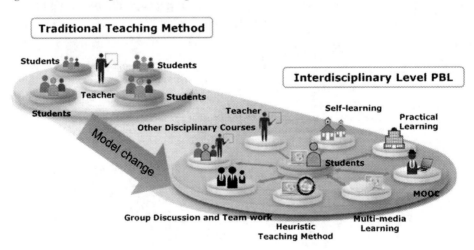

In student-centered teaching and learning mode, multiple methods could be used in interdisciplinary level PBL plan, such as group discussion, team work, multimedia learning, MOOC, practical learning, self-learning and so on. The Chinese concept of competition and Chinese codes of teamwork which elaborated should be considered. Students should choose the way they learn by themselves. Teachers should provide feedbacks in an improper way and promote students' face.

Assessment

In most PBL modes, students' assessment is composed by course score and project score. They each account for 50%. It is shown in figure 11 Course score is given by lecturers the same as traditional teaching mode and project score could be assess by different ways.

In interdisciplinary level PBL plan, it can use assessment method showed above, but it need more resources and policies supports from universities to manage student score. Another choice for assessment is to assess courses and project separately. And this method is easier to implement since it has minimal impact on existing score management systems. Course score could record the same as before, and project can be seen as a new course to record the project score.

Figure 12 describes the project assessment ways. In this interdisciplinary level PBL plan, presentation and reports are usually used to assess the projects. Presentation could be evaluated by teachers as well as other students. Reports include midterm report and final report. Generally speaking, final report is necessary for assessment, but midterm report is depending on different courses. Project also could be evaluated by students in the group and between groups.

Figure 11. Assessment

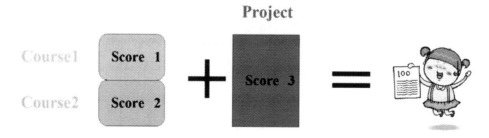

Figure 12. Project assessment ways

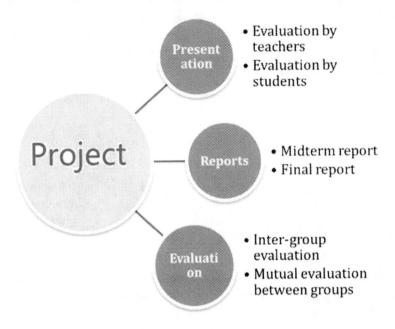

Case Study

In this section, a case for interdisciplinary level PBL is proposed and it will be set forth by the six aspects above respectively. We choose three disciplines in software college of NEU. They are software engineering, information security and digital media technology. And we choose two elective courses from each discipline respectively. Thus, we offer these six courses for students to choose. Course structure is shown in figure 13. We choose IOS Development Technologies (IDT) and Android Development Technologies (ADT) from software engineering discipline, Information Content Security (ICS) and Security Technologies of Data Communication (STDC) from information security discipline, Virtual Reality Design and Development (VRDD) and Computer Game Design and Development (CGDD) from digital media technology discipline. All the six courses are offered in the sixth semester for third year undergraduate students. There are 32 teaching hours and 2 credits for each course.

Figure 13. Course structure of case

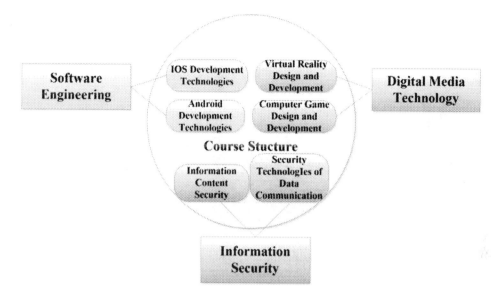

Figure 14 shows an example of credit allocate structure in this case. If a student from information security discipline selects 2 credits course ADT of software engineering discipline and 2 credits course CGDD of digital media technology discipline, he will get 4 credits for project and get 8 credits in total. And 4 credits equals 64 teaching hours in NEU. Therefore, students could use this 64 teaching hours to do projects.

Figure 14. Credit structure example of case

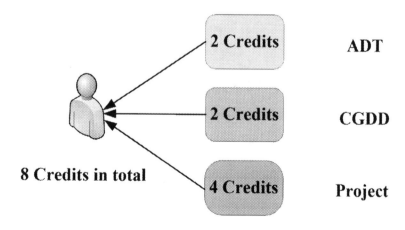

Students

Figure 15 describes team structure to compose groups. Student from different disciplines are encouraged to compose a group for PBL. In other words, one group is composed by three students who are from three different disciplines. As figure 15 shows, we choose 9 students from each discipline. Thus, 27 students compose 9 groups and 3 students in each group.

As students in a group from different disciplines, they need to know each other and choose a leader for the new team. NEU needs to offer space for groups to discuss and communicate. And relatively independent and privacy space is recommended. The leader in a team should be freely elected by team members after they know each other.

Figure 15. Team structure of case

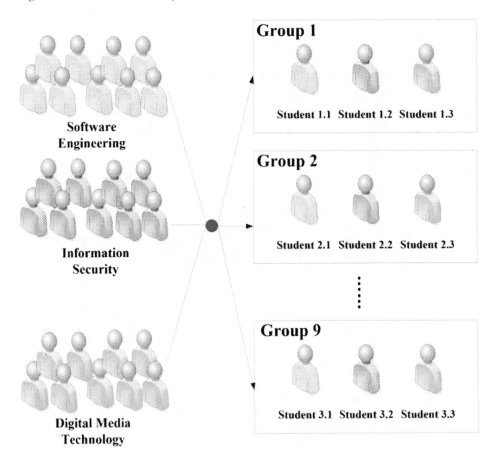

Teaching Staff

As it is described above, teacher's role is not only a lecturer, but also a facilitator. As a lecturer, teacher could organize teaching contents similar as before and adjust some contents and teaching methods. As a facilitator, teachers need to supervise students' group project. As figure 13 shows, there are maximum 6 teachers participated in this case and 2 teachers per discipline. Each discipline should assign at least one teacher as the project's mentor. And each mentor is responsible for 3 groups. It is shown in figure 16.

As a facilitator, teachers need to know each student's contribution in the project and progress and completion of each project they responsible for. Teachers also need to correct the final reports and participate in the final defense. As mentor is familiar with the 3 groups they responsible for, mentor's judging judgment on the workload of the students will account for a larger proportion.

Learning Goals

In NEU, each course has its own learning goals. As it is describes above, the goal includes four aspects: knowledge, technology, quality and competitiveness. Table 4 shows an example of STDC learning goals in information security discipline. Practical teaching is very important in this course. The purpose of the experiment is not only to verify the theoretical knowledge but also to enhance students' practical skills and the ability to apply knowledge and innovation. Through this experiment, students will gain basic knowledge of data communication and communication security, especially with regard to firewall issues. Students will learn how to use

Figure 16. Mentor allocation

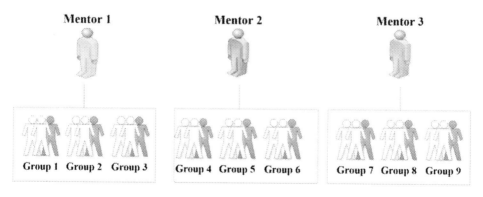

iptables packet filtering and iptables rules to audit and control network events, the basic configuration of a firewall, NAT principles and implementation, and finally they will build a secure enterprise network environment.

After the practical, students need to prepare and submit a report documenting their experiments. The report must include a brief description of the topics investigated, test data, results, problems encountered and solutions. The report should also include the listing of any codes, programs, instructions and scripts that they developed and used during the practical sessions. Students should also include in the test report their suggestions, comments and conclusions that arise from their experience of conducting the experiments.

If students from software engineering and digital media technology disciplines choose STDC, the learning goals of STDC should integrated in new course structure in interdisciplinary level PBL plan. For example, a student choose 3 courses in new course structure which shows in figure 13, learning goals should integrated in all the 3 courses.

Contents

As it is shows in figure 9, teaching contents consists of lecturer content and project content. Lecture content is depending on courses. While project content design is new compare to lecture content in interdisciplinary level PBL plan. Figure 17 illustrates the relationship between courses and project. Projects selection and design should relate to course content.

In this case, IDT and ADT are in mobile development area, ICS and STDC belong data and content security area, VRDD and CGDD are in computer game

Table 4. Learning Goals of STDC

Learning Goals	**Knowledge**	Computer and Network Security Threats, Computer and Network Security Techniques, Wireless WANs, Distributed Data Processing
	Technologies	Use iptables packet filtering and iptables rules to audit and control network events, Basic configuration of a firewall, NAT principles and implementation, Build a secure enterprise network environment
	Quality	Teamwork ability, Communication skills, Project management
	Competitiveness	Creative Competence

Figure 17. Relationship between courses and projects

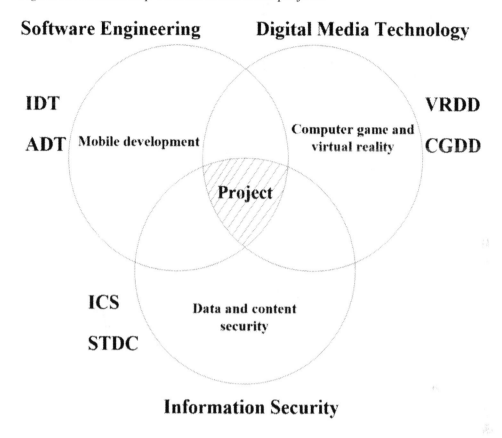

and virtual reality area. Projects should cover these 3 areas and it shows in shadow part in figure 17. Project design or problem selection should use of the knowledge and technologies of these courses.

Teaching and Learning Methods

For different teaching contents, we should adopt different teaching and learning methods. In this case, all the six courses are in computer science area. Table 5 shows teaching and learning methods of this case. For lecture content, classroom lecture teaching is a main method. In addition, practical learning, MOOC and multi-media learning are very suitable for lecture content. Regarding project content, teaching and learning methods should include group discussion, team work, self-learning and heuristic teaching methods and so on.

Table 5. Teaching and learning methods of case

Lecture Content	Classroom Teaching, MOOC, Practical Learning, Multimedia Learning......
Project Content	Group Discussion, Team Work, Self- Learning, Heuristic Teaching......

Assessment

In this case, students' assessment is composed by courses assessment and project assessment. With regard to course assessment, final exam, practical report and student's usual performance evaluation are 3 main assessment methods in traditional teaching in NEU. In order to minimize the impact on the traditional curriculum system, courses assessment could be the same as before. And courses assessment and project assessment are independent. Thus, project assessments score will use to assess extra allocate credits. For example, if a student chooses courses like figure 14, assessments for ADT, CGDD and project are independent which is showed in figure 18. In NEU, final scores in hundred mark system represent the assessments.

Figure 18. Assessment example of case

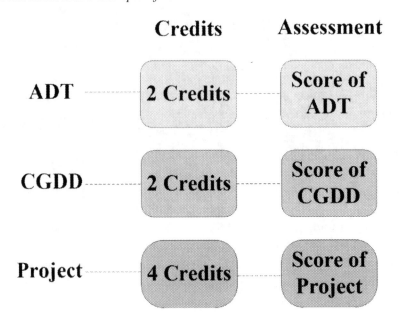

In interdisciplinary level PBL plan, presentation and final report are used to assess the project in this case. Presentation and final report each account for 50%. This plan needs policy support from NEU which the scores of project have to record into the NEU's teaching performance management system.

REFERENCES

Du, X., Su, L., & Liu, J. (2013). Developing sustainability curricula using the PBL method in a Chinese context. *Journal of Cleaner Production, 61*, 80–88. doi:10.1016/j.jclepro.2013.01.012

Kolmos, A. (2010). Premises for Changing to PBL. *International Journal for the Scholarship of Teaching and Learning, 4*(1), 4. doi:10.20429/ijsotl.2010.040104

APPENDIX

Table 6a. Syllabus of Security Technologies of Data Communication

Course No.	C0802000220	Course Name (Chinese)		数据通信安全技术				
Course Name (English)	Security Technologies of Data Communication							
Total Hours	40	Lecture Hours	32	**Laboratory Hours**	8	**Computer Hours**	0	**Responsible Instructor**	Nitin Naik
Credits	2.5							
College	Software College		**Major**	Information Security				
Evaluation and Grading Policy	Final grade 100% = regular performance 10% + laboratory 20% + final test 70%							
Prerequisites	Principles of Communication							
Course Type	☐Degree Course ■ Elective Course ☐ Prioritized Elective Course							
Textbooks	William Stallings: 《BUSINESS DATA COMMUNICATIONS SIXTH EDITION》 International paperback edition. ISBN-10: 0-13-606543-0 or ISBN-13: 978-0-13-606543-2, 2008-10.							
Reference Books	1 Subhendu Mondal: 《Data Communication and Computer Network: Basics of Computer Networking in Different Media》, ISBN:9783639371758, 2011-7. 2 Debashis Saha,Debashis Saha: 《Next Generation Data Communication Technologies: Emerging Trends》, ISBN: 9781613504772, 2011-12.							
Course Description	"Security Technologies of Data Communication" will look at a variety of issues related to security in the context of data communications. It will interpret the term "security" to include not only confidentiality and privacy of data but also the integrity of data and the capabilities of communications systems to deliver that data correctly ("quality of service"). The module will consider the various types of data that are important to a business deployment of data communication systems. The important area of firewalls is covered during practical sessions that will consider both the Microsoft and Linux environments as well as being addressed in lecture time.							
Connections Between Course Objectives and Graduation Requirements	Graduation Requirements CO 1. Knowledge of Engineering H 2. Problem Analysis M 3. Solution to Design/Development 4. Research 5. Using Modern Tools L 6. Engineering and Society 7.Environment and Sustained Development 8. Professional Ethics 9. People and Team 10. Communication 11. Project Management 12. Lifelong Learning 1.(1/H)Master the basic concepts and theories of data communication and apply them to solve problems. And main concepts include distributed data processing, circuit switching and packet switching, computer and network security techniques, wireless LAN and so on. 2.(2/M)Could use the theories and knowledge learned from this module to analysis the security problems in data communication system. 3.(5/L) Could use the library and the Internet to carry on the literature search and the data inquiry							

Table 6b. Syllabus of Security Technologies of Data Communication

	Course Content	Class Hours			Teaching Method
		Lecture	Computer	Laboratory	
Teaching Methods and Time Allocation	Chapter 1 Introduction	3			Classroom Instruction, Multimedia Presentations
	Chapter 2 Business Information	3			Classroom Instruction, Multimedia Presentations, Discussion Teaching
	Chapter 3 Distributed Data Processing	2			Classroom Instruction, Multimedia Presentations, Experimental Demonstration
	Chapter 4 Internet History and Architecture	3			Classroom Instruction, Multimedia Presentations
	Chapter 5 TCP/IP and OSI	2			Classroom Instruction, Multimedia Presentations,
	Chapter 6 Internet-Based Applications	4		8	Classroom Instruction, Multimedia Presentations, Experimental Demonstration
	Chapter 7 Circuit Switching and Packet Switching	4			Classroom Instruction, Multimedia Presentations, Discussion Teaching
	Chapter 8 Frame Relay and ATM	2			Classroom Instruction, Multimedia Presentations
	Chapter 9 Wireless WANs	3			Classroom Instruction, Multimedia Presentations
	Chapter 10 Computer and Network Security Threats	3			Classroom Instruction, Multimedia Presentations, Experimental Demonstration
	Chapter 11 Computer and Network Security Techniques	3			Classroom Instruction, Multimedia Presentations

continued on following page

Table 6b. Continued

Course Assessment and Sustained Improving Mechanism	Teaching Objectives: The Goal of this course is to let the student grasp the basic theory, elementary knowledge and security techniques of the data communication and the students are able to solve security problems of data communication system. Teaching Methods:Classroom instructions, class tests, assignment, and the final exam. Objective Assessment:Regular performance of students in class, the quality of laboratory report, as well as the scores of the final exam. Sustained Improving Mechanism: ①Since the course is taught in English and the students' mother tongue is Chinese, it is necessary to enhance pre-course reading and teaching trials such as providing lecture notes and class exercises before the start of this course, however it still need to explore more effective and efficient methods to assist the students in learning this course. ②The course takes two weeks and the time in classroom is limited, and it would be better to provide online learning platform, such as BB or MOOC platforms. It requires teaching research on the problem: how to make these platforms play a more active role in accordance with the classroom instructions.
Syllabus Approval	Written by: Jingping Song Co-written by: Fucai Zhou, Yuan Liu, Jiliang Zhang, Jian Xu Examined by: Fucai Zhou Approved by: Yuan Liu Date (Written/Revised):May, 2016

Chapter 9
Facilitating Cross–Cultural Communication:
A Global Dimension to Fostering International Talents and Innovation in University Foreign Affairs Management

Mei Li
Northeastern University, China & Aalborg University, Denmark

Zhiliang Zhu
Northeastern University, China

ABSTRACT

The purpose of this chapter is twofold: 1) to make a brief interpretation of global dimension mainly focusing on the criterion for "international talents" and the requirements for the internationalization of higher education and 2) to address foreign affairs management in universities plays a vital role in promoting the internationalization of teaching, research, and administrative management, which can be regarded as a key diver to develop global dimension of innovation in higher education. Accordingly, this chapter proposes potential strategies for innovation of the foreign affairs management in universities, which has important significances in studies on internationalization of higher education, cross-culture communication, and foreign affairs management.

DOI: 10.4018/978-1-5225-9961-6.ch009

INTRODUCTION

Current, although a lot of attention has been paid to a global dimension of higher education development that has achieved fruitful achievements. In 2002, De Wit (2002) stated that "as the international dimension of higher education gains more attention and recognition, people tend to use it in the way that best suits their purpose." (pp.114) This is even more the case now in view of this further proliferation of activities and terms. "Internationalization is changing the world of higher education, and globalization is changing the world of internationalization," remarks Jane Knight (2004). "Internationalization is a term that is being used more and more to discuss the international dimension of higher education and, more widely, postsecondary education. It is a term that means different things to different people and is thus used in a variety of ways. Although it is encouraging to see the increased use and attention being given to internationalization, there is a great deal of confusion about what it means." (pp.5) Therefore, some more efforts are still required to response questions such as: how to understand the role of universities in developing a global community in higher education? How to define "international talents" and what does "internalization" mean to universities? And, how can we understand foreign affairs management as a key driver to facilitate cross-culture communication and develop internationalization in higher education? All of the above questions are required to be deeper explored as a framework that indicates the importance of reform and innovation in foreign affairs management in universities.

Following above lines, this chapter will explore a discussion step by step and try to bridge significant relevance between a comprehensive understanding on developing a global community in higher education and the roles of innovation in foreign affairs management in universities. Thus, this will fill in a knowledge gap as indicated by questions proposed in above. Furthermore, this chapter will be structured into the following parts. Firstly, to discuss briefly on the challenges faced by universities under a background of globalization and internalization. Secondly, to make a deeper exploration on global dimension of universities from a new angle by interpretation of the word "globalization". At last, to focus on an analysis on innovation in foreign affairs management that contributes to strategies for better developing international universities in the future.

Challenges for Universities' International Development

Meaning of Global Community

With the dramatically changes in the way of knowledge production and information transfer in the 21st century, realization of worldwide communication is giving full play to the role of eliminating the obstacles of time and space, making the world become a smaller village and undergoing profound changes in economic, political, social and cultural life, whereas people around the world have become almost one community living together in the global atmosphere. Borrowing from Anthony Marsella, Deutsch (2012) has defined a global community as the interrelatedness of peoples, groups, communities, institutions, and nations that is facilitated by technology and includes political, economic, and social interdependence. Deutsch once wrote,"The global community is multicultural, multinational, and multiethnic and is affected systemically by world events and forces including technology and media, environmental conditions and changes, militarism and war, economic upheaval and inequality, disease pandemics, sexism, racism, and social injustices, and more." (pp. 300) This indicates that a global community is calling for more cross-culture communication, collaboration and integration between partners.

Change of Knowledge Production

University is the main site for knowledge production and talents cultivation. Expectations of what universities should accomplish in terms of knowledge production have been rising for many years and have accelerated a lot of discussion on the changes of knowledge production in information age and knowledge society. The world is being transformed by the information explosion with rapid development of science and technology on information communication technology, the production of knowledge also be deeply affected, changing from the traditional Mode 1 to the emerging Mode 2. In the book *The New Production of Knowledge: The Dynamics of Science and Research in Contemporary Societies* (Gibbons, M. et al. 2010), which discussed two types of knowledge production in science and technology: Mode 1 is university based, pure, disciplinary, homogeneous, expert-led, supply-driven, hierarchical, peer-reviewed; Out of Mode 1 grows Mode 2 knowledge production, which is applied, problem-focused, trans-disciplinary, heterogeneous, hybrid, demand-driven, entrepreneurial, accountability-tested, and embedded in networks.

This shift in knowledge production pattern has turned traditional single-type knowledge production into complex, systematic, problem-based and interdisciplinary teamwork. The knowledge generated by team may consist of people of very different backgrounds working together temporarily to solve a problem. The number of sites where such knowledge can be generated is greatly increased; they are linked by functioning networks of communication. And moreover, as people now living and working in a more global-oriented community, this teamwork and communication is under the globalization atmosphere calls for cross-culture communication and ability adapt to this change. In other words, individual creativity is the driving force of Mode 1 knowledge, while in Mode 2, creativity is based in the group, which may nevertheless contain members socialized in Mode 1 forms. The change of knowledge production mode is bound to put forward new development requirements for universities' education and teaching concepts, the talent training model of higher education should adapt to the transformation of this knowledge production mode, and it is more suitable to cultivate practical, inter-disciplinary and international talents in the context of global dimensions, who need to be mastered abilities and familiar with the rules communicating in global community and give full play of their creativity in teamwork and in any cross-culture communication activities.

Importance of Cross-Culture Communication

In general, we can understand 'communication' as the ability to share ideas and feelings with others that is the basis of all human contact. However, by looking through the literature, the definition of communication is fully of complexity. For example, over thirty years ago, Dance and Larson (1976) reviewed the literature on communication and they found 126 definitions on communication. Since then, countless others have been added to their list. If communication is complex and multidimensional, then it can be defined in the following way (Wood, 1997), "communication is a dynamic, systematic process in which meanings are created and reflected in human interaction with symbols." (pp.36) So the study of human communication is always complex and multidimensional in particular to in the discussion on issues cross-culture communication.

Culture and communication, although two different concepts, are so closely linked, and usually we cannot discuss only one without considering of the other. The two concepts are so inextricably bound that some anthropologists believe they are virtually synonymous. As Smith (1996) noted, "Whenever people interact

247

they communicate. To live in societies and to maintain their culture they have to communicate." (pp.122) Then, what is cross-culture communication? In its most general sense, cross-culture communication occurs when a member of one culture produces a message for consumption by a member of another culture. Most preciously, cross-culture communication is the communication between people whose cultural perceptions and symbol system are distinct enough to alter the communication event. Frequently, the term cross-culture communication is used when referring to communication between people from different cultures. And why cross-culture communication is important? Language and cultural misinterpretations can be avoided by increasing our understanding of other people and their cultures. The study of cross-culture communication addresses this need by examining the communications and interactions between people of different cultures and sub cultures. The fundamental principle of cross-culture communication is that it is through culture that people communicate. Globalization has made intercultural communication inevitable. (Prasanta Kumar Padhi, 2016)

In a global environment, the ability to communicate effectively can be both an opportunity and challenge. When entering a quite different cultural atmosphere, people may feel totally lost and experience the cultural conflict. Jonathan Turner (2005) defines cultural conflict as a conflict stemming from "differences in cultural values and beliefs that place people at odds with one another". (pp.87) This cultural conflict result in the cultural shock, as defined by Merriam-Webster Dictionary, means, "a sense of confusion and uncertainty sometimes with feelings of anxiety that may affect people exposed to an alien culture or environment without adequate preparation." (Merriam-Webster.com.) Culture shock is a strange psychological phenomenon which acts a barrier in communicating with others especially in a global environment. The term "culture shock" was first introduced in the 1950s by Kalvero Oberg (1960) to describe the phenomena people might experience after moving to a new environment, the feeling of disorientation experienced by a person suddenly subjected to an unfamiliar culture or way of life. It is the physical and emotional discomfort a person experience. (pp.177-182) As society becomes more globally connected the ability to communicate across cultural boundaries has gained increasing prominence. The cross-culture communication can avoid cultural misinterpretations by a better understanding of an alien culture. Understanding such impact of cross-culture communication is imperative for higher education to create a competitive advantage in the global community.

A Global Dimension of Universities

On Understanding of "Global Dimension"

'Global dimension' defines a departure of developing internalization among universities and contributes to a deeper understanding on 'global community'. We can view a 'global dimension' as 'exploring the world's interconnections', i.e. with a global dimension to the education, learners have a chance to engage with complex global issues and explore the links between their own lives and people, places and issues throughout the world, opens people's eyes and minds to the realities of the world, and encourages bringing about a world of greater justice, equity and human rights for all (https://globaldimension.org.uk/about/what-is-the-global-dimension/). This calls for educational institutions playing a vital role in helping their students to improve and recognize their responsibilities to be citizens of the global community. The young students are required to be equipped with knowledge, skills, and capabilities for developing successful cross-cultural collaboration and taking responsible actions. Therefore, the global dimension is now a core element when time and distance barriers have collapsed and the need to understand and appreciate the changes that are occurring has become ever important. Universities should capture the challenges to the development and implementation of the global dimensions and foster students with the ability to live and work in a closely connected modern society being economically, socially, and politically interdependent, in which "global citizenship" is the trend and call.

Fostering Cross-Culture Communication Abilities

The challenge of a fast-changing 'globalized' world offers enormous opportunities for higher education to make reform and innovation to equip the young generation with the knowledge, skills and values they need in order to survive in contemporary competitive society and to create the kind of world that they can live in happily and sustainably. To locate universities in a broader context, it should be mentioned that the development of technology and communication media has totally changed the way of life of human beings; different social groups are linked together in a globalized society by the interconnected and interdependent nature of the world with economic, political, and cultural exchange for mutual understanding and progress. The rapid development of economic globalization and information science has enabled people from different societies and cultural background to have frequent opportunities to interact, and cross-culture communication has become a prominent feature of the era of world integration.

The universities should respond to the challenges as mentioned above, and they should actively take measures for the cultivation of global citizenship that will be helpful for young students in learning how to communicate with people cross-culturally. The contemporary college students, as group members who are the most active in accepting new things, are undoubtedly facing the impact of multiculturalism. Accordingly, more attention should be paid to how to cultivate international talents who are able to adapt to the cultural diversity and cultural integration, which is one of the most urgent tasks facing by the higher education. It is suggested that now and for the future the emphasis should be much more on recognizing the complex linkage between local and global and what happens in one part of the world has a direct impact on another. In other words, fostering cross-culture communication abilities for future global citizenship requires dealing with issues of global interdependence, diversity of identities and cultures, sustainable development, peace & conflict and inequities of power, resources & respect. These global goals will need to be an integral part of higher education.

Moreover, it is necessary to look at a local context in China. In the process of comprehensive integration into economic globalization, the first bottleneck encountered in China's economic development is the shortage of international professionals. As suggested by McKinsey, the world-renowned consulting management company, in the report *Addressing China's Looming Talent Shortage* (Diana Farrell & Andrew Grant, 2005), there are many graduates in China, but less than 10% have the skills to work for foreign companies. The number of professionals who can meet the requirements of internationalization in China is extremely rare, and internationalized talents have become scarce resources in China.

International Talent and Interpretation of Globalization

Profile of International Talent

In order to respond growing challenges of globalization and fostering cross-culture communication abilities among young students, universities must undoubtedly shoulder the historical mission of cultivating innovative international talents and promoting the sustainable development of world's science, technology and economy.

However, what does "international talent" look like? There is a great deal of debate and discussion around this question. In the following lines, we learn a comprehensive definition from Oxfam (http://www.ideas-forum.org.uk/about-us/global-citizenship) which has indicated a global citizen as someone who:

- is aware of the wider world and has a sense of their own role as a world citizen
- respects and values diversity
- has an understanding of how the world works
- is outraged by social injustice
- participates in the community at a range of levels, from the local to the global
- is willing to act to make the world a more equitable and sustainable place
- takes responsibility for their actions

From above profile described, we can see that to be flexible, creative and proactive are the critical features of being qualified global citizens. Meanwhile, we should address abilities such as to think critically, communicate effectively, solve problems, make decisions, and work well in teamwork. These skills and qualities are increasingly recognized as being essential to be successful in the fierce competition among young students in their future career development.

Interpretation of the Word 'Globalization'

The profile of global citizens, as described in above section, is calling reform and innovation of higher education for fostering more qualified international talents in a global dimension. This drives authors in this chapter to rethink the meaning of 'globalization' and develop a new understanding and interpretation of the nine English letters "G, L, O, B, A, I, Z, T, N" that compose the word "globalization" through giving them some special meanings.

G: Global Thinking Mindset

The primary criterion for international talent is to have a global mindset. The so-called global mindset refers to the possess of three capitals: knowledgeable capital, psychological capital and social capital, i.e., the knowledge and skills in the professional and related fields used to deal with global affairs, the strong will and motivation to succeed in the context of internationalization, and the ability to build trust relationship among people with different cultural backgrounds. All in all, the global mindset is the willingness to actively integrate into the global community and keep up with the trend of the times. With the requirement to be a "global citizen", an international talent must persist in learning to expand knowledge, always strive to examine the world with an international perspective and gradually form an open mind to face challenge and change with a positive, optimistic and confident spirit in their professional practice.

L: Language Ability

Language is a tool for human thinking and understanding of the world. Mastering a language means mastering a method and habit of observing and understanding the world. The ever-changing modern technology has narrowed the temporal and spatial distance, making the whole world like a small village in the universe. The information, technology and cultural exchanges between countries and nations have become an indispensable important aspect of human life. This kind of communication across time, space and culture cannot be inseparable from the tool of language. The process of language communication is often the process of dissemination of culture and ideas. National language is an important carrier of national culture and national concept. William von Humboldt (1997) regards national language as the national spirit, and national spirit as the national language.(pp.50, pp.70) When a language spreads outward, the national culture and national concepts that the language loaded with will also spread. Moreover, compared with other forms of cultural output, the spread of cultures and concepts based on language communication is more natural and it is more likely to have subtle influences, and it is less likely to arouse resentment and resistance. Thus, mastering a foreign language not only means have an extra tongue, a pair of ears and eyes, but also a brain to rethink in a totally different cultural pattern. Therefore, an international talent must master foreign language abilities to achieve successful cross-culture communication

O: Occupational Skills

Occupational skills have been much emphasized by The Five in *Bill Gates's Top Ten Outstanding Staff Guidelines* (Guorong Lv, 2004): "Being visionary and improving professional knowledge and skills, i.e.: ①have a sharp insight on the surrounding things; ②live off one's past gains is the most horrible; ③continuous learning to improve work ability; ④master new knowledge and skills to adapt to future work;

⑤be a new type employee having the courage to be innovative." (pp.73-102) We should agree that occupational skills include both "hardware" and "software" possessed by each international talent; furthermore, what should also be emphasized here is that "hardware" and "software" must be updated. The frequency and speed of this kind of renewal should keep up with the international trend, adapt to the development of the times and always stand in the leading position of industry. Therefore, lifelong learning is necessary, as scientific and reasonable knowledge structure is fundamental, strong international awareness and communication skills is crucial to be an international talent who can effectively communicate information and solve problems in international exchange activities.

B: Background of Oversea Experience

The background of overseas study or work experience is not a necessary condition for defining an international talent. However, it is undeniable that only by integrating into the foreign environment and experiencing the real life of people in different cultural backgrounds can the culture be truly understood. For example, in China, more and more employers are looking for candidates to have overseas study or work experience, this requirement has increasingly abandoned the pursuit of "foreign diplomas" and more attention has been paid on the applicants' practical application of foreign languages and good command of international rules. Therefore, experience is more important than diploma. International talents should generally have the oversea studying or working experience, which enable them to have global psychological orientation, flexible expectations and capabilities for a complex and rapidly changing world, a slap-up approach to the intricacies of connections, an understanding attitude and a coordinated approach to cultural differences, as well as an optimistic attitude towards the unpredictable future. As addressed by Bussemaker (2014), who is the Dutch Minister of Education and who quoted Willam Maddux in her vision letter internalization to parliament: "People who have international experience are better problem solvers and display more creativity. What's more, we found that people with this international experience are more likely to create new businesses and products and to be promoted".

A: Ability for Cross-Culture Communication

The above discussion drives us to ask a question: "Global mindset + foreign language ability + occupational skills + background of oversea experience =?" What makes us concern about by this formula is not the final result, but the ultimate purpose of the reserve of the above criteria. We may answer the question as: all above discussion contributes to understand the important significances of the ability of cross-culture communication. Cross-culture communication refers to the communication between native speakers and non-native speakers, and also refers to the communication between people who have differences in language and cultural background. In general, when communicating with foreigners (due to differences in language and cultural backgrounds), what should be paid attention to is how to communicate properly and effectively. (Baidu Encyclopedia: http://baike.baidu.com/view/1017237.htm.) Therefore, only those who have the ability to communicate smoothly with people from different cultural backgrounds, achieving the cross-cultural management requirements of globalization, can be qualified as international talents. Ability for cross-culture communication is the focus of criterion to be an international talent.

I: Innovative Thinking Skill

If international talents want to win in international competition, global mindset is the premise, ability for cross-culture communication is the foundation, and innovative thinking skill is the key. Usually, we can understand innovative thinking skills as creativity that means generation of new and useful ideas. As quoted by Albert Einstein: "To raise new questions, new possibilities, to regard old questions from a new angle, requires creative imagination and marks real advances in science." And "The development of science and of the creative activities of the spirit in general requires still another kind of freedom, which may be characterized as inward freedom. It is this freedom of spirit which consists in the independence of thought from the restrictions of authoritarian and social prejudices as well as from unphilosophical routinizing and habit in general. This inward freedom is an infrequent gift of nature and a worthy objective for the individual...schools may favor such freedom by encouraging independent thought. Only if outward and inner freedom are constantly and consciously pursued is there a possibility of spiritual development and perfection and thus of improving man's outward and inner life." (Albert Einstein, 1940) The history of human society's development is a history of innovation, a history of taking creative thinking into practice. In other words, innovative thinking skill or creativity is the core of the international talents' intellectual structure. Creative thinking emphasizes pioneering and breakthrough, with a clear distinctive initiative characteristics, which is associated with creative activities and reflects novelty and uniqueness of the social value. As we can see creativity as one of elements of any innovation activities, while the fruits created by human beings are the externalization and materialization of creative thinking. Thus, we can understand innovation is the soul of a nation's progress and the inexhaustible motive force for the country's prosperity. Briefly, to foster innovative thinking skill and creativity among international talents should be on the top of agenda in higher education.

Z: Zigzag Manner

The term 'Zigzag Manner' means international talents require anti-frustration ability. As Zhou (2016) described, the complexity of the world is increasing; for example, in engineering practice, any engineering problems themselves are usually described as being complex. This means there are numbers of variables from diverse disciplines and aspects that require engineers have to consider a series of constraints on the solution such as technical function, economic feasibility, safety requirements, ethical issues, and resource considerations, etc. This further requires international talents to keep a zigzag manner for dealing with challenges from complexity of the world, in particular in the process of developing cross-cultural collaboration in their future career. There is a saying in English: "History moves in zigzags and by roundabout ways." The British philosopher Francis Bacon (2014) said: "Certainly if miracles be the command over nature, they appear most in adversity." Therefore, we must clearly understand that the twists and turns on the road of progress in solving any problems in any professional practice have certain positive significance for personal development to some extent. That is a kind of experience in life, enhance confidence, perseverance, clear ideas, and respond flexibly, meet complex challenges with optimistic spirit, twists and turns will become wealth, helping young people to drive out inertia and promote them to forge ahead.

T: Tangram Spirit

As mentioned in above, a healthy mentality and a positive attitude towards life is the most basic requirement for the psychological quality of an international talent in an era of rapid development. Furthermore, we should address a more comprehensive understanding on the exploration of criterion of fostering qualified international talents, so we propose an image of "tangram" as a metaphor on the above-mentioned abilities. The spirit of China's ancient traditional tangram game is concentrated in making people learn to adapt and cooperate. Such a game inspires us to emphasize that international talents must not only master the tangram in their hands, i.e., the above mentioned seven kinds of abilities, but also learn to be flexible, adopt win-win strategy to cooperate with others, thus a colorful life can be created (see figure 1).

As indicated by figure 1, we think all abilities mentioned above as an 'ability system', and different ability element interacts with each other and frame a common profile of a 'qualified international talent'. This also indicates in higher education, a new curriculum should be designed for developing multiple dimensions of skills required by young students. In addition, the section, foreign affairs management in universities should play more active roles in developing and facilitating international cooperation and collaboration that will bring more opportunities to international talents to understand national stance and worldwide vision, as discussed in the following lines.

N: National Stance and Worldwide Vision

The cultivation of international talents not means completely "westernization", but to pursuit cultural pluralism in the impact and collision between Chinese and Western cultures. The term 'cultural pluralism' refers to a country or a nation in

Figure 1. Tangram spirit

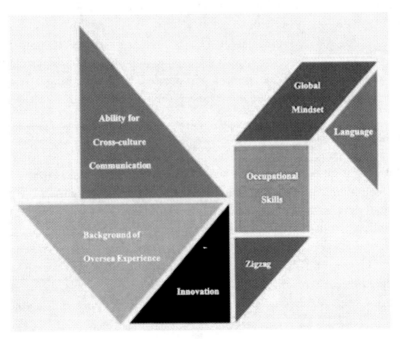

the process of social development, on the basis of inheriting the excellent culture of one's own, absorbing brilliant culture of other countries or nations, thus balance and assimilate each other, remain one's own characteristics to make it simpler. This can be concluded in a famous sentence in the *Analects of Confucius* (Chao Wang, 2015): "Striving for harmony but not sameness" (和而不同). Therefore, the international talents should not only have a worldwide vision, but a national stance, i.e., the attitude of learning from each other in the experience of cross-culture communication and collaboration. This also indicates the international talents should be prepared for innovative communication skills being able to improvise in unexpected situations and manage emerging conflicts.

In summary, we can describe the profile of "international talents" as: in the context of global integration, senior talents with international awareness and mind as well as world-class knowledge structure, whose vision and ability reaching international standards and is good at seize the opportunity and strive for the initiative in global competition. Followed by the new understanding on "international talents" is the discussion on how to realize the "global citizenship" education in universities through the internalization of higher education.

Internalization of Higher Education and Its Elements

Meaning of Internalization of Higher Education

The internationalization of higher education is a process and phenomenon in which the educational ideas, elements and behaviors of universities go across national borders and interact with each other. It is a process of integrating the "global dimension" into teaching, research and administrative management in universities. It is different nationalities with different cultural backgrounds penetrates into each other through education and achieves mutual understanding. It enables students to understand the existence of multiculturalism, fully communicate ideas in international science and technology, and be able to deal with problems from the broad perspective of the global community for the cultural exchanges. As the main body of education, universities must first establish an international talent training concept, rely on an elite faculty team who understands multiculturalism and international competition rules and is good at international exchanges, then establish an international talent training system to be brought in line with international criterion in scientific research cooperation, school-running mode, student structure, campus environment and administrative management level, thus maintain distinctive features in the fierce international competition.

DIVERSE ELEMENTS OF INTERNATIONALIZATION OF HIGHER EDUCATION

Internationalization of Teaching Staff

The lack of appropriate skills and knowledge amongst teaching staff has been identified as significant constraints in implementing the global dimension. An international staff team is a prerequisite for the cultivation of international talents. Teachers with international vision, teaching ability and experience are the most direct force to promote the goal of internationalized education. For example, in China, some attention has been paid to attract more and more overseas scholars to work in China through high-level talent introduction strategy, thus some universities have established good collaborations with partner universities, taking faculty exchange as a starting point to promote the interact and cooperation on scientific research, curriculum construction for further cooperation step by step. What should be emphasized is how to guarantee the teaching quality through effective supervision and management. Except for the developing collaboration between international intelligence, the importance of local intelligence should not be neglected. Accordingly, some measures should be taken in order to encourage potential faculty to undertake the task of assisting foreign experts and provide opportunity for them to be a visiting scholar going abroad for further study or participate in short-term training to pursue the advanced teaching methods.

Internationalization of Talent Training Mode

The quality of talent training is deeply influenced by the training objectives, methods, and content. Only by an international talent training mode can universities train international talents with international awareness, international knowledge and international communication skills that meet the requirements of the globalization era. The international curriculum construction is the top priority of the international talent training mode. The internationalization of curriculum refers to the addition of international content in the curriculum, which enables students to have a broad international vision and a comprehensive knowledge and capacity structure, focusing on improving students' competitiveness in an international environment. Such vision can be achieved through the adjustment of the existing curriculum system and the introduction of foreign advanced teaching resources, including foreign excellent courses, multimedia and online teaching resources, etc., which will benefit from the introduction, digestion and absorption of advanced teaching content and methods during the process of curriculum integration and curriculum reform. This not only meets the needs of the international talent training mode, but also adapts to the inevitable requirements for local development. As market becomes increasingly global, the innovation on knowledge production and transfer should refine curriculum to keep pace with and abreast of changing employer requirements and anticipate the future.

Internationalization of Cooperation on Scientific Research

International cooperation is a shortcut to rapidly improve the scientific research level of universities. In China, compared with the world-class universities, Chinese universities are lack of scientific and technological achievements, disciplines or majors and excellent faculty that can attract world's attention. Through international cooperation, Chinese researchers can broaden their horizons, find gaps, and explore new ways for development. Accordingly, universities in China should pay close attention to the forefront of science and technology development in contemporary era, through international academic exchanges aiming at establishing joint international research institutions and promoting high-level scientific research projects to tackle major problems for the global challenges hand in hand. The latest ideas, technologies, hardware and software environment in internationally renowned universities, research institutions or enterprises will provide a good research platform for teachers and students for promoting the transformation of technological achievements, forming a positive interact for teaching, scientific research and industry.

Internationalization of School-Running Mode

At present, universities choose different model of cooperation based on their own strength, student status, project design, partners and some other factors. However, in general, China has basically formed three major international school-running modes in the practice of Sino-foreign cooperative education, namely loose, convergent and grafted. (Li Liu, 2011) Loose mode is to invite foreign teachers to give lectures, provide opportunity for local teachers and students to go abroad for study, etc. in order to bring teaching in line with international approach. The convergent mode is to integrate the teaching mode of universities in China and foreign cooperative partners in the process of talent cultivation, and it includes the following three strategies: a) introducing partner's teaching plan, syllabus, materials and related teaching methods; b) inviting foreign teachers to give lectures and send local teachers abroad for self-improvement; and c) introducing teaching methods, such as class discussion, practice and case study, etc. The grafting mode is to fully retain the respective teaching mode. By mutual evaluation of the curriculum, recognition each other's credits, students have chance to receive the credits stipulated by universities from both home and aboard, receiving a dual degree become possible.

Internationalization of Student Structure

The education of international students is an important symbol of the internationalization level of universities. The proportion of foreign students is directly related to the degree of internationalization of a university. It is also an effective way to promote international talent training. Therefore, universities in China should continue to encourage more local students to go abroad for short-term study, competition or international conference to gain overseas experience. Meanwhile, endeavor should be made to increase the proportion of overseas students studying in China and gradually break barriers between teaching mode and method to make international students and local students to take lectures in the same class. The process of mutual communication will benefit the exchange of multiculturalism, enhance the understanding and recognition of each other's culture.

In the past five years, China's international talents field has undergone a rapid development. The number of students studying abroad continues to grow rapidly and more and more graduates choose to return to China. The overseas students studying in China also continues to increase by the Belt and Road Initiative. International talents are becoming an important force for China to achieve the goal of "Double Hundred Years" and realize the great rejuvenation of the Chinese nation, proving intellectual support for the realization of the Belt and Road Initiative and building of the community of shared future for mankind. Affected by the new trend, the growth rate of Chinese students studying abroad has also slowed down, but the number of overseas students studying in China continues to be the first around the world. In 2016, the total number of Chinese students studying abroad was 544,500. China is still the main source of foreign students in the United States, Canada, Australia, New Zealand, South Korea, Japan and other countries. Statistics show that Chinese students account for more than 30% of the total number of international students in the United States, Canada, Australia and New Zealand, and the proportion of Korean and Japanese international students is 57% and 49% respectively (see figure 2). All the statistics mentioned above come from the *Annual Report on the Development of Chinese Students Studying Abroad in Blue Book of Global Talent*. (Wang Huiyao & Miao Green, 2013)

Figure 2. Changes in the number of Chinese students studying abroad (2000-2016)

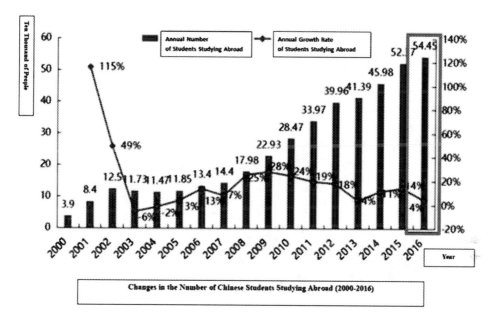

Under the guidance of the idea of "balance between study abroad and study in China", especially driven by the Belt and Road Initiative, in July 2016, according to the statistics from the Ministry of Education of China, the number of international students coming to China was 443,000, an increase of 44,000 compared with 2015, with a growth rate of 11.3%, reaching the highest level in recent years. In the top 15 countries where foreign students are sourced, there are 10 countries along the "Belt and Road" countries (see figure 3). All the statistics mentioned above come from the *Annual Report on the Development of Chinese Students Studying Abroad in Blue Book of Global Talent.* (Wang Huiyao & Miao Green, 2013)

Compared with studying abroad, there is a large "deficit" in the number of international students coming to China, which means there is still much room for the development of universities' internationalization of student structure. Only through improving the internationalization level of higher education, universities in China can provide necessary basic conditions to attract more foreign students who have the enthusiasm to study in China and experience Chinese culture. In other words, we can understand a key driver to embed the global dimension of the internationalization of higher education is the growth of overseas students studying in China. Attracting students from around the world will result in a far more diverse, multi-cultural student

Figure 3. Changes in the "deficit" of Chinese students studying aboard and foreign students studying in China (2004-2016)

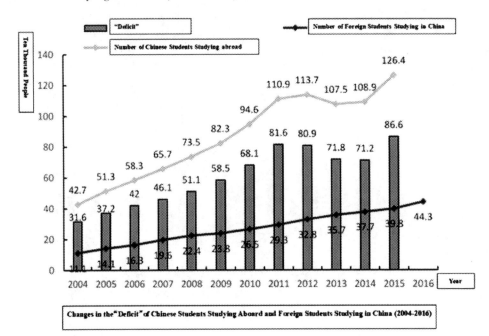

Changes in the "Deficit" of Chinese Students Studying Aboard and Foreign Students Studying in China (2004-2016)

population. The rapid development of studying in China provides talent support for international exchanges and cooperation, and provides a good opportunity for Chinese language and culture communication and Chinese culture to "go global".

Internationalization of Campus Environment

The internationalized campus environment refers to the improvement on both teaching facilities and living conditions. Firstly, teaching facilities must achieve "four modernizations", namely modern classrooms, modern laboratories, modern libraries and modern resource centers. The teaching facilities are equipped to reach the international level and guarantee the development of education, teaching and research activities. Secondly, the living conditions must achieve "two internationalizations", namely international apartments and international canteens. Such efforts provide convenient and comfortable working and living environment for foreign experts and students and contribute to the creation of international campus culture.

Internationalization of Teaching Management and Administrative Service

Internationalization process is complex and endures a long process, during which the teaching management and administrative service is an important safeguard. What we need nowadays is a professional and proficient team with international horizons to serve for the international exchange and cooperation, and pave way for the internationalization of higher education. Therefore, how to improve the foreign affairs management in universities should be an important question deserves discussion for the internationalization of high education.

International talent training should be understood from two aspects, respectively training objects and educational subject. From the perspective of training objects, it is to cultivate individual abilities and qualities, includes global vision, self-determination, innovation, openness, and cooperation. International talents should be equipped with composite knowledge, cross-culture communication competence, and adapt to the international environment and competition, thus create new values. From the perspective of the education subject, it is to build a platform and environment for the cultivation of international talents. In the process of international exchanges and cooperation, universities should actively change the traditional talent training ideas, aim at educating people and shaping talents, and constantly explore new ways and methods through teaching reform to move forward in the direction of internationalization, making the dream of training a large number of international talents with high awareness, good quality and strong ability for our nation's prosperity and revitalization come true.

Although much efforts has been made constantly on exploring the criterion for international talents and the requirements for internationalization of higher education, universities are meeting challenges of growing complexity of the world. So it should be emphasized that only continuous exploration and reform can make the qualitative description to be changed into quantitative indicators, accumulate experience in practice and make progress towards globalization.

REFORM AND INNOVATION OF FOREIGN AFFAIRS MANAGEMENT

Current Situation of University Foreign Affairs Management

Having explored the significance, goals and measures of global dimension of higher education in China, it is necessary to consider how to promote the internalization of higher education taking the reform and innovation of universities' foreign affaire management as a key driver. As there exists some weak points in its self-development in regards of the traditional institutional issues, so reform is imperative. Considering its importance, as long as foreign affair management dedicates to the institutional reform and conceptual innovation, its historical role as a key driver to the global dimension of higher education will surely come into play, and give rise to new vitality.

With the trend of the internationalization of higher education, the foreign affairs management in universities is developing towards an all-round, multi-level and wide-ranging direction, gradually integrating education, talent introduction, administrative management and service . The reasonable setting of foreign affairs agencies and working mechanism are the necessary factors to ensure the normal operation of foreign affairs management in universities. However, subject to the constraints of traditional institutional and personnel settings, apart from the International Exchange and Cooperation Office, as the direct agency for specific foreign affairs management, most colleges or departments do not have their own International Office. Most of the staff responsible for the foreign affairs is living under the house of Teaching Management Office or the Administrative Office, engaging in many administrative tasks besides foreign affairs. Obviously, the current situation is beneficial to make staff on foreign affairs be familiar with the objective law of teaching and administration. However, due to the vague job setting and unclear role positioning, they are trapped in the trivial matters, having not enough energy to improve the ability on foreign affairs management, and gradually lose their independence and the internal motivation and external feasibility to make reform and innovation. The backwardness of the system has resulted in the loose management of staff on foreign affairs, lack of overall layout. In the long run, foreign affairs personnel without unified leadership will eventually form a weak team.

Challenges of Reform in University Foreign Affairs Management

As mentioned above, in recent years, the concept of "internationalization of higher education" has pointed out a new path for the future development of higher education and become one of the most important guidelines for universities in China. Knight (1993) describes internationalization of higher education as 'the process of integrating an international/intercultural dimension into teaching, research and service functions of institution' (pp. 21). There are several key concepts in this definition, e.g. the idea of internationalization being a dynamic process and not a set of isolated activities, integration or infusion that contributes to the sustainability of the international dimension. Finally, this definition refers to the primary and universal functions of an institution of higher education, namely, teaching, research and service to society. As the bridge and tie between home and foreign universities, the important role played by the foreign affairs management in universities in the process of exchange and cooperation cannot be neglected. The linkage between the internationalization of higher education and reform and innovation for foreign affairs management in universities is bound to inspire new sparks, which brings not only unprecedented opportunities, but also new challenges.

Innovation cannot escape from reform and reform is bound to be painful. Faced with the ever-changing international situation and the ambition of universities to be internationalized, the foreign affairs management in universities can seize the opportunity by abandoning the conservative posture of self-restraint, struggling in the wave of reform to reach the destination of innovation. How to relieve the worries on the current situation of foreign affairs management, experience pain of reform and innovation, and revive in the difficulties to strive for the internationalization of higher education is worthy of consideration by every staff on foreign affairs. Where is the road for innovation? Where will the reform go? Following are some strategies for reference on the reform and innovation for foreign affairs management in universities.

STRATEGIES OF INNOVATION IN UNIVERSITY FOREIGN AFFAIRS MANAGEMENT

Clarifying Target of Foreign Affairs Management

The foreign affairs management in universities is the specific implementation of the internationalization development of higher education. In view of the current foreign affairs management of domestic universities, it mainly includes the following aspects: First, "connecting", it means to establish cooperative relations with foreign universities, international organizations or institutions and carry out cooperation projects; second, "inviting", it means to invite foreign teachers and experts and provide service for them according to teaching and research needs; Third, "going abroad", it means to organize faculty and students to study abroad, attend international academic conferences and competition, etc.; Fourth, "students management", it means to undertake management of international students, including management on enrollment, as well as management on both their learning and lives; Fifth, it is foreign affairs reception. Foreign affairs management promotes exchange and cooperation between universities and other research institutions home and abroad, and absorb advanced foreign education, teaching concepts and management methods, which is conducive to the cultivation of international talents and promote teaching, research and management to keep up pace with international standards, the competitiveness and internationalization level of universities can be steadily and comprehensively improved.

Restructuring Organization of Foreign Affairs Management

In view of the tasks shouldered by the foreign affairs management itself, the reform must start from restructuring. A stable, professional, efficient, cohesive, combative, and energetic team is the premise and guarantee for the development of foreign affairs management. In view of the complexity of foreign affairs, as each task cannot be accomplished by a single department, it is necessary for each college or department to have its own independent agency for handling foreign affairs and cooperate with other related departments in universities. The development of foreign affairs management has far exceeded some simple daily external liaison affairs, and various forms of cross-cultural, cross-international and even cross-disciplinary exchanges have become more and more frequent, which puts forward higher requirements for foreign affairs management. As involves teaching, research and administrative management, the foreign affairs management requires a leading figure who should be "professional, good at foreign language and management and excellent in communication" to make an overall planning for the guidance of a dynamic and energetic team of cooperation.

Improving Management Level of Foreign Affairs Management

- **Objective-Oriented and Performance Appraisal:** To optimize the operation mechanism of foreign affairs management, the concept should be changed first, and a scientific appraisal mode should be established, taking the necessary reward and punishment measures in the way of goals and performance appraisal, and improve the incentive mechanism. The staff on foreign affairs will be given appropriate rewards after fulfill the task to enhance their enthusiasm and fully tap their potential to promote the sustainable development of foreign affairs management.

- **Institutionalized Management:** Formulate relevant regulations to conduct rational supervision and control on the implementation of various tasks, and make the foreign affairs management become institutionalized and standardized, such as, Regulations on the Enrollment of Foreign Experts, Regulations on the Management of Faculty Going Abroad for Business Trip, Regulations on Students' International Exchange, Management on International Students, and Measures for the Implementation of Sino-foreign Cooperative Education, etc., to make foreign affairs management have regulations to follow and rules to articulate.

- **Process Management:** Process management can solve the problems of "who should do, how to do and how to do it well" for all kinds of complicated foreign affairs management, so the division of labor, process and responsible person can be seen at a glance. The process management eliminates departmental barriers and fills the gaps in functions. The clear role positioning will greatly enhance the overall operational efficiency, and improve the entire staff member's core competitiveness, so as to achieve the purpose of orderly operation of foreign affairs management with efficiency.

- **Archives and Informatization Management:** Foreign affairs archives of universities refer to materials, charts and audio-visual carriers with preservation value formed by universities in cooperation with foreign groups or individuals in academic exchanges, scientific research cooperation, and talent exchange. They are important portrayal and evidence of the foreign affairs management and have certain value and significance for social development. (Rui Li, 2013) Foreign affairs archives, as the original records formed in foreign affairs activities, play a vital role in foreign affairs activities. They truly record the entire foreign affairs activities, not only record the history, but also establish a bridge to communicate with the future. Foreign affairs management involves a wide range of content and a wide variety of issues which puts forward higher requirements for the collection and arrangement of foreign affairs archives in universities. Staff on foreign affairs should foster the awareness of keep files timely, learn the methods of archive management actively, improve the ability to use information platforms to deal with foreign affairs, and strive to build a "Foreign Affairs Management System" with such modules for the management on foreign experts, international student, faculty and student's application for going abroad and foreign affairs reception, etc., not only realizing a series of paperless office processes such as online approval, but also facilitating the retention of relevant foreign affairs archives and the classification and searching of data to achieve quick, efficient, accurate, reliable, convenient and multi-faceted sharing of information resources.

Improving Service Level of Foreign Affairs Management

- **Cultural Self-Confidence:** In addition to basic political stance, foreign language ability and service level, staff on foreign affairs must have a good intuitive sense for devotion. Furthermore, as the communication messenger for two cultures, cultural quality is indispensable. This kind of cultural quality not only contains self-confidence to the national culture, but also requires deep intercultural communication skills on both cultures. Cultural self-confidence refers to full affirmation of the intrinsic value of Chinese culture in the basis of cultural consciousness and the belief on Chinese culture's lasting vitality. (Xiaoyan Sun, 2012) Not underestimate our own culture can remain calm and self-reliant in exchanges with western culture and treat western culture inclusively, criticize it rationally and learn from it to make Chinese culture continue to be created and spread all over the world.

- **Cultural Accomplishment:** Affected by different customs, cultural heritage and other factors, staff on foreign affairs must be familiar with the cultural characteristics of different regions, so as to facilitate the preparation of foreign affairs management services. In addition, profound cultural accomplishment also helps to communicate with people from different cultural backgrounds, correctly and comprehensively understanding the information they intend to transmit, and fully reflect the service level.

- **Intercultural Communication Competence:** For staff on foreign affairs, only with cross-culture communication ability, can they truly understand Chinese and Western culture in both ancient and contemporary era on the basis of respecting cultural differences. With regard to the cultivation of cross-culture communication skills, proficiency in a foreign language is a tool, awareness of respecting different customs and habits is the way and to maintain the enthusiasm and ability of lifelong learning is the most important.

Innovation and Improvement of Working Methods

Make full use of the website in English version to increase the propaganda of foreign affairs management, transmit the relevant information and latest news to foreign partners, publicize the student exchange program and the international student enrollment project through Weibo, WeChat and other popular communication platforms, and make full use of the "Foreign Affairs Management System" to have good contact with relevant departments and student associations, etc., expand the audience and improve the efficiency of publicity, create a simple and easy work environment in line with international trends, such as a reception room for foreign guests and a display room for the achievements of international exchange.

To summarize, the foreign affairs management in universities is a key to achieve external relations. With the development of the times, the exchanges and cooperation between universities around the world have occupied an important position in the internationalization of higher education. Therefore, the foreign affairs management in universities should grasp the principle of "five services", i.e., services for education and teaching, for disciplines, for scientific research, for administrative management, and for teachers and students. However, there are full of challenges in developing new reform and facilitating innovation in university foreign affairs management. So the reform and innovation for foreign affairs management in universities cannot happen over one night, a systematic policy supports are required in Chinese universities that will further benefit to fostering more qualified international talents in the future.

CONCLUSION

The concept of "global dimension" means new opportunities and challenges for the international development of higher education in China. This indicates on the one hand, it has pointed out the direction and provided a stage for China's higher education to display its own characteristics. On the other hand, due to the constraints of traditional education concepts and systems, there is still much room for the development, and will certainly go through a long process. Only endeavor to keep up with the global trend and learning from each other can China gets own unique path. Higher education should be developed towards sustainability, shouldering the responsibility of cultivating international talents with global awareness and ability. This calling young international talents to master diverse skills and abilities such as: critical thinking, multi-disciplinary thinking, group work skills, and the ability to work across cultures and contexts, systems thinking and strong inter-personal and communication skills.

Universities need to prepare graduates with the skills and knowledge they will need to manage rapid change, uncertainty and complexity in their future professional practice. Students should also be prepared for life-long learning in a globalized society which enables them to cope with and adapt to this complexity, uncertainty and vulnerability in solving any professional problems. Universities will have to consider how to make innovation on the organization of teaching and learning. An effective reform to higher education has been to locate global dimension into the internationalization process aiming at training global citizenship that can have a better life in the global community.

The connotation of the global dimension is complex that involves many aspects of universities' education, teaching, research and management. As the connection and bond of these processes, university foreign affairs management is undergoing a period of unprecedented change under the call of global dimension, acting as a key driver for facilitating university changes towards internalization. However, it should address that the recognition of the necessity of foreign affairs management's reform and innovation is a key to integrate the global dimension into universities. With a clear target of facilitating cross-culture communication, the future of foreign affairs management is being framed by for the global forces which transcend national boundaries such as the exchange and cooperation of student, faculty as well as teaching and research among universities all over the world.

REFERENCES

Bacon. (2014). *Essays of Francis Bacon: Chapter 5 Of Adversity*. CreateSpace Independent Publishing Platform.

Baidu Encyclopedia. (n.d.). Retrieved from http://baike.baidu.com/view/1017237.htm

Bussemaker, J. (2014). *Letter on the government's vision on the international dimension of higher education and VET*. Government of the Netherlands. Retrieved from http://www.government.nl/ministries/ocw/documents-and-publications/letters/2014/07/21/government-s-vision-on-the-international-dimension-of-higher-education-and-vet.html

Dance, F. E. X., & Larson, C. E. (1976). *The functions of human communication: A theoretical approach*. New York: Holt, Rinehart and Winston.

De Wit, H. (2002). *Internationalization of Higher Education in the United States of America and Europe: A Historical Comparative and Conceptual Analysis*. Westport, CT: Greenwood.

Deutsch, M., Marcus, E. C., & Brazaitis, S. (2012). A framework for thinking about developing a global community. In *Psychological components of sustainable peace* (pp. 299–324). Springer New York. doi:10.1007/978-1-4614-3555-6_16

Farrell & Grant. (2005). *Addressing China's Looming Talent Shortage*. McKinsey & Company. Retrieved from http://www.ideas-forum.org.uk/about-us/global-citizenship https://globaldimension.org.uk/about/what-is-the-global-dimension/

Gibbons, Limoges, Nowotny, Schwartzman, Scott, & Trow. (2010). The New Production of Knowledge: The Dynamics of Science and Research in Contemporary Societies. SAGE Publications Ltd.

Guorong, Lv. (2004). *Ten Criteria for Excellent Staff of Bill Gates*. Beijing: Mechanical Industry Press.

Huiyao & Green. (Eds.). (2013). *Annual Report on the Development of Chinese Students Studying Abroad in Blue Book of Global Talent*. Social Science Literature Publishing House.

Knight, J. (1993). Internationalization: Management strategies and issues. *International Education Magazine, 9*(6), 21-22.

Knight, J. (2004, Spring). Internationalization Remodeled: Definition, Approaches, and Rationales. *Journal of Studies in International Education, 8*(1), 5–31. doi:10.1177/1028315303260832

Li, R. (2013). *Current Situation and Suggestions of Foreign Affairs Archives Management in Colleges and Universities*. Office Business.

Liu. (2011). Analysis of the School Running Mode of Sino-foreign Cooperation in Running Schools. *Business Management, 10*.

Oberg, K. (1960). Culture shock: Adjustment to new cultural environments. *Practical Anthropology, 7*(4), 177–182. doi:10.1177/009182966000700405

Padhi. (2016). The Rising Importance of Cross Cultural Communication in Global Business Scenario. *Quest Journals, Journal of Research in Humanities and Social Science, 4*(1), 20-26.

Smith, A. G. (1996). *Communication and Culture: Reading in the in the Codes of Human Interaction*. New York: Holt, Rinehalt & Winston.

Sun, X. (2012). *On the Understanding of the Subjectivity of National Culture*. Modern Communication.

Turner. (2005). *Sociology*. Prentice Hall.

von Humboldt, Heath, & Aarsleff. (1997). *On Language: The Diversity of Human Language-Structure and its Influence on the Mental Development of Mankind* (X. Yao, Trans.). Beijing: The Commercial Press.

Wang. (2015). *Lun Yu*. Beijing United Publishing Company.

Wood, J. T. (1997). *Gendered lives: Communication, gender and culture*. Belmont, CA: Wadsworth.

Zhou, C. (2016). Fostering creative problem solvers in higher education: a response to complexity of society. In C. Zhou (Ed.), *Creative Problem-Solving Skill Development in Higher Education* (pp. 1–24). Hershey, PA: IGI Global.

Chapter 10

Developing Engineering Creativity in STEM Programs in Chinese Universities

Chunfang Zhou
Aalborg University, Denmark

ABSTRACT

This chapter aims to formulate a proposal of developing engineering creativity by problem- and project-based pedagogies in STEM programs in university education in China. It will introduce the increasing needs of engineering creativity in China, deepen understanding of the concept of creativity and engineering creativity, and provide a review of diverse models of problem- and project-based pedagogies in STEM programs. This further brings a discussion on how to develop engineering creativity in STEM programs in Chinese universities in order to overcome the barriers caused by traditional education system and culture. A series of strategies will be proposed including supporting student group work, designing interdisciplinary project, facilitating staff development, and developing creative communities, etc. Briefly, this chapter has the significance of developing engineering creativity in China both theoretically and practically, and also implies how to develop problem- and project-based pedagogies in STEM programs in other cultures around the world.

DOI: 10.4018/978-1-5225-9961-6.ch010

UNDERSTANDING THE CONTEXT IN CHINA

In contemporary China, both 'innovation' and 'creativity' have been highly emphasized in the S&T policies initiated by the national government that grows the attention to roles of R&D centers in universities in the Chinese national system (Orcutt, & Shen, 2010). As suggested by Li (2011), the shift from 'Made in China' to 'Created in China' is underway, so the strategies for enhancing innovation capabilities have come to occupy an important position in China's development policy. In 2006, China initiated a 15-year 'Medium-to-Long-Term Plan for the Development of Science and Technology'. The Plan calls for China to become an 'innovative oriented society' by the year 2020, and a world leader in science and technology (S&T) by 2050 (Cao, Richard, & Denis, 2006). In the changes towards 'innovative nation', Chinese universities are one of key institutions carrying national engineering research projects. The fruitful research output arising from publicly financed research projects and a growing political pressure to change universities' traditional role of education and research, promote university entrepreneurship (Tang, 2009; Zhou et al., 2017).

However, policies have often failed to achieve their intended outcomes because the process of knowledge transfer is very complex and even sometimes the outcomes of policy are unpredictable (Brown, 2008). This can be indicated by the current debate on China's S&T capability in relation to set goals to become an 'innovative nation', which has reached almost two polar opposite conclusions. On the one hand, there is a pile of data shows China has increased its output in several S&T indicators. For example, China has dramatically increased the number of patents, scientific articles and engineers that it produces. China has also progressed in developing a high-tech manufacturing sector. This progress has led some to believe that China will soon overwhelm the rest of the world in engineering and technology. On the other hand, there is an equally large pile of data that suggests China's current technology capabilities are not that strong, and may remain weak for foreseeable future. Much of China's progress in patents, scientific articles and engineer formation could be described as involving improvements in 'quantity', such as numbers of publications and patents, but not necessarily 'quality' in terms of societal uptake and impact of new knowledge. In addition, China's improvements in high-tech manufacturing remain overly dependent on foreign technology transfer, as China has yet to develop domestic technology generation capabilities that truly rival those of the leading countries. Such debate calls us to rethink that studies on implementation processes must therefore take account of specific local contexts in which the policies are implemented. This also indicates engineering education in China is meeting crisis of fostering creative engineers who are able to develop original innovative work in their professional practice (Zhou et al., 2017).

Recently, the rethinking on STEM education innovation and creativity in China has driven that learning by projects and solving real-life problems has been considered as a promising pedagogy in STEM education on bachelor and postgraduate levels. For example, Project-Organized Groups (POGs) in some top universities. However, STEM education in China is still lecture-based model, the current application of student project models is to only one part within the traditional educational curriculum. Therefore, a systematic way of engineering education reform is required and to fostering creative learning culture is a condition. Accordingly, this chapter aims to propose developing problem and project-based pedagogies as a potential strategy to develop engineering creativity among STEM programmes in university education in China, which brings both theoretical discussions on creativity theories and practical suggestions for improving STEM education in China.

WHAT IS ENGINEERING CREATIVITY?

Engineering as a profession has come a long way from the era of Leonardo da Vinci and others when craft and science enjoyed a scared harmony to a widening recognition beyond technologies (Beder, 1999). In the book *Educating Engineers: Designing for the Future of the Field*, Sheppard and his colleagues (2009) discussed that today's engineers, like other professionals such as physicians, nurses and lawyers, have to deal with an ever-increasing complexity in their fields of work while considering changing societal needs. The explosion of new information technologies, robotics, biotechnology, and the increased blending of invention with scientific discovery are powerfully affecting everyday life in unexpected ways. For instance, information technologies are not only speeding up communication and information exchanges but also increasing the complexity in how tasks are carried out and how business is organized worldwide. Environmental and societal issues require local and global solutions (Feest, 2008), and engineers at work, at the center of all these developments, are frequently challenged to grapple with the ramifying consequences of such rapid innovation (Baillie & Catalano, 2008). This calls increasingly for creative problem-solving abilities among engineers. For example, The Engineer of 2020 (National Academy of Engineering, 2004) points out that engineers need 'creativity'- that is, the ability to respond to challenges by combining in new ways a broader range of interdisciplinary knowledge, and a greater focus on systemic constructs and outcomes (Zhou, 2012a).

Although there are different ways of definition, generally, creativity involves the ability to offer new perspectives, generate novel and meaningful ideas, raise new questions, and come up with solutions to ill-defined problems (Amabile, 1996). It has been demonstrated multiple manifestations of the conceptualization: personal cognitive and social or emotional processes, family aspects, education, characteristics of the domain and fields, social or cultural contextual aspects, as well as historical forces, event, and trends (Sternberg, 1999). The recent literature has demonstrated the growing attention to a systems approach to creativity in a framework of social-cultural theory (Zhou, 2012b). For example, the systems model (Csikszentmihalyi, 2014) shows creativity occurs at the interface of their subsystems: An individual who absorbs information from the culture and changes it in a way that will be selected by the relevant Field of gatekeepers for inclusion into the Domain, from whence the novelty will be accessible to the next generation. This means that in creativity, it makes no sense to say that a beneficial step was the result of a particular person alone, without taking into account environmental conditions. To be creative, a variation has to be adapted to its social environment, and it has to be capable of being passed on through time. It also means creativity is the engine that drives cultural evolution, as creativity always involves a change in a symbolic system - a change that, in turn, will affect the thoughts and feelings of other and feelings of other members of the culture. So creativity presupposes a community of people who share ways of thinking and acting, who learn from each other and imitate each other's actions (Csikszentmihalyi, 2014).

In short, creativity is a domain-general ability, a means of envisaging solutions and ways forward, of thriving in a complex social system with numerous different needs (Sternberg 1999). There have been increasing calls for creativity in everyday life - otherwise described as life-wide creativity (Craft, 2008) or life-wide resourcefulness in charting a course of action by seeing opportunities as well as overcoming obstacles. While someone may have a new idea about how to run a country or a company, artists may develop new types of music, and scientists may develop new techniques or knowledge that may have a profound impact on society. This type of creativity has sometimes been called 'big C' creativity. The everyday creativity has been described as 'little C' creativity that happens as people try to solve problems at work and at home, or on the road in between (Paulus, and Nijstad, 2003). In other words, 'little C' creativity may occur in personal and social matters or in undertaking an activity in a disciplinary or professional area. It is 'know-how', concerned with the skills involved in maneuvering and operating concepts and ideas in the physical and social world - including the skills of social interaction and engagement (Craft, 2005, 2006). In engineering practice, the concepts of 'little C' and 'know-how' should be particularly emphasized, as the role of creativity rests on its potential to develop new insight, make new connections and identify new solutions. Accordingly, creativity should be a part of engineering professional identity that is an embedded thinking skill in engineering life. From this sense, creativity can be regarded as a kind of scientific and technology literacy of engineers that is particularly related to the challenges of issues of sustainability, creativity, and engineering education innovation (Zhou, 2016).

Relating the general points of creativity to engineering practice, Zhou (2012a) discussed much on creativity is also a domain-specific conception in relation to understanding engineering creativity. Based on the work of Cropley and Cropley (2005), Zhou (2012b) also emphasized creativity is a vital factor in "good" engineering, and creativity in engineering clearly differs from creativity in the other domains. For example, by contrast creativity in fine arts - a manifestation of creativity with no functional purpose, only aesthetic purpose - engineering creativity results from creativity with a purpose. This purpose is to create products in the broadest sense of the word - including physical objects, complex systems, and processes. So the differences are pointed out that engineers produce devices or systems that perform tasks or solve problems. From this sense, engineering creativity has been defined as "functional creativity". The most important aspect is the devices systems that perform tasks or solve problem - that is, it practically useful products. Furthermore, a "four-dimensional model" for defining the creativity of engineering products has been outlined (Cropley and Cropley, 2005; Zhou, 2012b):

1. **Relevance and Effectiveness:** The product solves the problem it was intended to solve.
2. **Novelty:** The product is original and "surprising."
3. **Elegance:** The product is "beautiful" or pleasing, and goes beyond a simple mechanical solution.
4. **Generalizability:** The product is broadly applicable - it can be transferred to situations other than the present one and opens up perspectives for solving other problems.

The four-dimensional model is helpful to conceptualize the products of functional creativity as solutions to problems. Meanwhile, the most important aspect of this model is that the dimensions form a hierarchy, which indicates functional creativity as a system. As argued by Zhou (2012a), relevance and effectiveness on the one hand, and novelty on the other, are fundamental and necessary conditions for a creative product, but neither is sufficient on its own. Only when both are present is it possible to talk about creativity. Furthermore, the first criterion (effectiveness) must be met before the second (novelty) becomes relevant. Elegance and generalizability come lower in the hierarchy: It is possible to talk about creativity without them, and they are only interesting when the first two criteria have been met (Zhou, 2012a).

Accordingly, the definition of engineering creativity helps to deepen understanding characteristics of creativity in a particular situation of engineering practice. It also provides implications for thinking what kinds of particular abilities the students should master when they are encouraged to be creative. However, this point has not been paid enough attention in previous studies on fostering engineering creativity in higher education. Pedagogical strategies for creativity has been ignored to some extent because universities have traditionally concentrated on providing "hard technological knowledge" where the "soft skills" become the "appurtenant" in engineering education. Despite some efforts towards creativity development in engineering education have been made in recent years, progress has not been significant. According to Zhou (2012a), a series of prejudice of educators leads creativity blockers in engineering education, such as:

1. Engineering is serious business, engineers must be accurate not creative.
2. Creativity leads to chaos and disorder in the school and later to design uncertainties and therefore legal liabilities in practice.
3. Creative behavior contradicts or violates academic standards at school and national engineering standards in practice and standards.
4. Anyone can produce a draft design. Engineers must only use fundamentally sound equations and established procedures and precedents to design.
5. Engineers cannot take risks. The example of building bridges, making mistakes, and loss of lives comes up often.

These barriers include a lack of emotional engagement with engineering works on the part of the students, which in turn is mainly focused on the technical aspect of the curriculum. Furthermore, engineering educators face difficulties due to (1) the institution's role in promoting creativity and (2) figuring out how to integrate creativity into the engineering program. Moreover, most studies take a departure regarding creativity as a domain-general ability but among particular groups of engineers. On terms of designing curriculum models for fostering engineering creativity, little attention has been paid to a systematic way of thinking learning environment involving interplays between teaching, learning, and cultural contexts. Most efforts have been made on how to improve skills of creative problem solving by introducing creativity-training courses.

PEDAGOGIES FOR ENGINEERING CREATIVITY IN STEM PROGRAMMES

The recent study shows there is increasing recognition that by using student project as a pedagogical strategy, a creative learning environment will be fostered (Zhou, 2012b). According to Zhou (2016), by using student projects, there are at least five elements that play significant roles in fostering creativity: 1) group learning, 2) problem solving, 3) facilitation, 4) interdisciplinary learning, and 5) project management. These are influenced by each other within a student project context and commonly construct the learning context as a stimulus of social practice and appreciate conditions for motivating group interactions in order to generate both individual and group creativity. In other words, creativity happens in the interplay between these elements and the process of creativity development is embedded in a situated-learning community built by project work (Zhou, 2015a). Accordingly, Zhou (2015b) suggested a metaphor of regarding a student project as an 'extra group member' in relation to the context of group creativity development. This means that students' creativity can be developed out of 'conversations' between students and an 'extra group member' (the project). The conversations are 'back and forth' processes - the 'extra group member' (the project) 'asks' students to meet task challenges, 'calls for' group discussions, 'speeds up' group decision making, and 'remind' the deadline of project reports; the students react in collaborative ways in order to 'answer' the 'extra group member' (the project). This metaphor deepens us about the understanding that creativity is social-constructed as dialogic and not as unitary (Craft, 2005; Csikszentmihalyi, 2014). The 'relationship' in the construction of collaborative creativity can be seen as a form of dynamic interaction between learners and between learners and the discipline itself (Zhou, 2015b).

In pedagogical practice, diverse models of using student projects have been developed with the aim of fostering creative students have been explored in many educational institutions in various countries such as Denmark, U.K., Australia, Finland, Brazil, Spain, and elsewhere (Zhou, et al., 2010). There is Project-Led Education in Portugal, Project-Centered Learning in the USA, Problem and Project-Based Learning (PBL) in Denmark (Zhou, et al., 2010), Project-Organized Groups (POGs) in China, Design Thinking in German, Conceive-Design-Implement-Operate (CDIO) in Sweden, and Inquiry-Based Learning at University in Spain, etc. These models have common underlying assumptions that creativity can be stimulated by a suitable environment and using effective exercises and group work in practice (Zhou, et al., 2010). In practice, these models have been employed in different ways and levels in engineering education from context to context. For example, Problem and Project-Based Learning (PBL) has been employed as a whole university education model at Aalborg University in Denmark; Project-Organized Groups (POGs) has been only one part curriculum in master engineering programs in some Chinese universities; while Project-Led Education is also on course level education in Portugal. The influences of learning culture on creativity in different strategies also have been discussed. For example, PBL model in Denmark highlights students' ownership of learning that means students manage their project by themselves; however, POGs model in China highlights supervisors' leadership in project management that means students are not involved in project management (Zhou & Valero, 2015).

In addition, challenges in the shift from teacher-led to student-centered education (Dolmans, 2001) and culture issues of creativity development in STEM education should be addressed. As cognitive studies suggested (Newman, 2005), students will be more creative when internally motivated, when they feel some ownership of or control over the learning process, and when they look beyond one correct answer. Using student projects places high demands on the problems used and on the skills of the supervisor in order to ensure that cooperative learning in group work positively influences student learning or leads to better learning than individual learning (Zhou, 2016). This challenge should be particularly emphasized in Chinese context where has a long cultural tradition of collectivism, as suggested in the following.

BARRIERS TO DEVELOPING ENGINEERING CREATIVITY IN CHINA

Generally, China has a relative traditional educational context for STEM students. In China, students learn individually and lecture is the main way of knowledge delivery. Recently, some actions aiming to foster excellent students through project work have been taken in some universities in China. For example, learning in project-organized teams is considered as a promising strategy for postgraduate level education. By this strategy, students have opportunities to participate projects supported by government or company. Usually, the project teams consist of supervisors and their students from different levels and diverse backgrounds. However, there are always some new recruits to enter teams and the graduates leave at every semester, so high personnel turnover rate exists, while most projects are at least one-year-long with aims of solving real engineering problems needed in society. The supervisors are professors in universities with responsibilities of leaders in these teams, as well the experts in some fields of engineering education. Therefore, for the STEM students, learning is organized through practical problems and in collaborations among group members, which may develop skills of creative thinking along with problem solving process.

However, the recent study (Zhou & Valero, 2015) shows in STEM education in China, the students in project-organized teams have opportunity only to participate in projects rather than to design, plan, or manage projects on their own. The students are not encouraged to develop as many new ideas through risk taking and the supervisors tend to expect obedience or respect, expectations which are influenced by the project management system and the Confucian tradition. Thus, the current Chinese education policy and the traditional culture are potential barriers to develop creative talents in China.

In a previous study, Zhou (2016) suggested that advantages of using student project in Chinese universities are in providing a series of drivers to creative climate including group openness, task challenges, group diversity, and group leadership, etc., and some barriers including students' fear of authority, limited working time, and lacking of students' leadership of project management, etc. As Bush and Qiang (2000) argued, the Chinese culture remains in the place where a love of authority and leadership are balanced with hierarchy and collectivism. This influences learning activity where there is an emphasis on teaching through lectures rather than discussion or student questions. Such a culture influenced the students' behaviors in their project groups, leading to fear of asking questions, challenging authority, or worrying about a supervisor's unsatisfying response to questions that is negatively correlated with group creative climate (Rudowicz & Yue, 2002). So much reflection on future efforts against existing problems of student project strategies is about how to restructure the relationships between teachers and students in order to foster engineering creativity. In other words, the key for future improvement is about better applying the egalitarian approach.

STRATEGIES TO DEVELOPING ENGINEERING CREATIVITY IN CHINA

As discussed in the above, the issues of developing creativity in STEM education in China that are in line with general challenges of using student projects in traditional universities in other contexts around the world; however, this also requires overcoming the particular local cultural barriers in China. Therefore, it is necessary to design appropriate model of learning through student projects in STEM education in Chinese context; and meanwhile, in order to foster STEM creativity and applying student project pedagogy, the appropriate model of staff training programs among Chinese STEM educators also are required. Accordingly, the following strategies will be proposed and discussed.

Firstly, supporting students in group work should be encouraged in STEM programmes in Chinese universities. In order to solve complex problems in STEM field, collaboration among students is a key to the satisfying solutions. Thus, the traditional individual learning cannot face the challenges of complex engineering practice. Creativity needs a collaborative group learning context. As argued by Eteläpelto and Lahti (2008), in successful collaboration within collective learning setting, participants build on each other's ideas in order to reach an understanding that was not available to any of the participants initially. However, in order for this to happen, the participants need to be committed to the shared goals, and have sufficient trust in each other to join in the shared endeavour. The participants must also enter into critical and constructive negotiation of each other's suggestions. Well-grounded arguments and counter-arguments need to be shared and critically evaluated through collective communication. Thus, such participation is necessary in order to foster creative endeavours in collaboration.

Secondly, designing interdisciplinary project for students is necessary in STEM programmes in Chinese universities. Nijstad and Stroebe (2006) have suggested that task-related diversity enhances group performance. Increasing the diversity of group membership can improve the number and type of innovative ideas coming into the group. As Wenger (1998) suggested, competence and experience are in different relationships at the core and at the boundaries of practices. The innovation potential of a system lies in its combination of strong practices and active boundary processes - people who can engage across boundaries, but have enough depth in their own practice that they can recognize when something is really significantly new. Accordingly, efforts on developing interdisciplinary projects among student groups are necessary in STEM programmes in China. This also involves efforts on interdisciplinary collaboration between teaching staff and organizations in Chinese universities. Organizational changes towards a systematic model of problem and project-based pedagogies should be considered on institutional level.

Thirdly, facilitating changes from "teacher-led" education towards "student-centered" learning should be emphasized among STEM staff in Chinese universities. To hold on to the philosophy of "student-centered learning" is critical for teachers in problem and project-based pedagogies. There should be a good relationship between supervisors and students. The supervisors tended to encourage students to explore answers, sometimes joined in group work, and always ensure quality of group dynamics. As the literature (Kazerounian & Foley, 2007) shows, teacher's pedagogic strategies and attitudes can have an impact on creativity. The psychological research has examined that when researchers manipulated the learning environment in such a way that students felt that risky behaviour was more acceptable, students' creativity increased. Students were more excited about the potential to excel and less worried about the possibility of failure. It has been shown that students will be more creative when they are internally motivated and when they feel some ownership of or control over a learning process (Craft, 2005). This is matched with the core philosophy of "student-centered learning" of PBL. However, the Chinese Confucian tradition tends to get response of obedient behaviour from students and tend to control students' activities in classroom, which are barriers to construct creative learning environment. Thus, in order to foster creativity in STEM education, the barriers of traditional Confusion culture should be broken in the future. Therefore, a series of strategies on staff development should be considered.

Fourthly, facilitating staff development on teaching creativity should be considered in STEM programmes in Chinese universities. It should aim to change the traditional views and attitudes towards STEM education to the teaching staff. A comprehensive conceptualization of creativity is necessary to be shaped among Chinese educators. For example, a series of topics those educators should be able to understand clearly in teaching practice: What is creativity? Why do STEM students have problems with creativity? What kills creativity among STEM students? How can STEM students solve problems creatively? Meanwhile, the techniques related to creative thinking and learning, group creativity, creative project management should be provided to the staff, which will be helpful to support student groups in their project work. In addition, rethinking of creative teaching is needed for Chinese teaching staff. Only through a self-evaluation of the own culture, the elements that are blocking the populace, and the construction of more fertile creative soil can the teaching lead the students to new levels of creative achievement (Kim, 2007). So only when the educators pay more attention to creativity will the students have more opportunities to be creative (Zhou, 2012b).

Finally, the 'creative STEM community' should be encouraged and built by S&T policies in China. As the concept of 'community' can represent a network of embedded mutual relationships or it can imply designated social relationships. Communities provide synergy. Initially innovative communities tend to cluster in urban spaces, followed by a gradual reaching out, a process, which can generate socio-economic transformations in cities and region (Heinze et al. 2009). In this sense, the 'creative STEM community' meets the needs of building an 'innovation system' where should involve diverse actors such as university, private business, state-owned enterprise, and government research institution, etc. and their collaboration. As Tang (2009) discussed, in current China many universities have gained more autonomy in terms of deciding on tuition fees, enrolment of students, curricula design, employment of teaching staffs, scientific research and so on. In this context people-oriented and ability-oriented approaches are gaining ground, changing the value orientation of economic development and encouraging a new lifestyle, where work is combined with individual development and fulfilment, in university organizations.

In short, to build a creative learning environment in the classroom and a creative learning culture in institutions is the key to foster creativity in STEM education in China. So, an atmosphere that stimulates motivation, an open mind, taking risks, ownership, freedom, and psychological safety is the key focus to be planned, developed, evaluated, and improved in the future. Therefore, attention should be paid to ways that young STEM students can express their creative ideas and meanwhile the pedagogical strategies should support those creative ideas to be developed further in practice. In other words, this requires conversations between teaching and learning are centred by a key word of creativity, which interplays with creative institutional culture. Therefore, related efforts of making new institutional policies and curriculum changes are expected in Chinese STEM education.

CONCLUSION

STEM education issues have received a lot of attention in recent years and the attention has been paid to a sufficient number of students, teachers, and practitioners in different levels of curriculum and diverse culture. The growing concerns are not only on defining STEM education but also about how STEM education is implemented better in order to prepare more qualified young people for the society in dealing with increasing complexity in working practices in the areas of STEM. Accordingly, necessary skills and abilities have been discussed in STEM education and among which creativity is one of key topics. Meanwhile, some advanced pedagogical strategies or models also have been focused, for example, problem and project-based pedagogies. This chapter firstly discusses how to understand creativity, engineering creativity and requirements of developing creativity in STEM programmes. Linking these points to a context of STEM programmes development in university education in China, barriers and strategies of developing creativity in STEM education are also discussed and proposed. It requires needs the collaborated effort of educational institutions, business and the community for its coordinated development. A self-evaluation of influences of Chinese culture on creativity and innovation is required that contributes to further break traditional cultural barriers to creative climate of university and to provide references to policy makers. In other words, we must recognize that innovation is a complex concept and difficult to grasp in a single indicator. Along with the emergence of creative industry in China, the creative culture has been encouraged in the shift from 'made in China' to 'Created in China'. This involves changes of emphasis from product innovation to value innovation, from use value to symbolic value, from economic growth to economic development, from working hard to working, and so on. Such national culture changes also facilitate the organizational management in Chinese universities to change towards supporting creative education. In this sense, this chapter provides both theoretical understanding and practical guidelines of facilitating changes of STEM programmes towards problem and project-based strategies for the future. This also implies other contexts for manging challenges in developing creativity in STEM programmes in universities around the world.

REFERENCES

Amabile, T. M. (1996). *Creativity in Context: Update to the Social Psychology of Creativity*. New York: Crown.

Baillie, C., & Catalano, G. (2008). *Engineering and society, working toward social justice*. Morgan & Claypool Publishers.

Beder, B. S. (1999). Beyond technicalities: Expanding engineering thinking. *Journal of Professional Issues in Engineering Education and Practice, 125*(1), 12–18. doi:10.1061/(ASCE)1052-3928(1999)125:1(12)

Brown, H. (2008). *Knowledge and Innovation: A Comparative study of the USA, the UK, and Japan*. London: Routledge.

Bush, T., & Qiang, H. (2000). Leadership and culture in Chinese education. *Asia Pacific Journal of Education, 20*(2), 58–67. doi:10.1080/02188791.2000.10600183

Cao, C., Richard, P. S., & Denis, F. S. (2006). China's 15-year Science and Technology Plan. *Physics Today, 59*(December), 38–43. doi:10.1063/1.2435680

Craft, A. (2005). *Creativity in Schools: Tensions and Dilemmas*. New York: Routledge. doi:10.4324/9780203357965

Craft, A. (2006). Creativity in schools. In N. Jackson, M. Oliver, M. Shaw, & J. Wisdom (Eds.), *Developing Creativity in Higher Education: An Imaginative Curriculum* (pp. 19–28). London: Routledge.

Craft, A. (2008). Studying collaborative creativity: Implications for education. *Thinking Skills and Creativity, 3*(3), 241–245. doi:10.1016/j.tsc.2008.09.006

Cropley, D., & Cropley, A. (2005). Engineering creativity: a systems concept of functional creativity. In J. C. Kaufman & J. Baer (Eds.), *Creativity Across Domains: Faces of the Muse* (pp. 169–186). London: Lawrence Erlbaum Associates.

Csikszentmihalyi, M. (2014). *The Systems Model of Creativity: The Collected Works of Mihaly Csikszentmihalyi*. London: Springer. doi:10.1007/978-94-017-9085-7

Dolmans, D., Wolfhagen, I. H. A. P., van der Vleuten, C. P. M., & Wijnen, W. H. F. W. (2001). Solving problems with group work in Problem-based Learning: Hold on to the philosophy. *Medical Education, 35*(9), 884–889. doi:10.1046/j.1365-2923.2001.00915.x PMID:11555227

Eteläpelto, A., & Lahti, J. (2008). The resources and obstacles of creative collaboration in a long-term learning community. *Thinking Skills and Creativity*, *3*(3), 226–240. doi:10.1016/j.tsc.2008.09.003

Feest, T. (2008). Engineers: Going global. *Industry and Higher Education*, *22*(4), 209–213. doi:10.5367/000000008785201801

Heinze, T., Shapira, P., Rogers, J. D., & Senker, J. M. (2009). Oragnizational and Instituational Influences on Creativity in Scientific Research. *Research Policy*, *38*(4), 610–623. doi:10.1016/j.respol.2009.01.014

Kazerounian, K., & Foley, S. (2007). Barriers to creativity in engineering education: A study of instructors and students perceptions. *Journal of Mechanical Design*, *129*(7), 761–768. doi:10.1115/1.2739569

Kim, K. H. (2007). Exploring the interactions between Asian culture (Confucianism) and creativity. *The Journal of Creative Behavior*, *41*(1), 28–53. doi:10.1002/j.2162-6057.2007.tb01280.x

Li, W. (2011). How Creativity is Changing China (M. Keane, Ed.; H. Li & M. Guo, Trans.). Bloomsbury Academic.

National Academy of Engineering (NAE). (2004). *The engineer of 2020: vision of engineering in the new century*. Washington, DC: National Academies Press.

Nijstad, B. A., & Stroebe, W. (2006). Four principles of group creativity. In L. L. Thompson & H. S. Choi (Eds.), *Creativity and Innovation in Organizational Team* (pp. 161–177). London: Lawrence Erlbaum Associates.

Orcutt, J. L., & Hong, S. (2010). *Shaping China's Innovation Future: University Technology Transfer in Transition*. Edward Elgar.

Paulus, P. B., & Nijstad, B. A. (2003). Group creativity: an introduction. In P. B. Paulus (Ed.), *Group Creativity: Innovation through Collaboration* (pp. 3–11). New York: Oxford University Press. doi:10.1093/acprof:oso/9780195147308.003.0001

Rudowicz, E., & Yue, X. (2002). Compatibility of Chinese and creative personalities. *Creativity Research Journal*, *14*(3&4), 387–394. doi:10.1207/S15326934CRJ1434_9

Sheppard, F. S. D., Macatangay, K., William, A. C., & Sullivan, M. (2009). *Educating engineers, designing for the future*. San Francisco: Jossey-Bass.

Sternberg, R. J. (1999). *Handbook of creativity*. New York: Cambridge University Press.

Tang, M. F. (2009). *Technology Transfer from University to Industry: Insight into University Technology Transfer in the Chinese National Innovation Systems*. London: Adonis & Abbey Publishers Ltd.

Wenger, E. (1998). *Communities of Practice, Learning, Meaning and Identity*. New York: Cambridge University Press. doi:10.1017/CBO9780511803932

Zhou, C. (2012a). Fostering Creative Engineers: A Key to Face Complexity of Engineering Practice. *European Journal of Engineering Education, 37*(4), 343–353. doi:10.1080/03043797.2012.691872

Zhou, C. (2012b). *Group Creativity Development in Engineering Education in Problem and Project-Based Learning (PBL) Environment* (Ph.D. thesis). Aalborg: AK print.

Zhou, C. (2015a). Bridging creativity and group by elements of Problem-Based Learning (PBL). In A. Abraham, A. K. Muda, & Y.-H. Choo (Eds.), *Pattern Analysis, Intelligent Security and the Internet of Things* (pp. 1–10). London: Springer. doi:10.1007/978-3-319-17398-6_1

Zhou, C. (2015b). Student project as an 'extra group member': a metaphor for creativity development in Problem-Based Learning (PBL). *Academic Quarter*, 9223-235.

Zhou, C. (2016). Developing Creativity as a Scientific Literacy in Software Engineering Education towards Sustainability. In *2016 12th International Conference on Natural Computation, Fuzzy Systems and Knowledge Discovery (ICNC-FSKD 2016)*. IEEE Press. 10.1109/FSKD.2016.7603533

Zhou, C., Rasmussen, P., Chemi, T., & Luo, L. (2017). An Investigation of Creative Climate of University R&D Centers and Policy Implications for Innovation in China. In Y. Jing & S. Osborne (Eds.), *Public Service Innovations in China* (pp. 185–205). Singapore: Palgrave Macmillan. doi:10.1007/978-981-10-1762-9_9

Zhou, C., & Valero, P. (2015). A Comparison on Creativity in Project Groups in Science and Engineering Education between Denmark and China. In G. E. Corazza & S. Agnoli (Eds.), *Multidisciplinary Contributions to Science of Creative Thinking* (pp. 133–151). Springer.

ADDITIONAL READING

Awang, H., & Ramly, I. (2008). Creative thinking skill approach through Problem-Based Learning: Pedagogy and practice in the engineering classroom. *The International Journal of Social Sciences (Islamabad)*, *3*(1), 18–23.

Ayas, K., & Zeniuk, N. (2001). Project-based learning: Building communities of reflective practitioners. *Management Learning*, *32*(1), 61–76. doi:10.1177/1350507601321005

Baumard, P. (1999). *Tacit Knowledge in Organizations*. London: Sage Publications.

Boden, M. A. (2011). Creativity and artificial intelligence. *Artificial Intelligence*, *103*(1-2), 347–356. doi:10.1016/S0004-3702(98)00055-1

Brosnan, K., & Burgess, R. C. (2003). Web based continuing professional development – a learning architecture approach. *Journal of Workplace Learning*, *15*(1), 24–33. doi:10.1108/13665620310458794

Brosnan, M., & Lee, W. (1998). A cross-cultural comparison of gender differences in computer attitudes and anxieties: The United Kingdom and Hong Kong. *Computers in Human Behavior*, *14*(4), 559–577. doi:10.1016/S0747-5632(98)00024-7

Buzan, T. (1976). *Use Both Sides of Your Brain*. NY: E. P. Dutton & Co.

Claxton, G., Edwards, L., & Scale-Constantinou, V. (2009). Cultivating creative mentalities: A framework for education. *Thinking Skills and Creativity*, *1*(1), 57–61. doi:10.1016/j.tsc.2005.11.001

Daud, M. Y., & Zakaria, E. (2012). Web 2.0 application to cultivate creativity in ICT literacy. *Procedia: Social and Behavioral Sciences*, *59*, 459–466. doi:10.1016/j.sbspro.2012.09.301

De Graaff, E., & Ravesteijn, W. (2001). Training complete engineers: Global enterprise and engineering education. *European Journal of Engineering Education*, *26*(4), 419–427. doi:10.1080/03043790110068701

Defillippi, R. J. (2001). Introduction: Project-based learning, reflective practices and learning outcomes. *Management Learning*, *32*(1), 5–10. doi:10.1177/1350507601321001

Delic, K. A., & Dum, R. (2006). On the emerging future of complexity sciences, *ACM Ubiquity, 7*.

Ekvall, G. (1999). Creative climate. In M. A. Runco & S. R. Pritzker (Eds.), *Encyclopedia of Creativity* (pp. 403–412). San Diego: Academic Press.

Ferrari, A., Cachia, R., & Punie, Y. (2009). *Innovation and Creativity in Education and Training in the EU member States: Fostering Creative Learning and Supporting Innovative Teaching, Literature Review on Innovation in E&T in the EU Members States. Office for Official Publications of the European Communities.* Luxembourg: Romina Cachia and Yves Punie Luxembourg.

Gauntlett, D. (2011). *Making is Connecting: the Social Meaning of Creativity, from DIY and Knitting to YouTube and Web 2.0.* Cambridge: Polity.

Grossen, M. (2008). Methods for studying collaborative creativity: An original and adventurous blend. *Thinking Skills and Creativity, 3*(3), 246–249. doi:10.1016/j.tsc.2008.09.005

Hoegl, M., & Parboteeah, P. (2007). Creativity in innovative projects: How teamwork matters. *Journal of Engineering and Technology Management, 24*(1-2), 148–166. doi:10.1016/j.jengtecman.2007.01.008

Hughes, T. (2004). *Human-Built world: How to think about technology and culture.* Chicago: University of Chicago Press. doi:10.7208/chicago/9780226120669.001.0001

Illeris, K. (2007). *The three dimensions of learning.* Denmark: Roskilde University Press.

Kampylis, P. G., Bocconi, S., & Punie, Y. (2012). *Towards a Mapping Framework of ICT-enabled Innovation for Learning.* Scientific and Policy Report by the Joint Research Centre of the European Commission.

Littleton, K., Rojas-Drummond, S., & Miell, D. (2008). Introduction to the special issue: collaborative creativity: socio-cultural perspectives. *Thinking Skills and Creativity, 3*(3), 175–176. doi:10.1016/j.tsc.2008.09.004

Loveless, A. M. (2007). Creativity, technology and learning – a review of recent literature (No. 4 update). Last retrieved May 2009, from www. futurlab.org.dk/litereviews

Loveness, A., Burton, J., & Turvey, K. (2006). Developing conceptual frameworks for creativity, ICT and teacher education. *Thinking Skills and Creativity, 1*(1), 3–13. doi:10.1016/j.tsc.2005.07.001

Lubart, T. I. (1999). Creativity across cultures. In R. J. Sternberg (eds.), Handbook of Creativity. 339-350. New York: Cambridge University Press.

Mathisen, G. E., & Einarsen, S. (2009). A review of instruments assessing creative and innovative environments within organizations. *Creativity Research, 16,* 1–5.

Ng, A. K. (2001). *Why Asians are Less Creative than Westerners.* Singapore: Prentice-Hall.

Osborn, A. F. (1953). *Applied Imagination: Principles and Procedures of Creative Problem Solving.* NY: Scribners.

Paavola, S., Lipponen, L., & Hakkarainen, K. (2004). Models of innovative knowledge communities and three metaphors of learning. *Review of Educational Research, 74*(4), 557–576. doi:10.3102/00346543074004557

Pool, R. (1997). *Beyond engineering: How society shapes technology.* New York: Oxford University Press.

Rojas-Drummond, S. M., Albarrán, C. D., & Littleton, K. S. (2008). Collaboration, creativity and the co-construction of oral and written texts. *Thinking Skills and Creativity, 3*(3), 177–181. doi:10.1016/j.tsc.2008.09.008

Sawyer, R. K. (2003). Emergence in creativity and development. In R. K. Sawyer (Ed.), *Creativity and Development* (pp. 4–12). USA: Oxford University Press.

Shrader-Frechette, K., & Westra, L. (1997). *Technology and values.* Lanham: Rowman & Littlefield Publishers, Inc.

Sparrow, P., & Gaston, K. (1996). Generic climate maps: A strategic application of climate survey data? *Journal of Organizational Behavior, 17*(6), 679–698. doi:10.1002/(SICI)1099-1379(199611)17:6<679::AID-JOB786>3.0.CO;2-M

Sternberg, R. J. (1999). *Handbook of Creativity.* New York: Cambridge University Press.

Thompson, G., & Lordan, M. (1999). A review of creativity principles applied to engineering design. *Journal of Process Mechanical Engineering, 213*(1), 17–31. doi:10.1243/0954408991529960

Verbeek, P. P. (2011). *Moralizing technology: Understanding and designing the morality of things.* Chicago: The University of Chicago Press. doi:10.7208/chicago/9780226852904.001.0001

Wenger, E. (1998). *Communities of Practice: Learning, Meaning, and Identity.* New York: Cambridge University Press. doi:10.1017/CBO9780511803932

Wenger, E. (2006). *Communities of Practice - A Brief Introduction.* Available at: http://www.ewenger.com/theory/

Westbury, I., Hopmann, S., & Riquarts, K. (2000). *Teaching as a reflective practice: The german didaktik tradition.* Mahwah: Lawrence Erlbaum Associates, Publishers.

Winter, N., & Toyama, K. (2009). Human-Computer Interaction for Development: Mapping the Terrain. *Information Technologies and International Development*, *5*(4), iii–viii.

Yu, M., Zhou, C., & Xing, W. (2014). Change towards creative society: a developed knowledge model for IT in learning. In Li, S., Jin, Q., Jiang, X., Park, J. H. (eds.), Frontier and Future Development of Information Technology in Medicine and Education, Lecture Notes in Electrical Engineering: ITME 2013, vol. 269, pp. 3373-3377. Springer, Lecture Notes in Electrical Engineering. doi:10.1007/978-94-007-7618-0_437

Zhou, C. (2014). A student project as an 'extra group member': A metaphor for the development of creativity in Problem-Based Learning (PBL). *Akademisk Kvarter*, *9*, 223–235.

Zhou, C., & Purushothaman, A. (2015a). Improving creativity in collaborative process: a knowledge model based on communities of practice in organizational learning contexts. In: Ogunleye, J. (eds.) *Research Papers on Knowledge, Innovation and Enterprise* (pp. 57-68). 2015 International Conference on Knowledge, Innovation & Enterprise.

Zhou, C., & Purushothaman, A. (2015b). The need to foster creativity and digital inclusion among women users in developing context: Addressing second order digital divide in online skills. *International Journal of Emerging Technologies in Learning*, *10*(3), 69–74. doi:10.3991/ijet.v10i3.4248

Zhou, C., & Purushothaman, A. (2017). Developing creativity and learning design by Information and Communication Technology (ICT) in developing contexts. In The Encyclopedia of Information Science and Technology (4 ed., pp. 4178 - 4188). USA: IGI Global.

KEY TERMS AND DEFINITIONS

Big C: While someone may have a new idea about how to run a country or a company, artists may develop new types of music, and scientists may develop new techniques or knowledge that may have a profound impact on society. This type of creativity has sometimes been called "big C" creativity.

Creativity: Generally, creativity involves the ability to offer new perspectives, generate novel and meaningful ideas, raise new questions, and come up with solutions to ill-defined problems. It has been demonstrated multiple manifestations of the conceptualization: personal cognitive and social or emotional processes, family aspects, education, characteristics of the domain and fields, social or cultural contextual aspects, as well as historical forces, event, and trends.

Engineering Creativity: Creativity is a vital factor in "good" engineering, and creativity in engineering clearly differs from creativity in the other domains. For example, by contrast creativity in fine arts - a manifestation of creativity with no functional purpose, only aesthetic purpose – engineering creativity results from creativity with a purpose. This purpose is to create products in the broadest sense of the word – including physical objects, complex systems, and processes. The differences are pointed out that engineers produce devices or systems that perform tasks or solve problems. From this sense, engineering creativity has been defined as "functional creativity". The most important aspect is the devices systems that perform tasks or solve problem – that is, it practically useful products.

Little C: Creativity may occur in personal and social matters or in undertaking an activity in a disciplinary or professional area. It is "know-how," concerned with the skills involved in maneuvering and operating concepts and ideas in the physical and social world - including the skills of social interaction and engagement.

Project-Organized Teams: Learning in project-organized teams is considered as a promising strategy for postgraduate level education. By this strategy, students have opportunities to participate projects supported by government or company. Usually, the project teams consist of supervisors and their students from different levels and diverse backgrounds. However, there are always some new recruits to enter teams and the graduates leave at every semester, so high personnel turnover rate exists, while most projects are at least one-year-long with aims of solving real engineering problems needed in society. The supervisors are professors in universities with responsibilities of leaders in these teams, as well the experts in some fields of engineering education. Therefore, for the STEM students, learning is organized through practical problems and in collaborations among group members, which may develop skills of creative thinking along with problem solving process.

Glossary

Assessment for Learning: Assessment activities that are designed to provide feedbacks to improve learning.

Big C: While someone may have a new idea about how to run a country or a company, artists may develop new types of music, and scientists may develop new techniques or knowledge that may have a profound impact on society. This type of creativity has sometimes been called "big C" creativity.

Co-Creation: From an organizational management perspective, co-creation is a joint creation and evaluation of value with stakeholding individuals, intensified and enacted through platforms of engagements, virtualized and emergent from ecosystems of capabilities, and actualized and embodied in domains of experiences, expanding wealth-welfare-wellbeing. Introducing the concept of co-creation to an educational context, it means to design a curriculum by involving the following elements: 1) students' active and reflective participation, 2) changes of teachers' roles towards becoming facilitators of learning, 3) a dynamic and interactive process of teaching and learning, 4) multiple channels of resources of teaching and learning, and 5) increased levels of individual and collective students' responsibility for their learning.

Creative Society: It is an expansion or evolution of information and knowledge society. It has been defined both in a narrow sense and a broad sense. From a narrow sense, the creative society labels the society as being creative or interchangeably inventive; creativity is just the one of possible features, likely the most important one, which can be attributed to the contemporary society. From a broad sense, the creative society should be understood as a phenomenon; it is a name of the contemporary society, not limited only to one attribute as being creative, but emphasizing the creativity as state of the society, affecting all other attributes. Creativity and new technology are key enablers in developing a creative society.

Creativity: Generally, creativity involves the ability to offer new perspectives, generate novel and meaningful ideas, raise new questions, and come up with solutions to ill-defined problems. It has been demonstrated multiple manifestations of the conceptualization: personal cognitive and social or emotional processes, family aspects, education, characteristics of the domain and fields, social or cultural contextual aspects, as well as historical forces, event, and trends.

Engineering Creativity: Creativity is a vital factor in "good" engineering, and creativity in engineering clearly differs from creativity in the other domains. For example, by contrast creativity in fine arts - a manifestation of creativity with no functional purpose, only aesthetic purpose – engineering creativity results from creativity with a purpose. This purpose is to create products in the broadest sense of the word – including physical objects, complex systems, and processes. The differences are pointed out that engineers produce devices or systems that perform tasks or solve problems. From this sense, engineering creativity has been defined as "functional creativity". The most important aspect is the devices systems that perform tasks or solve problem – that is, it practically useful products.

Information and Communication Technology (ICT): ICT can be seen as a set of information technological tools that can be chosen as supporting educational environment. The technological resources can support the creation and development of ideas by stimulating the learners to engage into deeper learning process and activities.

Learning: Learning involves any process that in living organisms leads to permanent capacity change. Learning develops knowledge, abilities, understandings, emotions, attitudes, and sociality, which are important elements of the conditions and raw material of society.

Learning Activity: A recreation of organized learning.

Learning Goal: An end to which learning effort is directed.

Little C: Creativity may occur in personal and social matters or in undertaking an activity in a disciplinary or professional area. It is "know-how," concerned with the skills involved in maneuvering and operating concepts and ideas in the physical and social world - including the skills of social interaction and engagement.

Problem-Based Learning (PBL): As an innovative educational model, problem-based learning (PBL) has been widely used in diverse disciplines and cultures throughout the world. In PBL, students' learning centers on complex problems that do not have a single answer or solving real-life projects. Students work in collaborative groups to identify what they need to learn in order to solve the problems. The teacher acts to facilitate the learning process rather than to provide knowledge. So "student-centered learning" is the core philosophy of PBL.

Professional Knowledge: Knowledge about how to conduct professional activities.

Project-Organized Teams: Learning in project-organized teams is considered as a promising strategy for postgraduate level education. By this strategy, students have opportunities to participate projects supported by government or company. Usually, the project teams consist of supervisors and their students from different levels and diverse backgrounds. However, there are always some new recruits to enter teams and the graduates leave at every semester, so high personnel turnover rate exists, while most projects are at least one-year-long with aims of solving real engineering problems needed in society. The supervisors are professors in universities with responsibilities of leaders in these teams, as well the experts in some fields of engineering education. Therefore, for the STEM students, learning is organized through practical problems and in collaborations among group members, which may develop skills of creative thinking along with problem solving process.

Teaching Vision: A thought formed by imaging the results of teaching.

Transferable Skills: Skills that can be applied to different professional domains.

Transformative Learning: It refers to the process by which we transform our take-for-granted frames of reference (meaning perspectives, habits of mind, mindsets), to make them more inclusive, discriminating, open, emotionally capable of change, and reflective so that they may generate beliefs and opinions that will prove more true or justified to guide action. Through transformative learning, personality-integrated knowledge is developed on the basis of which associations can be freely made in all subjectively relevant contexts.

Compilation of References

Aalborg University – Knowledge for the World. (2018). Retrieved 2018, from https://www.en.aau.dk/about-aau

Albanese, M. A., & Mitchell, S. (1993). Problem-Based Learning: A Review of Literature on Its Outcomes and Implementation Issues. *Academic Medicine: Journal of the Association of American Medical Colleges*, 68(1), 52–81. doi:10.1097/00001888-199301000-00012 PMID:8447896

Algreen-Ussing, H., & Fruensgaard, N. O. (1990). *Metode i Projektarbejde*. Aalborg University Press.

Amabile, T. M. (1996). *Creativity in Context: Update to the Social Psychology of Creativity*. New York: Crown.

Anderson, L. W., & Krathwohl, D. R. (2001). *A Taxonomy for Learning, Teaching, and Assessing: A Revision of Bloom's Taxonomy of Educational Objectives*. New York: Longman.

Anette, K., de Graaff, E., & Du, X. (2009). Diversity of PBL-PBL learning principles and models. In *Research on PBL practice in engineering* (pp. 9–21). Rotterdam: Sense.

Araya, D. (2010). Educational policy in the creative economy. In D. Araya & M. A. Peters (Eds.), *Education in the Creative Economy: Knowledge and Learning in the Age of Innovation* (pp. 3–28). New York: Peter Lang.

Bacon. (2014). *Essays of Francis Bacon: Chapter 5 Of Adversity*. CreateSpace Independent Publishing Platform.

Baidu Encyclopedia. (n.d.). Retrieved from http://baike.baidu.com/view/1017237.htm

Baillie, C., & Catalano, G. (2008). *Engineering and society, working toward social justice.* Morgan & Claypool Publishers.

Bammer, G. (2013). *Disciplining Interdisciplinarity: Integration and Implementation Sciences for Researching Complex Real-World Problems.* ANU E Press.

Bammer, G., & Smithson, M. (2012). *Uncertainty and Risk: Multidisciplinary Perspectives.* Routledge. doi:10.4324/9781849773607

Barrett, M. J. (2006). Education for the environment: Action competence, becoming, and story. *Environmental Education Research, 12*(3-4), 503–511. doi:10.1080/13504620600799273

Barrow, R. (1987). Skill Talk. *Journal of Philosophy of Education, 21*(2), 187–195. doi:10.1111/j.1467-9752.1987.tb00158.x

Barrows, H. S. (1986). A taxonomy of problem-based learning methods. *Medical Education, 20*(6), 481–486. doi:10.1111/j.1365-2923.1986.tb01386.x PMID:3796328

Barrows, H. S. (1996). Problem-based learning in medicine and beyond: A brief overview. *New Directions for Teaching and Learning, 1996*(68), 3–12. doi:10.1002/tl.37219966804

Barrows, H. S., & Tamblyn, R. M. (1980). *Problem-Based Learning: An Approach to Medical Education.* New York: Springer.

Bedard, D., Lison, C., Dalle, D., & Boutin, N. (2010). Predictors of student's engagement and persistence in an innovative PBL curriculum: Applications for engineering education. *International Journal of Engineering Education, 26*(3), 511–522.

Beder, B. S. (1999). Beyond technicalities: Expanding engineering thinking. *Journal of Professional Issues in Engineering Education and Practice, 125*(1), 12–18. doi:10.1061/(ASCE)1052-3928(1999)125:1(12)

Berthelsen, J., Illeris, K., & Poulsen, S. C. (1977). *Projektarbejde.* København: Borgen.

Biesta, G. (2009). Pragmatism's contribution to understanding learning-in-context. In R. Edwards, G. Biesta, & M. Thorpe (Eds.), *Rethinking Contexts for Learning and Teaching* (pp. 61–72). London: Routledge.

Biggs, J. (1982). *Evaluating The Quality of Learning:The SOLO Taxonomy.* Academic Press.

Biggs, J. (1996). Enhancing teaching through constructive alignment. *Higher Education, 32*(3), 347–364. doi:10.1007/BF00138871

Biggs, J., & Tang, C. (2011). *Teaching For Quality Learning At University.* McGraw-Hill Education.

Bloom, B. S., Krathwohl, D. R., & Masia, B. B. (1984). *Taxonomy of educational objectives: the classification of educational goals.* Academic Press.

Blumberg, P. (2009). Maximizing learning through course alignment and experience with different types of knowledge. *Innovative Higher Education, 34*(2), 93–103. doi:10.100710755-009-9095-2

Boden, R., Cox, D., Nedeva, M., & Barker, K. (2004). Scientific Knowledge Production Processes. In Scrutinising Science (pp. 136–156). Academic Press. doi:10.1057/9781403943934_6

Borhan, M. T. (2014). Problem based learning (PBL) in teacher education: A review of the effect of PBL on pre-service teachers' knowledge and skills. *European Journal of Educational Sciences, 01*(01), 76–87. doi:10.19044/ejes.v1no1a9

Boud, D., & Feletti, G. (1991). *The Challenge of Problem-based Learning.* London: Kogan Page. Fraenkel, G. J. (1978). *McMaster Revisited. British Medical Journal, 2,* 1072–1076.

Breiting, S., & Wickenberg, P. (2010). The progressive development of environmental education in Sweden and Denmark. *Environmental Education Research, 16*(1), 9–37. doi:10.1080/13504620903533221

Brown, H. (2008). *Knowledge and Innovation: A Comparative study of the USA, the UK, and Japan.* London: Routledge.

Bruner, J. (2009). Culture, mind and education. In Contemporary Theories of Learning (pp. 179–188). Academic Press.

Bruner, J. S. (1965). EDITORIAL: The Process of Education. *The Physics Teacher, 3*(8), 369–370. doi:10.1119/1.2349211

Burr, V. (1995). *An Introduction to Social Constructionism.* London: Routledge. doi:10.4324/9780203299968

Bush, T., & Qiang, H. (2000). Leadership and culture in Chinese education. *Asia Pacific Journal of Education*, *20*(2), 58–67. doi:10.1080/02188791.2000.10600183

Bussemaker, J. (2014). *Letter on the government's vision on the international dimension of higher education and VET*. Government of the Netherlands. Retrieved from http://www.government.nl/ministries/ocw/documents-and-publications/letters/2014/07/21/government-s-vision-on-the-international-dimension-of-higher-education-and-vet.html

Cao, C., Richard, P. S., & Denis, F. S. (2006). China's 15-year Science and Technology Plan. *Physics Today*, *59*(December), 38–43. doi:10.1063/1.2435680

Castells, M. (2011). *The Rise of Network Society*. London: Wiley-Blackwell.

Chin, C., & Chia, L.-G. (2004). Problem-based learning: Using students' questions to drive knowledge construction. *Science Education*, *88*(5), 707–727. doi:10.1002ce.10144

Chunfang Zhou, A. K. A. J. D. N. (2012). A Problem and Project-Based Learning (PBL) Approach to Motivate Group Creativity in Engineering Education. *International Journal of Engineering Education*, *28*(1), 3–16.

Covey, S. R. (2016). *Primary Greatness: The 12 Levers of Success*. Simon and Schuster.

Craft, A. (2005). *Creativity in Schools: Tensions and Dilemmas*. New York: Routledge. doi:10.4324/9780203357965

Craft, A. (2006). Creativity in schools. In N. Jackson, M. Oliver, M. Shaw, & J. Wisdom (Eds.), *Developing Creativity in Higher Education: An Imaginative Curriculum* (pp. 19–28). London: Routledge.

Craft, A. (2008). Studying collaborative creativity: Implications for education. *Thinking Skills and Creativity*, *3*(3), 241–245. doi:10.1016/j.tsc.2008.09.006

Cropley, D., & Cropley, A. (2005). Engineering creativity: a systems concept of functional creativity. In J. C. Kaufman & J. Baer (Eds.), *Creativity Across Domains: Faces of the Muse* (pp. 169–186). London: Lawrence Erlbaum Associates.

Csikszentmihalyi, M. (2014). *The Systems Model of Creativity: The Collected Works of Mihaly Csikszentmihalyi*. London: Springer. doi:10.1007/978-94-017-9085-7

Cunningham, W., & Cunningham, M. (2014). *Cunningham, Environmental Science: A Global Concern*. McGraw-Hill Education.

Dalrymple, K. R., Wong, S., Rosenblum, A., Wuenschell, C., Paine, M., & Shuler, C. F. (2007). PBL Core Skills Faculty Development Workshop 3: Understanding PBL process assessment and feedback via scenario-based discussions, observation, and role-play. *Journal of Dental Education*, *71*(12), 1561–1573. PMID:18096882

Dance, F. E. X., & Larson, C. E. (1976). *The functions of human communication: A theoretical approach*. New York: Holt, Rinehart and Winston.

Daniels, H. (2016). *Vygotsky and Pedagogy*. Routledge. doi:10.4324/9781315617602

Daud, M. Y., & Zakaria, E. (2012). Web 2.0 application and cultivate creativity in ICT literacy. *Procedia: Social and Behavioral Sciences*, *59*, 459–466. doi:10.1016/j.sbspro.2012.09.301

De Graaf, E., & Kolmos, A. (2003). Characteristics of problem-based learning. *International Journal of Engineering Education*, 657–662.

de Graaff, A., & Kolmos, E. (2003). Characteristics of Problem-Based Learning. *Int. J. Engng Ed.*, *19*(5), 657-662.

De Graaff, E., & Kolmos, A. (2009). *Management of Change: Implementation of Problem-Based and Project-Based Learning in Engineering*. Sense Publishers.

De Wit, H. (2002). *Internationalization of Higher Education in the United States of America and Europe: A Historical Comparative and Conceptual Analysis*. Westport, CT: Greenwood.

Detel, W. (2001). Social Constructivism. In *International Encyclopedia of the Social & Behavioral Science* (pp. 14264–14267). Academic Press.

Deutsch, M., Marcus, E. C., & Brazaitis, S. (2012). A framework for thinking about developing a global community. In *Psychological components of sustainable peace* (pp. 299–324). Springer New York. doi:10.1007/978-1-4614-3555-6_16

Dewey, J. (1900). *The School and Society*. University of Chicago Press.

Dewey, J. (1965). *Experience and Education*. New York: Collier Books.

Dewey, J. (2007). *Experience And Education*. Simon and Schuster.

Dewey, J., & Bentley, A. F. (1949). *Knowing and the Known*. Boston: Beacon Press.

Dolmans, D. H. J. M., Diana, H. J., Snellen-Balendong, H., & van der Vleuten, C. P. M. (1997). Seven principles of effective case design for a problem-based curriculum. *Medical Teacher, 19*(3), 185–189. doi:10.3109/01421599709019379

Dolmans, D., Wolfhagen, I. H. A. P., van der Vleuten, C. P. M., & Wijnen, W. H. F. W. (2001). Solving problems with group work in Problem-based Learning: Hold on to the philosophy. *Medical Education, 35*(9), 884–889. doi:10.1046/j.1365-2923.2001.00915.x PMID:11555227

Dolog, P., Thomsen, L. L., & Thomsen, B. (2016). Assessing Problem-Based Learning in a Software Engineering Curriculum Using Bloom's Taxonomy and the IEEE Software Engineering Body of Knowledge. *ACM Transactions on Computing Education, 16*(3), 1–41. doi:10.1145/2845091

Duch, B. J. (2001). Writing problems for deeper understanding. In *The power of problem-based learning* (pp. 47–58). Stylus Publishing.

Du, X., Su, L., & Liu, J. (2013). Developing sustainability curricula using the PBL method in a Chinese context. *Journal of Cleaner Production, 61*, 80–88. doi:10.1016/j.jclepro.2013.01.012

Easton, T. A. (2017). *Taking Sides: Clashing Views on Environmental Issues*. McGraw-Hill Education.

Elamvazuthi, I., Lee, H. J., Ng, J. C., Song, H. L., Tiong, Y. X., Parimi, A. M., & Swain, A. K. (2015). Implementation of a New Engineering Approach for Undergraduate Control System Curriculum using a Robotic System. *Procedia Computer Science, 76*, 34–39. doi:10.1016/j.procs.2015.12.272

Elkjaer, B. (2009). Pragmatism: A learning theory for the future. In K. Illeris (Ed.), *Contemporary Theories of Learning* (Vol. 5, pp. 66–82). Taylor & Francis Routledge.

Engeströ, Y., Miettinen, R., & Punamaki, R. L. (1999). *Perspectives on Activity Theory*. Cambridge, UK: Cambridge University Press. doi:10.1017/CBO9780511812774

Eteläpelto, A., & Lahti, J. (2008). The resources and obstacles of creative collaboration in a long-term learning community. *Thinking Skills and Creativity, 3*(3), 226–240. doi:10.1016/j.tsc.2008.09.003

Farrell & Grant. (2005). *Addressing China's Looming Talent Shortage*. McKinsey & Company. Retrieved from http://www.ideas-forum.org.uk/about-us/global-citizenship https://globaldimension.org.uk/about/what-is-the-global-dimension/

Feest, T. (2008). Engineers: Going global. *Industry and Higher Education, 22*(4), 209–213. doi:10.5367/000000008785201801

Forehand, M. (2010). Bloom's taxonomy. In M. Orey (Ed.), Emerging perspectives on learning, teaching, and technology (pp. 41–47). Academic Press.

Fox, S. (2000). Communities of practice, Foucault and actor-network theory. *Journal of Management Studies, 37*(6), 853–867. doi:10.1111/1467-6486.00207

Frodeman, R. (2010). *The Oxford Handbook of Interdisciplinarity*. Oxford University Press.

Gao, S. (2018). *China Program for Higher Education Powers - Analysis of Basic Contradictions in New Era Education*. Tianjin University of Finance and Economics Higher Education Conference.

Gardner, H. (1983). *Frames of Mind: the Multiple Intelligences*. New York: Basic Books.

Gergen, K. J. (1994). *Realities and Relationships*. Cambridge, MA: Harvard University Press.

Gibbons, Limoges, Nowotny, Schwartzman, Scott, & Trow. (2010). The New Production of Knowledge: The Dynamics of Science and Research in Contemporary Societies. SAGE Publications Ltd.

Gibbons, M. (2003). A new mode of knowledge production. In Routledge Studies in Business Organizations and Networks. Academic Press. doi:10.4324/9780203422793.pt4

Gibbons, M., Limoges, C., Nowotny, H., Schwartzman, S., Scott, P., & Trow, M. (1994). *The New Production of Knowledge: The Dynamic of Science and Research in Contemporary Societies*. London: Sage Publications.

Gibbs, G., & Simpson, C. (2005). *Conditions under which assessment supports students' learning*. Learning and Teaching in Higher Education.

Gijselaers, W. H., Tempelaar, D. T., Keizer, P. K., Blommaert, J. M., Bernard, E. M., & Kasper, H. (1995). *Educational Innovation in Economics and Business Administration: The Case of Problem-Based Learning*. Springer Science & Business. doi:10.1007/978-94-015-8545-3

Graaff, E. de, & Bouhuijs, P. A. J. (Eds.). (1993). *Implementation of problem-based learning in higher education*. Amsterdam: Thesis Publishers.

Graaff, E. de, & Kolmos, A. (2003). Characteristics of problem-based learning. *International Journal of Engineering Education, 5*(19), 657–662.

Graham, R. H., & Royal Academy of Engineering (Great Britain). (2012). *Achieving Excellence in Engineering Education: The Ingredients of Successful Change*. Anchor Books.

Graham, R. H. (2012). *Achieving excellence in engineering education: the ingredients of successful change*. London: Royal Academy of Engineering.

Guilford, J. P. (1950). Creativity. *The American Psychologist, 5*(9), 444–454. doi:10.1037/h0063487 PMID:14771441

Guorong, Lv. (2004). *Ten Criteria for Excellent Staff of Bill Gates*. Beijing: Mechanical Industry Press.

Gwee, M. C. (2008). Globalisation of problem-based learning (PBL): Cross-cultural implications. *The Kaohsiung Journal of Medical Sciences, 3*(3Suppl), 14–22. doi:10.1016/S1607-551X(08)70089-5 PMID:18364282

Haggis, T. (2007). Conceptualizing the case in adult and higher education research: a dynamic system view. In J. Bogg & R. Geyer (Eds.), *Complexity, Science, and Society*. Oxford, UK: Radcliff.

Harper, W. (1969). The Oxford Handbook of Interdisciplinarity. *Theological Librarianship, 5*(2), 88–89.

Heinze, T., Shapira, P., Rogers, J. D., & Senker, J. M. (2009). Oragnizational and Instituational Influences on Creativity in Scientific Research. *Research Policy, 38*(4), 610–623. doi:10.1016/j.respol.2009.01.014

Heitmann, G. (1993). Project study and project organised curricula: a historical review of its intentions. *Project-organized curricula in engineering education, Proceedings of a SEFI-seminar held 5th*.

Hiim, H., & Hippe, E. (2004). *Learning through experience, understanding and action*. Gyldendal Uddannelse.

Hillen, H., Scherpbier, A., & Wijnen, W. (2010). History of problem-based learning in medical education. Lessons from Problem-based Learning, 5–12. doi:10.1093/acprof:oso/9780199583447.003.0002

Hmelo-Silver, C. E. (2004). Problem-Based Learning: What and how do student learn? *Educational Psychology Review*, *16*(3), 235–266. doi:10.1023/B:EDPR.0000034022.16470.f3

Holgaard, J. E. (2013). Information technology for sustainable development: A problem based and project oriented approach. In *Proceedings for Engineering Edu- cation for Sustainable Development 2013*. University of Cambridge.

Holgaard, J. E., Guerra, A., Kolmos, A., & Petersen, L. S. (2017). Getting a Hold on the Problem in a Problem-Based Learning Environment. *International Journal of Engineering Education*, *33*(3), 1070–1085.

Holten-Andersen, C., Schnack, K., & Wahlgren, B. (1983). *Invitation til projektarbejde*. Gyldendals pædagogiske bibliotek.

Huiyao & Green. (Eds.). (2013). *Annual Report on the Development of Chinese Students Studying Abroad in Blue Book of Global Talent*. Social Science Literature Publishing House.

Hung, W. (2006). The 3C3R Model: A Conceptual Framework for Designing Problems in PBL. *Interdisciplinary Journal of Problem-Based Learning*, *1*(1). doi:10.7771/1541-5015.1006

Ikeda, T., Okumura, A., & Muraki, K. (1998). Information classification and navigation based on 5W1H of the target information. *Proceedings of the 17th international conference on Computational linguistics*, 571–577.

Illeris, K. (1976). *Problemorienterad och deltagarstyrd undervisning: förutsättningar, planering och genomförande*. Academic Press.

Illeris, K. (2009). A comprehensive understanding of human learning. In K. Illeris (Ed.), *Contemporary Theories of Learning: Learning Theorists -- in Their Own Words* (pp. 7–20). Taylor & Francis Routledge. doi:10.4324/9780203870426

Illers, K. (2007). *How We Learn: Learning and Non-Learning in School and Beyond*. London: Routledge. doi:10.4324/9780203939895

Jackson, N. (2006). Imagining a different world. In N. Jackson, M. Oliver, M. Shaw, & J. Wisdom (Eds.), *Developing Creativity in Higher Education: an Imaginative Curriculum* (pp. 1–9). London: Routledge. doi:10.4324/9780203016503

Jansen, T., & van Kammen, A.-R. (1976). *Projectonderwijs: afleren en aanleren* [Project education: un-learning and re-learning]. Purmerend: Muusses.

Jarvis, P. (2009). The Routledge International Handbook of Lifelong Learning. Academic Press. doi:10.4324/9780203870549

Jensen, B. B., & Schnack, K. (1997). The Action Competence Approach in Environmental Education. *Environmental Education Research, 3*(2), 163–178. doi:10.1080/1350462970030205

Jing, Y., & Osborne, S. P. (2017). *Public Service Innovation in China.* Singapore: Palgrave. doi:10.1007/978-981-10-1762-9

Jonassen, D. H. (1991). Objectivism versus constructivism: Do we need a new philosophical paradigm? *Educational Technology Research and Development. ETR & D, 39*(3), 5–14. doi:10.1007/BF02296434

Jonassen, D. H. (2010). *Learning to Solve Problems: A Handbook for Designing Problem-Solving Learning Environments.* Routledge. doi:10.4324/9780203847527

Jonassen, D. H., & Hung, W. (2008). All Problems are Not Equal: Implications for Problem-Based Learning. *Interdisciplinary Journal of Problem-Based Learning, 2*(2). doi:10.7771/1541-5015.1080

Jørgensen, P. S. (1999). Hva er kompetence [What is competence]? *Uddannelse (Copenhagen, Denmark), 9*, 4–13.

Katzenbach, J. R., & Smith, D. K. (2015). *The Wisdom of Teams: Creating the High-Performance Organization.* Harvard Business Review Press.

Kaufman, A. (1985). *Implementing Problem-Based Medical Education: Lessons from Successful Innovations.* Springer Publishing Company. doi:10.1891/9780826146618

Kaufman, A. (Ed.). (1985). *Implementing Problem-based Medical Education. Lessons from Successful Innovations.* New York: Springer Publishing.

Kazerounian, K., & Foley, S. (2007). Barriers to creativity in engineering education: A study of instructors and students perceptions. *Journal of Mechanical Design, 129*(7), 761–768. doi:10.1115/1.2739569

Kegan, R. (2009). What "form" transforms? In K. Illeris (Ed.), *Contemporary Theories of Learning: Learning Theorists In Their Own Words.* Taylor & Francis Routledge.

Khoo, H. E. (2003). Implementation of problem-based learning in Asian medical schools and students' perceptions of their experience. *Medical Education, 37*(5), 401–409. doi:10.1046/j.1365-2923.2003.01489.x PMID:12709180

Kim, K. H. (2007). Exploring the interactions between Asian culture (Confucianism) and creativity. *The Journal of Creative Behavior, 41*(1), 28–53. doi:10.1002/j.2162-6057.2007.tb01280.x

Knight, J. (1993). Internationalization: Management strategies and issues. *International Education Magazine, 9*(6), 21-22.

Knight, J. (2004, Spring). Internationalization Remodeled: Definition, Approaches, and Rationales. *Journal of Studies in International Education, 8*(1), 5–31. doi:10.1177/1028315303260832

Kolb, D. A. (1984). *Experiental Learning. Experience as the source of learning and development*. Prentice Hall.

Kolb, D. A. (1984). *Experiential learning: Experience as the source of learning and development*. Prentice-Hall.

Kolmos, A. (2017). PBL Curriculum Strategies. In PBL in Engineering Education (pp. 1–12). Academic Press. doi:10.1007/978-94-6300-905-8_1

Kolmos, A., & De Graaff, E. (2014). Problem-based and project-based learning in engineering education. In A. Johri, & B. M. Olds (Eds.), *Cambridge handbook of engineering education research* (pp. 141-161). Cambridge University Press.

Kolmos, A., Fink, F. K., & Krogh, L. (Eds.). (2004). The Aalborg PBL Model – Progress, Diversity and Challenges. Aalborg: Aalborg University Press.

Kolmos, A., Holgaard, J., & Du, X. (2009). Transformation du curriculum: vers un apprentissage par problèmes et par projets. Innover dans l'enseignement supérieur, 151.

Kolmos, A. (1996). Reflections on Project Work and Problem-based Learning. *European Journal of Engineering Education, 2*(21).

Kolmos, A. (2002). Facilitating change to a problem-based learning model. *The International Journal for Academic Development, 7*(1), 63–74. doi:10.1080/13601440210156484

Kolmos, A. (2010). Premises for Changing to PBL. *International Journal for the Scholarship of Teaching and Learning*, *4*(1), 4. doi:10.20429/ijsotl.2010.040104

Kolmos, A. (2013). Problem- and project-based learning in a global perspective: community building or certification? In L. Krogh & A. A. Jensen (Eds.), *Visions, Challenges, and Strategies: PBL Principles and Methodologies in a Danish and Global Perspective* (pp. 47–66). Aalborg: Aalborg University Press.

Kolmos, A., & de Graaff, E. (2007). Process of changing to PBL. In E. de Graaff & A. Kolmos (Eds.), *Management of change: implementation of problem-based and project-based learning in engineering* (pp. 31–43). Rotterdam: Sense Publishers.

Kolmos, A., Du, X., Holgaard, J. E., & Jensen, L. P. (2008). *Facilitation in a PBL environment*. Aalborg: Center for Engineering Education Research and Development, Aalborg University.

Kolmos, A., Fink, F. K., & Krogh, L. (2004). The Aalborg Model- Problem-Based and Project-organized learning. In A. Kolmos, F. K. Fink, & L. Krogh (Eds.), *The Aalborg PBL Model-Progress, Diversity and Challenges* (pp. 9–18). Aalborg: Aalborg University Press.

Kolmos, A., Fink, F. K., & Krogh, L. (2004). *The Aalborg PBL model: progress, diversity and challenges*. Aalborg: Aalborg University Press.

Kolmos, A., & Graaff, E. D. (2007). Process of changing to PBL. In *Management of change: Implementation of problem-based and project-based learning in engineering* (pp. 31–44). Rotterdam: Sense Publishers.

Kolomos, A., Fink, F. K., & Krogh, L. (2004). *The Aalborg PBL Model: Progress, Diversity and Challenges*. Aalborg Universitetsforlag.

Krathwohl, D. R. (2002). A revision of Bloom's taxonomy: An overview. *Theory into Practice*, *41*(4), 212–218. doi:10.120715430421tip4104_2

Krathwohl, D. R., & Anderson, L. W. (2010). Merlin C. Wittrock and the Revision of Bloom's Taxonomy. *Educational Psychologist*, *45*(1), 64–65. doi:10.1080/00461520903433562

Lam, T. P., Wan, X. H., & Ip, M. S. (2006). Current perspectives on medical education in China. *Medical Education*, *40*(10), 940–949. doi:10.1111/j.1365-2929.2006.02552.x PMID:16987183

Lattura, L. R. (2002). Learning interdisciplinarity: Sociocultural perspectives on academic work. *The Journal of Higher Education, 73*(6), 711–739.

Levin, R. (2010). The Rise of Asia's Universities. *The New York Times*.

Levin, R. C. (2008). *The Work of the University*. Yale University Press.

Li, W. (2011). How Creativity is Changing China (M. Keane, Ed.; H. Li & M. Guo, Trans.). Bloomsbury Academic.

Li, H., & Du, X. (2018). *Educational Design for Future: Analysis of the Curriculum Model and Education Idea of Problem Based Learning at Aalborg University in Denmark*. Chongqing Higher Education Research.

Li, R. (2013). *Current Situation and Suggestions of Foreign Affairs Archives Management in Colleges and Universities*. Office Business.

Little, P., Ostwald, M., & Ryan, G. (Eds.). (1995). Research & Development in Problem Based Learning (Vol. 3). PROBLARC, University of Newcastle.

Liu. (2011). Analysis of the School Running Mode of Sino-foreign Cooperation in Running Schools. *Business Management, 10*.

Liu, L., Du, X., Zhang, Z., & Zhou, J. (2019). Effect of Problem-Based Learning in Pharmacology Education: A Meta-Analysis. *Studies in Educational Evaluation, 60*, 43–58. doi:10.1016/j.stueduc.2018.11.004

Marra, R. M., Jonassen, D. H., Palmer, B., & Luft, S. (2014). Why Problem-Based Learning Works: Theoretical Foundations. *Journal on Excellence in College Teaching, 25*(3&4), 221–238.

Mencius, B. I., & Ivanhoe, P. J. (2011). Mencius. Columbia University Press.

Mezirow, J. (2009). Transformative learning theory. In K. Illeris (Ed.), Contemporary Theories of Learning (pp. 114–128). Academic Press.

Mezirow, J. (2000). Learning to think like an adult: core conceptions of transformation theory. In J. Mezirow & ... (Eds.), *Learning as Transformation: Critical Perspectives on a Theory in Progress*. San Francisco: Jossey-Bass.

Mogensen, F. (1997). Critical thinking: A central element in developing action competence in health and environmental education. *Health Education Research, 12*(4), 429–436. doi:10.1093/her/12.4.429 PMID:10176372

Mogensen, F., & Schnack, K. (2010). The action competence approach and the "new" discourses of education for sustainable development, competence and quality criteria. *Environmental Education Research*, *16*(1), 59–74. doi:10.1080/13504620903504032

Morales Bueno, P., Bueno, P. M., & Rodas, R. S. (2018). Metacogntion and motivation relationship in a hybrid PBL approach. *ICERI2018 Proceedings*.

Mullen, C. A. (2017). *Creativity and Education in China: Paradox and Possibilities for an Era of Accountability*. New York: Routledge. doi:10.4324/9781315665856

Nandi, P. L., Chan, J. N. F., & Chan, C. P. K. (2000). Undergraduate medical education: Comparison of problem-based learning and conventional teaching. *Hong Kong Medical Journal*, *6*, 301–306. PMID:11025850

National Academy of Engineering (NAE). (2004). *The engineer of 2020: vision of engineering in the new century*. Washington, DC: National Academies Press.

Negt, O., & Kluge, A. (1972). Öffentlichkeit und Erfahrung: Zur Organisationsanalyse von bürgerlicher und proletarischer Öffentlichkeit. Frankfurt am Main: Academic Press.

Negt, O. (1968). *Soziologische Phantasie und exemplarisches Lernen*. Frankfurt am Main: Zur Theorie der Arbeiterbildung.

Neufeld, V., & Barrows, H. S. (1974). The McMaster Philosophy: An approach to medical education. *Journal of Medical Education*, *49*, 1040–1050. PMID:4444006

Nijstad, B. A., & Stroebe, W. (2006). Four principles of group creativity. In L. L. Thompson & H. S. Choi (Eds.), *Creativity and Innovation in Organizational Team* (pp. 161–177). London: Lawrence Erlbaum Associates.

Norman, G. R. (1986). Problem-solving skills, Solving problems and problem-based learning. *Medical Education*, *22*(4), 279–286. doi:10.1111/j.1365-2923.1988.tb00754.x PMID:3050382

Norman, G., & Schmidt, H. G. (1992). The psychological basis of problem-based learning: A review of the evidence. *Academic Medicine*, *67*(9), 557–565. doi:10.1097/00001888-199209000-00002 PMID:1520409

O'Grady, G., Yew, E., Goh, K. P. L., & Schmidt, H. (2012). *One-Day, One-Problem: An Approach to Problem-based Learning*. Springer Science & Business Media. doi:10.1007/978-981-4021-75-3

Oberg, K. (1960). Culture shock: Adjustment to new cultural environments. *Practical Anthropology, 7*(4), 177–182. doi:10.1177/009182966000700405

Olesen, H. S. (1989). *Adult Education and Everyday Life*. Roskilde: The Adult Education Group, Roskilde University.

Orcutt, J. L., & Hong, S. (2010). *Shaping China's Innovation Future: University Technology Transfer in Transition*. Edward Elgar.

Ostwald, M., & Kingsland, A. (Eds.). (1994). Research & Development in Problem Based Learning (Vol. 2). PROBLARC, University of Newcastle.

Padhi. (2016). The Rising Importance of Cross Cultural Communication in Global Business Scenario. *Quest Journals, Journal of Research in Humanities and Social Science, 4*(1), 20-26.

Pan, S., & Cui, L. (2016). *SPS Case Study Method: Process, Modeling and Examples*. Beijing: Peking University Press.

Parker, R. (2017). Essentials of Environmental Science (2nd ed.). Lulu.com.

Paulus, P. B., & Nijstad, B. A. (2003). Group creativity: an introduction. In P. B. Paulus (Ed.), *Group Creativity: Innovation through Collaboration* (pp. 3–11). New York: Oxford University Press. doi:10.1093/acprof:oso/9780195147308.003.0001

Piaget, J. (1977). *Psychology and Epistemology: Towards a Theory of Knowledge*. Academic Press.

Piaget, J. (1964). Part I: Cognitive development in children: Piaget development and learning. *Journal of Research in Science Teaching, 2*(3), 176–186. doi:10.1002/tea.3660020306

Post, G. J., & Graaff, E. de, & Drop, M. J. (1988). Efficiency of a Primary-Care Curriculum. *Annals of Community-Oriented Medical Education, 1*, 25–31.

Prince, M. J., & Felder, R. M. (2006). Inductive Teaching and Learning Methods: Definitions, Comparisons, and Research Bases. *Journal of Engineering Education, 95*(2), 123–138. doi:10.1002/j.2168-9830.2006.tb00884.x

Prince, M., & Felder, R. (2006). Inductive Teaching and Learning Methods: Definitions, Comparisons, and Research Bases. *Journal of Engineering Education, 2*(95).

Pucciarelli, F., & Kaplan, A. (2016). Competition and strategy in higher education: Managing complexity and uncertainty. *Business Horizons, 59*(3), 311–320. doi:10.1016/j.bushor.2016.01.003

Purushothaman, A., & Zhou, C. (2014). Change toward a creative society in developing contexts: Women's barriers to learning by Information and Communication Technology. *Gender, Technology and Development, 18*(3), 363–386. doi:10.1177/0971852414544008

Ramaswamy, V., & Ozcan, K. (2014). *The Co-creation Paradigm.* Stanford, CA: Stanford University Press.

Reimeris, R. (2016). Theoretical features of the creative society. *Creativity Studies, 9*(1), 15–24. doi:10.3846/23450479.2015.1088902

Resnick, M. (2007, December). Sowing the seeds for a more creative society. *Learning and Leading with Technology*, 18–22.

Rogers, C. (1961). *On becoming a person.* Boston: Houghton Mifflin.

Rudowicz, E., & Yue, X. (2002). Compatibility of Chinese and creative personalities. *Creativity Research Journal, 14*(3&4), 387–394. doi:10.1207/S15326934CRJ1434_9

Ryan, G. (Ed.). (1993). Research & Development in Problem Based Learning (Vol. 1). PROBLARC, University of Newcastle.

Sáenz, C. (2009). The role of contextual, conceptual and procedural knowledge in activating mathematical competencies (PISA). *Educational Studies in Mathematics, 71*(2), 123–143. doi:10.100710649-008-9167-8

Savery, J. R. (2006). Overview of problem-based learning: Definitions and distinctions. *Interdisciplinary Journal of Problem-Based Learning, 1*(1), 9–20. doi:10.7771/1541-5015.1002

Savin-Baden, M. (2000). *Problem-based Learning in Higher Education: Untold Stories.* Buckingham, UK: SRHE and Open University Press.

Savin-Baden, M. (2004). Understanding the impact of assessment on students in problem-based learning. *Innovations in Education and Teaching International, 41*(2), 221–233. doi:10.1080/1470329042000208729

Sawyer, R. K. (2005). *Social Emergence: Societies As Complex Systems.* New York: Cambridge University Press. doi:10.1017/CBO9780511734892

Schmidt, H. G. (1983). Problem-based learning: Rationale and description. *Medical Education, 17*(1), 1116. doi:10.1111/j.1365-2923.1983.tb01086.x PMID:6823214

Schmidt, H. G. (1993). Foundations of problem-based learning: Some explanatory notes. *Medical Education, 27*(5), 422–432. doi:10.1111/j.1365-2923.1993. tb00296.x PMID:8208146

Schmidt, H. G. (1995). Problem-Based Learning: An Introduction. *Instructional Science, 22*(4), 247–250. doi:10.1007/BF00891778

Schmidt, H. G. (2012). A Brief History of Problem-based Learning. In *One-Day* (pp. 21–40). One-Problem. doi:10.1007/978-981-4021-75-3_2

Schön, D. A. (2017). *The Reflective Practitioner: How Professionals Think in Action.* Routledge. doi:10.4324/9781315237473

Servant-Miklos, V. F. C. (2018). *Fifty Years on: A Retrospective on the World's First Problem-Based Learning Programme at McMaster University Medical School.* Health Professions Education.

Servant-Miklos, V. F. C. (2018). *The Harvard Connection: How the Case Method Spawned Problem-Based Learning at McMaster University.* Health Professions Education.

Shani, A. B., Mohrman, S. A., Pasmore, W. A., Stymne, B., & Adler, N. (2007). *Handbook of Collaborative Management Research.* SAGE Publications.

Sheppard, F. S. D., Macatangay, K., William, A. C., & Sullivan, M. (2009). *Educating engineers, designing for the future.* San Francisco: Jossey-Bass.

Smith, A. G. (1996). *Communication and Culture: Reading in the in the Codes of Human Interaction.* New York: Holt, Rinehalt & Winston.

Smith, B., & Enger, E. (2015). *Environmental Science.* McGraw-Hill Education.

Sockalingam, N., & Schmidt, H. G. (2011). Characteristics of Problems for Problem-Based Learning: The Students' Perspective. *Interdisciplinary Journal of Problem-Based Learning, 5*(1).

Sockalingam, N., & Schmidt, H. G. (2011). Characteristics of Problems for Problem-Based Learning: The Students' Perspective. *Interdisciplinary Journal of Problem-Based Learning*, 5(1). doi:10.7771/1541-5015.1135

Spaulding, W. P. (1969). The Undergraduate Medical Curriculum Model: McMaster University. *Canadian Medical Association Journal*, 100, 659–664. PMID:5776441

Spliid, C. C. M., Bøgelund, P., & Dahl, B. (2017). Student challenges when learning to become a real team in a PBL curriculum: Experiences from first year science, engineering and mathematics students. *International Research Symposium on Problem-Based Learning 2017*.

Sterling, S. R. (2001). *Sustainable Education: Re-visioning Learning and Change*. Green Books.

Sternberg, R. J. (1999). *Handbook of creativity*. New York: Cambridge University Press.

Sun, X. (2012). *On the Understanding of the Subjectivity of National Culture*. Modern Communication.

Tai, G. X.-L., & Yuen, M. C. (2007). Authentic assessment strategies in problem based learning. Proceedings of Ascilite Singapore, 983-993.

Tang, M. F. (2009). *Technology Transfer from University to Industry: Insight into University Technology Transfer in the Chinese National Innovation Systems*. London: Adonis & Abbey Publishers Ltd.

Tan, O. S. (2009). *Problem-Based Learning and Creativity*. Singapore: Cengage Learning Asia Pte Ltd.

The Core Curriculum Requirement. (2008). Retrieved from http://static.fas.harvard. edu/registrar/ugrad_handbook/2009_2010/chapter2/core02.html

The World Bank. (2013). *China 2030: Building A Modern, Harmonious, and Creative Society*. Washington, DC: The World Bank.

Thousand, J. S., & Villa, R. A. (1995). Managing Complex Change Towards Inclusive Schooling. In Creating an inclusive school (pp. 51–79). Academic Press.

Turner. (2005). *Sociology*. Prentice Hall.

Ulseth, R. (2016). Development of PBL Students as Self-Directed Learners. *2016 ASEE Annual Conference & Exposition Proceedings*. 10.18260/p.26823

UN. (2017). The 17 Sustainable Development Goals as one indivisible system. In Integrated Approaches for Sustainable Development Goals Planning (pp. 10–12). UN.

Van Woerden, W. M. (1991). *Het Projectonderwijs onderzocht* [Research into the project method of teaching] (Thesis). Enschede: University of Technology Twente.

Verstegen, D. M. L., de Jong, N., van Berlo, J., Camp, A., Könings, K. D., van Merriöenboer, J. J. G., & Donkers, J. (2016). How e-learning can support PBL groups: a literature review. In S. Bridges, L. K. Chan, & C. E. Hmelo-Silver (Eds.), *Educational Technologies in Medical and Health Sciences Education* (pp. 9–33). Springer International Publishing. doi:10.1007/978-3-319-08275-2_2

von Humboldt, Heath, & Aarsleff. (1997). *On Language: The Diversity of Human Language-Structure and its Influence on the Mental Development of Mankind* (X. Yao, Trans.). Beijing: The Commercial Press.

Wang. (2015). *Lun Yu*. Beijing United Publishing Company.

Wang, J., Zhang, W., & Qin, L. (2010). Problem-based learning in regional anatomy education at Peking University. *Anatomical Sciences Education*, *3*, 121–126. PMID:20496433

Weber, M. (1922). Die protestantische Ethik und der Geist des Kapitalismus. In M. Weber (Ed.), Gesammelte Aufsätze zur Religionssoziologie. Tübingen: Mohr Siebeck.

Wenger, E. (1998). *Communities of Practice, Learning, Meaning and Identity*. New York: Cambridge University Press. doi:10.1017/CBO9780511803932

Wickson, F., Carew, A. L., & Russell, A. W. (2006). Transdisciplinary research: Characteristics, quandaries and quality. *Futures*, *38*(9), 1046–1059. doi:10.1016/j.futures.2006.02.011

Wikipedia. (2018). Retrieved from Wikipedia: https://en.wikipedia.org/wiki/Interdisciplinarity

Wilkerson, L., & Gijselaers, W. H. (Eds.). (1996). *Bringing Problem-Based Learning to Higher Education: Theory and Practice*. San Francisco: Jossey-Bass Publishers.

Wood, J. T. (1997). *Gendered lives: Communication, gender and culture*. Belmont, CA: Wadsworth.

Woods, D. R. (1994). *Problem-based learning: how to gain the most from PBL*. Academic Press.

Wyness, L., & Dalton, F. (2018). The Value of Problem-Based Learning in Learning for Sustainability: Undergraduate Accounting Student Perspectives. *Journal of Accounting Education*, *45*, 1–19. doi:10.1016/j.jaccedu.2018.09.001

Zhang, G. (2002, October). Using problem based learning and cooperative group learning in teaching instrumental analysis. *The China Papers*, 4-8.

Zhang, J. (2016). Striking a Balance Between Environmental Protection and Rapid Development. In China in the Xi Jinping Era (pp. 151–185). Academic Press. doi:10.1007/978-3-319-29549-7_7

Zhiyu, L. (2012). Study on the Cultivation of College Students' Science and Technology Innovative Ability in Electrotechnics Teaching Based on PBL Mode. *IERI Procedia*, *2*, 287–292. doi:10.1016/j.ieri.2012.06.090

Zhong, D. (2017). *Connotations and Actions for Establishing the Emerging Engineering Education*. Research in Higher Education of Engineering.

Zhou, C. (2012). *Group Creativity Development in Engineering Education in Problem and Project-Based Learning (PBL) Environment*. Aalborg: akprint.

Zhou, C. (2012b). *Group Creativity Development in Engineering Education in Problem and Project-Based Learning (PBL) Environment* (Ph.D. thesis). Aalborg: AK print.

Zhou, C. (2015b). Student project as an 'extra group member': a metaphor for creativity development in Problem-Based Learning (PBL). *Academic Quarter*, 9223-235.

Zhou, C. (2016). Developing Creativity as a Scientific Literacy in Software Engineering Education towards Sustainability. In *2016 12th International Conference on Natural Computation, Fuzzy Systems and Knowledge Discovery (ICNC-FSKD 2016)*. IEEE Press. 10.1109/FSKD.2016.7603533

Zhou, C. (2017). Fostering Creative Problem Solvers in Higher Education. In Advances in Higher Education and Professional Development (pp. 1–23). Academic Press. doi:10.4018/978-1-5225-0643-0.ch001

Zhou, C. (2017). How Ha-Ha Interplays with Aha! Supporting a playful approach to creative learning environments. In T. Chemi, S. G. Davy, & B. Lund (Eds.), Innovative Pedagogy: A Recognition of Emotions and Creativity in Education (pp. 107-124). Rotterdam: Brill.

Zhou, C., & Purushothaman, A. (2017). Developing creativity and learning design by Information and Communication Technology (ICT) in developing contexts. In The Encyclopedia of Information Science and Technology (4th ed.; pp. 4178 - 4188). IGI Global.

Zhou, C., Rasmussen, P., Chemi, T., & Luo, L. (2017). An investigation of creative climate of university R&D centers and policy implications for innovation in China. In Y. Jing & S. Osborne (Eds.), Public Service Innovations in China (pp. 185-205). Singapore: Palgrave Macmillan. doi:10.1007/978-981-10-1762-9_9

Zhou, C. (2012a). Fostering Creative Engineers: A Key to Face Complexity of Engineering Practice. *European Journal of Engineering Education*, *37*(4), 343–353. doi:10.1080/03043797.2012.691872

Zhou, C. (2014). Student Project as an 'Extra Group Member': A Metaphor for Creativity Development in Problem-Based Learning (PBL). *Academic Quarter*, *9*, 223–235.

Zhou, C. (2015a). Bridging creativity and group by elements of Problem-Based Learning (PBL). In A. Abraham, A. K. Muda, & Y.-H. Choo (Eds.), *Pattern Analysis, Intelligent Security and the Internet of Things* (pp. 1–10). London: Springer. doi:10.1007/978-3-319-17398-6_1

Zhou, C. (2016a). Fostering creative problem solvers in higher education: a response to complexity of society. In C. Zhou (Ed.), *Creative Problem-Solving Skill Development in Higher Education* (pp. 1–24). Hershey, PA: IGI Global.

Zhou, C. (2016b). Going towards adaption, integration and co-creation: a conclusion of research on creative problem solving skills development in higher education. In C. Zhou (Ed.), *A Handbook Research on Creative Problem Solving Skills Development in Higher Education*. IGI Global.

Zhou, C. (2018). A Study on creative climate in Project-Organized Groups (POGs) in China and implications for sustainable pedagogy. *Sustainability*, *10*(114), 1–15. PMID:30607262

Zhou, C., Kolmos, A., & Nielsen, J. F. (2012). A problem and project-based learning (PBL) approach to motivate group creativity in engineering education. *International Journal of Engineering Education*, 3–16.

Zhou, C., & Luo, L. (2012). Group Creativity in Learning Context: Understanding in a Social-Cultural Framework and Methodology. *Creative Education*, *3*(4), 392–399. doi:10.4236/ce.2012.34062

Zhou, C., Otrel-Cass, K., & Børsen, T. (2015). Integrating Ethics into Engineering Education. In S. S. Sethy (Ed.), *Contemporary Ethical Issues in Engineering* (pp. 159–173). IGI Global. doi:10.4018/978-1-4666-8130-9.ch012

Zhou, C., & Shi, J. (2015). A Cross-Cultural Perspective to Creativity in Engineering Education in Problem-Based Learning (PBL) between Denmark and China. *International Journal of Engineering Education*, *31*(1A), 12–22.

Zhou, C., & Valero, P. (2015). A Comparison on Creativity in Project Groups in Science and Engineering Education between Denmark and China. In G. E. Corazza & S. Agnoli (Eds.), *Multidisciplinary Contributions to Science of Creative Thinking* (pp. 133–151). Springer.

Related References

To continue our tradition of advancing academic research, we have compiled a list of recommended IGI Global readings. These references will provide additional information and guidance to further enrich your knowledge and assist you with your own research and future publications.

Aburezeq, I. M., & Dweikat, F. F. (2017). Cloud Applications in Language Teaching: Examining Pre-Service Teachers' Expertise, Perceptions and Integration. *International Journal of Distance Education Technologies*, *15*(4), 39–60. doi:10.4018/IJDET.2017100103

Adera, B. (2017). Supporting Language and Literacy Development for English Language Learners. In J. Keengwe (Ed.), *Handbook of Research on Promoting Cross-Cultural Competence and Social Justice in Teacher Education* (pp. 339–354). Hershey, PA: IGI Global. doi:10.4018/978-1-5225-0897-7.ch018

Ahamer, G. (2011). How Technologies Can Localize Learners in Multicultural Space: A Newly Developed "Global Studies" Curriculum. *International Journal of Technology and Educational Marketing*, *1*(2), 1–24. doi:10.4018/ijtem.2011070101

Ahamer, G. (2015). Conclusions from Social Dynamics in Collaborative Environmental Didactics. *International Journal of Technology and Educational Marketing*, *5*(2), 68–92. doi:10.4018/IJTEM.2015070105

Ahamer, G. (2015). Designing and Analyzing Social Dynamics for Collaborative: Environmental Didactics. *International Journal of Technology and Educational Marketing*, *5*(2), 46–67. doi:10.4018/IJTEM.2015070104

Ahamer, G. (2017). Quality Assurance for a Developmental "Global Studies" (GS) Curriculum. In I. Management Association (Ed.), *Educational Leadership and Administration: Concepts, Methodologies, Tools, and Applications* (pp. 438-477). Hershey, PA: IGI Global. doi:10.4018/978-1-5225-1624-8.ch023

Ahamer, G. (2017). Quality Assurance for a Developmental "Global Studies" (GS) Curriculum. In I. Management Association (Ed.), *Educational Leadership and Administration: Concepts, Methodologies, Tools, and Applications* (pp. 438-477). Hershey, PA: IGI Global. doi:10.4018/978-1-5225-1624-8.ch023

Alegre de la Rosa, O. M., & Angulo, L. M. (2017). Social Inclusion and Intercultural Values in a School of Education. In S. Mukerji & P. Tripathi (Eds.), *Handbook of Research on Administration, Policy, and Leadership in Higher Education* (pp. 518–531). Hershey, PA: IGI Global. doi:10.4018/978-1-5225-0672-0.ch020

Ambikairajah, E., Sethu, V., Eaton, R., & Sheng, M. (2014). Evolving Use of Educational Technologies: Enhancing Lectures. In F. Alam (Ed.), *Using Technology Tools to Innovate Assessment, Reporting, and Teaching Practices in Engineering Education* (pp. 241–258). Hershey, PA: IGI Global. doi:10.4018/978-1-4666-5011-4.ch018

Anderson, K. M. (2017). Preparing Teachers in the Age of Equity and Inclusion. In I. Management Association (Ed.), *Medical Education and Ethics: Concepts, Methodologies, Tools, and Applications* (pp. 1532-1554). Hershey, PA: IGI Global. doi:10.4018/978-1-5225-0978-3.ch069

Awdziej, M. (2017). Case Study as a Teaching Method in Marketing. In D. Latusek (Ed.), *Case Studies as a Teaching Tool in Management Education* (pp. 244–263). Hershey, PA: IGI Global. doi:10.4018/978-1-5225-0770-3.ch013

Bain, B. (2014). Exploring Assessment of Critical Thinking Learning Outcomes in Online Higher Education. In V. Wang (Ed.), *Handbook of Research on Education and Technology in a Changing Society* (pp. 1191–1202). Hershey, PA: IGI Global. doi:10.4018/978-1-4666-6046-5.ch089

Banas, J. R., & York, C. S. (2017). Pre-Service Teachers' Motivation to Use Technology and the Impact of Authentic Learning Exercises. In L. Tomei (Ed.), *Exploring the New Era of Technology-Infused Education* (pp. 121–140). Hershey, PA: IGI Global. doi:10.4018/978-1-5225-1709-2.ch008

Bariso, E. U. (2015). Educational Policy Analysis Debates and New Learning Technologies in England. In M. Khosrow-Pour (Ed.), *Encyclopedia of Information Science and Technology* (3rd ed.; pp. 2371–2378). Hershey, PA: IGI Global. doi:10.4018/978-1-4666-5888-2.ch230

Beycioglu, K., & Wildy, H. (2015). Principal Preparation: The Case of Novice Principals in Turkey. In K. Beycioglu & P. Pashiardis (Eds.), *Multidimensional Perspectives on Principal Leadership Effectiveness* (pp. 1–17). Hershey, PA: IGI Global. doi:10.4018/978-1-4666-6591-0.ch001

Beycioglu, K., & Wildy, H. (2017). Principal Preparation: The Case of Novice Principals in Turkey. In I. Management Association (Ed.), Educational Leadership and Administration: Concepts, Methodologies, Tools, and Applications (pp. 1152-1169). Hershey, PA: IGI Global. doi:10.4018/978-1-5225-1624-8.ch054

Bharwani, S., & Musunuri, D. (2018). Reflection as a Process From Theory to Practice. In M. Khosrow-Pour, D.B.A. (Ed.), Encyclopedia of Information Science and Technology, Fourth Edition (pp. 1529-1539). Hershey, PA: IGI Global. doi:10.4018/978-1-5225-2255-3.ch132

Bisschoff, T., & Rhodes, C. (2011). Transformation through Marketing: A Case of a Secondary School in South Africa. In P. Tripathi & S. Mukerji (Eds.), *Cases on Innovations in Educational Marketing: Transnational and Technological Strategies* (pp. 263–272). Hershey, PA: IGI Global. doi:10.4018/978-1-60960-599-5.ch016

Bodomo, A. B. (2010). Educational Technologies (WebCT): Creating Constructivist and Interactive Learning Communities. In A. Bodomo (Ed.), *Computer-Mediated Communication for Linguistics and Literacy: Technology and Natural Language Education* (pp. 252–290). Hershey, PA: IGI Global. doi:10.4018/978-1-60566-868-0.ch010

Bohjanen, S. L., Cameron-Standerford, A., & Meidl, T. D. (2018). Capacity Building Pedagogy for Diverse Learners. In J. Keengwe (Ed.), *Handbook of Research on Pedagogical Models for Next-Generation Teaching and Learning* (pp. 195–212). Hershey, PA: IGI Global. doi:10.4018/978-1-5225-3873-8.ch011

Brewer, J. C. (2018). Measuring Text Readability Using Reading Level. In M. Khosrow-Pour, D.B.A. (Ed.), Encyclopedia of Information Science and Technology, Fourth Edition (pp. 1499-1507). Hershey, PA: IGI Global. doi:10.4018/978-1-5225-2255-3.ch129

Brown, S. L. (2017). A Case Study of Strategic Leadership and Research in Practice: Principal Preparation Programs that Work – An Educational Administration Perspective of Best Practices for Master's Degree Programs for Principal Preparation. In V. Wang (Ed.), *Encyclopedia of Strategic Leadership and Management* (pp. 1226–1244). Hershey, PA: IGI Global. doi:10.4018/978-1-5225-1049-9.ch086

Brzozowski, M., & Ferster, I. (2017). Educational Management Leadership: High School Principal's Management Style and Parental Involvement in School Management in Israel. In V. Potocan, M. Üngan, & Z. Nedelko (Eds.), *Handbook of Research on Managerial Solutions in Non-Profit Organizations* (pp. 55–74). Hershey, PA: IGI Global. doi:10.4018/978-1-5225-0731-4.ch003

Cannaday, J. (2017). The Masking Effect: Hidden Gifts and Disabilities of 2e Students. In P. Dickenson, P. Keough, & J. Courduff (Eds.), *Preparing Pre-Service Teachers for the Inclusive Classroom* (pp. 220–231). Hershey, PA: IGI Global. doi:10.4018/978-1-5225-1753-5.ch011

Capobianco, B. M., & Lehman, J. D. (2010). Fostering Educational Technology Integration in Science Teacher Education: Issues of Teacher Identity Development. In J. Yamamoto, J. Kush, R. Lombard, & C. Hertzog (Eds.), *Technology Implementation and Teacher Education: Reflective Models* (pp. 245–257). Hershey, PA: IGI Global. doi:10.4018/978-1-61520-897-5.ch014

Chao, G. H., Hsu, M. K., & Scovotti, C. (2013). Predicting Donations from a Cohort Group of Donors to Charities: A Direct Marketing Case Study. In J. Wang (Ed.), *Optimizing, Innovating, and Capitalizing on Information Systems for Operations* (pp. 196–214). Hershey, PA: IGI Global. doi:10.4018/978-1-4666-2925-7.ch010

Chauhan, A. (2015). Beyond the Phenomenon: Assessment in Massive Open Online Courses (MOOCs). In E. McKay & J. Lenarcic (Eds.), *Macro-Level Learning through Massive Open Online Courses (MOOCs): Strategies and Predictions for the Future* (pp. 119–140). Hershey, PA: IGI Global. doi:10.4018/978-1-4666-8324-2.ch007

Coffman, T. L., & Klinger, M. B. (2013). Managing Quality in Online Education. In G. Kurubacak & T. Yuzer (Eds.), *Project Management Approaches for Online Learning Design* (pp. 220–233). Hershey, PA: IGI Global. doi:10.4018/978-1-4666-2830-4.ch011

Contreras, E. C., & Contreras, I. I. (2018). Development of Communication Skills through Auditory Training Software in Special Education. In M. Khosrow-Pour, D.B.A. (Ed.), Encyclopedia of Information Science and Technology, Fourth Edition (pp. 2431-2441). Hershey, PA: IGI Global. doi:10.4018/978-1-5225-2255-3.ch212

Cook, R. G. (2011). Educational Marketing: Coming Down from the Cloud Using Landing Gear. In U. Demiray & S. Sever (Eds.), *Marketing Online Education Programs: Frameworks for Promotion and Communication* (pp. 26–31). Hershey, PA: IGI Global. doi:10.4018/978-1-60960-074-7.ch003

Cook, R. G., & Ley, K. (2015). Past, Future and Presents: Meeting New Online Challenges with Primal Marketing Solutions. *International Journal of Technology and Educational Marketing*, *5*(2), 19–33. doi:10.4018/IJTEM.2015070102

Cooley, D., & Whitten, E. (2017). Special Education Leadership and the Implementation of Response to Intervention. In F. Topor (Ed.), *Handbook of Research on Individualism and Identity in the Globalized Digital Age* (pp. 265–286). Hershey, PA: IGI Global. doi:10.4018/978-1-5225-0522-8.ch012

Cosner, S., Tozer, S., & Zavitkovsky, P. (2017). Enacting a Cycle of Inquiry Capstone Research Project in Doctoral-Level Leadership Preparation. In I. Management Association (Ed.), Educational Leadership and Administration: Concepts, Methodologies, Tools, and Applications (pp. 1460-1481). Hershey, PA: IGI Global. doi:10.4018/978-1-5225-1624-8.ch067

Crawford, C. M. (2018). Instructional Real World Community Engagement. In M. Khosrow-Pour, D.B.A. (Ed.), Encyclopedia of Information Science and Technology, Fourth Edition (pp. 1474-1486). Hershey, PA: IGI Global. doi:10.4018/978-1-5225-2255-3.ch127

Crosby-Cooper, T., & Pacis, D. (2017). Implementing Effective Student Support Teams. In P. Dickenson, P. Keough, & J. Courduff (Eds.), *Preparing Pre-Service Teachers for the Inclusive Classroom* (pp. 248–262). Hershey, PA: IGI Global. doi:10.4018/978-1-5225-1753-5.ch013

Curran, C. M., & Hawbaker, B. W. (2017). Cultivating Communities of Inclusive Practice: Professional Development for Educators – Research and Practice. In C. Curran & A. Petersen (Eds.), *Handbook of Research on Classroom Diversity and Inclusive Education Practice* (pp. 120–153). Hershey, PA: IGI Global. doi:10.4018/978-1-5225-2520-2.ch006

Dass, S., & Dabbagh, N. (2018). Faculty Adoption of 3D Avatar-Based Virtual World Learning Environments: An Exploratory Case Study. In I. Management Association (Ed.), Technology Adoption and Social Issues: Concepts, Methodologies, Tools, and Applications (pp. 1000-1033). Hershey, PA: IGI Global. doi:10.4018/978-1-5225-5201-7.ch045

Davison, A. M., & Scholl, K. G. (2017). Inclusive Recreation as Part of the IEP Process. In C. Curran & A. Petersen (Eds.), *Handbook of Research on Classroom Diversity and Inclusive Education Practice* (pp. 311–330). Hershey, PA: IGI Global. doi:10.4018/978-1-5225-2520-2.ch013

DeCoito, I. (2018). Addressing Digital Competencies, Curriculum Development, and Instructional Design in Science Teacher Education. In M. Khosrow-Pour, D.B.A. (Ed.), Encyclopedia of Information Science and Technology, Fourth Edition (pp. 1420-1431). Hershey, PA: IGI Global. doi:10.4018/978-1-5225-2255-3.ch122

DeCoito, I., & Richardson, T. (2017). Beyond Angry Birds™: Using Web-Based Tools to Engage Learners and Promote Inquiry in STEM Learning. In I. Levin & D. Tsybulsky (Eds.), *Digital Tools and Solutions for Inquiry-Based STEM Learning* (pp. 166–196). Hershey, PA: IGI Global. doi:10.4018/978-1-5225-2525-7.ch007

Delmas, P. M. (2017). Research-Based Leadership for Next-Generation Leaders. In R. Styron Jr & J. Styron (Eds.), *Comprehensive Problem-Solving and Skill Development for Next-Generation Leaders* (pp. 1–39). Hershey, PA: IGI Global. doi:10.4018/978-1-5225-1968-3.ch001

Demiray, U., & Ekren, G. (2018). Administrative-Related Evaluation for Distance Education Institutions in Turkey. In K. Buyuk, S. Kocdar, & A. Bozkurt (Eds.), *Administrative Leadership in Open and Distance Learning Programs* (pp. 263–288). Hershey, PA: IGI Global. doi:10.4018/978-1-5225-2645-2.ch011

Dickenson, P. (2017). What do we Know and Where Can We Grow?: Teachers Preparation for the Inclusive Classroom. In P. Dickenson, P. Keough, & J. Courduff (Eds.), *Preparing Pre-Service Teachers for the Inclusive Classroom* (pp. 1–22). Hershey, PA: IGI Global. doi:10.4018/978-1-5225-1753-5.ch001

Dickerson, J., & Coleman, H. V. (2012). Technology, E-Leadership and Educational Administration in Schools: Integrating Standards with Context and Guiding Questions. In V. Wang (Ed.), *Encyclopedia of E-Leadership, Counseling and Training* (pp. 408–422). Hershey, PA: IGI Global. doi:10.4018/978-1-61350-068-2.ch030

Dickerson, J., Coleman, H. V., & Geer, G. (2012). Thinking like a School Technology Leader. In V. Wang (Ed.), *Technology and Its Impact on Educational Leadership: Innovation and Change* (pp. 53–63). Hershey, PA: IGI Global. doi:10.4018/978-1-4666-0062-1.ch005

Donne, V., & Hansen, M. (2017). Teachers' Use of Assistive Technologies in Education. In L. Tomei (Ed.), *Exploring the New Era of Technology-Infused Education* (pp. 86–101). Hershey, PA: IGI Global. doi:10.4018/978-1-5225-1709-2.ch006

Donne, V., & Hansen, M. A. (2018). Business and Technology Educators: Practices for Inclusion. In I. Management Association (Ed.), Business Education and Ethics: Concepts, Methodologies, Tools, and Applications (pp. 471-484). Hershey, PA: IGI Global. doi:10.4018/978-1-5225-3153-1.ch026

Dreon, O., Shettel, J., & Bower, K. M. (2017). Preparing Next Generation Elementary Teachers for the Tools of Tomorrow. In M. Grassetti & S. Brookby (Eds.), *Advancing Next-Generation Teacher Education through Digital Tools and Applications* (pp. 143–159). Hershey, PA: IGI Global. doi:10.4018/978-1-5225-0965-3.ch008

Drinka, D., Voge, K., & Yen, M. Y. (2005). From Principles to Practice: Analyzing a Student Learning Outcomes Assessment System. *Journal of Cases on Information Technology*, 7(3), 37–56. doi:10.4018/jcit.2005070103

Durak, H. Y., & Güyer, T. (2018). Design and Development of an Instructional Program for Teaching Programming Processes to Gifted Students Using Scratch. In J. Cannaday (Ed.), *Curriculum Development for Gifted Education Programs* (pp. 61–99). Hershey, PA: IGI Global. doi:10.4018/978-1-5225-3041-1.ch004

Egorkina, E., Ivanov, M., & Valyavskiy, A. Y. (2018). Students' Research Competence Formation of the Quality of Open and Distance Learning. In V. Mkrttchian & L. Belyanina (Eds.), *Handbook of Research on Students' Research Competence in Modern Educational Contexts* (pp. 364–384). Hershey, PA: IGI Global. doi:10.4018/978-1-5225-3485-3.ch019

Ekren, G., Karataş, S., & Demiray, U. (2017). Understanding of Leadership in Distance Education Management. In I. Management Association (Ed.), Educational Leadership and Administration: Concepts, Methodologies, Tools, and Applications (pp. 34-50). Hershey, PA: IGI Global. doi:10.4018/978-1-5225-1624-8.ch003

Elmore, W. M., Young, J. K., Harris, S., & Mason, D. (2017). The Relationship between Individual Student Attributes and Online Course Completion. In K. Shelton & K. Pedersen (Eds.), *Handbook of Research on Building, Growing, and Sustaining Quality E-Learning Programs* (pp. 151–173). Hershey, PA: IGI Global. doi:10.4018/978-1-5225-0877-9.ch008

Ercegovac, I. R., Alfirević, N., & Koludrović, M. (2017). School Principals' Communication and Co-Operation Assessment: The Croatian Experience. In I. Management Association (Ed.), Educational Leadership and Administration: Concepts, Methodologies, Tools, and Applications (pp. 1568-1589). Hershey, PA: IGI Global. doi:10.4018/978-1-5225-1624-8.ch072

Everhart, D., & Seymour, D. M. (2017). Challenges and Opportunities in the Currency of Higher Education. In K. Rasmussen, P. Northrup, & R. Colson (Eds.), *Handbook of Research on Competency-Based Education in University Settings* (pp. 41–65). Hershey, PA: IGI Global. doi:10.4018/978-1-5225-0932-5.ch003

Farmer, L. S. (2017). Managing Portable Technologies for Special Education. In V. Wang (Ed.), *Encyclopedia of Strategic Leadership and Management* (pp. 977–987). Hershey, PA: IGI Global. doi:10.4018/978-1-5225-1049-9.ch068

Farmer, L. S. (2018). Optimizing OERs for Optimal ICT Literacy in Higher Education. In J. Keengwe (Ed.), *Handbook of Research on Mobile Technology, Constructivism, and Meaningful Learning* (pp. 366–390). Hershey, PA: IGI Global. doi:10.4018/978-1-5225-3949-0.ch020

Fındık, L. Y. (2017). Self-Assessment of Principals Based on Leadership in Complexity. In I. Management Association (Ed.), Educational Leadership and Administration: Concepts, Methodologies, Tools, and Applications (pp. 978-991). Hershey, PA: IGI Global. doi:10.4018/978-1-5225-1624-8.ch047

Flor, A. G., & Gonzalez-Flor, B. (2018). Dysfunctional Digital Demeanors: Tales From (and Policy Implications of) eLearning's Dark Side. In I. Management Association (Ed.), The Dark Web: Breakthroughs in Research and Practice (pp. 37-50). Hershey, PA: IGI Global. doi:10.4018/978-1-5225-3163-0.ch003

Floyd, K. K., & Shambaugh, N. (2017). Instructional Design for Simulations in Special Education Virtual Learning Spaces. In T. Kidd & L. Morris Jr., (Eds.), *Handbook of Research on Instructional Systems and Educational Technology* (pp. 202–215). Hershey, PA: IGI Global. doi:10.4018/978-1-5225-2399-4.ch018

Giovannini, J. M. (2017). Technology Integration in Preservice Teacher Education Programs: Research-based Recommendations. In M. Grassetti & S. Brookby (Eds.), *Advancing Next-Generation Teacher Education through Digital Tools and Applications* (pp. 82–102). Hershey, PA: IGI Global. doi:10.4018/978-1-5225-0965-3.ch005

Good, S., & Clarke, V. B. (2017). An Integral Analysis of One Urban School System's Efforts to Support Student-Centered Teaching. In J. Keengwe & G. Onchwari (Eds.), *Handbook of Research on Learner-Centered Pedagogy in Teacher Education and Professional Development* (pp. 45–68). Hershey, PA: IGI Global. doi:10.4018/978-1-5225-0892-2.ch003

Grobler, B. (2015). The Relationship between Emotional Competence and Instructional Leadership and Their Association with Learner Achievement. In K. Beycioglu & P. Pashiardis (Eds.), *Multidimensional Perspectives on Principal Leadership Effectiveness* (pp. 373–407). Hershey, PA: IGI Global. doi:10.4018/978-1-4666-6591-0.ch017

Hamidi, F., Owuor, P. M., Hynie, M., Baljko, M., & McGrath, S. (2017). Potentials of Digital Assistive Technology and Special Education in Kenya. In C. Ayo & V. Mbarika (Eds.), *Sustainable ICT Adoption and Integration for Socio-Economic Development* (pp. 125–151). Hershey, PA: IGI Global. doi:10.4018/978-1-5225-2565-3.ch006

Heavin, C., & Neville, K. (2015). Addressing the Learning Needs of Future IS Security Professionals through Social Media Technology. In M. Khosrow-Pour (Ed.), *Encyclopedia of Information Science and Technology* (3rd ed.; pp. 4766–4775). Hershey, PA: IGI Global. doi:10.4018/978-1-4666-5888-2.ch468

Henderson, L. K. (2017). Meltdown at Fukushima: Global Catastrophic Events, Visual Literacy, and Art Education. In R. Shin (Ed.), *Convergence of Contemporary Art, Visual Culture, and Global Civic Engagement* (pp. 80–99). Hershey, PA: IGI Global. doi:10.4018/978-1-5225-1665-1.ch005

Hismanoglu, M. (2012). Important Issues in Online Education: E-Pedagogy and Marketing. In I. Management Association (Ed.), *E-Marketing: Concepts, Methodologies, Tools, and Applications* (pp. 676-701). Hershey, PA: IGI Global. doi:10.4018/978-1-4666-1598-4.ch041

Howard, B. C. (2008). Common Features and Design Principles Found in Exemplary Educational Technologies. *International Journal of Information and Communication Technology Education*, 4(4), 31–52. doi:10.4018/jicte.2008100104

Howard, B. C., & Tomei, L. A. (2008). The Classroom of the Future and Emerging Educational Technologies: Introduction to the Special Issue. *International Journal of Information and Communication Technology Education*, 4(4), 1–8. doi:10.4018/jicte.2008100101

Hudgins, T., & Holland, J. L. (2018). Digital Badges: Tracking Knowledge Acquisition Within an Innovation Framework. In I. Management Association (Ed.), Wearable Technologies: Concepts, Methodologies, Tools, and Applications (pp. 1118-1132). Hershey, PA: IGI Global. doi:10.4018/978-1-5225-5484-4.ch051

Ion, G., Tomàs, M., Castro, D., & Salat, E. (2015). Analysis of the Tasks of School Principals in Secondary Education in Catalonia: Case Study. In K. Beycioglu & P. Pashiardis (Eds.), *Multidimensional Perspectives on Principal Leadership Effectiveness* (pp. 39–58). Hershey, PA: IGI Global. doi:10.4018/978-1-4666-6591-0.ch003

Janus, M., & Siddiqua, A. (2018). Challenges for Children With Special Health Needs at the Time of Transition to School. In I. Management Association (Ed.), Autism Spectrum Disorders: Breakthroughs in Research and Practice (pp. 339-371). Hershey, PA: IGI Global. doi:10.4018/978-1-5225-3827-1.ch018

Jesus, R. A. (2018). Screencasts and Learning Styles. In M. Khosrow-Pour, D.B.A. (Ed.), Encyclopedia of Information Science and Technology, Fourth Edition (pp. 1548-1558). Hershey, PA: IGI Global. doi:10.4018/978-1-5225-2255-3.ch134

Kaplan-Rakowski, R., & Rakowski, D. (2011). Educational Technologies for the Neomillennial Generation. In E. Dunkels, G. Franberg, & C. Hallgren (Eds.), *Interactive Media Use and Youth: Learning, Knowledge Exchange and Behavior* (pp. 12–31). Hershey, PA: IGI Global. doi:10.4018/978-1-60960-206-2.ch002

Karpinski, A. C., D'Agostino, J. V., Williams, A. K., Highland, S. A., & Mellott, J. A. (2018). The Relationship Between Online Formative Assessment and State Test Scores Using Multilevel Modeling. In M. Khosrow-Pour, D.B.A. (Ed.), Encyclopedia of Information Science and Technology, Fourth Edition (pp. 5183-5192). Hershey, PA: IGI Global. doi:10.4018/978-1-5225-2255-3.ch450

Kats, Y. (2017). Educational Leadership and Integrated Support for Students with Autism Spectrum Disorders. In I. Management Association (Ed.), *Educational Leadership and Administration: Concepts, Methodologies, Tools, and Applications* (pp. 101-114). Hershey, PA: IGI Global. doi:10.4018/978-1-5225-1624-8.ch007

Kaya, G., & Altun, A. (2018). Educational Ontology Development. In M. Khosrow-Pour, D.B.A. (Ed.), *Encyclopedia of Information Science and Technology, Fourth Edition* (pp. 1441-1450). Hershey, PA: IGI Global. doi:10.4018/978-1-5225-2255-3.ch124

Keough, P. D., & Pacis, D. (2017). Best Practices Implementing Special Education Curriculum and Common Core State Standards using UDL. In P. Dickenson, P. Keough, & J. Courduff (Eds.), *Preparing Pre-Service Teachers for the Inclusive Classroom* (pp. 107–123). Hershey, PA: IGI Global. doi:10.4018/978-1-5225-1753-5.ch006

Kilburn, M., Henckell, M., & Starrett, D. (2018). Factors Contributing to the Effectiveness of Online Students and Instructors. In M. Khosrow-Pour, D.B.A. (Ed.), *Encyclopedia of Information Science and Technology, Fourth Edition* (pp. 1451-1462). Hershey, PA: IGI Global. doi:10.4018/978-1-5225-2255-3.ch125

Konecny, L. T. (2017). Hybrid, Online, and Flipped Classrooms in Health Science: Enhanced Learning Environments. In I. Management Association (Ed.), *Flipped Instruction: Breakthroughs in Research and Practice* (pp. 355-370). Hershey, PA: IGI Global. doi:10.4018/978-1-5225-1803-7.ch020

Kowch, E. G. (2013). Towards Leading Diverse, Smarter and More Adaptable Organizations that Learn. In J. Lewis, A. Green, & D. Surry (Eds.), *Technology as a Tool for Diversity Leadership: Implementation and Future Implications* (pp. 11–34). Hershey, PA: IGI Global. doi:10.4018/978-1-4666-2668-3.ch002

Krezmien, M., Powell, W., Bosch, C., Hall, T., & Nieswandt, M. (2017). The Use of Tablet Technology to Support Inquiry Science for Students Incarcerated in Juvenile Justice Settings. In I. Levin & D. Tsybulsky (Eds.), *Optimizing STEM Education With Advanced ICTs and Simulations* (pp. 267–295). Hershey, PA: IGI Global. doi:10.4018/978-1-5225-2528-8.ch011

Leach, L. F., Winn, P., Erwin, S., & Benedict, L. P. (2015). What 21st Century Students Want: Factors that Influence Student Selection of Educational Leadership Graduate Programs. *International Journal of Technology and Educational Marketing*, *5*(1), 15–28. doi:10.4018/ijtem.2015010102

Leng, H. K. (2014). An Update on the Use of Facebook as a Marketing Tool by Private Educational Institutions in Singapore. In I. Lee (Ed.), *Trends in E-Business, E-Services, and E-Commerce: Impact of Technology on Goods, Services, and Business Transactions* (pp. 191–205). Hershey, PA: IGI Global. doi:10.4018/978-1-4666-4510-3.ch011

Leone, S. (2018). An Open Learning Format for Lifelong Learners' Empowerment. In M. Khosrow-Pour, D.B.A. (Ed.), Encyclopedia of Information Science and Technology, Fourth Edition (pp. 1517-1528). Hershey, PA: IGI Global. doi:10.4018/978-1-5225-2255-3.ch131

Ley, K., & Gannon-Cook, R. (2010). Marketing a Blended University Program: An Action Research Case Study. In S. Mukerji & P. Tripathi (Eds.), *Cases on Technology Enhanced Learning through Collaborative Opportunities* (pp. 73–90). Hershey, PA: IGI Global. doi:10.4018/978-1-61520-751-0.ch005

Loose, W., & Marcos, T. (2016). Instructional Design for Millennials: Instructor Efficiency in Streamlining Content, Assignments, and Assessments. In P. Dickenson & J. Jaurez (Eds.), *Increasing Productivity and Efficiency in Online Teaching* (pp. 1–25). Hershey, PA: IGI Global. doi:10.4018/978-1-5225-0347-7.ch001

Lovell, K. L. (2017). Development and Evaluation of Neuroscience Computer-Based Modules for Medical Students: Instructional Design Principles and Effectiveness. In J. Stefaniak (Ed.), *Advancing Medical Education Through Strategic Instructional Design* (pp. 262–276). Hershey, PA: IGI Global. doi:10.4018/978-1-5225-2098-6.ch013

Manuel, N. N. (2016). Angolan Higher Education, Policy, and Leadership: Towards Transformative Leadership for Social Justice. In N. Ololube (Ed.), *Handbook of Research on Organizational Justice and Culture in Higher Education Institutions* (pp. 164–188). Hershey, PA: IGI Global. doi:10.4018/978-1-4666-9850-5.ch007

Marouchou, D. V. (2015). The Impact of Academic Beliefs on Student Learning. In M. Khosrow-Pour (Ed.), *Encyclopedia of Information Science and Technology* (3rd ed.; pp. 4796–4804). Hershey, PA: IGI Global. doi:10.4018/978-1-4666-5888-2.ch471

McCormack, V. F., Stauffer, M., Fishley, K., Hohenbrink, J., Mascazine, J. R., & Zigler, T. (2018). Designing a Dual Licensure Path for Middle Childhood and Special Education Teacher Candidates. In D. Polly, M. Putman, T. Petty, & A. Good (Eds.), *Innovative Practices in Teacher Preparation and Graduate-Level Teacher Education Programs* (pp. 21–36). Hershey, PA: IGI Global. doi:10.4018/978-1-5225-3068-8.ch002

McDaniel, R. (2017). Strategic Leadership in Instructional Design: Applying the Principles of Instructional Design through the Lens of Strategic Leadership to Distance Education. In V. Wang (Ed.), *Encyclopedia of Strategic Leadership and Management* (pp. 1570–1584). Hershey, PA: IGI Global. doi:10.4018/978-1-5225-1049-9.ch109

Memon, R. N., Ahmad, R., & Salim, S. S. (2018). Critical Issues in Requirements Engineering Education. In I. Management Association (Ed.), Computer Systems and Software Engineering: Concepts, Methodologies, Tools, and Applications (pp. 1953-1976). Hershey, PA: IGI Global. doi:10.4018/978-1-5225-3923-0.ch081

Mendenhall, R. (2017). Western Governors University: CBE Innovator and National Model. In K. Rasmussen, P. Northrup, & R. Colson (Eds.), *Handbook of Research on Competency-Based Education in University Settings* (pp. 379–400). Hershey, PA: IGI Global. doi:10.4018/978-1-5225-0932-5.ch019

Mense, E. G., Griggs, D. M., & Shanks, J. N. (2018). School Leaders in a Time of Accountability and Data Use: Preparing Our Future School Leaders in Leadership Preparation Programs. In E. Mense & M. Crain-Dorough (Eds.), *Data Leadership for K-12 Schools in a Time of Accountability* (pp. 235–259). Hershey, PA: IGI Global. doi:10.4018/978-1-5225-3188-3.ch012

Mense, E. G., Griggs, D. M., & Shanks, J. N. (2018). School Leaders in a Time of Accountability and Data Use: Preparing Our Future School Leaders in Leadership Preparation Programs. In E. Mense & M. Crain-Dorough (Eds.), *Data Leadership for K-12 Schools in a Time of Accountability* (pp. 235–259). Hershey, PA: IGI Global. doi:10.4018/978-1-5225-3188-3.ch012

Mestry, R., & Naicker, S. R. (2017). Exploring Distributive Leadership in South African Public Primary Schools in the Soweto Region. In I. Management Association (Ed.), Educational Leadership and Administration: Concepts, Methodologies, Tools, and Applications (pp. 1041-1064). Hershey, PA: IGI Global. doi:10.4018/978-1-5225-1624-8.ch050

Monaghan, C. H., & Boboc, M. (2017). (Re)Defining Leadership in Higher Education in the U.S. In V. Wang (Ed.), *Encyclopedia of Strategic Leadership and Management* (pp. 567–579). Hershey, PA: IGI Global. doi:10.4018/978-1-5225-1049-9.ch040

Related References

Muthee, J. M., & Murungi, C. G. (2018). Relationship Among Intelligence, Achievement Motivation, Type of School, and Academic Performance of Kenyan Urban Primary School Pupils. In M. Khosrow-Pour, D.B.A. (Ed.), Encyclopedia of Information Science and Technology, Fourth Edition (pp. 1540-1547). Hershey, PA: IGI Global. doi:10.4018/978-1-5225-2255-3.ch133

Naranjo, J. (2018). Meeting the Need for Inclusive Educators Online: Teacher Education in Inclusive Special Education and Dual-Certification. In D. Polly, M. Putman, T. Petty, & A. Good (Eds.), *Innovative Practices in Teacher Preparation and Graduate-Level Teacher Education Programs* (pp. 106–122). Hershey, PA: IGI Global. doi:10.4018/978-1-5225-3068-8.ch007

Nkabinde, Z. P. (2017). Multiculturalism in Special Education: Perspectives of Minority Children in Urban Schools. In J. Keengwe (Ed.), *Handbook of Research on Promoting Cross-Cultural Competence and Social Justice in Teacher Education* (pp. 382–397). Hershey, PA: IGI Global. doi:10.4018/978-1-5225-0897-7.ch020

Nkabinde, Z. P. (2018). Online Instruction: Is the Quality the Same as Face-to-Face Instruction? In J. Keengwe (Ed.), *Handbook of Research on Digital Content, Mobile Learning, and Technology Integration Models in Teacher Education* (pp. 300–314). Hershey, PA: IGI Global. doi:10.4018/978-1-5225-2953-8.ch016

O'Connor, J. R. Jr, & Jackson, K. N. (2017). The Use of iPad® Devices and "Apps" for ASD Students in Special Education and Speech Therapy. In Y. Kats (Ed.), *Supporting the Education of Children with Autism Spectrum Disorders* (pp. 267–283). Hershey, PA: IGI Global. doi:10.4018/978-1-5225-0816-8.ch014

Okolie, U. C., & Yasin, A. M. (2017). TVET in Developing Nations and Human Development. In U. Okolie & A. Yasin (Eds.), *Technical Education and Vocational Training in Developing Nations* (pp. 1–25). Hershey, PA: IGI Global. doi:10.4018/978-1-5225-1811-2.ch001

Paciga, K. A., & Hoffman, J. L. (2015). Realizing the Potential of e-Books in Early Education. In M. Khosrow-Pour (Ed.), *Encyclopedia of Information Science and Technology* (3rd ed.; pp. 4787–4795). Hershey, PA: IGI Global. doi:10.4018/978-1-4666-5888-2.ch470

Paulson, E. N. (2017). Adapting and Advocating for an Online EdD Program in Changing Times and "Sacred" Cultures. In I. Management Association (Ed.), Educational Leadership and Administration: Concepts, Methodologies, Tools, and Applications (pp. 1849-1876). Hershey, PA: IGI Global. doi:10.4018/978-1-5225-1624-8.ch085

Petersen, A. J., Elser, C. F., Al Nassir, M. N., Stakey, J., & Everson, K. (2017). The Year of Teaching Inclusively: Building an Elementary Classroom for All Students. In C. Curran & A. Petersen (Eds.), *Handbook of Research on Classroom Diversity and Inclusive Education Practice* (pp. 332–348). Hershey, PA: IGI Global. doi:10.4018/978-1-5225-2520-2.ch014

Pfannenstiel, K. H., & Sanders, J. (2017). Characteristics and Instructional Strategies for Students With Mathematical Difficulties: In the Inclusive Classroom. In C. Curran & A. Petersen (Eds.), *Handbook of Research on Classroom Diversity and Inclusive Education Practice* (pp. 250–281). Hershey, PA: IGI Global. doi:10.4018/978-1-5225-2520-2.ch011

Preast, J. L., Bowman, N., & Rose, C. A. (2017). Creating Inclusive Classroom Communities Through Social and Emotional Learning to Reduce Social Marginalization Among Students. In C. Curran & A. Petersen (Eds.), *Handbook of Research on Classroom Diversity and Inclusive Education Practice* (pp. 183–200). Hershey, PA: IGI Global. doi:10.4018/978-1-5225-2520-2.ch008

Randolph, K. M., & Brady, M. P. (2018). Evolution of Covert Coaching as an Evidence-Based Practice in Professional Development and Preparation of Teachers. In V. Bryan, A. Musgrove, & J. Powers (Eds.), *Handbook of Research on Human Development in the Digital Age* (pp. 281–299). Hershey, PA: IGI Global. doi:10.4018/978-1-5225-2838-8.ch013

Rawlins, P., & Kehrwald, B. (2010). Education Technology in Teacher Education: Overcoming Challenges, Realizing Opportunities. In R. Luppicini & A. Haghi (Eds.), *Cases on Digital Technologies in Higher Education: Issues and Challenges* (pp. 50–63). Hershey, PA: IGI Global. doi:10.4018/978-1-61520-869-2.ch004

Rell, A. B., Puig, R. A., Roll, F., Valles, V., Espinoza, M., & Duque, A. L. (2017). Addressing Cultural Diversity and Global Competence: The Dual Language Framework. In L. Leavitt, S. Wisdom, & K. Leavitt (Eds.), *Cultural Awareness and Competency Development in Higher Education* (pp. 111–131). Hershey, PA: IGI Global. doi:10.4018/978-1-5225-2145-7.ch007

Riel, J., Lawless, K. A., & Brown, S. W. (2017). Defining and Designing Responsive Online Professional Development (ROPD): A Framework to Support Curriculum Implementation. In T. Kidd & L. Morris Jr., (Eds.), *Handbook of Research on Instructional Systems and Educational Technology* (pp. 104–115). Hershey, PA: IGI Global. doi:10.4018/978-1-5225-2399-4.ch010

Roberts, C. (2017). Advancing Women Leaders in Academe: Creating a Culture of Inclusion. In S. Mukerji & P. Tripathi (Eds.), *Handbook of Research on Administration, Policy, and Leadership in Higher Education* (pp. 256–273). Hershey, PA: IGI Global. doi:10.4018/978-1-5225-0672-0.ch012

Rodgers, W. J., Kennedy, M. J., Alves, K. D., & Romig, J. E. (2017). A Multimedia Tool for Teacher Education and Professional Development. In C. Martin & D. Polly (Eds.), *Handbook of Research on Teacher Education and Professional Development* (pp. 285–296). Hershey, PA: IGI Global. doi:10.4018/978-1-5225-1067-3.ch015

Romanowski, M. H. (2017). Qatar's Educational Reform: Critical Issues Facing Principals. In I. Management Association (Ed.), Educational Leadership and Administration: Concepts, Methodologies, Tools, and Applications (pp. 1758-1773). Hershey, PA: IGI Global. doi:10.4018/978-1-5225-1624-8.ch080

Ruffin, T. R., Hawkins, D. P., & Lee, D. I. (2018). Increasing Student Engagement and Participation Through Course Methodology. In M. Khosrow-Pour, D.B.A. (Ed.), Encyclopedia of Information Science and Technology, Fourth Edition (pp. 1463-1473). Hershey, PA: IGI Global. doi:10.4018/978-1-5225-2255-3.ch126

Rutaisire, J. (2011). Innovations in Technology for Educational Marketing: Stakeholder Perceptions and Implications for Examinations System in Rwanda. In P. Tripathi & S. Mukerji (Eds.), *Cases on Innovations in Educational Marketing: Transnational and Technological Strategies* (pp. 214–233). Hershey, PA: IGI Global. doi:10.4018/978-1-60960-599-5.ch013

Sabina, L. L., Curry, K. A., Harris, E. L., Krumm, B. L., & Vencill, V. (2017). Assessing the Performance of a Cohort-Based Model Using Domestic and International Practices. In I. Management Association (Ed.), Educational Leadership and Administration: Concepts, Methodologies, Tools, and Applications(pp. 913-929). Hershey, PA: IGI Global. doi:10.4018/978-1-5225-1624-8.ch044

Santamaría, A. P., Webber, M., & Santamaría, L. J. (2017). Effective School Leadership for Māori Achievement: Building Capacity through Indigenous, National, and International Cross-Cultural Collaboration. In I. Management Association (Ed.), Educational Leadership and Administration: Concepts, Methodologies, Tools, and Applications (pp. 1547-1567). Hershey, PA: IGI Global. doi:10.4018/978-1-5225-1624-8.ch071

Santamaría, L. J. (2017). Culturally Responsive Educational Leadership in Cross-Cultural International Contexts. In I. Management Association (Ed.), Educational Leadership and Administration: Concepts, Methodologies, Tools, and Applications (pp. 1380-1400). Hershey, PA: IGI Global. doi:10.4018/978-1-5225-1624-8.ch064

Sarafidou, J., & Xafakos, E. (2015). Transformational Leadership and Principals' Innovativeness: Are They the "Keys" for the Research and Innovation Oriented School? In K. Beycioglu & P. Pashiardis (Eds.), *Multidimensional Perspectives on Principal Leadership Effectiveness* (pp. 324–348). Hershey, PA: IGI Global. doi:10.4018/978-1-4666-6591-0.ch015

Segredo, M. R., Cistone, P. J., & Reio, T. G. (2017). Relationships Between Emotional Intelligence, Leadership Style, and School Culture. *International Journal of Adult Vocational Education and Technology, 8*(3), 25–43. doi:10.4018/IJAVET.2017070103

Shaik, N., & Ritter, S. (2012). Social Media Based Relationship Marketing. In I. Management Association (Ed.), E-Marketing: Concepts, Methodologies, Tools, and Applications (pp. 88-110). Hershey, PA: IGI Global. doi:10.4018/978-1-4666-1598-4.ch006

Shalev, N. (2017). Empathy and Leadership From the Organizational Perspective. In Z. Nedelko & M. Brzozowski (Eds.), *Exploring the Influence of Personal Values and Cultures in the Workplace* (pp. 348–363). Hershey, PA: IGI Global. doi:10.4018/978-1-5225-2480-9.ch018

Siamak, M., Fathi, S., & Isfandyari-Moghaddam, A. (2018). Assessment and Measurement of Education Programs of Information Literacy. In R. Bhardwaj (Ed.), *Digitizing the Modern Library and the Transition From Print to Electronic* (pp. 164–192). Hershey, PA: IGI Global. doi:10.4018/978-1-5225-2119-8.ch007

Siozos, P. D., & Palaigeorgiou, G. E. (2008). Educational Technologies and the Emergence of E-Learning 2.0. In D. Politis (Ed.), *E-Learning Methodologies and Computer Applications in Archaeology* (pp. 1–17). Hershey, PA: IGI Global. doi:10.4018/978-1-59904-759-1.ch001

Siu, K. W., & García, G. J. (2017). Disruptive Technologies and Education: Is There Any Disruption After All? In I. Management Association (Ed.), Educational Leadership and Administration: Concepts, Methodologies, Tools, and Applications (pp. 757-778). Hershey, PA: IGI Global. doi:10.4018/978-1-5225-1624-8.ch037

Related References

Skibba, K., Moore, D., & Herman, J. H. (2013). Pedagogical and Technological Considerations Designing Collaborative Learning Using Educational Technologies. In J. Keengwe (Ed.), *Research Perspectives and Best Practices in Educational Technology Integration* (pp. 1–27). Hershey, PA: IGI Global. doi:10.4018/978-1-4666-2988-2.ch001

Slagter van Tryon, P. J. (2017). The Nurse Educator's Role in Designing Instruction and Instructional Strategies for Academic and Clinical Settings. In J. Stefaniak (Ed.), *Advancing Medical Education Through Strategic Instructional Design* (pp. 133–149). Hershey, PA: IGI Global. doi:10.4018/978-1-5225-2098-6.ch006

Slattery, C. A. (2018). Literacy Intervention and the Differentiated Plan of Instruction. In *Developing Effective Literacy Intervention Strategies: Emerging Research and Opportunities* (pp. 41–62). Hershey, PA: IGI Global. doi:10.4018/978-1-5225-5007-5.ch003

Smith, A. R. (2017). Ensuring Quality: The Faculty Role in Online Higher Education. In K. Shelton & K. Pedersen (Eds.), *Handbook of Research on Building, Growing, and Sustaining Quality E-Learning Programs* (pp. 210–231). Hershey, PA: IGI Global. doi:10.4018/978-1-5225-0877-9.ch011

Souders, T. M. (2017). Understanding Your Learner: Conducting a Learner Analysis. In J. Stefaniak (Ed.), *Advancing Medical Education Through Strategic Instructional Design* (pp. 1–29). Hershey, PA: IGI Global. doi:10.4018/978-1-5225-2098-6.ch001

Spring, K. J., Graham, C. R., & Ikahihifo, T. B. (2018). Learner Engagement in Blended Learning. In M. Khosrow-Pour, D.B.A. (Ed.), Encyclopedia of Information Science and Technology, Fourth Edition (pp. 1487-1498). Hershey, PA: IGI Global. doi:10.4018/978-1-5225-2255-3.ch128

Stocklin, S. (2015). Building Capacity by Managing a Mission. In J. Feng, S. Stocklin, & W. Wang (Eds.), *Educational Strategies for the Next Generation Leaders in Hotel Management* (pp. 115–139). Hershey, PA: IGI Global. doi:10.4018/978-1-4666-8565-9.ch005

Storey, V. A., Anthony, A. K., & Wahid, P. (2017). Gender-Based Leadership Barriers: Advancement of Female Faculty to Leadership Positions in Higher Education. In V. Wang (Ed.), *Encyclopedia of Strategic Leadership and Management* (pp. 244–258). Hershey, PA: IGI Global. doi:10.4018/978-1-5225-1049-9.ch018

Stottlemyer, D. (2018). Develop a Teaching Model Plan for a Differentiated Learning Approach. In *Differentiated Instructional Design for Multicultural Environments: Emerging Research and Opportunities* (pp. 106–130). Hershey, PA: IGI Global. doi:10.4018/978-1-5225-5106-5.ch005

Stottlemyer, D. (2018). Developing a Multicultural Environment. In *Differentiated Instructional Design for Multicultural Environments: Emerging Research and Opportunities* (pp. 1–27). Hershey, PA: IGI Global. doi:10.4018/978-1-5225-5106-5.ch001

Swami, B. N., Gobona, T., & Tsimako, J. J. (2017). Academic Leadership: A Case Study of the University of Botswana. In N. Baporikar (Ed.), *Innovation and Shifting Perspectives in Management Education* (pp. 1–32). Hershey, PA: IGI Global. doi:10.4018/978-1-5225-1019-2.ch001

Swanson, K. W., & Collins, G. (2018). Designing Engaging Instruction for the Adult Learners. In M. Khosrow-Pour, D.B.A. (Ed.), Encyclopedia of Information Science and Technology, Fourth Edition (pp. 1432-1440). Hershey, PA: IGI Global. doi:10.4018/978-1-5225-2255-3.ch123

Swartz, B. A., Lynch, J. M., & Lynch, S. D. (2018). Embedding Elementary Teacher Education Coursework in Local Classrooms: Examples in Mathematics and Special Education. In D. Polly, M. Putman, T. Petty, & A. Good (Eds.), *Innovative Practices in Teacher Preparation and Graduate-Level Teacher Education Programs* (pp. 262–292). Hershey, PA: IGI Global. doi:10.4018/978-1-5225-3068-8.ch015

Taliadorou, N., & Pashiardis, P. (2015). Emotional Intelligence and Political Skill Really Matter in Educational Leadership. In K. Beycioglu & P. Pashiardis (Eds.), *Multidimensional Perspectives on Principal Leadership Effectiveness* (pp. 228–256). Hershey, PA: IGI Global. doi:10.4018/978-1-4666-6591-0.ch011

Taliadorou, N., & Pashiardis, P. (2017). Emotional Intelligence and Political Skill Really Matter in Educational Leadership. In I. Management Association (Ed.), Educational Leadership and Administration: Concepts, Methodologies, Tools, and Applications (pp. 1274-1303). Hershey, PA: IGI Global. doi:10.4018/978-1-5225-1624-8.ch060

Tam, F. W., & Kwan, P. Y. (2011). School Images, School Identity, and How Parents Select Schools for Their Children: The Case of Hong Kong. In P. Tripathi & S. Mukerji (Eds.), *Cases on Innovations in Educational Marketing: Transnational and Technological Strategies* (pp. 87–103). Hershey, PA: IGI Global. doi:10.4018/978-1-60960-599-5.ch005

Tandoh, K. A., & Ebe-Arthur, J. E. (2018). Effective Educational Leadership in the Digital Age: An Examination of Professional Qualities and Best Practices. In J. Keengwe (Ed.), *Handbook of Research on Digital Content, Mobile Learning, and Technology Integration Models in Teacher Education* (pp. 244–265). Hershey, PA: IGI Global. doi:10.4018/978-1-5225-2953-8.ch013

Tinoca, L., Pereira, A., & Oliveira, I. (2014). A Conceptual Framework for E-Assessment in Higher Education: Authenticity, Consistency, Transparency, and Practicability. In S. Mukerji & P. Tripathi (Eds.), *Handbook of Research on Transnational Higher Education* (pp. 652–673). Hershey, PA: IGI Global. doi:10.4018/978-1-4666-4458-8.ch033

Tobin, M. T. (2018). Multimodal Literacy. In M. Khosrow-Pour, D.B.A. (Ed.), Encyclopedia of Information Science and Technology, Fourth Edition (pp. 1508-1516). Hershey, PA: IGI Global. doi:10.4018/978-1-5225-2255-3.ch130

Torres, M. L., & Ramos, V. J. (2018). Music Therapy: A Pedagogical Alternative for ASD and ID Students in Regular Classrooms. In P. Epler (Ed.), *Instructional Strategies in General Education and Putting the Individuals With Disabilities Act (IDEA) Into Practice* (pp. 222–244). Hershey, PA: IGI Global. doi:10.4018/978-1-5225-3111-1.ch008

Toulassi, B. (2017). Educational Administration and Leadership in Francophone Africa: 5 Dynamics to Change Education. In S. Mukerji & P. Tripathi (Eds.), *Handbook of Research on Administration, Policy, and Leadership in Higher Education* (pp. 20–45). Hershey, PA: IGI Global. doi:10.4018/978-1-5225-0672-0.ch002

Umair, S., & Sharif, M. M. (2018). Predicting Students Grades Using Artificial Neural Networks and Support Vector Machine. In M. Khosrow-Pour, D.B.A. (Ed.), Encyclopedia of Information Science and Technology, Fourth Edition (pp. 5169-5182). Hershey, PA: IGI Global. doi:10.4018/978-1-5225-2255-3.ch449

Usman, L. M. (2011). Adult Education and Sustainable Learning Outcome of Rural Widows of Central Northern Nigeria. *International Journal of Adult Vocational Education and Technology*, 2(2), 25–41. doi:10.4018/javet.2011040103

Vettraino, L., Castello, V., Guspini, M., & Guglielman, E. (2018). Self-Awareness and Motivation Contrasting ESL and NEET Using the SAVE System. In M. Khosrow-Pour, D.B.A. (Ed.), Encyclopedia of Information Science and Technology, Fourth Edition (pp. 1559-1568). Hershey, PA: IGI Global. doi:10.4018/978-1-5225-2255-3.ch135

Wang, V. C. (2013). Marketing Educational Programs through Technology and the Right Philosophies. In P. Tripathi & S. Mukerji (Eds.), *Marketing Strategies for Higher Education Institutions: Technological Considerations and Practices* (pp. 15–24). Hershey, PA: IGI Global. doi:10.4018/978-1-4666-4014-6.ch002

Wiemelt, J. (2017). Critical Bilingual Leadership for Emergent Bilingual Students. In I. Management Association (Ed.), Educational Leadership and Administration: Concepts, Methodologies, Tools, and Applications (pp. 1606-1631). Hershey, PA: IGI Global. doi:10.4018/978-1-5225-1624-8.ch074

Williams, D. D. (2006). Measurement and Assessment Supporting Evaluation in Online Settings. In D. Williams, M. Hricko, & S. Howell (Eds.), *Online Assessment, Measurement and Evaluation: Emerging Practices* (pp. 1–9). Hershey, PA: IGI Global. doi:10.4018/978-1-59140-747-8.ch001

Wolf, F., Seyfarth, F. C., & Pflaum, E. (2018). Scalable Capacity-Building for Geographically Dispersed Learners: Designing the MOOC "Sustainable Energy in Small Island Developing States (SIDS)". In U. Pandey & V. Indrakanti (Eds.), *Open and Distance Learning Initiatives for Sustainable Development* (pp. 58–83). Hershey, PA: IGI Global. doi:10.4018/978-1-5225-2621-6.ch003

Woodley, X. M., Mucundanyi, G., & Lockard, M. (2017). Designing Counter-Narratives: Constructing Culturally Responsive Curriculum Online. *International Journal of Online Pedagogy and Course Design*, *7*(1), 43–56. doi:10.4018/IJOPCD.2017010104

Woods, P. A., & Woods, G. J. (2011). Lighting the Fires of Entrepreneurialism?: Constructions of Meaning in an English Inner City Academy. *International Journal of Technology and Educational Marketing*, *1*(1), 1–24. doi:10.4018/ijtem.2011010101

Yell, M. L., & Christle, C. A. (2017). The Foundation of Inclusion in Federal Legislation and Litigation. In C. Curran & A. Petersen (Eds.), *Handbook of Research on Classroom Diversity and Inclusive Education Practice* (pp. 27–52). Hershey, PA: IGI Global. doi:10.4018/978-1-5225-2520-2.ch002

Zhao, J. (2011). China Special Education: The Perspective of Information Technologies. In P. Ordóñez de Pablos, J. Zhao, & R. Tennyson (Eds.), *Technology Enhanced Learning for People with Disabilities: Approaches and Applications* (pp. 34–43). Hershey, PA: IGI Global. doi:10.4018/978-1-61520-923-1.ch003

Related References

Zinger, D. (2016). Developing Instructional Leadership and Communication Skills through Online Professional Development: Focusing on Rural and Urban Principals. In A. Normore, L. Long, & M. Javidi (Eds.), *Handbook of Research on Effective Communication, Leadership, and Conflict Resolution* (pp. 354–370). Hershey, PA: IGI Global. doi:10.4018/978-1-4666-9970-0.ch019

Zutshi, A., Pogrebnaya, M., & Fermelis, J. (2014). Wellness Programs in Higher Education: An Australian Case. In N. Baporikar (Ed.), *Handbook of Research on Higher Education in the MENA Region: Policy and Practice* (pp. 391–419). Hershey, PA: IGI Global. doi:10.4018/978-1-4666-6198-1.ch017

About the Contributors

Zhiliang Zhu, Ph.D., doctoral supervisor, Professor, Director of Academic Affairs Department at Northeastern University (NEU), China, Expert of wining the Special Government Allowance of the State Council, China. Prof. Zhu is a fellow of China Institute of Communications (CIC), and an academic leader on a provincial level in institutions of higher education in Liaoning. He has been selected into the Provincial Hundreds and Thousands of Talents Project (level of Hundreds), and one of the Leading Academics of Shenyang City. He is a member of the Teaching Steering Committee of Software Engineering (Ministry of Education) and a member of Subcommittee on SOA Standards (Ministry of Industry and Information Technology). He is executive council member of Branch of Teaching Research of China Association of Higher Education (CAHE), executive council member of Chinese Association of Suzhi Education, and Vice President of Liaoning Branch of the National Institute of Laboratory Work in Colleges and Universities (CULABS). As a project leader, Prof. Zhu has wined twice the National Teaching Achievement Award (the Second Prize). Two of his courses have been evaluated as National Top-quality Courses. As the head of National Experimental Teaching Demonstration Center in Software College of Northeastern University, Prof. Zhu is leading a National Teaching Team. So far Prof. Zhu has published more than 200 papers, including more than 40 papers indexed by SCI (as the first or corresponding author), 4 most-cited papers by ESI, and 5 books. Additionally, 5 of his research outcomes have wined awards respectively by Scientific and Technological Progress Award of Liaoning Education Commission (the first, second prize), and Scientific and Technological Progress Award of Liaoning Government (the second and third prize).

Chunfang Zhou, Ph.D., Associate Professor in Department of Planning, Aalborg University (AAU), Denmark. Chunfang has an interdisciplinary and cross-cultural educational background; she finished bachelor degree (Industry Automation and Information Engineering) and master degree (Philosophy of Science and Technology) in China; since 2008, Chunfang has worked in Denmark started by a Ph.D. project on Engineering Creativity in Problem and Project-Based Learning (PBL) at

UNESCO Center of PBL at AAU. Chunfang locates her research in area of Science, Technology and Society (STS), with a particular focus on creativity and its relations to innovation process, with interests in diverse domains including digitalization, human-centered design, sustainability, group collaboration, knowledge management, Problem-Based Learning (PBL) and STEM education. Recently, she has done cross-cultural contributions to creativity research, especially by her Individual Independent Research Project *Fostering Creativity in Higher Education: A Comparative Study on Pedagogical Strategies of Learning by Projects between Denmark and China,* funded by Danish Research Council (2013-2016). Currently she is coordinating *Designing, Participation and Facilitation of Problem and Project-Based Learning (PBL)* between Northeastern University (NEU), China and AAU, Denmark; she is leading *Creativity in Technology Design: Developing a Sino-Danish Research Network for Future Digital Societies,* funded by Danish Research Council (2019-2020). Chunfang has authored or co-authored over 80 peer-review publications. Chunfang is member of research group Techno-Anthropology and Participation, member of Danish Center for Health Informatics, member of Chinese Creativity Research Network, and board member of Danish Development Research Network (DDRN).

* * *

Fenghua Li, Ph.D., Associate Professor in Department of Resources and Environment, Northeastern University (NEU), China. Since 2004, Fenghua has been working in School of Metallurgy majoring Environmental Science at NEU, after she finished her bachelor and master degree (Metallurgical Physics and Chemical) and doctor degree (Materials Science) at NEU. She was the visiting professor in Department of Planning at the Aalborg University (AAU, Denmark) in 2018. She received research funding grants from the National Natural Science Foundation of China and Liaoning Provincial Natural Science Foundation in China, and authored over 30 publications on superconductors and resource recycling. Fenghua has an interdisciplinary research area covering Environment and Materials, mainly focusing on eco-design of materials and energy materials, such as superconductor, photo-catalytic materials and semiconductor solar cells. She cares about the relationship between education and sustainability, and is a member of the international non-profit organization Pour un Monde Meilleur via l'Education (PMME).

Mei Li, Ph.D. in the School of Marxism, Northeastern University (NEU), China and guest Ph.D. in the Department of Planning, Aalborg University (AAU), Denmark. Mei has an educational background and work experience of education and cross-culture communication. She has finished her bachelor degree (English Language Teaching) at Harbin Normal University and master degree (English Language and

Literature) at Northeast Forestry University, China. She has once been a faculty member in School of Foreign Studies of East University of Heilongjiang. She has worked in the Administrative Office of Software College in NEU as secretary on foreign affairs from 2010 to 2016 and be responsible for student international exchange program in the International Cooperation and Exchange Department of NEU from 2016 to 2017. Since 2017, she has become a Ph.D. in School of Marxism of NEU (Philosophy of Science and Technology). Mei locates her research in several areas of Cross-culture Communication, with particular focuses on translation, internationalization of higher education and foreign affairs management in universities, etc. She has published several related papers and participated in the project "Exploration and Practice of Innovative Internationalized Talents Training Mode in Software Engineering Specialty" when working in the Software College of NEU, which has won the grand prize of Teaching Achievement Award of NEU and second prize of Teaching Achievement Award of Liaoning Province, China. Now, Mei is studying in the Department of Planning of AAU as a guest Ph.D., devoting herself to the research on communication, culture and technology.

Jingping Song, Ph.D., Lecturer in Software College of Northeastern University (NEU), China. Jingping has an interdisciplinary and cross-cultural educational background; he finished his bachelor degree (Communication Engineering) and master degree (Communication and Information System) at NEU in China; from 2012 to 2016, Jingping has been working in United Kingdom and got a Ph.D. degree (Computer Science) at Aberystwyth University. Jingping's research work focus on Chaotic Security Communication, Machine Learning and Information Security. Jingping worked in High Education Evaluation Center of Ministry of Education of the People's Republic of China from 2017 to 2018. And he learned PBL (Problem Based Learning) at UNESCO Center of PBL at Aalborg University in Denmark from 2018 to 2019. Recently, he has authored or co-authored over 20 publications in Chaotic Security Communication and Machine Learning. And he chaired and participated 6 research funding granted by NSFC, Liaoning Natural Science Fund and so on.

Xiu Song, Ph.D., Associate Professor in the department of Materials Science, School of Materials Science and Engineering, Northeastern University (NEU), China. Xiu Song has obtained Bachelor degree in Materials Science and Engineering in 2005 at NEU in China, and Ph.D degree in Materials Science in 2011 at NEU. She has been in Institute of Materials Research (IMR), Tohoku University, Japan, as a joint doctoral student supported by China Scholarship Council (CSC) for two years, from 2008 to 2010. She was also appointed as a visiting Professor at Aalborg University (AAU) in Denmark for half a year in 2018. She was an associate professor in the

School of Materials Science and Engineering at NEU from 2011, and became an associate Professor since 2015. Her current research activities in Prof. Lei Wang's research group at NEU are relatively focused on the microstructure controlling and improving of mechanical properties of high performance structure materials, mainly including Ti alloy used for biomedical applications or aerospace applications and superalloy also used for aerospace applications. She has independently done over 7 project grants supported by National Natural Science Foundation of China (NSFC), Liaoning Natural Science Foundation, Fundamental Research Funds for the Central Universities, and so on. And she has also participated in several other projects supported by the National High Technology Research and Development Program of China (863 Program) and Major State Basic Research Development Program of China (973 Program). She has already published more than 30 papers about the microstructure controlling and improving of mechanical properties of high performance structure materials as the first author or co-authors.

Xinbo Sun, Ph.D., Professor in Department of Organization and Management, Associate Dean in School of Business Administration, Northeastern University (NEU), China. Xinbo has Industrial Automation, Marketing Administration, Business Administration, Management Science and Engineering educational background; He finished his bachelor's degree, master's degree and Ph.D. in China; He is interested in Management Philosophy, Organizational and Strategy Management, Leadership and Motivation, Innovation and Entrepreneurship; His teaching experience included Management Philosophy, Principle of Management, Management Philosophy and Leadership, Project Management, Outward Bound, I Ching(The book of change) and Chinese Managerial Art and so forth. So far, he has supervised 170 master's and doctoral students. He has published more than 140 academic papers and 17 books and textbooks. He has presided over two general projects of the national natural science foundation of China, participated in one major project of the national social science foundation of China, participated in three projects of the national natural science and social science foundation of China, He has presided over more than 50 provincial and enterprise-level projects. Xinbo has provided "management philosophy" and "leadership" training to more than 10,000 managers of hundreds of companies in China. He is currently executive director of the EMBA education center at Northeastern University and director of the global enterprise transformation research center. He is also a member of the academic committee of the Confucius institute. He is also a member of the academic committee of "China · practice · management", a member of the undergraduate teaching committee of Northeastern University. He is the executive director of the professional committee of organizational behavior and human resource management of China management modernization research association.

Fei Wang, Ph.D., Associate Professor, doctor supervisor in Faculty of Robot Science & Engineering, Northeastern University (NEU), China. He received the BSc. and MSc. degrees in Mechanical Engineering from Harbin Institute of Technology (HIT), China in 1997 and 1999 respectively, and Ph.D. degree in Functional System from the University of Tokushima, Japan in 2004. He is also currently the head of BSc. Programme of Robot Engineering and vice director of experimental center. He was visiting professor in Michigan State University (MSU), US., University of Tokushima (UT), Japan and Aalborg University (AAU), Denmark in 2010, 2014 and 2018 respectively. He is currently the Member of the Robotics Committee of the China Society of Automation, the Robotics Branch of the China Society of Mechanical Engineering. He received over 30 research funding granted by NSFC, Ministry of Science & Technology and Ministry of Education of P.R. China. He has authored or co-authored over 50 publications primarily in bio-signal processing, robot control and human-robot collaboration. He is the editor of the *Handbook of Industrial Robot* (to be published 2019 by Chemical Industry Press). Now, his research interests include pattern recognition, human-robot interaction and assistive robotics.

Jian-Hua Wang, Ph.D. Professor, Vice President of Northeastern University, China. Dr. Jian-Hua Wang was born in 1962 in Shandong Province, China. He received his under-graduate and graduate education at Nankai University (1981-1985) and Jilin University (1985-1988), respectively. After employment at Yantai Normal University, China (1988-1997), he spent one year at the University of Delaware for conducting research on analytical applications of tandem mass spectrometry (1997-1998). He was awarded a PhD degree in analytical chemistry by the Technical University of Denmark in 2002 with Professor Elo Harald Hansen as supervisor, and afterwards he joined Northeastern University in 2003. Jian-Hua Wang is currently a Professor in Analytical Chemistry at Research Center for Analytical Sciences, Department of Chemistry, Northeastern University, China. Jian-Hua Wang's research interests currently include flow analysis and sample pretreatment, microfluidic/mesofluidic analytical systems and applications in life sciences, metallomics and atomic spectrometry/mass spectrometry. His research has been financially supported by the National Natural Science Foundation of China (NSFC), where he received national science fund for distinguished young scholars, NSFC key projects for twice as well as major international joint research project. He has published more than 300 peer-reviewed papers and received a few awards including FIA Award for Science (the Japan Society for Analytical Chemistry, 2014) and Natural Science Award of the Ministry of Education, China (2008). He has been an Associate Editor for Talanta since Dec. 2004. He is also a member for the Editorial Advisory Board for Journal of Analytical Atomic Spectrometry (RSC, 2007-2011), Chinese Journal of

Analytical Chemistry (2006-), Spectroscopy and Spectral Analysis (2008-), Journal of Analytical Science (2008-) and Chinese Journal of Analysis Laboratory (2004-).

Xufang Zhang, Ph.D., Associate Professor in the School of Mechanical Engineering and Automation, the Northeastern University in China. He received the BA in Education, MSc. in Mechanical Education, and PhD in Civil Engineering from the Shenyang Normal University, the Northeastern University, and the University of Waterloo (Canada) in 2001, 2008, and 2013, respectively. He was appointed as a postdoctoral research fellow at the Katholieke Universiteit Leuven (KU-Leuven, Belgium) in 2017 and the visiting professor at the Aalborg University (AAU, Denmark) in 2018. He received several research funding grants from the National Natural Science Foundation of China and the Ministry of Education in China, and authored over 40 publications on the stochastic mechanics and the data-driven structural reliability algorithms. Now, his research interests are about smart surrogate modelling and data-driven techniques in risk-based assessment of renewable energy infrastructures.

Yin Zhang, Ph.D., Associate Professor in School of Computer Science and Engineering, Northeastern University (NEU), China. Yin has an educational background in Computer Science; he finished his bachelor degree (Computer Science and Engineering) and doctor degree (Computer Application Technology) at Northeastern University, China; since 2012, Yin has been working in NEU as a lecturer and postdoc. Yin locates his research in several areas of Computer Science (CS), with particular focuses on Searching as Learning (SaL) and Education as Engineering (EaE), which try to introduce and integrate CS research and education. Recently, he has made many contributions to SaL and EaE research, especially by his Individual Independent Research Project *Study on an Information Foraging Based Exploratory Search Query Recommendation Method,* funded by the National Natural Science Foundation of China (2016-2018). Currently, he is leading *Research and Practice of an Intercourse Problem Based Learning (PBL) Model to Foster Competencies of Multi-side Full Stack Integrated Development*, funded by Ministry of Education of the People's Republic of China, and Tencent Holding Limited (2019-2020). Yin is a member of China Computer Federation (CCF).

Index

A

assessment 6, 12, 18, 45, 52, 56-57, 62, 65,
    78-80, 84, 87, 108, 110-111, 123, 133,
    135-137, 140, 144-145, 149-150, 154,
    161-162, 175, 179, 184, 186-187, 189-
    190, 195, 198, 200, 203, 207-208, 210,
    212, 214, 217, 219, 228, 231-232, 238
assessment of learning 87, 110

B

big C 276, 293
BSc programme 172

C

case 44, 55-56, 58, 63, 65, 70, 84, 93, 104,
    108, 125, 130, 133, 137-138, 148,
    153-155, 170, 187, 190, 210, 217,
    219, 232-239, 245, 260
case study 232, 260
Chinese context 1, 146, 280, 282
Chinese universities 1, 3, 6, 10, 16-21, 36,
    47, 91, 107, 122, 130-133, 135-138,
    145-146, 148-150, 152-155, 196, 219,
    259, 269, 273-274, 280-283, 285
civil engineering 184, 195-196, 204
co-creation 11, 16-18, 20, 30, 42-43
collaborative education 32, 43, 46, 49-51, 53
Computer Science education 55-56
course group design 176
creative society 1-6, 16, 20-21, 30

creativity 2, 4-5, 10, 15-17, 20, 30, 34, 70,
    80, 107, 131, 134, 148, 152, 169, 219,
    247, 253-255, 273-285, 293
critical thinking 56, 61, 88, 92-94, 107,
    118, 125, 137, 141, 171, 191, 195,
    201, 203, 218, 229, 269
cross-culture communication 244-250,
    252-254, 257, 263, 270
curriculum design 10, 12, 16, 65, 101,
    106-107, 132, 136, 142, 155, 169-170,
    176, 184, 219

D

discipline construction 41, 159

E

education innovation 275, 277
education supply-side reform 34
engineering creativity 273, 275, 277-282,
    285, 293
engineering education 9-10, 130-137, 145-
    146, 149-150, 155, 166-168, 170, 195,
    208, 217, 275, 277-278, 280-281, 293
environmental education 88-92, 95, 99,
    120-121, 124-125
environmental science 89-92, 99

F

facilitator 17, 105, 118, 120, 125, 139,
    171, 185, 188-189, 200-201, 219,

226-228, 235

foreign affairs management 244-245, 256, 263-266, 268-270

G

global citizenship 249-250, 257, 270

Global Information Technology Revolution 32-33

globalization 10, 20, 46, 95, 125, 131, 135, 155, 245, 247-251, 254, 258, 263

H

higher education 10, 16, 18, 20, 32-36, 39-40, 42, 44, 50-51, 53, 84, 103, 125, 131, 136, 138-140, 160, 164-165, 169-170, 176, 244-245, 247-251, 255-258, 261, 263-265, 269-270, 278

I

implementation 9, 20, 32, 36, 49-51, 101, 106, 114, 123, 130, 133, 137, 155, 164-165, 176, 184, 197-200, 203-204, 206-208, 210, 223-225, 236, 249, 265, 274

Information and Communication Technology (ICT) 10, 19, 30

innovation 1-2, 5, 12, 18-21, 32, 35, 41-50, 53, 84, 95, 99-100, 116, 131-132, 134, 136-137, 141, 146, 160, 165, 169-170, 176, 217-218, 235, 244-245, 249, 251, 254-255, 259, 263-265, 268-270, 274-275, 277, 282, 284-285

institutional culture 284

integration education 50

interdisciplinarity 15, 90-91, 96, 99-100, 124, 140, 183, 186, 195-197, 200, 205-207

interdisciplinary 9-10, 15, 18, 34, 40, 53, 56, 59, 61, 63, 88, 90, 98-101, 124, 130-132, 134-135, 160, 169, 173-174, 187-189, 195-198, 200-201, 203-207, 220, 223-224, 227-232, 236, 239, 247, 273, 276, 279, 282-283

interdisciplinary course 189, 195, 200-201, 203

internalization 245, 249, 253, 257, 263, 270

international talent 250-260, 263

L

learning 1, 3, 5-15, 17-20, 30-35, 39-43, 46-49, 51-53, 55-70, 72, 76, 78, 80-81, 84, 87-88, 90-99, 101-108, 110-113, 117, 119-125, 130-153, 160-165, 168-171, 174, 176-179, 183-196, 198-205, 207-208, 210, 214-215, 217-220, 222, 225-226, 228-231, 235-237, 250, 252-253, 257, 266, 269, 275, 279-284, 293

learning activity 78, 87, 281

learning goal 65, 87, 179, 187

learning motivation 138

lifelong learning 7, 13, 35, 40, 48, 61, 88, 90, 95, 102, 125, 160, 194-196, 253

little C 276-277, 293

O

organizational change 150, 161, 164, 207

P

PBL 1, 3, 6-11, 15-20, 30-33, 36, 44, 46-47, 49-51, 53, 55-56, 59-63, 65-66, 68-71, 81, 83-84, 88, 95-96, 98, 102-107, 111-113, 117, 119-121, 123-125, 130, 132-133, 137-150, 152-155, 159-160, 162, 164-166, 170-172, 175-176, 178-179, 183-208, 210, 219-220, 222-232, 234, 236, 239, 280, 283

PBL models 10, 61, 66, 130, 133, 140, 142, 155, 171, 183, 186, 197, 207-208

PBL principles 11, 104-105, 130, 133, 140-141, 154-155, 160

practical implementation 200

problem and project-based pedagogies 275, 283, 285

Problem-Based Learning (PBL) 1, 3, 6-8, 19, 30, 33, 46-47, 56, 66, 88, 95, 98-99, 104-106, 113, 117, 119, 121, 123, 125,

132, 138, 143, 170, 178, 185, 219-220
professional knowledge 15, 71, 80, 87, 90,
    95, 169, 175, 252
PROGRAMME LEVEL 170, 172
project-organized teams 281, 293

R

reflection 11, 13, 15, 32, 43, 51, 90, 97, 102,
    109-110, 117, 119, 135, 145, 147-148,
    165, 174, 179, 184, 189, 202-203, 210,
    219, 222, 281
robot engineering 159, 166-168, 170, 172,
    175-179

S

Schematic diagram 50
STEM education 275, 280-285
student cultivation 131, 159, 168-172,
    175-176

student-centered learning 9, 15, 20, 31, 70,
    130, 138, 142, 147, 149, 160, 184-185,
    191, 200-202, 207, 283
sustainability 19, 91-92, 95, 125, 188, 265,
    269, 277

T

teaching philosophy 46, 49, 90, 168, 184,
    210, 216, 222
teaching practice 32, 44, 46, 283
Teaching Vision 71, 87
traditional engineering curriculum 183
transferable skills 56, 59, 61, 69-71, 80, 87,
    93, 132, 134, 142, 151-152, 228-229
transformative learning 13-14, 31, 88, 94,
    98, 125

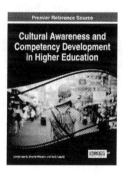

Ensure Quality Research is Introduced to the Academic Community

Become an IGI Global Reviewer for Authored Book Projects

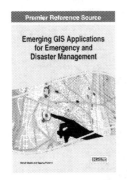
Premier Reference Source

Emerging GIS Applications for Emergency and Disaster Management

Premier Reference Source

Managerial Strategies and Green Solutions for Project Sustainability

Premier Reference Source

Comparative Approaches to Using R and Python for Statistical Data Analysis

Premier Reference Source

Solutions for High-Touch Communications in a High-Tech World

The overall success of an authored book project is dependent on quality and timely reviews.

In this competitive age of scholarly publishing, constructive and timely feedback significantly expedites the turnaround time of manuscripts from submission to acceptance, allowing the publication and discovery of forward-thinking research at a much more expeditious rate. Several IGI Global authored book projects are currently seeking highly qualified experts in the field to fill vacancies on their respective editorial review boards:

Applications may be sent to:
development@igi-global.com

Applicants must have a doctorate (or an equivalent degree) as well as publishing and reviewing experience. Reviewers are asked to write reviews in a timely, collegial, and constructive manner. All reviewers will begin their role on an ad-hoc basis for a period of one year, and upon successful completion of this term can be considered for full editorial review board status, with the potential for a subsequent promotion to Associate Editor.

If you have a colleague that may be interested in this opportunity, we encourage you to share this information with them.

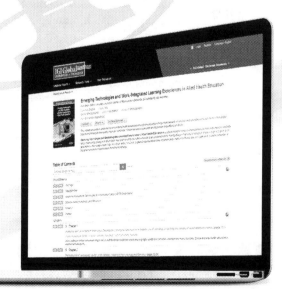

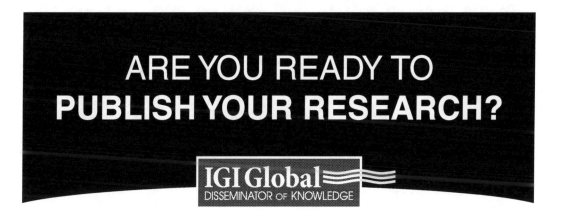

Printed in the United States
By Bookmasters